Concepts in the Brain

Concepts in the Brain

The View from Cross-Linguistic Diversity

David Kemmerer

Oxford University Press is a department of the University of Oxford. It furthers
the University's objective of excellence in research, scholarship, and education
by publishing worldwide. Oxford is a registered trade mark of Oxford University
Press in the UK and certain other countries.

Published in the United States of America by Oxford University Press
198 Madison Avenue, New York, NY 10016, United States of America.

CIP data is on file at the Library of Congress
ISBN 978–0–19–068262–0

1 3 5 7 9 8 6 4 2

Printed by Sheridan Books, Inc., United States of America

CONTENTS

PREFACE

For those who do not share the conviction that bits of knowledge laid end to end lead to wisdom, the articulation of the bits becomes a challenge separate from that of unearthing them. When the knowledge in question is knowledge about human behavior, the emergent image must bear a human face. If it doesn't, the mind goes blank when we look at it, irrespective of how detailed or precise it is. So there are two tasks, really: first, the assembly of the pieces, and second, the discernment of a human face.
—Melvin Konner (2002, p. xvi)

For the past 15 years, a framed reproduction of a prehistoric cave painting has been hanging above the fireplace in my home. The original pictograph is located at one of the many ancient rock art sites in southern Africa, some of which are at least 27,000 years old. Following traditions of style and content that were maintained for millennia, it portrays, in shades of maroon, yellow, black, and white, a variety of giraffes, elephants, rhinoceros, and eland, as well as several small groups of very tall, thin people, some carrying spears and others torches.

For me, this beautiful work of art is not just a nice decoration; it is also a vivid reminder of the lifeways that our hunter-gatherer ancestors led for over 90% of human history (Reich, 2018). Although those lifeways were quite different from our own, they undoubtedly depended on languages that were no less expressive than those currently spoken all over the world. After all, people then had essentially the same cognitive capacities that we have now, including the ability to weave the fabrics of their cultures with words. That is why, if I extrapolate rather liberally from recent findings about the conversational patterns of contemporary Ju/'hoan (!Kung) Bushmen in southern Africa, I can easily imagine that their forebears in the deep past—forebears like the people illustrated in my painting— devoted most of their day talk to the nitty-gritty details of food sharing, kinship dues, and land rights, whereas at night they gathered around their fires to relax and tell elaborate stories that were richly embellished with gestures, sound effects, and bursts of song, that were by turns amusing, exciting, and endearing, and that took listeners on virtual journeys through space and time so as to inform them about the social and emotional intricacies of marriage, intergroup relations, and trance healing (Weissner, 2014).

But while it is not hard for me to imagine *in general terms* what the people in my painting tended to talk about so many years ago, it is nearly impossible for me to get *a specific sense* of what their language was like, especially regarding the aspects of it that interest me most—namely, the meanings of its major symbolic units, which is to say, its morphemes, words, idioms, and grammatical constructions. This is not just because the language in question existed before the invention of writing and hence was never recorded, or because its referential resources cannot be fully reconstructed from information about the contemporary tongues that descended from it. It is also, and more fundamentally, because even though there are many similarities in how human languages carve up the world into multifarious conceptual categories, there are far more differences. Indeed, these differences are so dramatic that when speakers of one language—say, English—first encounter some of the words and phrases that are frequently used by speakers of an unrelated language—say, Central Yup'ik (Eskimo-Aleut, Alaska), or Tzeltal (Mayan, Mexico), or Yélî Dnye (Papuan, Rossel Island)[1]—they often find the meanings of those expressions to be quite surprising and peculiar, if not, in some cases, exotic. As Evans (2010, p. 45) observes, even seasoned scholars are frequently gobsmacked by what they discover in the course of their research: "One of the most exciting things about linguistic fieldwork is the way it continuously pushes the bounds of preconceived possibility, by stumbling upon 'unimaginable' languages—those that would never have been thought possible."

According to the best current estimate, nearly 6,500 mutually unintelligible languages are (or recently were) spoken on the planet (Hammarström, 2016).[2] And as Pagel (2012, p. viii) points out, "this is more different systems of communication in a single mammal species—for that is what we are—than there are mammal species." Unfortunately, however, many living languages are either endangered or already dying, and it is likely that at least half of them will go extinct during this century, as a few dominant ones, such as English and Mandarin Chinese, gradually take over the world (Crystal, 2000). This is nothing short of tragic, since every language not only provides a unique window into the workings of the human mind, but is also bound up with an ethnic group's identity and self-esteem. In a recent article in the *New York Times* about an inspiring effort to preserve one particular language—specifically, Southern Haida (Haida, British Columbia)—the anthropologist Wade Davis captured the significance of the project in a rather poignant manner: "The loss of one language is akin to clear-cutting an old-growth forest of the mind. The world's complex web of myths, beliefs and ideas—the ethnosphere—is torn, just as the loss of a species weakens the biosphere" (Porter, 2017).

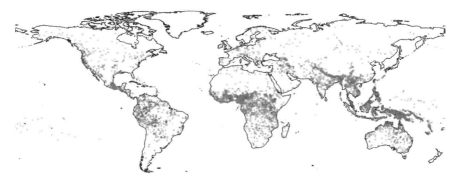

Figure. The roughly 6,500 attested and mutually unintelligible spoken languages of the world rendered with one dot per language at the center of its geographical location. A language is given a red dot if it is extinct and a green dot otherwise. A color version is in the color plates section. From Hammarström, 2016, p. 20.

---

[1] Throughout this book, for languages that may not be familiar to the reader, the family classification and geographical location are provided in parentheses.
[2] For details, see the websites for Ethnologue (https://www.ethnologue.com) and Glottolog (http://glottolog.org).

Table. Numbers of languages and families (including isolates) across macro-areas.

	Number of Languages		Number of Families	
Greater New Guinea Area	1797	28.0%	127	29.9%
South America	490	7.6%	109	25.7%
North America	558	8.7%	71	16.7%
Africa	1845	28.8%	50	11.7%
Eurasia	1423	22.2%	35	8.2%
Australia	292	4.5%	32	7.5%
	6409	100%	424	100%

From Hammarström, 2016, p. 23.

On the bright side, however, the rate at which vulnerable languages are being described and compared has been accelerating, and as a result the database has been rapidly growing (e.g., see the Mouton Grammar Library[3] and the World Atlas of Language Structures Online[4]). Within the broad field of linguistics, the division that concentrates on cross-linguistic similarities and differences is called typology, and within it the branch that focuses even more narrowly on conceptual representation is called semantic typology (e.g., Evans, 2010, 2011; Malt & Majid, 2013; Moore et al., 2015). Although this area of specialization is still maturing, it has begun to flourish during the past few decades, as shown by increasingly systematic and insightful studies of numerous conceptual realms, including colors, plants and animals (i.e., ethnobiology), body parts, landscapes, spatial relations, possession, and several spheres of action, such as giving, cutting and breaking, putting and taking, and eating and drinking. These investigations have shown that far-flung languages all over the world display many intriguing correspondences in both the content and structure of the concepts they encode—correspondences that may stem from commonalities in people's bodies, brains, communicative behaviors, and physical and social environments. At the same time, however, these investigations have also revealed a tremendous amount of cross-linguistic diversity in the lexical partitioning and packaging of particular semantic domains, and in the aspects of experience that speakers must regularly express in grammatical constructions and hence habitually track.

Now, in response to such variation, one could just throw up one's hands and exclaim, "So what? It all originates from the same underlying semantic system." Such an attitude, however, would treat as disproportionately special whatever universal constraints on meaning turn out to be true, and downplay as comparatively trivial all of the cross-linguistic conceptual differences that have been disclosed. In sharp contrast, an increasing number of scholars have been arguing that if there is any asymmetry of significance, it actually goes the other way, since cross-linguistic differences in meaning come primarily from culture, and culture is what ultimately explains the evolutionary success of our species (e.g., Tomasello, 1999, 2014; Richerson & Christiansen, 2013;

---

[3] https://www.degruyter.com/view/serial/16099#
[4] http://wals.info

Henrich, 2016; Boyd, 2018; Heyes, 2018). Here is how Stephen Levinson, one of the most influential semantic typologists, recently put it (Levinson, 2012b, p. 397):

> In the language sciences, there is a slow, growing realization that this diversity is the most striking feature of human language—there is no other animal on the planet, as far as we know, which has such myriad variants of form and meaning at every level in its communication system. What this feature of language ought to convey to us with special force is that culture is the peculiar human adaptive trick that has made it possible for us to invade and dominate almost every terrestrial niche on the planet. Classical cognitive science treats humans like an asocial species without culture, and in doing so, it misses the heart of the human phenomenon.

Semantic typology has already had a strong influence on developmental psychologists who investigate the acquisition of language during childhood (e.g., Bowerman & Levinson, 2001; Guo et al., 2008) and on cognitive scientists who explore the relation between language and thought (e.g., Gentner & Goldin-Meadow, 2003; Malt & Wolff, 2010). Unfortunately, however, it has not yet had much impact on the sizable branch of cognitive neuroscience that studies the organization, representation, and processing of concepts in the brain. To be sure, this field of research has been making spectacular progress in illuminating the large-scale cortical networks—and, to some extent, the fine-grained cell assemblies—that subserve both verbal and nonverbal concepts (e.g., Binder & Desai, 2011; Pulvermüller, 2013a; Yee et al., 2013; Clarke & Tyler, 2015; Kemmerer, 2015c; Lambon Ralph et al., 2017). But it has been laboring, for the most part, under the mistaken assumption that the concepts found in English and a few other familiar languages exemplify those found in languages worldwide. Because of this powerful bias, which is usually implicit, very few scholars have voiced any concern about the fact that the lion's share of empirical and theoretical work has been based on what Henrich et al. (2010) provocatively call WEIRD societies—i.e., societies that are Western(ized), educated, industrial, rich, and democratic. Consequently, the field as a whole has so far failed to take into account the huge variety of semantic systems that are manifested in the roughly 6,500 living languages around the globe and that are also, *ipso facto*, implemented in the brains of the speakers.

In light of these considerations, the main goal of this book is to raise awareness about the many ways in which semantic typology can contribute to cognitive neuroscience, with an eye toward showing that no neuroscientific theory of human conceptual knowledge can ever achieve comprehensive, species-wide coverage unless it accommodates the remarkable range of cross-linguistic similarities and differences in the lexical and grammatical representation of meaning.

The purpose of Part I is to elaborate the typological and neuroscientific approaches to studying concepts. Chapter 1, "The Perspective from Semantic Typology," begins by describing the widespread tendency to incorrectly assume that one's own language maps onto reality in a natural and impartial way. Then it devotes separate sections to lexical and grammatical semantics, in each case reviewing cross-linguistic research on universals and idiosyncrasies, conceptual fields, and coding patterns. Next, Chapter 2, "The Perspective from Cognitive Neuroscience," first elaborates how, in this area of inquiry, most theories of conceptual knowledge posit both modal (i.e., sensory, motor, and affective) and transmodal (i.e., integrative) levels of representation. Then it goes on to discuss representational similarity spaces in the brain, the lack of sufficient neuroscientific attention to grammatical semantics, and the captivating notion that linguistic communication involves brain-to-brain coupling.

The aim of Part II is to show that a synthesis of the two approaches surveyed in Part I can lead to a more unified and inclusive understanding of several domains of concrete meaning—domains that I have deliberately chosen so as to maximize the potential for inter-disciplinary cross-fertilization.[5] Most importantly, all three of the chapters in this central part of the book (but especially Chapters 3 and 4) make two overarching points: on the one hand, many cross-linguistic conceptual phenomena conform to, and hence help to substantiate, salient results and ideas in cognitive neuroscience; on the other hand, current neuroscientific theories and research programs may need to be revised and expanded to handle the full range of semantic variation.

Here's a brief preview of the main topics that are covered. Chapter 3, "Objects," first discusses four conceptual domains that have received substantial attention in both semantic typology and cognitive neuroscience—namely, plants, animals, artifacts, and body parts—and then it turns to two realms of grammatical meaning that have been studied much more intensively in the former field than in the latter—namely, possession and nominal classification systems. Chapter 4, "Actions," has a similar structure. It initially addresses several conceptual domains that have been explored from the dual perspectives of typology and neuroscience—namely, motion events, and events of cutting, breaking, and opening—and then it shifts to some other semantic spheres and representational strategies that have been carefully examined in typology but mostly, if not completely, neglected in neuroscience—namely, events of putting and taking, serial verb constructions, and verbal classification systems. Lastly, Chapter 5, "Spatial Relations," focuses on how people talk about the locations of objects and actions. It begins by describing how three different kinds of spatial relations—namely, topological, projective, and deictic—have been studied in great detail in semantic typology, and then it discusses the surprising fact that, for reasons that remain obscure, so far only a few sectors of this rich conceptual terrain have been mined by cognitive neuroscientists.

Scattered throughout the neuroscience sections of these three core chapters, there are suggestions for new experiments involving various languages. The main purpose of these proposals is to demonstrate that, when one takes the perspective of semantic typology, one can formulate novel predictions about the cortical architecture of conceptual knowledge. Some of these experiments could potentially be conducted. But because others concern languages spoken by small groups of people in remote parts of the world, it is unlikely that the predictions could ever be tested. In such cases,

---

[5] Both semantic typology and cognitive neuroscience have been making significant headway in the investigation of abstract concepts, but this book is restricted mainly to concrete concepts, largely in order to keep the length within reasonable limits. In addition, I should note that although much of the book is about various conceptual domains, I will refrain from trying to formulate a precise definition of the term *domain*, and will instead allow it to remain fairly intuitive, in keeping with current practice in both semantic typology and cognitive neuroscience. I will also use the terms *domain, realm, field, sphere,* and *arena* more or less interchangeably, as well as the terms *conceptual* and *semantic*.

however, the suggestions may still serve as useful thought exercises, since they deal with theoretically and empirically important, yet hitherto unrecognized, aspects of the neural representation of concepts—aspects that are most clearly viewed from the vantage point of typology.

Part III rounds off the book by addressing two questions of a more general nature. Chapter 6, "How Do Language-Specific Concepts Relate to Cognition?," tackles the classic issue of whether language affects thought and perception. The following argument is advanced: many forms of cognition do not necessarily rely on language-specific concepts; nonetheless, such concepts do sometimes influence a variety of cognitive processes, as predicted by Whorf's (1956) linguistic relativity hypothesis. In addition, this chapter emphasizes the need for more neuroscientific work on this topic, and it exposes some interpretive challenges facing recent evidence that verbal and nonverbal semantic tasks often have partly shared cortical underpinnings. Finally, Chapter 7, "Are We Ever Conscious of Concepts?," follows Jackendoff (1987, 2012), Prinz (2012), and several other scholars in defending the counter-intuitive position that concepts always operate below the surface of awareness. It also shows that, if this position is right, it raises serious problems for what are now the two most prominent neuroscientific theories of consciousness—namely, the Global Neuronal Workspace Theory (Dehaene & Naccache, 2001; Dehaene & Changeux, 2011; Dehaene, 2014; Dehaene et al., 2014, 2017) and the Integrated Information Theory (Tononi, 2004, 2008, 2012a, 2012b; Oizumi et al., 2014; Tononi & Koch, 2015; Tononi et al., 2016; Massimini & Tononi, 2018).

Before commencing, some acknowledgments are in order. As I was writing this book, I benefited greatly from the encouragement of several friends and colleagues, especially Larry Barsalou, Rutvik Desai, Ed Fox, Ad Foolen, Elaine Francis, and Brad Mahon. In addition, Asifa Majid and Jamie Reilly were kind enough to read the whole manuscript and provide valuable feedback—Asifa from the perspective of semantic typology, and Jamie from that of cognitive neuroscience. This led to many improvements, and I'm very grateful to both of them. Furthermore, Joan Bossert, my editor at Oxford University Press, has been supportive from the very outset. And finally, I owe the greatest debt of gratitude to my wonderful wife, Natalya Kaganovich, who has boosted my spirits during the rough stages of this project, shared my joys during the smooth ones, and frequently reminded me, with her laughter, kindness, and companionship, that, amazingly enough, there's actually much more to life than wondering about the neural substrates of seemingly exotic languages.

PART I

Two Perspectives on Concepts

1

THE PERSPECTIVE FROM SEMANTIC TYPOLOGY

I emphasize the range of linguistic variation because *that's the fundamentally interesting thing* about language from a comparative point of view. We are the only known species whose communication system is profoundly variable in both form and content. . . .
—Stephen Levinson (2003a, p. 29)

INTRODUCTION

The primary purpose of every human language is to convey meaning, and semantic typology is the branch of linguistic typology that explores how different languages fulfill this function not only in ways that reflect deep underlying regularities, but also in ways that are remarkably diverse. This chapter provides a synopsis of this explicitly cross-linguistic approach to studying concepts, with the aim of giving readers enough background to understand and appreciate the more detailed typological data covered in Part II (see also Harrison, 2007; Koptjevskaja-Tamm et al., 2007; Evans, 2010, 2011; Malt & Majid, 2013; Majid, 2015; Moore et al., 2015; Bohnemeyer, 2019). The first section focuses on the fact that most people, including cognitive neuroscientists, are highly susceptible to mistakenly thinking that the concepts conveyed by the words in their language represent the world in an objective manner that is self-evident and inevitable. The next two sections then introduce some basic aspects of semantic typology by discussing a variety of cross-linguistic similarities and differences in the encoding of concepts, first with regard to lexical semantics, and then with regard to grammatical semantics.

THE APPARENT NATURALNESS
OF ONE'S OWN LANGUAGE

We humans are extremely group-minded creatures. Indeed, some scholars have argued that our extraordinary success as a species derives primarily from our zoologically unique ability to form complex cultures in which everyone cooperatively thinks and acts according to certain standards that are not only collectively understood and adopted, but also transmitted across generations, with the consequence that innovations gradually accumulate through a kind of ratchet effect (Tomasello, 1999, 2014; Richerson & Boyd, 2006; Sterelny, 2012; Richerson & Christiansen, 2013; Henrich, 2016; Laland, 2017; Boyd, 2018; Heyes, 2018). According to one version of this story, namely Tomasello's (2014) "shared intentionality hypothesis," during late hominin evolution, perhaps around 200,000 years ago, increases in population size and inter-group competition led to cognitive adaptations for constructing the essential elements of *cultural common ground*—that is, the practices, customs, attitudes, institutions, etc., that define a particular society and form the bedrock of its members' group identity. Examples of such shared knowledge and skills include tool-making methods, food-sharing rules, religious rituals, and so on. As Tomasello (2014, p. 92) puts it, "there are collectively accepted perspectives on things (e.g., how we classify the animals of the forest, how we constitute our governing council) and collectively known standards for how particular roles in particular cultural practices should be performed—indeed, must be performed—if one is to be a member of the group." This passage highlights the important point that because this group-level or "we" mode of thinking and acting evolved to promote efficient coordination among the members of a particular culture, it typically has a normative slant, encouraging people to not only conform to the traditional lifeways of their community, but also regard those lifeways as natural and appropriate.

Now, for any given society, cultural common ground consists largely of conceptual common ground, and conceptual common ground consists largely of word meanings. After all, word meanings are essentially conventional—i.e., socially sanctioned and shared—ways of categorizing experiences for communicative purposes, and even the smallest modern lexicons contain thousands of items (Pawley, 2006). According to Tomasello (2014), this has tremendous cognitive significance because it implies that, from early childhood onward, people do not have to invent their own ways of conceptualizing things; instead, they just have to learn the prepackaged concepts that are encoded by the words in the local language and that embody, in crystallized form, the collective intelligence amassed by the entire cultural group over a long period of historical time (see also Gelman & Roberts, 2017).

Moreover, consistent with the normative nature of the community standards that hold cultures together, people often develop the intuition that the ready-made and widely shared words in their language capture inherent, objective, and obvious aspects of the world. For instance, Malt and Majid (2013) observe that because monolingual English speakers routinely distinguish between *green* and *blue, cup* and *glass, slice* and *chop, on* and *in*, etc., they tend to think that such familiar, collectively endorsed conceptual distinctions map onto reality in a fairly straightforward and impartial manner. In the same vein, Wierzbicka (2014, p. 6) notes that "the conviction that the words of our native language fit the world as it really is, is deeply rooted in the thinking of many people." She also shows, however, that the proclivity to treat the meanings of English words as being "given" by the world is rampant not only among ordinary English speakers, but also among Anglophone scholars, especially those who have never had the psychologically disorienting experience of learning a foreign language and thereby being forced to recognize the cultural contingency of their native language. Such scholars, including those who study human cognition and behavior, are often unaware that although English has both global prestige and a scientific glow, most of its conventionalized concepts are actually rather parochial, reflecting forms of attention and strategies of categorization that differ significantly from those exhibited by other languages. This is exemplified by the fact that, as Wierzbicka (2014) demonstrates, seemingly natural terms like *mouse, table, creek, morning, lunch, teenager, niece, anger, kindness, commonsense, privacy*, and *cooperation* have no exact translation equivalents in many, if not most, of the roughly 6,500 languages scattered around the globe. Even more strikingly, Evans and Levinson (2009) point out that some languages lack what most English speakers would consider to be quite elementary and indispensable expressions, such as spatial notions like *left of*, numerals like *seven*, and logical connectives like *or*.

In the current context, the reason this matters is because it underscores one of the fundamental ways in which semantic typology can expand the scope of cognitive neuroscience and help it overcome its biases and limitations. As mentioned in the Preface, and in keeping with Wierzbicka's (2014) remarks about Anglophone scholars in other fields, it appears that the vast majority of cognitive neuroscientists who study concepts erroneously presuppose that a substantial proportion of the concepts encoded in English are self-evident and hence likely to be encoded in other languages as well. As a result, these researchers tend to assume that the human brain contains a single, albeit broadly distributed, conceptual system whose content and design are more or less the same for everyone everywhere, regardless of what language they happen to speak. This unwarranted assumption, which is usually tacit, frequently fuels another unwarranted assumption, which is also usually tacit, namely that whenever new discoveries are made about the neural representation and organization of English word meanings, they can safely be generalized to other languages. To be sure, a variety of factors do constrain the cross-linguistic encoding of concepts, and some of them may reflect universal, perhaps even innate, properties of the brain. But make no mistake: there is also a huge amount of diversity in the meanings expressed by the thousands of languages currently spoken on the planet, and this diversity bears directly on cognitive neuroscience, since it must ultimately be accommodated by any adequate theory of how concepts are implemented in the brain.

Part II of this book summarizes a number of detailed typological studies of the cross-linguistic representation of particular conceptual domains, and discusses how they can contribute to cognitive neuroscience. Here, however, the aim is much simpler: to convey a general sense of how semantic typology works and what it can reveal about the nature of concepts. To that end, the next two sections describe some of the major ways in which languages converge and diverge in the encoding of both lexical and grammatical aspects of meaning.

LEXICAL SEMANTICS

Loosely speaking, lexical semantics encompasses the meanings of nouns, verbs, and adjectives, which are usually regarded as the three main "open classes" of words, since their inventories are often in flux as old items fall into disuse and new ones are created.[1] More strictly speaking, however, lexical semantics includes only the grammatically

---

[1] It is worth noting, however, that some languages, like Kalam (Trans-New Guinea, Papua New Guinea) have very small and fairly fixed inventories of verbs (this is illustrated later in this chapter, and also in the section on serial verb constructions in Chapter 4). In addition, some languages, like Kham (Tibeto-Burman, Nepal), only have a few adjectives (Dixon, 2010b), and others, like Lao (Tai Kadai, Laos), arguably have none at all (Enfield, 2007).

irrelevant conceptual features of these word classes, i.e., the features that do not affect the range of morphological and/or syntactic constructions that the words can occur in. This can be clarified by considering the two English nouns *book* and *mud*. Prototypically, the former word has to do with collections of printed, written, or blank sheets of paper, whereas the latter word has to do with soft, wet, dark earth. These are the sorts of rich, informative conceptual features that give each word its unique meaning, and they fall under the rubric of lexical semantics because they have no influence on the grammatical behavior of the words. It is apparent, however, that the two words do differ grammatically—for instance, *book* can easily be pluralized (*There are three books on the porch*), whereas *mud* cannot (**There are three muds on the porch*).[2] But this particular difference cannot be traced to any of the conceptual features mentioned earlier; instead, it derives from the fact that *book* specifies a type of discrete object, thereby making it a pluralizable count noun, whereas *mud* specifies a type of substance, thereby making it a non-pluralizable mass noun. Because these highly schematic specifications affect the grammatical possibilities of the words, they belong to the realm of grammatical semantics—a topic addressed further below.

Lexical-semantic idiosyncrasies and universals

As already noted, it is often assumed that languages worldwide have myriad commonalities regarding the concepts encoded in their lexicons. For instance, Li and Gleitman (2002, p. 266) begin their paper with the following paragraph:

> Language has means for making reference to the objects, relations, properties, and events that populate our everyday world. It is possible to suppose that these linguistic categories and structures are more-or-less straightforward mappings from a pre-existing conceptual space, programmed into our biological nature: humans invent words that label their concepts. This perspective would begin to account for the fact that the grammars and lexicons of all languages are broadly similar, despite historical isolation and cultural disparities among their users.

Lupyan (2016, p. 521) points out that this passage exemplifies a fairly widespread view (e.g., Pinker, 1994; Bloom, 2002; Clark, 2004; Waxman & Gelman, 2009). Extensive typological research has shown, however, that such a view is deeply misguided. Despite the pervasive availability of easy-to-use computer programs that make translation seem effortless and trivial,[3] there is now abundant evidence that most of the words in any given language do not really have true matches, with identical denotational and connotational ranges, in the vocabularies of other languages (for an authoritative review, see Malt & Majid, 2013, and for an illuminating literary demonstration, see Weinberger & Paz, 1987).

---

[2] A qualification: Some people might argue that the sentence *There are three muds on the porch* can in fact be felicitous, but I submit that this is only possible under the special "variety" or "kind" construal of *muds,* and not under the standard "counting" construal (Langacker, 1987).

[3] For example: https://translate.google.com

Such exuberant lexical-semantic diversity may seem surprising, but it actually follows from the fact that every language is the outcome of a massive constraint satisfaction problem for which there are countless possible solutions. On the one hand, in all domains of experience, such as shapes, movements, and emotions, people can make innumerable discriminations, any of which could potentially be judged worthy of conventionalizing with separate words. But on the other hand, every language must restrict itself to a limited number of labeled categories so as to avoid overwhelming its speakers' learning and memory capacities. Thus, the precision of lexical-semantic content must always be traded off—at least to some degree, and often to a large degree—against the need for cognitive and communicative efficiency. As a result, there is immense variation in how different languages end up classifying the vast multidimensional realm of human experiences.[4]

Examples of idiosyncratic, language-particular forms of expression are legion in the semantic typology literature, and also in the rest of this book, so for present purposes just a few provocative illustrations should suffice. Here is an especially arresting case: Although most languages have a large inventory of verbs, others have a much smaller stock of them, and this leads to a very peculiar mode of event description. One such language, namely Kalam (Trans-New Guinea, Papua New Guinea), has only about 130 verb roots, and just 15 of them account for a whopping 89% of all verb occurrences in texts (Pawley, 1987, 1993, 2008, 2011). In this extremely unusual system, complex actions are not encoded by individual, semantically specific verbs, but rather by sequences of generic verbs, as in this rough translation of the English verb *massage*:

wyk	*d*	*ap*	*tan*	*d*	*ap*	*yap*	*g*
rub	hold	come	ascend	hold	come	descend	do

Turning to a more predictable kind of lexical-semantic variation, some languages develop sizable specialized vocabularies that are devoted to topics of great cultural importance. This is nicely exemplified by Central Yup'ik (Eskimo-Aleut, Alaska), which has no term corresponding to the English noun *boot,* but instead has a proliferation of terms for particular types of boots, as shown in Table 1.1 (Mithun, 2004). In addition, every language has lots of words with quite distinctive meanings that may seem quite marvelous when one first encounters them. For instance, Mundari (Austro-Asiatic, India) has a mellifluous term, *rawadawa*, that refers to "the sensation of realizing that you can get away with doing something wicked because no one is there to witness it" (Evans, 2010). Wagiman (Gunwingguan, Australia) has a verb (more precisely, a coverb), *murr,* that means "to walk along in the water looking for something with one's feet" (Wilson, 1999). Navajo (Athabaskan, Southwestern United States) has separate names, *-yá* and *-áázh,* for "walking alone" and "walking in pairs" (Mithun, 2004). And Zurich German, but not Standard German, has a term, *schärme*, that denotes "a place where it does not rain when it rains all around" (Bickel, 2014).

---

[4] This variation is not, however, completely unlimited, as demonstrated below with regard to color (see also Kemp et al., 2018).

Table 1.1. Central Yup'ik (Eskimo-Aleut, Alaska) lacks a general term equivalent to the English noun *boot*, but it has a large inventory of more specific terms for particular types of boots.

Terms for Boots	Meanings
nanilnguaraq	short skin boot
amirak	fishskin boot
ayagcuun	thigh-high boot with fur on the outside
catquk	dyed sealskin boot
ciuqalek	fancy dyed sealskin boot with dark fur over the shin
iqertaq	sealskin boot with fur inside
ivrarcuun	wading boot
ivruciq	waterproof skin boot
atallgaq	ankle-high skin boot
kameksak	ankle-high skin boot, house slipper
qaliruaq	ankle-high skin boot for dress wear
piluguk	skin boot
sap'akiq	manufactured boot or shoe

From Mithun (2004).

Given all this cross-linguistic diversity, it is natural, of course, to ask whether there are any genuinely universal lexical-semantic structures (von Fintel & Matthewson, 2008). This continues to be a controversial question, but some researchers believe the answer is yes. According to the Natural Semantic Metalanguage research program that Anna Wierzbicka has been directing for over 30 years, all languages do share a small set of symbolic units that encode the very same basic concepts (e.g., Goddard & Wierzbicka, 1994, 2002; Wierzbicka, 1996; Goddard, 2008). These concepts are frequently called semantic primes or atoms because their content is putatively undecomposable. Approximately 70 such primes have been posited so far, and a large proportion of them are lexical-semantic rather than grammatical-semantic in character, falling under such headings as substantives (*thing, body*), relational substantives (*kind, part*), evaluators (*good, bad*), descriptors (*big, small*), mental predicates (*want, think, know, feel, see, hear*), speech (*say, words*), events (*do, happen, move, touch*), and life and death (*live, die*). Even some of these apparently incontrovertible candidates for lexical-semantic universals have been challenged, however. For example, Evans (1994, 2007) argues that there is no counterpart to *want* in Kayardild (Tangic, Australia) and that neither *think* nor *know* map straightforwardly onto the mental predicates of Dalabon (Gunwingguan, Australia).

Lexical-semantic fields

In every language, the meanings of most words are defined partly in relation to the meanings of other words, especially those that fall within the same semantic field. For example, Levin (1993) sorted over 3,000 English verbs into approximately 50 classes and 200 subclasses. Representative classes include verbs of contact by impact (e.g., *tap, poke, pound, swat*), verbs of throwing (e.g., *toss, fling, hurl, lob*), verbs of creation (e.g., *build, assemble, sculpt, weave*), and verbs of ingesting (e.g., *eat, chew, gobble, devour*). The verbs in a particular class collectively provide a richly detailed categorization of the relevant semantic field by making distinctions, sometimes of a remarkably fine-grained nature, along a number of different parameters. As an illustration, verbs of destruction are distinguished by the composition of the entity to be destroyed (e.g., *tear* vs. *smash*), the degree of force (e.g., *tear* vs. *rip*), and the extent of deformation (e.g., *tear* vs. *shred*). In addition, the verbs in a particular class are organized according to principled semantic relations such as the following (Fellbaum, 1998): synonymy, in which two verbs have nearly identical meanings (e.g., *shout* and *yell*); antonymy, in which two verbs have opposite meanings (e.g., *lengthen* and *shorten*); hyponymy, in which one verb occupies a higher taxonomic level than another (e.g., *talk* and *lecture*); and cohyponymy, in which two verbs occupy the same taxonomic level (e.g., *bow* and *curtsy*). Interestingly, a speaker's choice of which verb to use in a certain situation may have social repercussions affecting his or her rights, duties, and accountability. For instance, Enfield (2015a, p. 217) cites a case, originally reported by Sidnell and Barnes (2013), in which "two children dispute whether one of them had 'tapped' an object or 'poked' it, with obvious implications for culpability depending on whose version is accepted."

The languages of the world display numerous similarities and differences in how they lexically subdivide the same semantic fields, and in recent years an increasing amount of research has been devoted to documenting the extent of this variation, identifying the factors that drive and constrain it, and determining whether it is significantly greater for some fields than others. Comparative studies involving anywhere from a handful of languages to well over a hundred have already addressed a wide range of domains, including plants and animals (e.g., Berlin, 1992), body parts (e.g., Enfield et al., 2006), household containers (e.g., Malt et al., 1999), landscapes (e.g., Burenhult & Levinson, 2008), colors (e.g., Kay & Maffi, 2005), temperatures (e.g., Koptjevskaja-Tamm, 2015), odors (Majid & Burenhult, 2014), spatial relations (e.g., Levinson & Wilkins, 2006a), kinship (e.g., Kemp & Regier, 2012), numbers (e.g., Comrie, 2005), emotions (e.g., Wierzbicka, 1999), and several categories of action, such as locomoting (e.g., Slobin et al., 2014), giving (e.g., Newman, 1998), reciprocating (e.g., Evans et al., 2011), cutting and breaking (e.g., Majid & Bowerman, 2007), putting and taking (e.g., Kopecka & Narasimhan, 2012), and eating and drinking (e.g., Newman, 2009). All of these studies, and many others as well, demonstrate that languages differ multifariously in their lexical partitioning of the same semantic fields while still tending to exhibit overarching patterns. Several studies of some of the fields just mentioned are discussed at length in Part II of this volume, together with pertinent neuroscientific findings. To get an initial sense here of how such research is conducted, we will briefly consider a topic that is not covered later—namely, the intensively investigated domain of colors.

Color is a very salient aspect of human visual experience, and the number of shades that people can perceptually distinguish is enormous—approximately two million just noticeable differences (JNDs). In semantic typology, one of the oldest issues involves the degree to which languages converge and diverge in their use of basic color terms to classify this broad spectrum of sensations. To qualify as a basic color term, a word must be monolexemic and familiar to most speakers, and it must also denote a range of colors that is not subsumed within the range of a separate term. Some English words that satisfy these criteria are *red, yellow*, and *purple*. Some others that clearly do not are *forward fuchsia, solaria*, and *euphoric lilac*, which are on the flamboyant list of over 1,500 paint colors available from Sherwin-Williams. Because the typological literature on color is quite large, only a small part of it is summarized here, with special emphasis on some key methods and results.

Building on classic work by Berlin and Kay (1969), Kay et al. (2009) carried out the World Color Survey (WCS), which explored the color lexicons of 110 geographically and genealogically disparate languages from non-industrialized societies. The stimuli consisted of a standardized array of 330 colored chips representing 40 equally spaced, maximally saturated Munsell hues at 8 levels of lightness, as well as 10 achromatic shades extending from white to gray to black (Figure 1.1). In each language community, a fieldworker asked speakers (mean $n = 24$, range = 6–30) to not only name the color of each chip in the grid (a task designed to identify the breadth of each category), but also indicate which chip best exemplified the meaning of each term (a task designed to identify the prototype or focus of each category).

The main results reinforced and extended those from Berlin and Kay's (1969) previous study. Cross-linguistically, basic color terms denote three general types of categories: (1) primary color categories, of which there are precisely six—white, black, red, yellow, green, and blue; (2) composite color categories, which are fuzzy unions of the primaries—e.g., green/blue, where "/" indicates "or"; and (3) derived color categories, which are mixtures of the primaries—e.g., pink, which is a mixture of white and red. In addition, color term systems tend to evolve over historical time in a manner that proceeds through a succession of increasingly fine-grained partitions of perceptual color space. In fact, of the 110 languages in the WCS, 91 (83%) have systems that fall along the central line of development shown in Figure 1.2. For each kind of system illustrated in this figure, a representative language is mentioned in Table 1.2. These findings reveal several interesting aspects of typological variation and uniformity in the lexical encoding of color concepts (see also Haynie & Bowern, 2016). For instance, there are languages that fail to distinguish between red and yellow, and there are also languages that fail to distinguish between green and blue, but as a system develops, the former contrast always emerges before the latter, and this evolutionary pattern justifies the following implicational universal: if a language distinguishes between green and blue, then it also distinguishes between red and yellow.

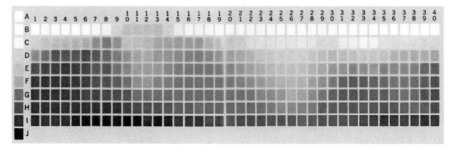

Figure 1.1. The World Color Survey stimulus palette. A color version is in the color plates section. From Kay & Regier (2003, p. 9086).

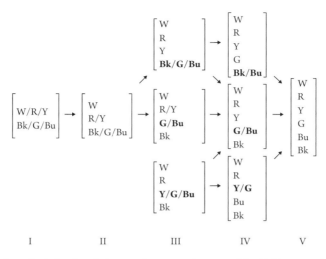

Figure 1.2. A typological and evolutionary scheme covering most of the 110 languages in the World Color Survey. Letters represent basic color categories according to the following conventions: W = White; R = Red; Y = Yellow; Bk = Black; G = Green; Bu = Blue. Composite categories are marked with "/", which means "or." Each bracketed set of letters represents a type of color term system, and nine different systems are shown to evolve over five historical stages (marked I through V), with the system(s) at each successive stage containing one or more term(s) than at the previous stage, reflecting the progressive differentiation of color space. Derived categories (e.g., pink) usually appear after stage V and are not included here because showing all of the possible combinations would lead to pointless complexity. From Kay et al. (2009, p. 11).

Statistical analyses of the WCS data have yielded many more insights. Kay and Regier (2003) compared the centroids—i.e., the centers of mass of the named sets of chips—of all color categories in all 110 languages, and found that they not only clustered around certain points in perceptual color space, but did so in a way that was significantly greater than chance (Figure 1.3; see also Lindsey & Brown, 2006).

Table 1.2. Representative languages with the color term systems shown in Figure 1.2.

Systems	Representative Languages
Stage I	Dani (Trans-New Guinea, Papua New Guinea)
Stage II	Ejagham (Bantoid, Nigeria/Cameroon)
Stage III-top	Kwerba (Tor-Kwerba, Indonesia)
Stage III-middle	Múra-Pirahã (unclassified, Brazil)
Stage III-bottom	Karajá (Karajá, Brazil)
Stage IV-top	Martu-Wangka (Pama-Nyungan, Australia)
Stage IV-middle	Bhili (Indo-European, India)
Stage IV-bottom	Cree (Algonquian, Canada)
Stage V	Kamano-Kafe (Trans-New Guinea, Papua New Guinea)

Data drawn from Kay et al. (2009).

(a)

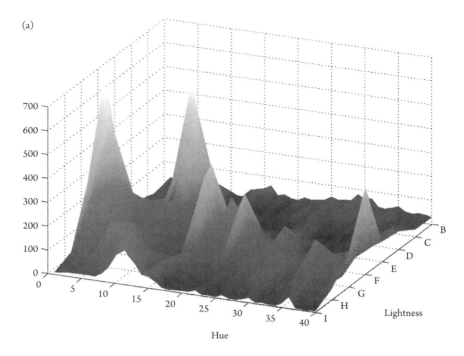

(b)

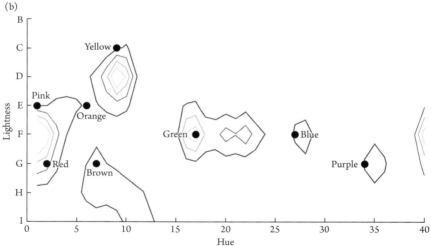

Figure 1.3. Distribution of centroids (i.e., centers of mass of named sets of chips) of all color categories in all 110 languages in the World Color Survey (WCS). (a) The floor plane corresponds to the chromatic portion of the color stimulus array shown in Figure 1.1. The height of the surface at each point in the plane denotes the number of speaker centroids in the WCS data set that fall at that position in color space. (b) The distribution of *a* is viewed from above by a contour plot. For each cluster, the outermost contour represents a height of 100 centroids, and each subsequent contour represents an increment in height of 100 centroids. The centroids of English color terms are represented by labeled, filled circles. Those for purple, blue, green, and brown fall at or near the peaks of the WCS distribution, and those for the other English terms are in the neighborhood of WCS peaks. The WCS peak midway between green and blue reflects the fact that most WCS languages have a composite term that spans those two categories. Similarly, the reason the centroids for English red and yellow seem to deviate from the nearest WCS peaks is because most WCS languages have composite terms that lump pink with red on the one hand, and orange with yellow on the other. From Kay & Regier (2003, p. 9088).

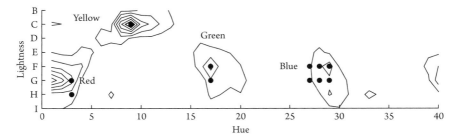

Figure 1.4. Contour plot of the best-example choices of all color categories in all 110 languages in the World Color Survey (WCS), compared with those for English, and mapped on the chromatic portion of the color stimulus array shown in Figure 1.1. The outermost contour of each cluster represents 100 hits, and each subsequent inner contour represents an increment of 100 hits. The black dots indicate the best examples of the English color terms, provided by one speaker, as reported by Berlin and Kay (1969). The best examples in the WCS data cluster at or near those in the English data, suggesting that these regions in perceptual color space are organized around universal foci. From Regier et al. (2005, p. 8387).

Subsequently, Regier et al. (2005) examined the best-example choices for all color categories in all 110 languages, and found that they fell near the prototypes of English white, black, red, yellow, green, and blue—a discovery which suggests that these particular categories may be anchored in universal foci (Figure 1.4). Furthermore, using computer simulations, Regier et al. (2007) created color term systems with 2, 3, 4, 5, and 6 categories that were theoretically optimal—i.e., well-formed insofar as they maximized perceptual similarity within categories and minimized it between them— and found that the models placed category boundaries in roughly the same places as many real languages with the corresponding terms (Figure 1.5). Taken together, these results support the view that although color naming strategies vary substantially across the world's languages, they are by no means random, since they tend to coalesce around a constrained set of categories that partition the semantic field of color in fairly predictable ways (see also Lindsey & Brown, 2009; Abbott et al., 2016).

At the same time, however, many questions remain open. For instance, some languages, such as Russian (Winawer et al., 2007) and Greek (Thierry et al., 2009), have two basic color terms for blue—essentially, one for dark blue and another for light blue—but it is unclear why this split sometimes occurs. Another concern has to do with the fact that the colored chips in the WCS were fully saturated. As Roberson and Hanley (2010) point out, most of the non-industrialized communities that were included in the WCS lacked printing and dyeing facilities and hence may not have had much, if any, prior exposure to such colorful stimuli. As a consequence, it is possible that individual speakers, and perhaps even entire groups of speakers, differed in their willingness to apply their basic color terms to those stimuli. There is also continuing uncertainty as to the origin(s) of the putatively universal aspects of color naming, with competing hypotheses involving properties of the physical environment (e.g., Shepard, 1992), sociolinguistic factors underlying communicative efficiency (e.g., Steels & Belpaeme, 2005), and biological mechanisms of color vision (e.g., Skelton et al., 2017). Finally, and of greatest relevance here, so far relatively little research has addressed the neural substrates of the meanings of basic color terms, either in English

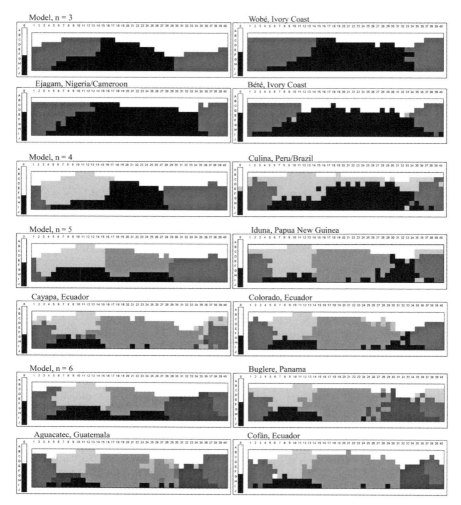

Figure 1.5. Models of optimal partitions for systems of 3, 4, 5, and 6 color categories, each compared with color naming schemes of selected languages from the World Color Survey, and mapped on the chromatic portion of the color stimulus array shown in Figure 1.1. A color version is in the color plates section. From (Regier et al., 2007, p. 1439).

or in other languages, leaving this topic ripe for further investigation (Chao & Martin, 1999; Pulvermüller & Hauk, 2006; Tan et al., 2008; Siok et al., 2009; Thierry et al., 2009; Kwok et al., 2011; Mo et al., 2011; Rogers et al., 2015; see also Figure 6.2 and the associated text in Chapter 6 of this volume).

Lexicalization patterns

Woven into the fabric of every language are certain lexicalization patterns—that is, preferences as to which components of concepts are systematically mapped onto which classes of words. As with other aspects of lexical semantics, these preferences differ substantially, but not without limit, across languages. One could argue, however, that this kind of diversity is especially interesting, since it reveals cross-cultural variation in some of the most fundamental forms of information packaging for communicative purposes.

Consider, for example, how the geometric properties of objects are lexicalized by different languages. In English and other familiar European languages, these properties are usually encoded by object nouns; indeed, several studies have shown that shape is among the most critical semantic features of object nouns in English (Vinson & Vigliocco, 2008; Hoffman & Lambon Ralph, 2013; Binder et al., 2016). In many other languages, however, the majority of object nouns encode material essence rather than shape, and the latter information is expressed through other lexical categories.

For instance, in Yucatec (Mayan, Mexico) the word *ha'as* has a very general meaning—something like "banana stuff"—and its specific spatial interpretation in a given context depends on a co-occurring element called a classifier (Lucy, 1992). As discussed in detail in Chapter 3, classifiers characterize objects along a variety of semantic parameters—most notably, animacy, shape, size, constitution, and function/interaction—and some languages have as many as several hundred of them. According to Levinson (1996, p. 185), to refer to a discrete entity in Yucatec, a classifier is required "to impose individuation on the material, metaphorically in much the way that a cookie-cutter cuts up undifferentiated dough!" The examples on the left side of Table 1.3 show how Yucatec speakers employ different shape-related

Table 1.3. In Yucatec (Mayan, Mexico), whenever a speaker wants to refer to a certain number of objects of a particular type, he or she must use a construction that includes not only the appropriate quantifier and noun, but also the appropriate classifier. Because many nouns encode formless substances, classifiers provide essential information about the schematic shapes of the designated entities. In this manner, they serve important geometrically mediated unitizing functions.

Different Classifiers, Same Noun	*Same Classifier, Different Nouns*
un-tz'iit ha'as	*un-tz'iit ha'as*
one-NUM.CL:1D banana.stuff	one-NUM.CL:1D banana.stuff
"one 1D banana (i.e., the fruit)"	"one 1D banana (i.e., the fruit)"
un-waal ha'as	*un-tz'iit kib'*
one-NUM.CL:2D banana.stuff	one-NUM.CL:1D wax
"one 2D banana (i.e., the leaf)"	"one 1D wax (i.e., a candle)"
un-p'iit ha'as	*un-tz'iit che'*
one-NUM.CL:BIT banana.stuff	one-NUM.CL:1D wood
"one bit banana (i.e., a bit of the fruit)"	"one 1D wood (i.e., a stick)"
un-kuuch ha'as	*un-tz'iit nal*
one-NUM.CL:LOAD banana.stuff	one-NUM.CL:1D corn
"one load banana (i.e., a bunch)"	"one 1D corn (i.e., an ear)"

Abbreviations: NUM.CL = numeral classifier; 1D = one-dimensional; 2D = two-dimensional.
Data drawn from Lucy (1992).

classifiers to convey different structural construals of the otherwise formless "banana stuff" denoted by *ha'as*. Orthogonally, when the same classifier is applied to different nouns, it performs more or less the same kind of geometrically specified unitizing role, as shown by the examples on the right side of Table 1.3.

Yet another lexicalization pattern involves mapping the geometric properties of objects onto elements known as dispositional predicates (Ameka & Levinson, 2007). For instance, Tzeltal (Mayan, Mexico) has over 250 such items, which are derived from verb roots, and which encode precise distinctions of shape, position, orientation, and configuration. As in Yucatec, most nouns in Tzeltal are mass-like, and partly for this reason, when Tzeltal speakers describe the location of an object, they often use a dispositional predicate to specify its spatial characteristics, thereby indicating not only where it is, but also what it looks like (Brown, 1994; Bohnemeyer & Brown, 2007). Here are several examples that convey the flavor of this phenomenon: *waxal*, "be-located, of a tall oblong-shaped container or solid object canonically standing"; *pakal*, "be-located, of a blob with a distinguishably flat surface lying face-down"; *lechel*, "be-located, of a wide flat object lying flat"; and *bech'el*, "be-located, of a long thin flexible object coiled around another object." These items, and dozens of others, attest to a peculiar lexicalization pattern in which extensive geometric information about objects is provided not by nouns, but rather by words derived from verb roots (for further details see the section on events of putting and taking in Chapter 4, and the discussion of topological relations in Chapter 5).

Shifting to a different conceptual domain, cross-linguistic studies have also disclosed a number of contrasting lexicalization patterns for motion events. In fact, this has been one of the hottest areas of typological research for nearly 40 years (e.g., Talmy, 1985, 1991, 2000; Matsumoto, 2003; Slobin, 2004, 2006; Levinson & Wilkins, 2006a; Filipović, 2007b; Beavers et al., 2010; Croft et al., 2010; Imbert, 2012; Goschier & Stefanowitsch, 2013; Levin & Rappaport Hovav, in press; see also the references in footnote 1 of Slobin et al., 2014). But because this topic is addressed in depth in Chapter 4, we will look at only a few of the major findings here.

First of all, most if not all languages treat motion events as having at least four basic semantic components: (1) the *figure*, which is the entity that moves, such as a person, animal, or inanimate object; (2) the *manner*, which is how the figure moves relative to its internal frame of reference, such as walking, swimming, or spinning; (3) the *path*, which is where the figure moves relative to its external frame of reference, such as into, onto, or across something; and (4) the *ground*, which is an entity that serves as a landmark for determining the path, such as the source or goal of motion. To take a simple example, in an ordinary scene in which a man walks across a street, the figure is the man, the manner of motion is walking, the path of motion is the trajectory that leads from one side of the street to the other, and the ground is the street itself.

Now, although languages worldwide distinguish between the four rudimentary semantic components of motion events just mentioned, they vary in how these components are preferentially encoded. In English, all of the components tend to be realized in a single clause such as *The bottle floated into the cave*, where the figure and ground entities are expressed by separate noun-phrases, the manner of motion is expressed by the verb *floated*, and the path of motion is expressed by the preposition *into*. This lexicalization pattern is fairly common cross-linguistically, but many other languages adopt a different strategy whereby the path component is encoded by the main-clause verb, forcing the manner component to take on adjunct status in an optional adverbial clause, as in the following sentence from Spanish:

La	*botella*	*entró*	*a*	*la*	*cueva*	(*flotando*)
The	bottle	entered	to	the	cave	(floating)

In Chapter 4 we will see that a lot depends on which of these two lexicalization patterns is dominant in a given language. For instance, the pattern found in languages like English gives rise to relatively large inventories of manner of motion verbs, whereas the one found in languages like Spanish is more often associated with relatively small inventories.

Among the other known lexicalization patterns for motion events, perhaps the most intriguing involves mapping features of the moving entity—i.e., the figure—onto the verb. To be sure, English does have a construction like this, but its use is highly restricted, being applied primarily to weather events—e.g., *It rained/hailed/ snowed in through the window*. In contrast, some languages employ this kind of pattern quite regularly, as illustrated by the sampling of verb roots from Atsugewi (Hokan, Northern California) in Table 1.4. Along similar lines, the Athabaskan languages of North America are renowned for having parallel sets of verbs for events of giving, taking, handling, etc., with each set consisting of multiple verbs that differ with regard to the type of object that is involved (Davidson et al., 1963; Carter, 1976; Rice, 1998; Mithun, 1999). For example, there is no general verb for "toss" in Navajo; instead, there are multiple verbs that are sensitive to the size, shape, rigidity, and constituency of the thing being tossed, as shown in Table 1.5. As with Atsugewi, what we have here is a situation in which familiar conceptual components—namely, the physical properties of objects—are systematically lexicalized in unfamiliar ways—namely, in verbs rather than nouns. Not surprisingly, such phenomena have significant implications for the neural substrates of lexical semantics, as discussed in Chapter 4.

Table 1.4. In Atsugewi (Hokan, Northern California), many verb roots encode detailed spatial information about the figure entity.

Verb Roots	Meanings
-lup-	for a small shiny spherical object (e.g., a round candy, an eyeball, a hailstone) to move/be-located
-i-	for a small planar object that can be functionally affixed (e.g., a stamp, a clothing patch, a button, a shingle) to move/be-located
-caq-	for a slimy lumpish object (e.g., a toad, a cow dropping) to move/be-located
-swal-	for a limp linear object suspended by one end (e.g., a shirt on a clothesline, a hanging dead rabbit) to move/be-located
-qput-	for loose dry dirt to move/be-located
-staq-	for runny icky material (e.g., mud, manure, rotten tomatoes, guts, chewed gum) to move/be-located

From Talmy (2000, p. 58).

Table 1.5. In Navajo (Athabaskan, Western United States), there are parallel sets of verbs for giving, taking, handling, etc., with each set consisting of multiple verbs that differ with regard to the size, shape, rigidity, and constituency of the thing being manipulated. This is illustrated here with verbs of tossing.

Verb Roots	Meanings
-łne'	to toss a small, round object such as a stone, ball, loaf of bread, coin, or bottle
-łjool	to toss something amorphous in texture such as a loose wad of wool or a bunch of hay
-łtłéé'	to toss wet, mushy matter like dough or a wet rag
-'ah	to toss a flat, flexible object such as a blanket, tablecloth, bedsheet, towel, or sheet of paper
-łdééL	to toss a slender, flexible object such as a string of beads, piece of rope, belt, chain, or paired objects such as socks, gloves, shoes, scissors, or pliers, or a conglomerate such as a set of tools or the unspecified contents of one's pockets
łt'e'	to toss a stiff, slender object such as a match, pencil, cigarette, stick of gum, broom, or rifle, or an animate object such as an animal or a doll
-yí	to toss something bulky, massive, and heavy in the form of a pack or load, such as a quiver of arrows or a medicine pouch
-łkaad	to toss something in an open container such as a glass of water, bowl of soup, dish of food, bucket of sand, box of apples, or dirt in a shovel
-nil	to toss a conglomeration of objects that can be readily visualized, such as several books, eggs, or boxes

From Mithun (2004, p. 125).

GRAMMATICAL SEMANTICS

Whereas the lexical-semantic specifications of a sentence provide the bulk of its conceptual content, the grammatical-semantic specifications provide a relational framework for structuring that content. Three different types of grammatical-semantic notions can be distinguished on purely formal grounds. As mentioned earlier, one type, which is always coded covertly, involves the grammatically relevant semantic features of open-class items, like the conceptual properties of *book* and *mud* that make the former a count noun and the latter a mass noun. Another type, which is always coded overtly, involves the meanings of closed-class items—i.e., items that usually form small, restricted sets that change very slowly over historical time. Some closed-class items are always bound to stems, like the English past-tense suffix -*ed*. Many others, however, are free-standing elements that are often called function words or, more simply, functors. Some English examples include articles like *a* and *the*, demonstratives like *this* and *that*, pronouns like *he* and *she*, modal verbs like *may* and *must*, prepositions like *in* and *on*, and conjunctions like *and* and *or*. The third and final manifestation of grammatical semantics involves the covertly coded meanings of morphological and syntactic constructions. For example, the English Caused Motion

Construction consists of a particular clausal pattern—roughly, "Subject Verb Object Oblique"—that is directly associated with a particular schematic meaning—roughly, "X causes Y to move along path Z." Evidence for this complex pairing of syntax and semantics comes from sentences like *She sneezed the foam off the cappucino*, since the construction itself is what allows the typically intransitive verb *sneeze* to be used transitively (Goldberg, 1995).

To get a better sense of the differences between lexical and grammatical semantics, it is useful to consider Talmy's (1988, pp. 172–173) analysis of the sentence *A rustler lassoed the steers*. The top part of Table 1.6 focuses on the lexical-semantic aspects of the overall meaning, and the bottom part focuses on the grammatical-semantic aspects. As Talmy observes, the lexical elements "are fewer in number, but their specifications

Table 1.6. Talmy's analysis of the lexical-semantic and grammatical-semantic aspects of the sentence *A rustler lassoed the steers*.

	Lexical Elements	Semantic Features
a.	*rustler*	a person, property ownership, illegality, mode of activity, etc.
b.	*steer*	object of particular appearance, physical makeup, relation to animal kingdom, castration, etc.
c.	*lasso*	certain objects (a body and a lasso) in particular configurations, certain movement sequences, accompanying cognitive intending, directing, monitoring, etc.
	Grammatical Elements	Semantic Features
a.	*-ed*	occurring at a time before that of the present communication
b.	*the*	has ready identifiability for the addressee
c.	*a*	not before in discussion or otherwise readily identifiable for the addressee
d.	*-s*	multiple instantiation of object
e.	*a . . . -ø*	unitary instantiation of object
f.	the grammatical category of "verb" for *lasso*	event character
g/h.	the grammatical category of "noun" for *rustler/steer*	entity character
i/j.	the grammatical relations of "subject"/"object" for *rustler/steer*	agent/patient (among the possibilities)
k.	active voice	point-of-view at the agent
l.	intonation, word order, pattern of auxiliaries	the speaker knows the situation to be true and asserts it

From Talmy (1988, pp. 172–173).

are greater in quantity and complexity, and function more to contribute content than structure." In contrast, the grammatical elements "seem more spare and simpler," and they serve to "establish the main delineations of the scene organization and communicative setting. . . ." These differences can be brought out even more sharply by independently manipulating one or the other type of meaning. Thus, if we change just the lexical elements, as in *A machine stamped the envelopes*, we get a very different referential scene, but one with the same basic structural mold. Conversely, if we change just the grammatical elements, as in *Will the rustlers lasso a steer?*, we alter the schematic organization of the scene and the discourse-pragmatic properties of the utterance, but the most contentful concepts are preserved. (See also Sapir's [1921, pp. 86–98] famous discussion of the sentence *The farmer killed a duckling*.)

Grammatical-semantic idiosyncrasies and universals

Every language requires its speakers to routinely track certain dimensions of experience, since these dimensions must be expressed as certain grammatical-semantic notions in certain frequently occurring contexts. Languages vary greatly, however, as to precisely which aspects of reality are given such preferential treatment. This insight was originally made by Franz Boas, an anthropological linguist who elaborated the idea in the early 20th century by comparing the English sentence *The man is sick* with the corresponding sentences in a variety of North American Indian languages. He noted that in several Siouan languages distributed across the Great Plains, one would have to indicate whether the man is moving or at rest; that in a Wakashan language of Southwestern Canada called Kwakiutl, one would have to specify whether he is visible or nonvisible to the speaker, and also whether he is near the speaker, the hearer, or a third person; and that in a language of the Eskimo-Aleut family spoken way up on Baffin Island in Northern Canada, one would just say "man sick" without having to encode definiteness, tense, visibility, or location. Boas remarked that "when we consider for a moment what this implies, it will be recognised that in each language only a part of the complete concept that we have in mind is expressed, and that each language has a peculiar tendency to select this or that aspect of the mental image which is conveyed by the expression of the thought" (Boas, 1911/1966, pp. 38–39; for further discussion, see Jakobson, 1959, and Slobin, 1996).

More recent typological research has documented extensive cross-linguistic diversity regarding not only which dimensions of experience speakers are forced to track for grammatical-semantic purposes, but also which distinctions they are forced to make along those dimensions. Here are just three representative examples from the vast literature on this complicated topic (for a broad overview, see Dixon, 2010a, 2010b, 2012). First, in many languages speakers must use so-called evidential markers to indicate the source of information for *all* statements expressed in the past tense and declarative mood (Aikhenvald & Dixon, 2014; Aikhenvald, 2018b). Some evidential systems make just a two-way contrast between eyewitness and non-eyewitness, but others make up to five distinctions, as shown in Table 1.7. Second, more than 20 Australian Aboriginal languages in different geographic regions have complex personal pronoun systems that are sensitive to kinship or moiety relations, requiring speakers to attend to such factors as whether people are in even-numbered generations (such as siblings, spouses, or grandkin) or odd-numbered generations (such as parents or

Table 1.7. In a number of languages of the Tucanoan family (Columbia/Brazil), if a speaker wants to say that the dog ate the fish, he or she must include one of five evidentiality markers.

Type	Use
Visual	The speaker saw the dog eat the fish.
Nonvisual	The speaker heard the dog in the kitchen (but did not see it), or the speaker smelled fish on the dog's breath.
Apparent	There are fish bones spread on the floor around the dog, which looks satisfied, as if after a good meal.
Reported	Someone told the speaker that the dog ate the fish.
Assumed	The fish was raw, and people do not eat raw fish, so it must have been the dog that took it.

From Dixon (1997, p. 120).

children) with respect to each other (Evans, 2003). Third, although English speakers are accustomed to a simple tense system that only distinguishes between past, present, and future, some languages have more highly developed systems that obligate speakers to provide further information about when an event occurred relative to the time of utterance (Dahl & Velupillai, 2005). For instance, whenever a speaker of Yagua (Peba-Yaguan, Peru) wants to refer to an event in the past, he or she must specify one of five different degrees of remoteness from the present, as shown in Table 1.8. In Part II, we will encounter many other interesting grammatical-semantic notions, specifically involving the conceptualization of objects, events, and spatial relations.

Are there any universals in this realm of linguistic knowledge? Only a few attempts have been made to generate an actual list of concepts that are putatively represented in all grammatical systems. Most notably, the chief advocates of the Natural Semantic

Table 1.8. Remoteness distinctions in the past-tense system of Yagua (Peba-Yaguan, Peru).

Name	Use	Suffix	Example
Proximate 1	a few hours before the time of utterance	-jásiy	*ray-jiya-jásiy* 1SG-go-PROX1 "I went (this morning)"
Proximate 2	one day before the time of utterance	-jay	*ray-junnúúy-jay-níí* 1SG-see-PROX2-3SG "I saw him (yesterday)"
Past 1	roughly 1 week ago to 1 month ago	-sij	*sa-díí-sij-maa* 3SG-die-PST1-PERF "He has died (between a week and a month ago)"
Past 2	roughly 1 to 2 months ago up to 1 to 2 years ago	-tíy	*sa-díí-tíy-maa* 3SG-die-PST2-PERF "He has died (between 1 to 2 months and a year ago)"
Past 3	distant or legendary past	-jada	*ray-rupay-jada* 1SG-be.born-PST3 "I was born (a number of years ago)"

From Dahl & Velupillai (2005, p. 269).

Metalanguage research program, which we discussed earlier in the context of lexical semantics, have argued that a variety of atomic grammatical-semantic notions are universally encoded in one way or another (e.g., Goddard & Wierzbicka, 1994, 2002; Wierzbicka, 1996; Goddard, 2008). They are grouped into categories such as determiners (*this, the same, other/else*), quantifiers (*one, some, all, many/much*), location, existence, possession, and specification (*be somewhere, be someone/something, there is, have*), time (*when, now, before, after*), space (*where, here, above, below, near, far, side, inside*), logical concepts (*not, maybe, can, because, if*), intensifiers and augmentors (*very, more*), and similarity (*like/as*). This approach, however, has not attracted many supporters in the field of typology.

Instead, more effort has been devoted to understanding why the grammatical systems of languages worldwide tend to incorporate certain *kinds* of concepts rather than others. For instance, nouns are frequently inflected for object-related features like number, case, gender, definiteness, and possession, but not, say, color; and verbs are frequently inflected for event-related features like tense, aspect, mood, modality, and voice, but not, say, ambient temperature (Talmy, 1988; Croft, 1991). According to Slobin (2001), such tendencies follow naturally from the fact that the only kinds of concepts that are psychologically capable of being encoded by grammar are those that can easily be stored and retrieved, and that are also applicable to a wide range of discourse contexts. As he points out, if English speakers had to inflect all object nouns for color, this would lead to innumerable communication breakdowns. For example, "when a newscaster reports a bomb explosion in the Paris Metro, he would have to know the color of the bomb, or the Metro, or the explosion" (Slobin, 2001, p. 436). Similar problems would also arise if we had to mark verbs for the ambient temperature of the designated events: "if I wanted to tell you a juicy bit of gossip, I would have to remember whether the reported event (or the time of my hearing about it) occurred on a warm or a cool day" (Slobin, 2001, p. 436).[5] Nevertheless, Slobin acknowledges that there do not appear to be any rigid cognitive limitations on the kinds of concepts that can, in principle, be grammatically encoded, and it is clear from the data already presented (e.g., intricately kin-sensitive pronouns) that which concepts do end up achieving this status varies considerably across languages, presumably because of significant differences in cultural preoccupations. Many more examples of such diversity are discussed in Part II, together with their implications for the neural substrates of meaning.

Grammatical-semantic fields

A large proportion of typological research has been devoted to investigating cross-linguistic similarities and differences in both the conceptual organization and the formal expression of particular grammatical-semantic fields. One way in which such studies are conducted is by focusing on a well-defined domain and systematically

---

[5] Another reason why color and temperature never seem to be grammaticized may be that they are often—not always, but often—predictable. For instance, many objects have prototypical colors, and if one knows that an event occurred in, say, the winter, one can safely assume that the temperature was cold. From an information-theoretic perspective, it would be optimal for a communication system to minimize the obligatory encoding of features like these that have a fairly high degree of predictability. I thank Rutvik Desai for these observations.

exploring its treatment in a representative sample of the world's languages, not only by elucidating the range and patterning of distinctions that are made in the given conceptual territory, but also by identifying, and ranking according to preference, the kinds of grammatical devices that are used to encode those distinctions. For instance, Stassen (2009) investigated how the seemingly straightforward topic of predicative possession (e.g., *The boy has a bicycle*) is semantically and syntactically treated in a globally balanced sample of 425 languages. He found that this is actually a rather complex realm, as reflected in part by the fact that many languages lack an equivalent to the verb *have*. Another strategy that is often pursued is to concentrate on a specific kind of grammatical device and examine the sorts of meanings that it encodes cross-linguistically. This approach is exemplified by Aikhenvald's (2000) analysis of nominal classifiers in about 500 languages from every major family and area around the world. As mentioned earlier, and as discussed in depth in Chapter 3, classifiers co-occur with nouns and characterize the designated entities along a variety of semantic parameters, including animacy, shape, size, constitution, and function/interaction (for some examples, see again Table 1.3).

In recent years, some of the most interesting and influential work in this branch of typology has made use of novel graphic representations that are referred to as language-specific semantic maps across universal conceptual spaces (e.g., Croft, 2001; Haspelmath, 2003; see also the special 2010 issue of *Linguistic Discovery* called "Semantic Maps: Methods and Applications"). It is well-established that grammatical morphemes and constructions tend to be multifunctional or polysemous, which is to say that they usually have several closely related meanings. Moreover, the sets of meanings that are encoded by comparable elements in different languages frequently overlap to varying degrees. This suggests that they collectively form a network, and that different languages capture different portions of that network, like alternative snapshots of the same landscape. These considerations have led to the proposal that such networks constitute universal conceptual spaces, and that the different coverages of those spaces by different languages constitute contrasting semantic maps.

To ease visualization, a conceptual space is usually depicted on a two-dimensional page. Meanings are plotted as points, but the only ones that are included are those that are formally expressed by different grammatical devices in at least one language. In addition, meanings that are maximally similar, as reflected by common marking in at least one language, are placed maximally close to each other on the page, often with lines connecting them. The polysemous contents of particular grammatical morphemes or constructions are illustrated by drawing boundaries around the relevant portions of the conceptual space, and such demarcations are then interpreted as language-specific semantic maps. Importantly, because the overall configuration of a conceptual space is arrived at inductively through cross-linguistic comparisons, it can be regarded as a tentative but well-motivated hypothesis about the universal cognitive organization of the given domain.

These ideas can be fleshed out by examining a domain that is typically expressed by prepositions, postpositions, and case markers—namely, the domain of instrumentals and related functions. Based on convergences and divergences in the grammatical encoding of this domain in a dozen or so languages, Haspelmath (2003) created the conceptual space shown in Figure 1.6a. The structural arrangement of this space stems from, and hence enables the efficient graphic portrayal of, a multitude of intersecting

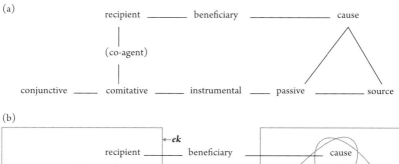

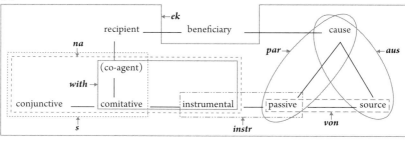

Figure 1.6. (a) Universal conceptual space for the domain of instrumentals and related functions. (b) Language-specific semantic maps for English *with*, Nkore-Kiga *na*, Russian instrumental case (abbreviated as *instr*) and preposition *s*, German *von* and *aus*, French *par*, and Seychelles Creole *ek*. A color version is in the color plates section. Based on Haspelmath (2003).

patterns of polysemy, some of which are plotted as language-specific semantic maps in Figure 1.6b.

Looking first at the left side of this figure, we can see that the English preposition *with* has both an instrumental meaning (e.g., *Sarah cracked the nut with a nutcracker*) and a comitative (i.e., accompaniment) meaning (e.g., *Sancho Panza arrived with Don Quixote*). It is also used to specify a "co-agent," which is a comitative-like participant that takes active part in the event (e.g., *Bill fought with Jake*), but the label for this meaning is enclosed in parentheses because Haspelmath did not have good cross-linguistic evidence for its placement as a link between comitative and recipient. Interestingly, many African languages have grammatical morphemes that capture not only the meanings of instrumental and comitative (plus co-agent), but also the conjunctive notion of "and." This is exemplifed by the Nkore-Kiga (Bantu, Uganda) preposition *na*:

Instrumental: *n' enyondo*
                "with a hammer"

Comitative: *na Mugasho*
                "(together) with Mugasho"

Conjunctive: *emeeza n' entebe*
                "a table and a chair"

It is also noteworthy, however, that these and other meanings are expressed by distinct devices in Russian. The case marker *-om/-em* specifies both instruments (e.g.,

Konstantin raskolol orex kamn-em "Konstantin cracked the nut with a stone") and passive agents (e.g., *Orex byl raskolot Konstantin-om* "The nut was cracked by Konstantin"), whereas the preposition *s* has both a comitative (plus co-agent) meaning (e.g., *Sancho Pansa prishel s Don Kixotom* "Sancho Panza arrived with Don Quixote") and a conjunctive meaning (e.g., *starik so staruxoj* "the old man and [literally 'with'] the old woman").

Turning now to the right side of the figure, it is apparent that German has one preposition, *von*, for both passive agents (e.g., *Ich wurde von Hunden gebissen* "I have been bitten by dogs") and sources (e.g., *Ich bekomme eine Pension von der Regierung* "I get a pension from the government"), and another preposition, *aus*, for both sources (e.g., *aus Paris* "from Paris") and causes (e.g., *aus Hass* "out of hatred"). In addition, French *par* captures the remaining two-way combination of meanings by specifying both passive agents (e.g., *par des chiens* "by some dogs") and sources (e.g., *par hazard* "by accident").

Finally, the last semantic map in Figure 1.6b encompasses every meaning in the entire conceptual space except beneficiary. This reflects the full coverage of a highly polysemous preposition, *ek*, in Seychelles Creole (French-based, Seychelles archipelago):

Instrumental: *Nou fer servolan, nou file ek difil.*
                        "We made a kite, we let it fly with a string."

Comitative: *Mon 'n travay ek Sye Raim.*
                        "I have worked with Mr. Raim."

Conjunctive: *dan zil Kosmoledo ek Asonpsyon*
                        "On the islands of Cosmoledo and Assomption."

Passive agent: *Mon 'n ganny morde ek lisyen.*
                        "I have been bitten by many dogs."

Source: *Mon ganny pansyon ek gouvernman.*
                        "I get a pension from the government."

Cause: *Pa kapab reste laba ek moustik.*
                        "It was impossible to stay there because of the mosquitos."

Recipient: *Mon 'n donn larzan ek li.*
                        "I gave the money to him."

Overall, Figures 1.6a and 1.6b clearly demonstrate that the domain of instrumentals and related functions can be thought of as a richly structured conceptual space that gets carved into a multitude of cross-crossing semantic sectors by the various coding devices of different languages. It is important to realize, however, that while these maps may seem complicated, they only capture some of the complexity of the given domain. This is because, as noted earlier, they derive from Haspelmath's (2003) analysis of only a dozen or so languages. In fact, a subsequent investigation of the same domain that took into account data from 200 languages disclosed a more convoluted conceptual space with a number of additional nodes and connections (Narrog & Ito, 2007).

The method of plotting language-specific semantic maps across putatively universal conceptual spaces has also been applied to many other domains of grammatical meaning, including tense/aspect (Anderson, 1982; Janda, 2007; Croft & Poole, 2008), modality (Anderson, 1986; Van der Auwera & Plungian, 1998), evidentiality (Boye, 2010), voice (Kemmer, 1993; Croft, 2001), pronouns (Haspelmath, 1997a; Cysouw, 2007), case-marking (Rice & Kabata, 2007), spatial and temporal relations (Haspelmath, 1997b; Levinson & Meira, 2003), intransitive predication (Stassen, 1997), and secondary predication (Van der Auwera & Malchukov, 2005). Furthermore, there has been growing interest in using multivariate statistics and other computational techniques to improve the descriptive and inferential rigor of these kinds of studies (Cysouw, 2007, 2010; Croft & Poole, 2008; Majid, 2008; Wälchli, 2010; Regier et al., 2013). In several sections of Part II, but especially in Chapter 5, we will return to this line of work and discuss it in connection with pertinent neuroscientific research.

Grammaticalization patterns

Semantic maps like those in Figure 1.6b show how particular languages represent particular domains at particular times in history, but the demarcations of grammatical meanings that they portray are not really static; rather, they change, albeit very slowly, over the course of hundreds of years. For instance, the comitative use of English *with* existed before, and gradually gave rise to, the instrumental use—a process of meaning extension that has also been documented in many other languages and that apparently never goes in the opposite direction (Narrog & Ito, 2007).

This kind of historical change constitutes a grammaticalization pattern. Such patterns have been intensively studied during the past few decades, and they typically involve either the gradual transformation of lexical categories into grammatical categories, or the gradual transformation of certain grammatical categories into others (Narrog & Heine, 2011). Some of the most common grammaticalization patterns are illustrated in Figure 1.7, which is based on a prior survey of over 400 well-attested patterns from over 500 languages worldwide (Heine & Kuteva, 2002). This diagram portrays six different levels of grammatical evolution, with clusters of categories at the same level having roughly the same degree of grammaticalization, as determined by their relation to both the categories they derive from (at higher, earlier levels) and the categories they develop into (at lower, later levels). Most of the categories shown here are fairly comprehensive (e.g., "pronoun" instead of "personal pronoun" or "indefinite pronoun"). But it is still clear that, generally speaking, historical progressions lead from open-class to closed-class items, from concrete to abstract meanings, and from functions that are relatively independent and referential to those that involve intra- and inter-clausal relations.

Given the recent explosion of psychological and neuroscientific research on embodied cognition (Shapiro, 2014), it is notable that body part terms serve as some of the most frequent sources of grammaticalization patterns (Heine et al., 1991; Svorou, 1993; Heine, 1997a; Heine & Kuteva, 2002). For instance, such terms are especially likely to be employed in an anthropomorphic manner to indicate the locations of objects, as illustrated by the following kinds of derivational processes: a noun for "head" evolves into a preposition for "up," "on top of," or "in front of"; a noun

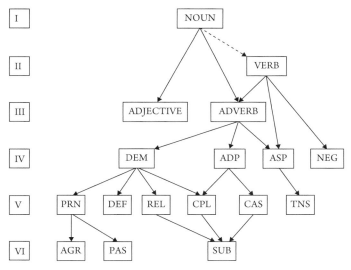

Figure 1.7. Six vertically arranged levels of historical grammatical development. Categories at the same level have roughly the same degree of grammaticalization vis-à-vis both those they emerge from and those they give rise to. These grammaticalization patterns are among the most commonly attested, but far more have been documented. Moreover, many of the categories included here are characterized in general rather than specific terms (e.g., "pronoun" instead of "personal pronoun" or "indefinite pronoun").
Abbreviations: ADP = adposition; AGR = agreement marker; ASP = (verbal) aspect; CAS = case marker; CPL = complementizer; DEF = definiteness marker ("definite article"); DEM = demonstrative; NEG = negative marker; PAS = passive marker; PRN = pronoun; REL = relative clause marker; SUB = subordinating marker of adverbial clauses; TNS = tense marker. Based on (Heine & Kuteva, 2007, p. 111).

for "butt" evolves into a preposition for "down" or "behind"; and a noun for "belly" or "stomach" evolves into a preposition for "in." These sorts of patterns are discussed more fully in Chapter 5, together with relevant neuroscientific research.

In a similar vein, verbs for basic human postures and movements are often grammaticalized into tense/aspect markers. In particular, verbs for sitting, standing, and lying commonly become markers for continuous aspect, and phrases like *go to* frequently turn into markers for intention and future tense (Heine & Kuteva, 2002). Indeed, the latter process occurred in English, as reflected by the following sentences from Bybee (2003; for a detailed semantic analysis see Langacker, 2011; see also Tyler & Jan, 2017):

Movement:	*We are going to Windsor to see the King.*
Intention:	*We are going to get married in June.*
Future:	*The trees are going to lose their leaves.*

It bears mentioning that in the two sentences expressing intention and future tense, but not in the one expressing physical movement, the phrase *going to* can easily be reduced to *gonna*, which is entirely consistent with the tendency for grammaticalization chains to involve phonological erosion.

CONCLUSION

Humans have evolved to learn and accept the unique practices, traditions, beliefs, etc.—in short, the collectively understood norms—of the particular cultures they belong to, and partly for this reason they often assume that the lexical and grammatical symbols in the language they happen to speak represent the world in a fairly natural way. What semantic typology has shown, however, is that even though the conceptual systems of the roughly 6,500 languages around the globe do display some universal tendencies, they also manifest many differences—differences that range from relatively superficial idiosyncrasies of word meaning (e.g., *rawadawa* in Mundari) to deeper contrasts involving such variables as the partitioning of entire semantic fields (e.g., color), the regular conflation of certain semantic components rather than others (e.g., whether motion verbs conventionally incorporate the manner, path, or figure), and the multifunctionality of polysemous grammatical elements (e.g., whether instrumental prepositions and case markers also have comitative and/or conjunctive uses, among other possibilities). Of course, the numerous similarities that have been found among the conceptual systems of the world's languages are quite significant, since they may reflect commonalities in people's bodies, brains, communicative behaviors, and physical and social environments. But the abundant cross-linguistic conceptual differences that have also been found are equally, if not more, interesting and important, since they indicate that most of the linguistic symbols that people employ are filters that sift human experience in culture-specific ways. In the current context, the key point is that both kinds of typological data can inform the branch of cognitive neuroscience that deals with concepts because, as demonstrated in much greater detail in Part II, together they provide essential information about both the uniformity and the diversity of the linguistically encoded meanings that are somehow supported by the complex cortical networks lodged inside our heads.

2

THE PERSPECTIVE FROM COGNITIVE NEUROSCIENCE

Conceptual processing does not operate in a stand-alone manner but instead relies on regions of modality-specific pathways.
—Lawrence Barsalou (2016, p. 1131)

INTRODUCTION

Ever since cognitive neuroscience first emerged as a coherent field of research in the 1980s, it has been advancing at a remarkably rapid pace, due in large part to continuing breakthroughs in brain mapping methods. These breakthroughs have allowed investigators to probe with increasing precision the neural substrates of essentially all aspects of our mental lives, including both verbal and nonverbal conceptual knowledge. In fact, the literature on how concepts are organized, represented, and processed in the human brain is now enormous, much bigger than the literature comparing the meanings of words and constructions across the roughly 6,500 languages of the world. As noted in the Preface, a limitation of this body of work is that the lion's share of it has been restricted to the kinds of concepts that are encoded by open-class words in English and a few other familiar languages. Despite this shortcoming, however, a tremendous amount has already been learned about the cortical underpinnings of semantic memory, and exciting new discoveries are being made all the time.

This chapter provides a concise and selective summary of some major theoretical and empirical developments in this area of inquiry, with the goal of establishing a foundation for the neurobiological data covered in Part II (for other reviews and perspectives, see Martin, 2007, 2009; Meyer & Damasio, 2009; Mahon & Caramazza, 2009, 2011; Binder & Desai, 2011; Kiefer & Pulvermüller, 2012; Meteyard et al., 2012; Hauk & Tschentscher, 2013; Pulvermüller, 2013a; Yee et al., 2013; Chen & Rogers, 2014; Lambon Ralph, 2014; Binder & Fernandino, 2015; Clarke, 2015; Kemmerer, 2015c; Hauk, 2016; Lambon Ralph et al., 2017; note also that several special issues of journals have recently been devoted to concepts and semantic cognition: *Neuropsychologia, 76*, 2015; *Psychonomic Bulletin & Review, 23/4*, 2016; *Cognitive Neuropsychology, 33/3–4*, 2016; and *Neuropsychologia, 105*, 2017). The first and longest section of this chapter describes some of the most widely endorsed, but still vigorously debated, ideas about the implementation of concepts in the brain. Then several shorter sections address the following topics: the increasingly popular notion of representational similarity spaces; the relatively neglected realm of grammatical semantics; and the provocative view that linguistic communication involves brain-to-brain coupling or alignment.

FLEXIBLE, MULTILEVEL MODELS OF THE NEURAL SUBSTRATES OF CONCEPTS
Some widely shared assumptions

Although this field of research is fraught with controversy, there is mounting evidence for a variety of complex network approaches such as the following:

- the convergence-divergence zone model (Damasio, 1989a, 1989b; Damasio et al., 2004; Meyer and Damasio, 2009; Man et al., 2013)
- the similarity-in-topography model (Simmons & Barsalou, 2003)
- the hub-and-spoke model (Patterson et al., 2007; Jefferies, 2013; Lambon Ralph, 2014; Patterson & Lambon Ralph, 2016; Lambon Ralph et al., 2017)
- the embodied abstraction model (Binder & Desai, 2011; Binder & Fernandino, 2015; Binder, 2016)
- the semantic pointer model (Eliasmith et al., 2012; Eliasmith, 2013; Blouw et al., 2016)
- the cell assembly model (Pulvermüller, 2013a, 2013b; Garagnani & Pulvermüller, 2016; Tomasello et al., 2017)
- the GRAPES (i.e., grounding representations in action, perception, and emotion systems) model (Martin, 2016)
- the grounding-by-interaction model (Mahon & Caramazza, 2008; see also Mahon, 2015a, 2015b)

These models differ in their specific architectural, representational, and computational claims, but at the same time most of them—not all, but most—share several fundamental assumptions. Of greatest salience and importance, perhaps, are the following common views: *in order to accommodate the available data, any viable framework must posit both modal and transmodal levels of representation, while also allowing online processing to be flexibly modulated by multiple factors such as task, context, and individual experience.* Before we consider some of the ways in which these widely held assumptions are empirically supported, we will first flesh them out in general theoretical terms.

Although a growing amount of neuroscientific research has explored abstract concepts, by far the most work has focused on concrete concepts, and it is largely for this reason that one of the hottest topics in recent years has been the notion that such concepts are grounded in modal systems for perception, action, and emotion. This idea has deep historical roots going back to ancient Greek philosophers like Aristotle (4th century BC/1961) and Epicurus (4th century BC/1994), British empiricists like Locke (1690/1959) and Hume (1739/1978), late 19th century neuropsychiatrists like Wernicke (1900; see also Gage & Hickok, 2005) and Freud (1891/1953), and late 20th century thinkers like Searle (1980) and Harnad (1990). In the contemporary scene, conceptual grounding and its close cousin, embodiment, are extremely popular ideas, penetrating virtually every corner of the cognitive, social, and affective neurosciences (e.g., Barsalou, 2008; Semin & Smith, 2008; Shapiro, 2014; Coello & Fischer, 2015; Fischer & Coello, 2015; Matheson & Barsalou, 2018). Despite all this attention, however, the exact nature of grounding is still unclear, and much more research is needed to understand it better. The most straightforward and promising approach, though, is probably that it involves *neural reuse*, as described below (Barsalou, 2016; see also Anderson, 2010).

The primary function of concepts is, of course, to abstract away from and generalize across the minutiae of specific conscious experiences so that certain aspects of them can be treated as instances of broad, similarity-based categories (see Chapter 7). For example, whenever we recognize an object that we see, touch, or hear, our brains project sensory signals in a bottom-up manner through complex hierarchies of successively smaller neural populations that capture successively richer conjunctions of perceptual features, thereby giving rise to successively more idealized representations that ultimately enable us to identify the object as a member of a particular class. This is illustrated in an oversimplified way in Figure 2.1a, which shows how such a "compression" hierarchy can implement the concept of a table—or, more precisely, its visual shape component. At the lower levels of this little network, images of different tables, or even images of the same table viewed from different distances or vantage points, trigger different patterns of activity across the neural populations, but at higher levels the critical feature combinations that allow these images to be regarded as exemplars of the category of tables are progressively extracted, so that the topmost node functions effectively as a table detector. In the figure this node is called a semantic pointer, but that's only because the figure happens to come from a paper about the semantic pointer

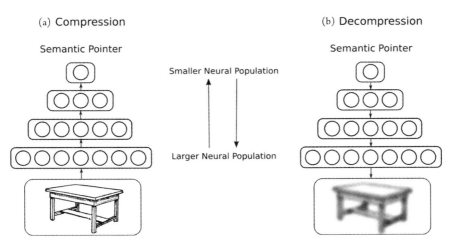

Figure 2.1. Hierarchical populations of neurons used for the compression and decompression of perceptual data. The number of nodes in each layer corresponds to the dimensionality of the representation. The low-dimensional semantic pointer at the top of the hierarchy in (a) is thus a compressed representation of a percept, and the high-dimensional representation at the bottom of the hierarchy in (b) amounts to a partial recovery of this percept from the appropriate semantic pointer. From Blouw et al. (2016, p. 1133).

model (Blouw et al., 2016). Importantly, most of the other models mentioned earlier posit similar devices, but with different names.

Now, in the current context the key claim is that, as shown in Figure 2.1b, the very same network can also serve as a "decompression" hierarchy that runs in the opposite direction, allowing table representations to be reconstructed with varying degrees of specificity, depending on how far down the signals are propagated. Such partial simulations of perceptual states are believed to occur during both verbal and nonverbal thoughts involving tables, and while they can certainly lead to conscious imagery, they can also occur beneath the surface of awareness (again, see Chapter 7). From a theoretical point of view, what matters most is simply that there is some degree of overlap between the neural resources underlying perception and conceptualization. It is this *neural reuse* of perceptual systems for conceptual purposes that constitutes conceptual grounding, and the same sort of reuse is assumed to take place in systems for action and emotion too.

Still, it is worth emphasizing that the specific cortical mechanisms that underlie grounding, such as the involvement of different laminar layers and different electrophysiological rhythms in bottom-up and top-down computations, are only beginning to be elucidated (Martin, 2016). Moreover, although most of the models mentioned earlier maintain that grounding plays a central, indeed a constitutive, role in the representation of concrete concepts, one of them—namely, the grounding-by-interaction framework—does not ascribe it such a high status (for in-depth arguments, see Mahon & Caramazza, 2008; Mahon, 2015a, 2015b). Also, as Hauk (2016, p. 785) points out in a recent review of this literature, while it is true that "most authors acknowledge that sensory-motor systems may contribute to semantic processing at some stage, the main controversy surrounds the issue of how relevant or essential these contributions really are, and whether the existing evidence tells us anything interesting about how we represent and process meaning. . . ." We will return to this critical issue further below, as well as at several points in Parts II and III.

Moving on, it is notable that some concrete concepts have primarily, or even exclusively, unimodal content. To take a few examples, the meaning of *thunder* is almost entirely auditory, whereas the meaning of *purple* is almost entirely visual. Most concrete concepts, however, have multimodal content. For instance, the word *scissors* has a complex meaning with specifications not only for shape, sound, and visual motion, but also for action planning as well as proprioceptive and tactile feedback. Not surprisingly, most of the models mentioned earlier assume that multimodal concepts like this have multimodal grounding, albeit with different attributes having different weights. This is illustrated in the part of Figure 2.2 labeled "perceptual simulation," which contains oversimplified semantic pointer and decompression hierarchies for the visual, tactile, and auditory components of the concept of a dog. Turning to the brain, because the cortical regions that house different modal systems are anatomically segregated from each other, it follows that the content of any multimodal concept does not reside in a single region; instead, different fragments of it are distributed across different areas according to the sensory/motor/affective content of the type of information that is represented, as shown by the yellow areas in Figure 2.3 (note that many of the cortical areas in this illustration are labeled in the parallel Figure 2.4).

Although modal systems are thought to subserve much of the content of concrete concepts, there is growing agreement that they cannot implement all aspects

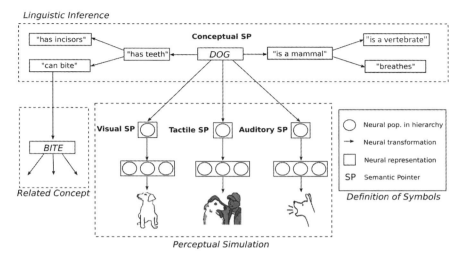

Figure 2.2. Schematic of the semantic pointer model. The diagram shows some of the possible transformations triggered by a semantic pointer for the concept labeled "DOG." Transforming the semantic pointer can result in perceptual simulations, linguistic inferences, and the consideration of related concepts. An occurrence of the concept DOG, on this account, is a process through which a set of these possible transformations is realized. All the representations and transformations depicted here have been implemented in a neurobiologically plausible computer model.
From Blouw et al. (2016, p. 1135).

of semantic cognition. This is because higher-level transmodal systems, also known as hubs, are required for a variety of integrative, organizational, and computational purposes (Lambon Ralph, 2014; Binder, 2016). Anatomically, these systems are located in certain associative sectors of the temporal and parietal lobes (see the red regions in Figure 2.3), and they are reciprocally connected with multiple modal systems via long-distance bidirectional fiber tracts. Due to this unique arrangement, they are ideally suited to detect and store cross-modal conjunctions of experiential features through convergent sensory/motor/affective input, and then later, during semantic tasks, reconstruct those distributed modal representations, with varying degrees of precision, through divergent top-down projections. For instance, Figure 2.2 shows that the transmodal semantic pointer for the concept of a dog, labeled "Conceptual SP," can, when necessary, trigger segregated yet time-locked modal simulations of the appearance, feel, and sound of this type of animal. Another critical function of transmodal systems is to guide categorization according to genuine conceptual criteria rather than merely superficial properties. As an illustration, consider the fact that while the word *chair* is often associated with the kind of four-legged, straight-backed, wooden artifact customarily used for sitting at a dining table, chairs can actually have any number of legs (even zero, as with beanbag chairs), they need not have backs (just think of some modern ergonomic designs), and they can be made of many types of material (wood, metal, plastic, etc.). Finally, transmodal systems enable the formation of distilled or chunked conceptual representations that can be thematically linked in long-term memory (e.g., *dog-bone* or *paper-pencil*) and transiently combined

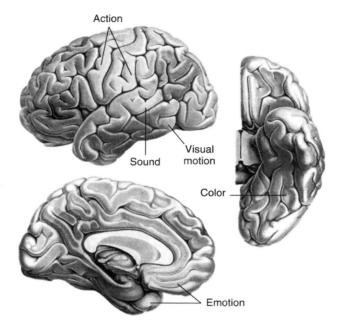

Figure 2.3. Modality-specific sensory, motor, and affective systems (yellow regions) are reciprocally connected with transmodal temporal and parietal convergence zones (red regions) that store increasingly compressed representations of entity and event knowledge. Inferior prefrontal and dorsomedial prefrontal cortices (blue regions) control the goal-directed activation and selection of semantic information stored in other regions. The posterior cingulate gyrus, precuneus, and retrosplenial cortex (green regions) may function as an interface between the semantic network and the hippocampal memory system, helping to encode meaningful events into episodic memory. A similar but somewhat less extensive semantic network exists in the right hemisphere, although the functional and anatomical differences between left and right brain semantic systems are still unclear. A color version is in the color plates section. From Binder & Desai (2011, p. 531).

during online processing (e.g., during the production and comprehension of novel sentences).

Speaking of online processing, the cortical scheme depicted in Figure 2.3 incorporates two additional systems that frequently contribute to the mental manipulation of concepts, regardless of modality (Binder & Desai, 2011). First, the pars triangularis of the left inferior frontal gyrus, which is often engaged together with the left dorsomedial prefrontal cortex (both regions are shown in blue), is well-established as controlling the goal-directed activation and selection of semantic structures stored in other parts of the brain. And second, although it is not yet clear what roles are served by several medial parietal regions—specifically, the posterior cingulate gyrus, precuneus, and retrosplenial cortex (shown in green)—one hypothesis is that they function as transmodal mechanisms that help relay meaningful experiences to the hippocampal episodic memory system.

Another important point is that even though the models mentioned earlier accommodate both verbal and nonverbal concepts, when words enter the architecture they sculpt it in many ways, since they are essentially language-particular coding

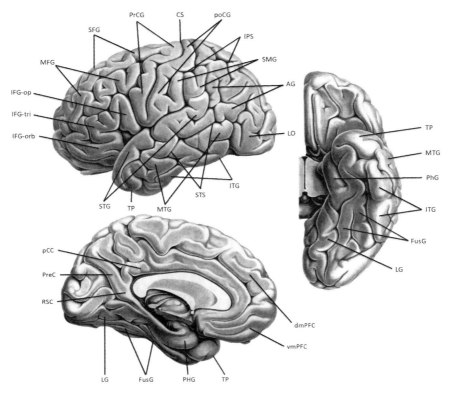

Figure 2.4. Labeled gyri and sulci on left lateral (top), ventral (right), and medial (bottom) brain figures like those in Figure 2.3.
Abbreviations extend through the temporal, occipital, parietal, and frontal lobes as follows: STG = superior temporal gyrus; TP = temporal pole; MTG = middle temporal gyrus; STS = superior temporal sulcus; ITG = inferior temporal gyrus; LG = lingual gyrus; FusG = fusiform gyrus; PhG = parahippocampal gyrus; LO = lateral occipital cortex; AG = angular gyrus; SMG = supramarginal gyrus; IPS = inferior parietal sulcus; poCG = postcentral gyrus; CS = central sulcus; prCG = precentral gyrus; MFG = middle frontal gyrus; IFG-op/tri/orb = inferior frontal gyrus-opercularis/triangularis/orbitalis.

devices that have been culturally designed to package concepts for communicative purposes, as described in Chapter 1. Following Firth's (1957, p. 11) famous dictum "You shall know a word by the company it keeps," some scholars have proposed that the statistical co-occurrence patterns of word forms across large corpora can give rise to a completely "disembodied" form of conceptual knowledge (e.g., see the "linguistic inferences" in Figure 2.2). And in fact a number of computational studies have shown that on the basis of such contextual associations among word forms, it is possible to account for a variety of psycholinguistic phenomena, including priming effects, sentence completions, implicit stereotypes, ambiguity resolution, and the extraction of gist from texts (for reviews and comparisons of different approaches, see Sahlgren, 2008; Baroni & Lenci, 2010; Turney & Pantel, 2010; Erk, 2012; Landauer et al., 2013; Pereira et al., 2016; Greenwald, 2017; see also Lupyan & Lewis, in press, for further insights). At the same time, however, many researchers have argued that when tasks require meticulous, analytic processing of concrete concepts, it is usually helpful, if not necessary, to draw on one or more of the modal systems that putatively subserve the most pertinent embodied representations (Barsalou et al., 2008; Simmons et al., 2008; Lynott & Connell, 2010; Dove, 2011; Louwerse, 2011; Andrews et al., 2014). And as indicated later in this chapter (in the section titled "Representational similarity spaces in the brain"), some of the semantic metrics used by computational analyses of word distributions may not really be as far removed from modal systems as previously thought, since at least one fMRI study suggests that they are capable of capturing many aspects of the representational geometry of cortical activity patterns in those systems (Carlson et al., 2014).

This brings us to the last widely shared assumption of the models mentioned earlier, which is that the engagement of modal systems during online processing is not an all-or-nothing affair, but rather a graded and flexible phenomenon that is sensitive to numerous factors, including task, context, and individual experience. We will consider these factors later on, after first reviewing some evidence that both modal and transmodal systems do in fact contribute to the representation of concepts in the brain.

Modal systems

As just indicated, one of the most intensively investigated topics in the cognitive neuroscience of conceptual knowledge is the hypothesis that the modality-specific components of word meanings—e.g., how the things we call *apples* typically look, taste, and smell, and how we typically interact with them—depend on some of the same modality-specific cortical systems that subserve perception, action, and emotion. Although this proposal remains controversial, it has been bolstered by increasing evidence from all of the major brain mapping methods. To get an initial sense of what these findings are like, we will begin by summarizing some representative results from research on the auditory and motor features of word meanings.

Starting with auditory features, Kiefer et al. (2008) conducted two experiments, one using functional magnetic resonance imaging (fMRI), which has good spatial resolution, and the other using electrophysiology, which has good temporal resolution. In both experiments, participants made lexical decisions (i.e., yes/no decisions as to whether letter strings are real words) for 100 printed real words and 100 printed pseudowords. Note that this kind of task does not require deliberate, effortful processing of word meanings; hence whatever semantic access does occur is mostly automatic and implicit (Chumbley & Balota, 1984; Binder et al., 2003). Crucially, the 100 real words in Kiefer et al.'s study consisted of two subsets that differed in the relevance of auditory features (e.g., *bell* vs. *desk*). When the investigators analyzed the fMRI data, they found that, in contrast to the words without auditory features, those with such features significantly engaged tertiary auditory regions in the left posterior superior and middle temporal gyri (pSTG/pMTG)—regions that, importantly, were also significantly engaged in a separate condition in which the participants heard familiar sounds produced by animals and artifacts (Figure 2.5a; see also Kellenbach et al., 2001; Noppeney & Price, 2002; Goldberg et al., 2006b). In addition, when the investigators analyzed the electrophysiological data, they found that the waveforms evoked by the two types of words diverged significantly during a time window of

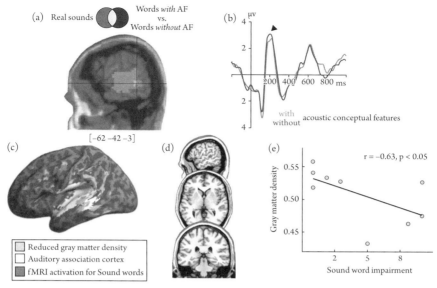

Figure 2.5. Data suggesting that the auditory features of word meanings depend on auditory regions in the left posterior superior/middle temporal gyri (pSTG/pMTG). (a) Compared to words without auditory features (AF, e.g., *table*), those with auditory features (e.g., *thunder*) activated a sector of the left pSTG/pMTG that was also activated by the perception of real sounds. (b) The electrophysiological waveforms evoked by words with vs. without auditory features diverged during a time window of 150–190 msec, with the most likely neural source being the left pSTG/pMTG. (c) Reduced gray matter density in patients with logopenic progressive aphasia (LPA, orange) affects regions of auditory association cortex (white) that were activated by words with auditory features in an fMRI study with healthy participants (blue). (d) Slices showing overlap (green) between reduced gray matter density in LPA patients and fMRI activation for words with auditory features in healthy participants. (e) Significant relationship between reduced gray matter density and impaired recognition of words with auditory features in LPA patients. A color version is in the color plates section. (a–b): Kiefer et al. (2008, pp. 12227–12228; (c–e): Bonner & Grossman (2012, p. 7989).

150–190 msec, with the most likely neural source being, once again, the left pSTG/pMTG (Figure 2.5b). Overall, as Kiefer et al. (2008, p. 12229) put it, "the implicitness of the conceptual task, the selective modulation of left pSTG/pMTG activity by acoustic feature relevance, the early onset of this activity at 150 msec, and its anatomical overlap with perceptual sound processing show that the left pSTG/pMTG represents auditory conceptual features in a modality-specific manner." What's more, it has also been shown that damage to the left pSTG/pMTG induces greater semantic processing deficits for words with auditory features than for words without them (Figure 2.5c, d, e; Bonner & Grossman, 2012; Trumpp et al., 2013). These findings are especially valuable because they confirm the causal involvement of high-level auditory areas in the comprehension of lexically encoded sound concepts.

Shifting to motor features, there is substantial evidence that these aspects of the meanings of both tool nouns and action verbs are underpinned primarily by both the left supramarginal gyrus and the left precentral motor cortices (for reviews, see Kemmerer, 2015a, 2015c, 2015d, 2015e; see also Chapters 3 and 4 in this volume).

Here, however, we will restrict our attention to data supporting the contribution of the left precentral motor cortices to the motor features of action verbs. For one thing, many fMRI studies have shown that, across a variety of implicit and explicit semantic processing tasks, verbs for leg/foot actions (e.g., *stomp*), arm/hand actions (e.g., *grab*), and face/mouth actions (e.g., *bite*) engage the corresponding somatotopically mapped motor areas (Figure 2.6a; e.g., Hauk et al., 2004; Kemmerer et al., 2008; Raposo et al., 2009; de Grauwe et al., 2014; see also Figure 4.8 in Chapter 4). In addition, several electrophysiological and magnetoencephalographic studies have shown that action verbs ignite these areas very quickly, within 200 msec after presentation, and within 100 msec after identification (Figure 2.6b; e.g., Klepp et al., 2014; Shtyrov et al., 2014; Grisoni et al., 2016; Yang et al., 2017). Importantly, such rapid somatotopic motor activations are independent of task-related brain responses (Dalla Volta et al., 2018). Furthermore, numerous studies using transcranial magnetic stimulation (TMS) have shown that, depending on the protocol, selectively perturbing body-part-specific motor areas can either facilitate or disrupt the semantic processing of action verbs with congruent body-part-specific motor features (e.g., Pulvermüller et al., 2005; Gerfo et al., 2008; Kuipers et al., 2013; Repetto et al., 2013). Finally, neuropsychological studies have shown that

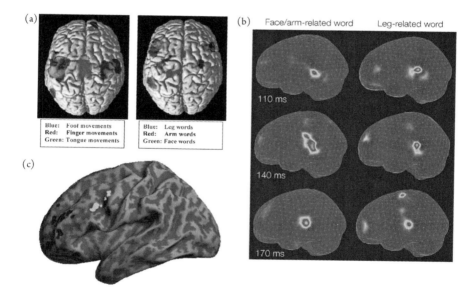

Figure 2.6. Data suggesting that the motor features of verb meanings depend on somatotopically mapped premotor and primary motor cortices. (a) Verbs for leg/foot actions (e.g., *stomp*), arm/hand actions (e.g., *grab*), and face/mouth actions (e.g., *bite*) engage some of the same precentral motor areas that are engaged during the execution of body-part congruent movements (Hauk et al., 2004, p. 304). (b) In a speech perception experiment, the Finnish verb *hotki* ("eat") activated a left inferior central site after only 140 msec, and the Finnish verb *potki* ("kick") activated a left superior central site just 30 msec later, with the slight delay potentially reflecting the spread of neural activity from perisylvian to dorsal motor cortices (Pulvermüller, 2005, p. 579). (c) Reduced gray matter density in patients with amyotrophic lateral sclerosis (green) is significantly related to poor understanding of action verbs in left lateral premotor and inferior prefrontal cortices (purple). A color version is in the color plates section. York et al. (2014, p. 1076).

damage to left frontal motor areas frequently impairs knowledge of action verbs (Figure 2.6c; e.g., Bak & Hodges, 2004; Grossman et al., 2008; Kemmerer et al., 2012; York et al., 2014; see also Figure 4.13 in Chapter 4), sometimes in ways that correlate closely with performance on nonverbal motor tasks (Desai et al., 2015).

Now let's step back from all of these detailed findings for a moment. It's worth noting that the only reason we have concentrated so far on just two aspects of concrete word meanings—namely, auditory and motor features—is to keep the discussion concise. Importantly, there is mounting evidence that other modality-specific components of concrete word meanings also depend on some of the corresponding modality-specific cortical regions. For instance, this has been supported for such attributes as color (e.g., Simmons et al., 2007), shape (e.g., Wheatley et al., 2005), visual motion (e.g., Wallentin et al., 2011), taste (Barrós-Loscertales et al., 2012), and smell (e.g., González et al., 2006). In addition, although the vast majority of studies have focused on individual attributes like these, a few have gone farther by investigating several attributes simultaneously.

An excellent example comes from Fernandino et al. (2015), who used fMRI to determine whether the combination of five sensory/motor attributes—specifically, sound, color, shape, visual motion, and manipulation—could predict the distributed patterns of brain activity elicited by particular words. The researchers began by employing a six-point scale to collect crowd-sourced ratings on the relevance of each attribute to 900 English words, 600 of which were relatively concrete nouns and 300 of which were relatively abstract nouns, with the two sets of words being matched for nuisance variables like length and frequency. As expected, the concrete nouns received significantly higher ratings than the abstract nouns for all five attributes (Figure 2.7). Next, the researchers asked a separate group of participants to make yes/no

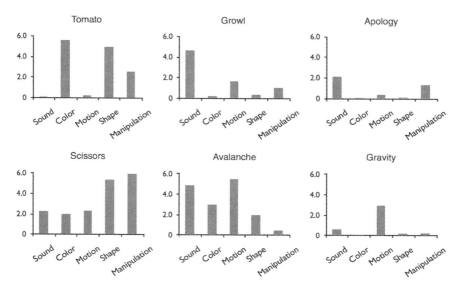

Figure 2.7. Examples of words used in Fernandino et al.'s (2015) fMRI study. Each word had a mean rating for each of the five semantic attributes.
From Fernandino et al. (2015, p. 19).

concreteness judgments for all 900 words while in the scanner. Data analyses then proceeded in several steps. First, by taking into account both the rating data and the imaging data for just 820 words, the researchers were able to create five attribute maps (AMs) that revealed the activity patterns associated with the five attributes of word meaning. Second, for each of the remaining 80 words (40 concrete and 40 abstract), they generated a predicted map that showed the given word's expected activity pattern, based on a linear combination of the five AMs, with each AM weighted by the corresponding attribute rating for that word. Finally, for each of these 80 words, they compared the predicted map with the observed map (i.e., the activity pattern that was actually evoked during the concreteness judgment task) by calculating voxel-by-voxel pairwise correlations. The main results were as follows. Activity patterns were predicted significantly better than chance for the 40 concrete words, but not for the 40 abstract words, which is consistent with the fact that the former words were rated as having much more sensory/motor content than the latter. In addition, although prediction accuracies increased linearly with the number of attributes included in each predicted map, no significant differences emerged between the relative contributions of the five attributes. This suggests that, in keeping with grounded theories of conceptual knowledge, all of the attributes played important roles in specifying the neural signatures of the various word meanings.

These findings are certainly quite impressive, but they are still rather limited because they only cover some of the most saliently embodied aspects of conceptual knowledge. To address this shortcoming, several research groups have been developing more comprehensive and sophisticated frameworks for characterizing the content of both concrete and abstract concepts, and for investigating the implementation of that content in the brain. For instance, one approach treats word meanings as sets of weightings across the following 12 dimensions: sensation, action, emotion, space, time, quantity, social interaction, morality, polarity (which involves positive or negative feelings), thought (which involves mental activity, ideas, opinions, and judgments), ease of teaching (which reflects the distinction between experiential observation and verbal instruction), and ease of modifying (which indexes the contextual availability of a noun according to the range of modifying adjectives it can take) (Troche et al., 2014; see also Troche et al., 2017). Another approach, which is similar to the first but more complex, treats word meanings as sets of weightings across not just 12 but 65 dimensions that are based on neurobiological considerations and are referred to as "experiential attributes" (Binder et al., 2016). Table 2.1 shows how these attributes fall into several categories, and Figure 2.8 shows how they can be used to represent the meanings of three words—*egg, bicycle,* and *agreement.* Both of these approaches have helped to illuminate the topography of semantic space and have also inspired new psycholinguistic and neurolinguistic experiments (Primativo et al., 2017; Anderson et al., 2017). In addition, and of special importance in the current context, both of them demonstrate that the scope of conceptual grounding is not restricted to such familiar and well-studied modal systems as perception and action, but encompasses a number of other neurocognitive spheres as well, some of which can also be regarded as modal, at least under a broad interpretation of that term (Barsalou, 2016).

Table 2.1. Binder et al.'s (2016) componential approach to conceptual analysis included 65 experiential attributes from 14 categories.

Category	Attributes
Vision	vision, bright, dark, color, pattern, large, small, motion, biomotion, fast, slow, shape, complexity, face, body
Somatic	touch, temperature, texture, weight, pain
Audition	audition, loud, low, high, sound, music, speech
Gustation	taste
Olfaction	smell
Motor	head, upper limb, lower limb, practice
Spatial	landmark, path, scene, near, toward, away, number
Temporal	time, duration, long, short
Causal	caused, consequential
Social	social, human, communication, self
Cognition	cognition
Emotion	benefit, harm, pleasant, unpleasant, happy, sad, angry, disgusted, fearful, surprised
Drive	drive, needs
Attention	attention, arousal

Note: See Figure 2.8 for application to the meanings of the words *egg, bicycle,* and *agreement.*
Adapted from Binder et al. (2016, p. 133).

Transmodal systems

We noted earlier that, according to most of the models listed at the outset, semantic cognition depends not only on modal systems, but also on transmodal ones,[1] with the latter serving a variety of functions, such as integrating the widely distributed components of multimodal concepts, transcending superficial criteria for categorization, and forming unitary, distilled, and relatively abstract representations that can easily be accessed and combined. Although the precise cortical underpinnings of transmodal semantic systems are currently controversial, accumulating evidence suggests that they reside primarily in certain temporal and parietal association areas. These regions are well positioned to perform the sorts of functions just mentioned because within the complex, progressively intertwined sensory/motor hierarchies that stretch across much of the cerebral cortex, they house the uppermost levels of

[1] Some researchers have characterized these representations as "amodal"; however, this term may be misleading. Barsalou (2016, p. 1126) notes that "Martin (personal communication) has been asking researchers who use the term 'amodal' what they mean by it. Overwhelmingly, he finds that they mean *multimodal*, not amodal." And I would argue that "multimodal" is more or less synonymous with "transmodal."

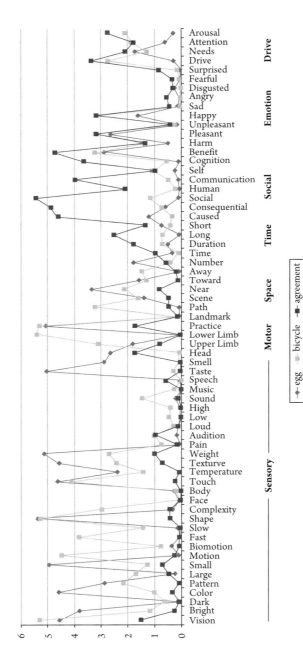

Figure 2.8. Mean ratings for the words *egg*, *bicycle*, and *agreement* across 65 experiential attributes that fall into 14 categories (see also Table 2.1). A color version is in the color plates section.

From Binder et al. (2016, p. 161).

representation that not only receive convergent input from, but send divergent output back to, multiple lower levels that represent different types of unimodal information (Meyer & Damasio, 2009; Sepulchre et al., 2012; Man et al., 2013; Margulies et al., 2015; Murphy et al., 2017; Huntenburg et al., 2018).

Some striking evidence that transmodal systems for conceptual knowledge depend, in part, on several sectors of the temporal and parietal association cortices comes from an interesting fMRI study by Fernandino et al. (2016). They re-analyzed the imaging data from their prior investigation (i.e., the one discussed earlier) and succeeded in identifying a broad array of brain regions that responded to bimodal, trimodal, and even more richly multimodal conjunctions of the five sensory/motor attributes of word meaning that they considered—namely, sound, color, shape, visual motion, and manipulation. For instance, as shown by the dark green patches in Figure 2.9, the posterior superior temporal sulcus and the adjacent posterior middle temporal gyrus responded to lexical-semantic specifications for both sound and motion—a bimodal conjunction that fits with other research implicating the same territory in audiovisual integration during perception (e.g., Beauchamp et al., 2004; Werner & Noppeney, 2010). In addition, as shown by the orange patches in Figure 2.9, the lateral occipitotemporal cortex and the anterior supramarginal gyrus, as well as a few regions in the precentral and postcentral gyri, responded to lexical-semantic specifications for two other attributes—shape, which is perceived both visually and

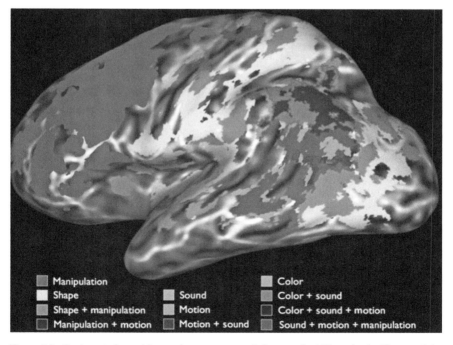

Figure 2.9. During a task requiring yes/no concreteness judgments for 900 words, significant activity was found in a wide range of temporal and parietal regions that responded to various conjunctions of five sensory/motor attributes of word meaning: manipulation, shape, sound, visual motion, and color. A color version is in the color plates section.
From Fernandino et al. (2016, p. 2029).

haptically, and manipulation, which draws on visual, motor, and proprioceptive information. Importantly, a large literature has linked these areas with the representation of object-directed actions, regardless of whether they are executed, observed, or linguistically coded (e.g., Caspers et al., 2010; Kemmerer et al., 2012; Lingnau & Downing, 2015). Yet another significant finding was that, as shown by the purple and brown patches in Figure 2.9, the angular gyrus was sensitive to several conjunctions of conceptual attributes, including color and sound, as well as color, sound, and motion. This, too, dovetails with prior work (e.g., Bonner et al., 2013; Bonnici et al., 2016; see also Seghier, 2013; Ramanan et al., 2018).

What's even more interesting, however, is that parts of the angular gyrus, along with a few medial areas not visible in Figure 2.9—specifically, the retrosplenial cortex, precuneus, and parahippocampal gyrus—were among the only regions that responded to all five attributes. They constitute cortical hubs that reside at the very top of the multifarious hierarchies of bidirectional information flow. The exact roles of these regions are still mysterious, but further evidence that they contribute to the high-level representation and processing of concepts comes from several sources, including a number of fMRI studies that have found them to be reliably engaged during the following contrasts between experimental conditions: real words vs. pseudowords; high- vs. low-frequency words; strongly vs. weakly associated words; and coherent sentences vs. unrelated word lists (for a review, see Binder, 2016; for a discussion of complications involving the angular gyrus, see Box 3 in Lambon Ralph et al., 2017).

Another brain region that often shows up in such contrasts is the anterior temporal lobe (ATL). In fact, this region has been the focus of extensive research during the past 20 years, and a wealth of data from all of the major brain mapping methods suggests that it makes vital contributions to the transmodal coding of concepts (for reviews, see Lambon Ralph, 2014; Patterson & Lambon Ralph, 2016; Lambon Ralph et al., 2017; for alternative perspectives, see Wong & Gallate, 2012; Martin et al., 2014). The following discussion only highlights a few of the key findings, however, since a broader survey would take us too far afield.

First, consider semantic dementia (SD), which is a devastating neurodegenerative disease that is characterized in its initial stages by focal atrophy and hypometabolism in the ATLs (bilaterally but with a left > right asymmetry) and by structural and functional disconnections between these regions and multiple modality-specific regions (Hodges & Patterson, 2007; Acosta-Cabronero et al., 2011; Guo et al., 2013; Collins et al., 2017; see also Kemmerer, 2015c, for an overview within the larger context of the cognitive neuroscience of language). Patients suffering from SD display progressively worse performance on essentially all verbal and nonverbal tasks that require them to retrieve and process concepts for objects, events, and abstract notions. Thus, they perform poorly when asked to define words, name pictures, draw pictures, match words with pictures, sort words according to similarity, sort pictures according to similarity, or recognize nonverbal stimuli based on sight, sound, touch, taste, or smell. Across many diverse tasks, and across many diverse categories and modalities of semantic content, patients consistently make errors that reflect difficulties with discrimination and generalization (Lambon Ralph & Patterson, 2008). These errors suggest that in SD the higher-order structural coherence of concepts gradually dissolves, starting with knowledge of the distinctive features that define and differentiate specific concepts, and extending to knowledge of the shared features that characterize entire groups of concepts. In object naming tasks, for instance, patients exhibit a steadily declining ability to distinguish between the subtypes of particular categories, resulting in errors like calling an eagle a duck at a relatively early stage of the disease, calling the very same stimulus just a generic bird at a middle stage, and calling it a horse, which is completely outside the avian domain, at a relatively late stage (Table 2.2; Hodges et al., 1995; Woollams et al., 2008). Similarly, in categorization tasks involving either pictures or words, patients tend to both overgeneralize (e.g., by treating a chihuahua as a cat) and undergeneralize (e.g., by not treating a hairless Sphynx cat as a cat) (Lambon Ralph et al., 2010; Mayberry et al., 2011). These findings, among many others, support the view that the ATL not only merges the multimodal attributes of concepts, but processes them in a nonlinear manner so that judgments can be based on underlying semantic similarities rather than superficial properties (for related data from picture-naming errors in early Alzheimer's disease, see Domoto-Reilly et al., 2012).

This view is bolstered by computational investigations (Rogers et al., 2004; Schapiro et al., 2013) and by numerous studies of neurologically normal subjects performing semantic tasks while undergoing PET (e.g., Vandenberghe et al., 1996; Sharp et al., 2004), fMRI (e.g., Visser et al., 2010a, 2012; Visser & Lambon Ralph, 2011), magnetoencephalography (e.g., Marinkovic et al., 2003; van Ackeren et al., 2014), TMS (e.g., Pobric et al., 2007, 2009, 2010; Lambon Ralph et al., 2009), or direct intracranial stimulation/recording (e.g., Chan et al., 2011; Shimotake et al., 2015; Chen et al., 2016b; see also Lin et al., 2007; Quiroga, 2012). With regard to fMRI, some studies, like the one by Fernandino et al. (2016) described earlier, have not found the ATL to be involved in conceptual processing, but this is usually because of methodological limitations, such as an insufficient field-of-view, an inappropriate baseline task, or a failure to correct for the reduced signal-to-noise ratio that is known to occur in this part of the brain. When all of these limitations are overcome, the ATL does turn out to be reliably linked with the transmodal representation of both verbal and nonverbal

Table 2.2. Picture naming responses of a patient with semantic dementia who was assessed longitudinally every six months for two years.

Item	September 1991	March 1992	September 1992	March 1993
Bird	+	+	+	Animal
Chicken	+	+	Bird	Animal
Duck	+	Bird	Bird	Dog
Swan	+	Bird	Bird	Animal
Eagle	Duck	Bird	Bird	Horse
Ostrich	Swan	Bird	Cat	Animal
Peacock	Duck	Bird	Cat	Vehicle
Penguin	Duck	Bird	Cat	Part of animal
Rooster	Chicken	Chicken	Bird	Dog

Note: + denotes a correct response.

Adapted from Hodges et al. (1995).

concepts. Moreover, the specific part of the ATL that is most frequently engaged during semantic tasks is the ventrolateral sector, which covers both the anterior inferior temporal gyrus and the anterior fusiform gyrus (Visser et al., 2010b; Rice et al., 2015). In a terrible twist of fate, this is also the sector that incurs the greatest atrophy in SD, and the degree to which patients are impaired on semantic tasks correlates most strongly with the degree to which this particular region is disrupted (Galton et al., 2001; Butler et al., 2009; Mion et al., 2010; see also Binney et al., 2010).

It should come as no surprise, however, that the representational organization of the ATL is much more complex than this, as reflected by several independent strands of work (for a review, see Wong & Gallate, 2012). Here we will restrict our attention to the hypothesis that the semantic architecture of this cortical territory is graded along the lines shown in Figure 2.10 (Rice et al., 2015). As just noted, the ventrolateral sector, which is colored white in this figure, seems to be the "center of gravity," so to speak, because it responds to the widest range of both concrete and abstract concepts—a finding which suggests that it conducts the greatest amount of transmodal semantic structuring. In contrast, although other sectors also display transmodal activations, their functions appear to be somewhat more selective in nature, consistent with their differing patterns of connectivity with other brain regions. The main trends that have been identified so far are as follows. The posterior and ventromedial parts of the ATL are richly connected with the visual system and are preferentially engaged by concepts that have many specifications in this modality (e.g., Tyler et al., 2013; Liuzzi et al.,

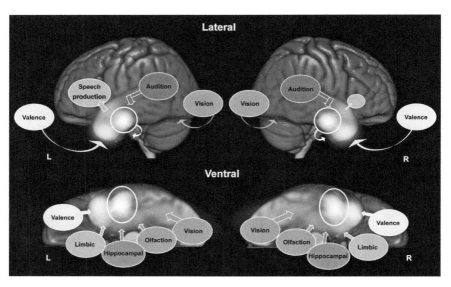

Figure 2.10. According to the "graded hub" hypothesis regarding the representational architecture of the anterior temporal lobe (ATL), the central region is the ventrolateral sector, shown in white. This area is most reliably engaged across semantic categories and tasks, and it incurs the greatest atrophy in semantic dementia. Neighboring sectors of the ATL, shown in other colors, also display transmodal activations, but their functions appear to be somewhat more modality-selective, in keeping with their differing patterns of connectivity with other brain regions. A color version is in the color plates section. From Rice et al. (2015, p. 4384).

2015; Bonner et al., 2016). The superior sector of the ATL is richly connected with auditory-verbal areas and is preferentially engaged not only by concepts with heavily weighted auditory attributes, but also by abstract and social concepts, which are closely related to spoken language (e.g., Visser & Lambon Ralph, 2011; Hoffman et al., 2015; Binney et al., 2016). And lastly, the anterior (i.e., polar) division of the ATL is richly connected with affective regions and is preferentially engaged by emotionally imbued social concepts (Olson et al., 2013; Binney et al., 2016; Mellem et al., 2016).

Flexible processing

One of the most significant insights to have emerged from recent psycholinguistic and neurolinguistic research on concepts is that even the most entrenched features of word meanings are not always activated in an immediate and automatic manner. This is illustrated in an especially compelling way by several studies that have focused on color terms. In the classic Stroop paradigm, when people are asked to name the font colors of color terms, their reaction times are slower when the two colors are incongruent (e.g., the word *green* in red font) than when they are congruent (e.g., the word *green* in green font). This interference effect has historically been treated as evidence that the color features of color terms—and, by extension, the central semantic properties of other words—are accessed involuntarily. However, it can be reduced or even eliminated by a variety of experimental manipulations, such as varying the proportion of congruent to incongruent trials (Jacoby et al., 2003), varying the frequency of congruent and incongruent trials for specific word-color pairings (Jacoby et al., 2003), coloring a single letter in the color term instead of the whole word (Besner et al., 1997), or priming the notion of dyslexia (Goldfarb et al., 2011). It can also be diminished or abolished by the post-hypnotic suggestion that the terms are meaningless symbols (for a review, see Lifshitz et al., 2013; for an alternative perspective, see Augustinova & Ferrand, 2014).

How should the lack of a consistent interference effect in the Stroop paradigm be interpreted? Surely it does not entail that the color features of color terms are not genuine components of the meanings. Instead, the main theoretical implication seems to be that we should abandon the traditional but simplistic assumption that all aspects of concepts are reliably retrieved in an invariant, involuntary fashion, and replace it with the more nuanced and realistic view that different attributes of concepts may be accessed to different degrees and with different time courses across different situations, depending on such factors as task, context, and individual experience (Lebois et al., 2015). Importantly, the sorts of multilevel models described earlier are well suited to accommodate such flexibility in semantic processing, and many of their chief proponents have already begun to address, at both theoretical and empirical levels of analysis, the many manifestations of variability in conceptual grounding effects—i.e., in behavioral and neural markers of the retrieval of modal representations during semantic processing (Binder & Desai, 2011; Kiefer & Pulvermüller, 2012; Connell & Lynott, 2014; Kemmerer, 2015a; Barsalou, 2016; Hauk, 2016; Yee & Thompson-Schill, 2016).

First, let's consider the factor of task. Earlier we looked closely at two fMRI studies by Fernandino et al. (2015, 2016), both of which required subjects to make yes/no concreteness judgments about words. The authors acknowledge that because this fairly deep semantic processing task may have induced subjects to generate conscious mental imagery, a critic might argue that some of the activity patterns, particularly those in modality-specific cortical regions, may have reflected purely perceptual simulations (i.e., conscious mental images) rather than genuinely conceptual representations. In defense of the conceptual account, however, the authors note that when fMRI studies employ tasks in which semantic processing is shallow, like lexical decision, the relevant modal systems still tend to be engaged (e.g., Kiefer et al., 2008, 2012; Bonner & Grossman, 2012; de Grauwe et al., 2014). To be sure, the specific patterns of cortical activity that are evoked in such conditions often differ somewhat from those that are associated with deliberate imagery, with the former patterns typically being less extensive and involving higher levels of modal decompression hierarchies than the latter (Willems et al., 2010b). But these discrepancies are entirely in keeping with the view that concept retrieval is not an all-or-nothing affair but rather a matter of degree, with relatively schematic and implicit access at one end of the continuum, and highly detailed, explicit imagery at the other. Now, this line of thinking leads quickly to thorny questions about the complex relation between concepts and consciousness, but we will refrain from tackling them until Chapter 7. The key claim here is simply that, as Fernandino et al. (2015, p. 25) put it, "concept retrieval can involve a variable amount of sensory/motor reenactment, where the extent of the reenactment depends on the specific demands of the task."

Further support for this position comes from numerous studies, including some that focus on the motor features of word meanings. For instance, in an fMRI study, van Dam et al. (2012) found that the anterior supramarginal gyrus—which, as noted earlier, contributes to the representation of object-directed actions—was engaged significantly more by Dutch nouns with salient motor features (e.g., *haarborstel* "hairbrush") than by Dutch nouns without such features (e.g., *douchekop* "showerhead"), but this difference was much greater when the subjects were asked to think about how the objects are used than when they were asked to think about what the objects look like (see also Hoenig et al., 2008). Likewise, in a TMS study, Papeo et al. (2009) found that the level of activity in hand-related primary motor cortex was enhanced when subjects were told to focus on the motor specifications of hand-related Italian verbs (e.g., *mescolo* "I stir"), but not when they were told to count the number of syllables in the very same words. These studies clearly indicate that the degree to which tool nouns and action verbs engage parietal and frontal motor areas can be influenced by task (see also Tomasino & Rumiati, 2013). But this kind of variability does not necessarily challenge the assumption—which is shared by most theories of grounded conceptual knowledge—that the motor features of these word meanings reside in these brain regions. Instead, it merely shows that, just like the color features of color terms, they do not always need to be fully accessed whenever the words are encountered.

This point is also relevant to the interpretation of several neuropsychological studies that some researchers have regarded as threatening the notion of conceptual grounding, specifically with respect to the motor features of word meanings. Although the relevant data and arguments apply to both tool nouns and action verbs, here we will concentrate on the latter. We noted earlier, in the discussion of modal systems, that the disruption of precentral motor cortices, either transiently by TMS or chronically by lesions, typically affects the comprehension of action verbs (for reviews, see Kemmerer, 2015a, 2015c, 2015d, 2015e). However, there are a few reports of brain-damaged patients who have action production deficits due to parietal and/or frontal disturbances but nevertheless display intact understanding of action verbs (Papeo et al., 2010; Arévalo et al., 2012; Kemmerer et al., 2013; Maieron et al., 2013; Vannuscorps et al., 2016). These findings have sometimes been treated as evidence against the hypothesis that the motor features of action verbs depend in part on the precentral motor cortices. But an alternative explanation is that those features are not always essential for adequate task performance, since a relatively high level of accuracy can often be achieved by drawing mainly on other sources of information. For example, determining that *rip* is more like *tear* than *fold* normally engages not only arm/hand-related precentral regions that presumably underpin the unique motor specifications of the three verbs, but also posterior middle temporal regions that presumably underpin their unique visual motion specifications (Kemmerer et al., 2008). And even though the former features most likely facilitate the conceptual comparison process, it is certainly possible that an accurate decision could be reached by relying on the latter features instead. Indeed, this may be why patients with Parkinson's disease, whose precentral motor cortices are dysfunctional, can still perform this particular task as well as healthy participants (Kemmerer et al., 2013). It is also noteworthy that according to the kinds of multilevel models described earlier, one might be able to accomplish various less demanding verb comprehension tasks by retrieving, say, just the transmodal representations in the ATL, or just the statistical co-occurrence patterns of the word forms. On the other hand, these models cannot be so supple that they can handle any type of result; otherwise they would be unfalsifiable. The upshot of this little discussion is simply that, together, the multiple levels of representation in current neuroscientific theories of conceptual knowledge, and the variety of task effects documented by a growing number of experimental studies, have made the interpretation of neuropsychological data more challenging that it once was.

   Another form of flexibility in semantic processing involves the pervasive influence of context (for a broad overview, see Yee & Thompson-Schill, 2016). This can be illustrated, once again, by focusing on the motor features of action verbs. As an example of linguistic context effects, in an fMRI study Raposo et al. (2009) found that although somatotopically mapped precentral motor cortices were engaged when subjects heard action verbs in isolation (e.g., *kick*) and in literal phrases (e.g., *kick the ball*), they were not engaged when subjects heard such verbs in idiomatic phrases (e.g., *kick the bucket*) (for similar results, see Aziz-Zadeh et al., 2006; Desai et al., 2013; Schuil et al., 2013; for contrary results, but from post-sentence recordings, see Boulenger et al., 2009). And as an example of nonlinguistic context effects, in another fMRI study Papeo et al. (2012) found that when subjects silently read a series of verbs after first performing a mental rotation task using a motor strategy instead of a visuospatial one, precentral motor cortices responded not only to action verbs but also, rather surprisingly, to purely stative ones. These studies support the view that verb-induced motor activity does not occur in a rigid, invariant manner, but is instead quite sensitive to the given situation (see also Tettamanti et al., 2008; Moody & Gennari, 2010; Aravena et al., 2012, 2014; Lam et al., 2017). As argued above, however, the mere fact that there is some variability regarding when and how the motor features of verb meanings are retrieved does not imply that those features are not really long-term components of the concepts or that they are not really subserved by the precentral motor cortices. It simply requires that we move closer to the kinds of multilevel models described earlier, in which the activation of modal semantic features is not deterministic, but is instead dynamically conditioned by many factors.

The last factor that we will consider is individual experience, and it can easily be elaborated by continuing with the theme of the motor features of action verbs (for research on other kinds of concepts, see Kan et al., 2006; Kiefer et al., 2007; Weisberg et al., 2007; Oliver et al., 2009; Hoenig et al., 2011). For instance, in an fMRI study, Willems et al. (2010a) showed that handedness modulates the hemispheric asymmetry of cortical activity patterns when subjects process manual action verbs like *throw*, such that right-handers engage predominantly left-lateralized hand-related premotor areas, whereas left-handers engage predominantly right-lateralized hand-related premotor areas (for different results that may reflect a different task, see Hauk & Pulvermüller, 2011). And in another fMRI study that focused on a much more specific kind of expertise, Beilock et al. (2008) found that skilled hockey players not only understood sentences about hockey maneuvers better than novices, but also exhibited greater activity in the left dorsal premotor cortex while processing such sentences (see also Lyons et al., 2010). Given the current context, it is also notable that in the large literature on the human mirror neuron system, many studies have reported significant expertise effects involving nonlinguistic action recognition, specifically showing that greater skill at executing certain kinds of actions correlates with greater engagement of body-part-congruent motor areas when those kinds of actions are perceived (Calvo-Merino et al., 2006; Aglioti et al., 2008; Cross et al., 2009; Candidi et al., 2014; Makris & Urgesi, 2015). These results reinforce the general point that individual differences in sensory/motor experience can cause concepts to vary in their representational richness and specificity.

REPRESENTATIONAL SIMILARITY SPACES IN THE BRAIN

During the past 15 years, increasingly sophisticated multivariate approaches to analyzing fMRI data have allowed researchers to describe and compare, in remarkable detail, the multifaceted mental representations that are instantiated by cortically distributed patterns of neural activity (for reviews, see Kriegeskorte & Kievit, 2013; Haxby et al., 2014; Charest & Kriegeskorte, 2015; Haynes, 2015). Needless to say, these methodological advances have greatly enhanced the whole field of cognitive neuroscience, including the branch that investigates the implementation of conceptual knowledge in the brain (e.g., Mitchell et al., 2008; Huth et al., 2012, 2016; Coutanche & Thompson-Schill, 2015; Malone et al., 2016). To illustrate the power of these new imaging tools, we will first consider a few insights that have emerged from studies that have used a technique called "representational similarity analysis" (RSA; Kriegeskorte et al., 2008b), and then briefly discuss another method that concentrates on pattern classification.

RSA is based on the well-established assumption that any given brain region can be regarded as a high-dimensional representational space. Each neuron—or, in the case of fMRI, each voxel—corresponds to a single dimension with a certain range of values, and a particular pattern of activity across the entire region corresponds to a point in the multidimensional space. If two different stimuli evoke two different patterns of activity in the region, the degree to which they are similar can be plotted as the distance between their corresponding points. Thus, the way in which the region responds to a large set of stimuli can be portrayed as a richly structured representational geometry that reflects fine-grained groupings of items, medium-sized clusters of items, and large categories of items. It is also noteworthy that from this perspective, neural computation can be construed as the transformation of representational geometries along processing pathways.

In fMRI studies, a common procedure for conducting RSA is as follows. First, the multivoxel activity patterns evoked by a set of stimuli are compared with each other by measuring their pairwise correlations. Then these results are entered into a square representational dissimilarity matrix (RDM) that is indexed horizontally and vertically by labels for the stimuli, and that shows in each cell the color-coded degree of dissimilarity between the two activity patterns associated with the two stimuli specified by the row and column labels. Next, another RDM is created that pertains to the same stimuli but derives from a different source, such as (a) explicit judgments of the similarity relations among the stimuli, (b) computational measures of the similarity relations among the stimuli, or (c) multivoxel activity patterns evoked by the stimuli in a different brain area. Finally, the two RDMs are directly compared with each other, and the extent to which their representational geometries match is determined.

A recent study by Carlson et al. (2014) exemplifies how an expanded version of this approach can shed light on the degree to which concrete concepts are grounded in modal systems. The researchers began by taking some previously published fMRI data from Kriegeskorte et al. (2008a)—specifically, two neural RDMs that captured the relationships among the activity patterns evoked in the primary visual cortex and the object-sensitive ventral temporal cortex by 67 pictures of entities from four general categories: human faces and bodies, animal faces and bodies, natural objects, and man-made objects. Then the researchers created six additional RDMs that reflected, in different ways, the semantic similarities between the English nouns for the 67 objects (Table 2.3). One of these RDMs was based on explicit judgments of the conceptual

Table 2.3. 67 words used in Carlson et al.'s (2014) investigation employing representational similarity analysis (RSA). These words were judged to be the most appropriate names for the pictures used in Kriegeskorte et al.'s (2008a) fMRI study, and they constitute the consecutive labels for the rows and columns in the two matrices shown in Figure 2.11.

Category	*Nouns*
Human faces & bodies	hand, ear, chef, dancer, woman, eye, man, pointing, fist, child
Animal faces & bodies	armadillo, camel, snake, wolf, monkey, ostrich, zebra, elephant, sheep, frog, cow, goat, dog, alligator, giraffe, lion
Natural objects	carrots, grapes, potato, tree, pepper, lettuce, kiwi, cucumber, leaf, apple, radish, eggplant, lake, pine cone, banana, tomato, garlic, path, pineapple, pear, waterfall
Man-made objects	city, bottle, lightbulb, sign, cassette, church, flag, key, pliers, arch, door, hammer, chair, gun, house, dome, umbrella, phone, stove

relatedness of the nouns. Three other RDMs were based on computational measures of their conceptual relatedness in WordNet, an electronic lexical database (Fellbaum, 1998). And the last two RDMs were based on computational measures of their conceptual relatedness in two programs for calculating the statistical co-occurrence patterns of word forms in large corpora—Latent Semantic Analysis (LSA; Landauer & Dumais, 1997) and the Correlated Occurrence Analogue to Lexical Semantics (COALS; Rohde et al., 2005). For illustrative purposes, two RDMs are shown in Figure 2.11—one reflecting the relationships among the activity patterns evoked in the ventral temporal cortex by the 67 pictured objects, and another reflecting the relationships among the 67 nouns for those objects, as measured by LSA.

The principal analyses consisted of comparing the six word-based semantic RDMs with the two picture-based neural RDMs to uncover any correspondences. Not surprisingly, none of the word-based RDMs matched the picture-based RDM for the primary visual cortex. But three of the word-based RDMs—specifically, the one derived from explicit similarity judgments and the two derived from LSA and COALS—did correlate significantly with the picture-based RDM for the ventral temporal cortex, and the strongest correspondences between those RDMs involved the associations among items within each of the four general categories. These findings suggest that at a relatively fine-grained level of organization, the representational geometry of the semantic relationships between words for certain kinds of objects closely resembles the representational geometry of the activity patterns that are evoked in the ventral temporal cortex by pictures of those objects. And this in turn supports the view that the meanings of object nouns are grounded, at least partly, in the visual system, especially in the higher-order mechanisms for representing shape, color, and texture that are known to reside in the ventral temporal cortex (for a review, see Kravitz et al., 2013, and for further information see Chapter 3 in this volume). At the same time, however, it is important to note that even though the correspondences between some of the RDMs were significant, they were far from perfect. This outcome highlights the fact that the language-dependent conceptualization of objects cannot be completely reduced to the language-independent perception of objects. Finally, it also bears mentioning that none of the three RDMs derived from WordNet matched the RDM for the ventral temporal cortex. According to Carlson et al. (2014), it is possible that the short definitions and sparse hierarchies in WordNet are too simplistic to capture the predominantly visual aspects of word meaning that appear to depend on the ventral temporal cortex.

Other fMRI studies have used RSA to explore some of the ways in which other brain areas contribute to conceptual knowledge. For instance, returning to the transmodal ATL, there is growing evidence (despite some inconsistencies) that in several sectors of this highly integrative region, the functional topography of activity patterns reflects the semantic distances not only between object pictures, but also between object nouns (Peelen & Caramazza, 2012; Bruffaerts et al., 2013; Clarke & Tyler, 2014; Liuzzi et al., 2015). In addition, a few other transmodal cortical areas—most notably, the pMTG and precuneus—have been found to implement neural similarity spaces that correspond closely to conceptual similarity spaces (Devereux et al., 2013; Fairhall & Caramazza, 2013). Furthermore, in a brilliant study that took this line of work in a creative new direction, Zinszer et al. (2016) discovered that when separate groups of English and Mandarin Chinese speakers read words with roughly equivalent meanings in their respective native languages, the resulting patterns of cortical activity could be

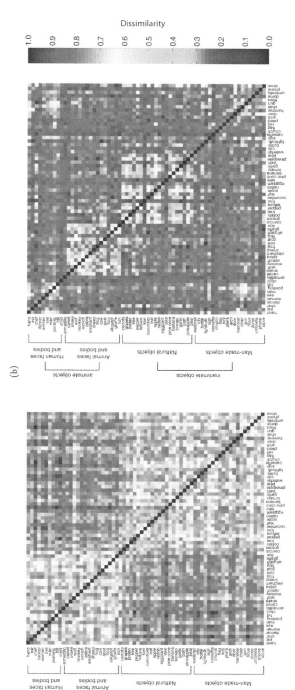

Figure 2.11. Two representational dissimilarity matrices (RDMs) from Carlson et al.'s (2014) investigation. (a) Relationships among the activity patterns evoked in the ventral temporal cortex by 67 pictured objects whose names constitute the labels for the rows and columns (see Table 2.3 for clarification). (b) Relationships among the 67 words for those objects, as measured by Latent Semantic Analysis (LSA; again, see Table 2.3 for clarification). A color version is in the color plates section. From Carlson et al. (2014, p. 121).

used to structurally align the word meanings in one group of speakers with the corresponding word meanings in the other group. This finding is especially valuable because, as the authors point out, it opens up exciting opportunities for investigating the neural substrates of not just translation symmetries between languages, but also translation asymmetries, which, as indicated in Chapter 1 and elaborated in greater detail in Part II, are far more common.

It is also worth emphasizing that RSA is just one of many pattern-based fMRI methods that could potentially be harnessed to study how cross-linguistic similarities and differences in conceptual knowledge are implemented in the brain. Another popular approach is frequently referred to as "neural decoding" or "brain reading" (for a simple introduction, see Smith, 2013; for a more technical discussion, see Haynes, 2015). Many different versions of this technique are currently being explored, but all of them share the same basic procedure: researchers first train a computer program to associate certain kinds of stimuli with certain kinds of activity patterns, and then they test the program by determining how well it can classify the activity patterns elicited by new stimuli. This method has already helped to illuminate how a wide range of mental representations are carried by complex sets of brain signals, and in Chapter 4 we will see how it has been applied to the study of action concepts (Wurm & Lingnau, 2015; see the section of Chapter 4 on events of cutting, breaking, and opening).

WHAT ABOUT THE NEURAL SUBSTRATES OF GRAMMATICAL SEMANTICS?

In Chapter 1 we contrasted lexical semantics with grammatical semantics, noting that while the former aspects of meaning provide most of the content of sentences, the latter aspects establish what Talmy (1988, p. 173) describes as "the main delineations of the scene organization and communicative setting." Grammatical semantics has received a great deal of attention in both linguistics and psycholinguistics, but unfortunately it has not attracted much interest in neurolinguistics, and for this reason its cortical underpinnings are still, for the most part, *terra incognita*. Nevertheless, there are a few corners of this multifaceted conceptual realm that cognitive neuroscientists have begun to explore.

For instance, I and others have taken some steps toward elucidating the neural substrates of locative prepositions, such as *in, on, around, through, between, above, below, left of, right of, in front of*, and *in back of*. The short story is that PET and fMRI studies with healthy subjects, as well as lesion studies with brain-damaged patients, suggest that the meanings of these words depend primarily on parts of the left inferior parietal lobule that lie near areas important for spatial perception, in keeping with grounded theories of conceptual knowledge (Damasio et al., 2001; Tranel & Kemmerer, 2004; Noordzij et al., 2005; Amorapanth et al., 2010, 2012; Struiksma et al., 2011; see also Chatterjee, 2008; Kemmerer, 2006b, 2010). This topic is discussed in detail in Chapter 5.

Another form of grammatical semantics that some researchers have started to relate to the brain involves the schematic meanings of verb-based argument structure constructions. According to the increasingly popular "constructionist" approach to syntax (Hoffman & Trousdale, 2013), argument structure constructions are clausal patterns that directly encode certain idealized types of events (Goldberg, 1995). This is illustrated in Table 2.4, which shows how the English verb *kick* can occur in at least nine

Table 2.4. Nine verb-based argument structure constructions in English, each of which is characterized here according to its name, form, meaning, and instantiation in an example sentence involving the verb *kick*.

Construction	Form	Meaning	Example
1. Transitive	Subject verb Object	X acts on Y	Bill kicked the ball.
2. Caused Motion	Subject verb Object Oblique	X causes Y to move along path Z	Bill kicked the ball into the lake.
3. Conative	Subject verb Oblique$_{at}$	X attempts to contact Y	Bill kicked at the ball.
4. Ditransitive	Subject verb Object$_1$ Object$_2$	X causes Y to receive Z	Bill kicked Bob the ball.
5. Resulative	Subject verb Object Complement	X causes Y to become Z	Bill kicked Bob black and blue.
6. Possessor Ascension	Subject verb Object Oblique$_{in/on}$	X contacts Y in/on body-part Z	Bill kicked Bob in the knee.
7. Contact *against*	Subject verb Object Oblique$_{against}$	X causes Y to contact Z	Bill kicked his foot against the chair.
8. X's *way*	Subject verb *X's way* Oblique	X makes progress by performing action	Bill kicked his way through the crowd.
9. Habitual	Subject verb	X performs action habitually	That horse kicks.

different active-voice constructions, each of which consists of a symbolic association between a particular syntactic structure and a particular semantic structure. For example, in the sentence *Bill kicked his way through the crowd*, the general concept of "motion of the subject referent along a path" comes from the "X's way" construction itself, and the more specific concept of "forceful outward foot movement" comes from *kick*.

In a recent fMRI study, van Dam and Desai (2016) attempted to isolate the neural correlates of the "caused motion" construction, which is the second one listed in Table 2.4. The main experimental stimuli consisted of both concrete and abstract sentences instantiating this construction (e.g., *You threw the ball to her* and *You delegated the task to her*), and the baseline stimuli consisted of both concrete and abstract sentences instantiating an intransitive construction (e.g., *You waved at her whole family* and *You thought about her feelings*). When the researchers contrasted the former sentences against the latter, they found significant activation in several parietal regions that have been implicated in the high-level planning of object-directed arm/hand actions. This led them to conclude that, regardless of concreteness, sentences instantiating the caused motion construction "activate a caused motion schema, which is grounded through areas controlling reaching and grasping actions" (van Dam & Desai, 2016, p. 703). This interpretation is certainly plausible, but it is limited by the fact that the design of the study did not allow the researchers to disentangle the neural correlates of the syntactic and semantic aspects of the construction of interest (see also Allen et al., 2012, which has the same shortcoming).

Relatedly, it is worth noting that in some of my own neuropsychological work, I have obtained evidence that focal brain damage can disrupt knowledge of the semantic aspects of several verb-based constructions and/or knowledge of the grammatically relevant semantic aspects of the verbs themselves, while preserving knowledge of the syntactic aspects of the constructions as well as knowledge of the grammatically irrelevant semantic aspects of the verbs (Kemmerer, 2000a, 2003; Kemmerer & Wright, 2002; for a review, see Kemmerer, 2006a; and for similar studies involving adjective-based constructions, see Kemmerer, 2000b; Kemmerer et al., 2009). For instance, one study focused on the so-called possessor ascension construction, which is the sixth one listed in Table 2.4, and which has a schematic meaning that can be characterized roughly as "X contacts Y in/on body-part Z" (Kemmerer, 2003). Due to this meaning, the construction only allows, for the most part, verbs that encode contact. This criterion is satisfied by three of the verb classes in Levin's (1993) large taxonomy—specifically, verbs of touching (e.g., *touch, pat, caress*), verbs of poking (e.g., *poke, jab, prick*), and verbs of contact by impact (e.g., *hit, bump, tap*)—but it is violated by many other verb classes, including pure change-of-state verbs, like verbs of breaking (e.g., *break, smash, tear*). That's why it would be perfectly fine to say *Steve hit Scott on the arm*, but very odd—indeed, quite ungrammatical—to say **Steve broke Scott on the arm*. The neuropsychological study revealed that two patients who suffered left-hemisphere strokes could no longer make these kinds of naturalness judgments, but they could still rearrange sets of randomly ordered words into well-formed possessor ascension sentences, and they could still discriminate between subtle aspects of verb meaning that are invisible to the construction (e.g., the differences between *poke, jab*, and *prick*, all three of which can occur in the construction). Taken together, these results suggest that the patients' deficits were grammatical-semantic in nature, selectively affecting their knowledge of the schematic meaning of the construction and/or their knowledge of just those aspects of verb meaning that are relevant to it. Interestingly, the two patients' lesions overlapped in the anterior supramarginal gyrus and the posterior inferior frontal gyrus, and the other studies cited above also found that both verb-based and adjective-based grammatical-semantic impairments tend to be associated with damage in these areas, though not with complete consistency. Figure 2.12 shows the distribution of gray and white matter damage in one

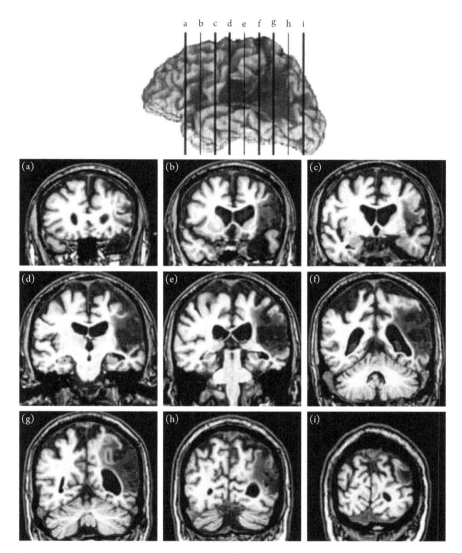

Figure 2.12. Lesion reconstruction for a stroke patient who displayed selectively impaired knowledge of grammatical semantics in several studies involving verb-based and adjective-based constructions. The vertical lines in the lateral view of the left hemisphere indicate the planes of the coronal sections shown beneath it. Note also that the patient's left temporal pole has less anterior extension that his right temporal pole.
From Kemmerer & Tranel (2003, p. 426).

patient who manifested selective grammatical-semantic deficits across the entire series of studies.

As this brief review indicates, the meanings of locative prepositions and argument structure constructions are slowly beginning to be investigated with the tools of cognitive neuroscience. It is important to bear in mind, however, that these are only a few of the many manifestations of grammatical semantics, and most of this rich and complex conceptual territory has not yet been explored from a neuroscientific perspective, let alone mapped in any detail. In Chapters 3, 4, and 5, we will survey a variety of cross-linguistic similarities and differences in several grammatical-semantic domains involving objects, actions, and spatial relations, with the aim of examining how these sorts of typological findings could potentially inform future research on the cortical underpinnings of concepts.

LINGUISTIC COMMUNICATION AS BRAIN-TO-BRAIN COUPLING

There is now abundant evidence that much of human social perception and cognition is based on a unique kind of interpersonal alignment that some researchers call "brain-to-brain coupling" (Hasson et al., 2012; see also Keysers & Gazzola, 2006). This phenomenon often takes the form of implicit embodied simulations of other people's actions, sensations, and emotions, as illustrated by the following examples. Whenever you watch someone perform an ordinary action like reaching for a cup of coffee, motor areas in your own brain are engaged, as if you were the one doing the reaching (e.g., Filimon et al., 2007, 2014; Rizzolatti et al., 2014; see also Kemmerer, 2015d). Whenever you see someone touch something, somatosensory regions in your own brain are activated, as if you were the one experiencing the tactile sensation (e.g., Hasson et al., 2004; Keysers et al., 2005; Blakemore et al., 2005). And whenever you observe someone's face take on an expression of disgust after they have detected a foul odor, some of the neural structures that underlie the feeling of disgust in your own brain are ignited, as if you were the unlucky individual who smelled the awful scent (e.g., Calder et al., 2000; Adolphs et al., 2003; Wicker et al., 2003).

These points are pertinent to language because a major goal of verbal communication is to set up "the same thought" in the receiver's brain as is currently taking place in the sender's brain, and this process can easily be construed as another form of brain-to-brain coupling, one that is similar in some respects to those just mentioned. After all, as argued throughout much of this chapter, words and sentences, especially those with concrete content, also tend to evoke implicit embodied simulations of sensory/motor/affective states. At the same time, however, linguistic symbols are clearly special because, as described in Chapter 1, they reflect historically shaped and, for the most part, culturally idiosyncratic conventions for conceptual coordination. That is to say, words and sentences are not just verbally coded cues for covertly recapitulating certain kinds of modal and transmodal states; they are *language-specific* cues for doing so. It therefore seems likely that much of the linguistically based brain-to-brain coupling that occurs between people in any given society involves embodied simulations that are sculpted in various ways by the distinctive semantic structures of the particular language that happens to be employed. Although many of those meanings are unique to that language, they collectively constitute the bulk of the community's conceptual common ground and hence provide a firm foundation for creating rich semantic alignments between group-mates (Tomasello, 2014). In Chapters 3, 4, and 5, we will see that these considerations, which derive partly from recent developments in semantic typology, have significant implications for the branch of cognitive neuroscience that concentrates on the representation, organization, and processing of concepts.

CONCLUSION

As with all of the other branches of cognitive neuroscience, research on how concepts are implemented in the brain has been advancing at a meteoric rate. Although many theoretical issues are still hotly debated, several fundamental assumptions have gradually come to be widely adopted. There is broad agreement, for instance, that concrete concepts tend to be grounded in modal systems for perception, action, and emotion, such that a great deal of semantic processing involves the partial reconstruction of sensory, motor, and affective states. There is also a growing consensus that transmodal systems are necessary to integrate the cortically distributed features of multimodal concepts, transcend superficial criteria for categorization, and form unitary, distilled representations that can easily be accessed and combined. Yet another common view is that a relatively shallow and "disembodied" level of semantic processing can often be achieved, largely for heuristic purposes, by relying solely on the statistical co-occurrence patterns of word forms. Finally, in the face of mounting evidence, most researchers now acknowledge that semantic processing is not a rigid affair, but is instead quite flexible, being modulated by multiple factors such as task, context, and individual experience. As highly sensitive brain mapping methods like RSA and neural decoding continue to evolve, the ability of researchers to characterize concepts in cortical terms will become progressively more sophisticated. On the other hand, it is essential to realize that the neuroscientific coverage of conceptual space will remain woefully incomplete until proper attention is devoted to the richly structured realm of grammatical semantics and, even more importantly, to the tremendous range of cross-linguistic similarities and differences that semantic typology has revealed.

PART II

Conceptual Domains

3

OBJECTS

Disparate languages are not just collections of different names for the same concepts in a hypothetical "mentalese" that is the same for speakers of all languages. Rather, many of the concepts we use to apprehend the world are built up in the very process of learning to speak—with the result that our conceptual stock differs markedly with our language background.
—Nicholas Evans (2010, p. 159)

INTRODUCTION

In Chapter 1 we saw that even though the lexical and grammatical concepts encoded by the roughly 6,500 languages of the world exhibit some universal tendencies, what stands out most strongly is their enormous diversity. Still, it is reasonable to suppose that this cross-linguistic semantic variation may be greater for some domains than others. One prominent view maintains that object concepts are more likely to be "given by the world" than relational concepts, and that, as a result, the meanings of concrete count nouns should be more similar across languages than the meanings of, say, action verbs and spatial prepositions/postpositions (Gentner & Boroditsky, 2001). This view is quite plausible, and it has recently been supported by typological research (Majid et al., 2015). However, it would be wrong to infer that all languages represent objects in more or less the same way. To be sure, there are many interesting cross-linguistic similarities in the lexical and grammatical encoding of objects at multiple levels of generalization, but there are also myriad differences that are equally striking. The goal of this chapter is to show that both sorts of findings are relevant to cognitive neuroscience. While the typological convergences provide valuable clues about how the human brain is naturally inclined to structure the semantic realm of objects, the typological divergences illuminate the degree to which this neural structuring can be influenced by cultural and environmental variation.

We begin by considering four domains of objects that are usually expressed by open-class nouns: plants, animals, artifacts, and body parts. All of these conceptual domains have been explored by both typologists and neuroscientists, but in different combinations. Specifically, although both research communities have often studied body part concepts by themselves, typologists have customarily investigated plant and animal concepts together, analyzing them separately from artifact concepts, whereas neuroscientists have tended to directly compare all three of these domains. In an effort to accommodate these mismatching approaches, the first main section of the chapter discusses plant, animal, and artifact concepts jointly, but in a manner that still respects their different treatments by typologists and neuroscientists. Then the subsequent section, which is much simpler but no less interesting, focuses on the fourth domain, namely body parts. Next, we consider some of the ways in which objects are represented by the following kinds of closed-class items and constructions: grammatical-semantic splits involving possession, and nominal classification systems. Although both of these forms of object representation have been intensively investigated in typology, they have been almost completely neglected in neuroscience; hence, they are especially pertinent to the latter field of study.

PLANTS, ANIMALS, AND ARTIFACTS
Typology

For millennia people everywhere have been fascinated with plants and animals. All cultures, it seems, have traditions for naming living things, sorting them into groups, predicting their behaviors and life cycles, and using them for food, clothing, weapons, medicines, recreational drugs, and many other purposes. During the past 50 years, a great deal of typological research has focused on how diverse societies refer to their local flora and fauna. Most of this work has been conducted within the branch of anthropology known as ethnobiology (a.k.a. folkbiology), and it has revealed numerous similarities and differences in how various languages, and the people who speak them, categorize the natural world (e.g., Berlin et al., 1973; Hunn, 1977; Hays, 1983; Brown, 1984; Atran, 1990; Berlin, 1992; Malt, 1995; López et al., 1997; Medin & Atran, 1999; Atran & Medin, 2008). The following survey focuses on an assembly of salient findings that, as discussed further below, are especially relevant to cognitive neuroscience.

Like the Linnaean tree of life, it appears that all systems of ethnobiological classification have a taxonomic structure with several ranks or levels of inclusiveness—usually between three and six—that are independent of idiosyncratic cultural beliefs. This is illustrated by Figure 3.1, which shows a small fragment of the English folk taxonomy, with the hierarchical levels labeled according to the framework developed by Berlin (1992): unique beginner (e.g., *plant*), life form (e.g., *tree*), generic (e.g., *oak*), specific (e.g., *white oak*), and varietal (e.g., *swamp white oak*). Cross-linguistically, terms at the top three levels tend to be morphemically simple, whereas those below the generic rank are usually two- or three-term compounds that make their subordinate status transparent, as in the English examples just given. Furthermore, in most systems at least some generic categories branch off directly from a unique beginner, bypassing the life form level. For example, although an octopus is clearly a kind of animal, it is certainly not a fish, nor does it seem to belong to any other life form (and the fact that, technically, an octopus is a mollusk is part of scientific knowledge, not folk knowledge).

There is widespread agreement among ethnobiological researchers that the heart of every system is the generic level. This is the level at which one always finds the largest number of categories, as illustrated by Tables 3.1 and 3.2, which show some representative results from elicitation-based fieldwork in a variety of non-industrialized societies (Berlin, 1992). Looking first at Table 3.1, it can be seen that across 17 societies the

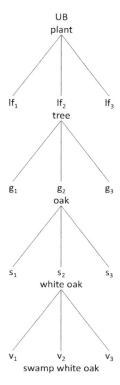

Figure 3.1. Fragment of the English folk taxonomy for plants.
Abbreviations: UB = unique beginner; lf = life form; g = generic; s = specific; v = varietal.

number of generic types of plants ranges from 137 to 956, with cultivators usually recognizing more categories (mean = 520) than non-cultivators (mean = 197). It is also apparent that cultivators are more likely to occupy tropical regions with rich biodiversity, which suggests that their bigger ethnobotanical inventories may reflect environmental factors as much as, if not more than, cultural ones. Turning to Table 3.2, the reported numbers of generic animal categories across 10 societies range from 186 to 606 (mean = 390). Although this sample is too small to determine whether the size of a society's ethnozoological lexicon is related to its mode of subsistence, there are some hints that as the number of animal species in a region increases, so does the number of animal names.

Another robust discovery is that folk systems of plant and animal classification exhibit substantial correspondences with scientific taxonomies. These correspondences are often manifested at both supra-generic and sub-generic levels of inclusiveness, but they are most frequent at the generic rank (for a review, see Malt, 1995). This is consistent with the fact that the generic rank is the one at which the coherently correlated morphological, behavioral, and ecological properties of organisms are most discernible. As Berlin (1992, p. 53) put it, the large but finite set of generic categories "is special in each system because its members stand out as beacons on the landscape of biological reality, figuratively crying out to be named."

Table 3.1. Reported numbers of generic plant categories in 17 relatively complete ethnobiological descriptions.

Group and Location	Number of Generic Categories
Traditional non-cultivators	
1. Lillooet (Canada)	137
2. Bella Coola (Canada)	152
3. Haida (Canada)	167
4. Anindilyakwa (Australia)	199
5. Navajo (USA)	201
6. Sahaptin (USA)	213
7. Seri (Mexico)	301
	Mean = 197
Traditional cultivators	
8. Quechua (Peru)	238
9. Mixe (Mexico)	383
10. Ndumba (New Guinea)	385
11. Chinantec (Mexico)	396
12. Tzeltal (Mexico)	471
13. Wayampí (French Guiana)	516
14. Aguaruna (Peru)	566
15. Taubuid (Philippines)	598
16. Tobelo (Indonesia)	689
17. Hanunóo (Philippines)	956
	Mean = 520

From Berlin (1992, p. 98).

Table 3.2. Reported numbers of generic animal categories in 10 relatively complete ethnobiological descriptions.

Group and Location	Number of Generic Categories
1. Ndumba (New Guinea)	186
2. Sahaptin (USA)	236
3. Piaroa (Venezuela)	305
4. Tzeltal (Mexico)	335
5. Kalam (New Guinea)	345
6. Anindilyakwa (Australia)	417
7. Tobelo (Indonesia)	420
8. Hanunóo (Philippines)	461
9. Wayampí (French Guiana)	589
10. Aguaruna (Peru)	606
	Mean = 390

From Berlin (1992, p. 100).

A closely related finding is that people from disparate cultures are strongly inclined to conceptualize every generic plant and animal category as having a hidden teleological essence that determines how that type of organism looks, develops, and reproduces (e.g., Keil, 1989; Atran, 1990; Gelman, 2003). This commonsense intuition is what lies behind people's understanding that a caterpillar and a butterfly are actually the same kind of creature, despite having very different forms, behaviors, and habitats. It also drives the insightful judgments that preschoolers make about many aspects of living things, such as that a raccoon with a stripe painted down its back is still a raccoon and not a skunk, but a dog whose insides have been removed is not really a dog any more and can no longer perform typical canine actions. Indeed, because parents hardly ever talk about the underlying identities of plants and animals, it is possible that children's predisposition to attribute hidden essences to them reflects an innate component of human ethnobiological cognition, one that facilitates learning and reasoning about natural kinds.

It is also noteworthy, however, that people's knowledge and use of ethnobiological terms depend very much on their interests. In all of the foraging societies that have been studied, people are routinely in intimate contact with the local flora and fauna from a fairly young age, and this is a major reason why they find the generic level of categorization to be the most basic—i.e., the one that they learn first, talk about most frequently, and recognize and recall most easily. In sharp contrast, the vast majority of people in urban societies have become estranged from the natural world, and as a result their basic level of ethnobiological classification has risen up to the higher rank of life form. This was dramatically demonstrated by Dougherty (1981), who found that while speakers of Tzeltal (Mayan, Mexico) typically categorized plants and animals at the generic level (e.g., by using terms equivalent to *oak, starling,* and *trout*), English speakers were much more likely to categorize them at the life form level (e.g., by using terms like *tree, bird,* and *fish*). It is crucial to realize, however, that even though Tzeltal speakers, as well as people in other foraging societies, may appear to have an extraordinary degree of ethnobiological expertise, this is only because we are viewing them from the novice perspective shared by most members of urban societies. If instead we adopt the more objective vantage point of evolutionary anthropology, we can see that the scale of ethnobiological competence evinced by foraging societies is actually the norm or default for *Homo sapiens*, since these societies are far more similar to ancestral populations than urban ones. The notion that modernization induces a significant decrease in ethnobiological knowledge is discussed in depth by Atran and Medin (2008), and the same issue is also addressed by Henrich et al. (2010, p. 7), who make the following quip: "studying the cognitive development of folkbiology in urban children would seem the equivalent of studying 'normal' physical growth in malnourished children."

Substantial group differences have also been documented for typicality and similarity judgments involving ethnobiological categories. Based on classic work in cognitive psychology, it is often thought that a good example of a plant or animal category is one that exhibits the central tendency in terms of physical properties (Smith et al., 1974; Rosch & Mervis, 1975). For instance, robins are usually rated as being representative of birds. It turns out, however, that these findings are rather parochial, since they come from studies with American undergraduates, most of whom are, as just mentioned, ethnobiological novices. Very different outcomes have come from comparable studies with people in foraging societies, virtually all of whom know a tremendous amount about the local flora and fauna (Atran & Medin, 2008). Importantly, these people base their typicality judgments not on central tendency, but rather on size, salience, and cultural importance—factors that collectively reflect idealness. As an illustration, for speakers of Itza' (Mayan, Mexico), the three "truest" or "most representative" birds are the ocellated turkey, crested guan, and great curassow, all three of which are large, morphologically striking, and highly edible galliformes (i.e., wild fowl). It is also notable that members of foraging societies diverge from American undergraduates in how they sort plants and animals according to similarity (Atran & Medin, 2008). For instance, while American undergraduates generally keep passerines (i.e., small songbirds) in a single group, Itza' speakers tend to spread them out across the hierarchy. This is probably because the Itza' interact regularly with their environment, and passerines don't play as prominent a role in this commerce as, say, large game birds. The upshot: how people mentally structure their ethnobiological categories is strongly influenced by how they deal with those kinds of objects in the real world.

In this connection, it is quite significant that, unlike scientific classification systems, ethnobiological ones, especially those developed by foraging societies, characterize numerous kinds of living things not only in terms of their shapes, behaviors, and ecological properties, but also in terms of their utility to the given culture. This occurs at all taxonomic levels, as described below.

Starting with supra-generic categories, many languages lack a lexical distinction corresponding to the seemingly obvious English contrast between *plant* and *animal*. Instead, they distinguish between other higher-order classes of organisms, drawing on features that are particularly relevant to human concerns. Here are three examples. First, ||Gana (Khoe-Kwadi, Botswana) posits the following large-scale groups of organisms: *kxʼooxo* ("eat things"), which are edible; *paaxo* ("bite things"), which are harmful; and *goōwahaxo* ("useless things"), which are neither edible nor harmful (Harrison, 2007). Second, Mohawk (Iroquoian, Ontario) does not recognize a single, all-encompassing domain of animals, but rather makes a fundamental cut between *kário* ("wild animals"), which cannot be possessed, and *katshé:nen'* ("domestic animals"), which usually are (Mithun, 2004). Third, Jahai (Mon-Khmer, Malaysia) has a top-level category of "forest things" that breaks down into leafy vegetables, starchy foods, ripe fruits, and edible animals; there are also two kinds of starchy foods—those in the ground and those on trees—as well as two kinds of edible animals—river game and land game; in addition, the category of land game subdivides into ground game and tree game (Levinson & Burenhult, 2009). What's more, many of the nouns for these types of living things have semantically parallel verbs that denote object-specific eating and foraging behaviors. In particular, there are distinct verbs for eating leafy vegetables, starchy foods, ripe fruits, and edible animals, as well as distinct verbs for foraging by plucking vegetables, digging, casting nets, and hunting game; there is even a more precise verb for hunting game in a particular manner—namely, by blowpiping (Levinson & Burenhult, 2009).

Turning to generic categories, the most compelling case for the relevance of cultural utility probably comes from Berlin's (1978; Berlin et al., 1974) analyses of Tzeltal (Mayan, Mexico) and Aguaruna (Jivaroan, Peru). For each language, he separated all of the generic plant categories into four groups: cultivated; protected but not cultivated; useful but not protected; and of no known use. He found that in both languages, fully two-thirds of the categories fell into one of the first three groups. Thus, a substantial majority of the lexicalized generic plant categories were defined partly in terms of their cultural value.

Finally, there is considerable evidence that, as Atran and Medin (2008, p. 34) observe, "the subordinate ranks of folkspecific and varietal correspond to ranges of perceptible natural variation that humans are most apt to appropriate and manipulate as a function of their cultural interests." In the domain of plants, folkspecific and varietal categories tend to have agricultural, medicinal, or ritual significance; and in the domain of animals, such categories are often the targets of hunting or selective breeding/domestication. For instance, seals have special significance for Eskimos, so it is not surprising that Central Yup'ik (Eskimo-Aleut, Alaska) has separate terms not only for different species of seals, but also for the same species at different stages of life, such as *amirkaq* ("young bearded seal"), *maklaaq* ("bearded seal in its first year"), and *maklassuk* ("bearded seal in its second year") (Mithun, 2004). Similarly, many speakers of Todzhu (Northern Turkic, Siberia) are reindeer herders, and their language has a large set of terms that categorize reindeer according to age, sex, rideability, fertility, and tameness (Harrison, 2007). This impressive degree of lexical-conceptual integration is nicely illustrated by the following examples:

- *döngür:* a male domesticated reindeer from second fall to third fall; first mating season; may be castrated or not, and if not, will probably be allowed to mate
- *myndyzhak:* a female domesticated reindeer in her first autumn of mating
- *chary:* a five-year-old male castrated reindeer; the most useful kind for riding

Even more remarkable, perhaps, is Kayapó (Northern Jean, Brazil), many of whose speakers can name 56 kinds of bees and group them into 15 families depending on their flight pattern, aggressive behavior, sound, habitat, edibility of larvae, quality of wax, and, most importantly, quality of honey (Posey, 1990). As one would expect, given their peculiar ethnoentomological obsession with bees, the Kayapó love to harvest and eat honey.

So far, we have seen that while there is certainly a great deal of uniformity across ethnobiological classification systems, there is also a substantial amount of diversity, due in large part to the critical role that human interests, and especially cultural concerns, play in the recognition and construal of plants and animals. Considerably less typological research has been devoted to artifact concepts, but one productive line of work has revealed a number of intriguing cross-linguistic similarities and differences in a domain which is seemingly mundane but actually quite informative from a semantic point of view—namely, the domain of household containers.

In a study that used as stimuli a set of 60 common containers such as bottles, jars, jugs, boxes, and so forth, Malt et al. (1999, 2003) asked speakers of English, Argentinian Spanish, and Mandarin Chinese to not only name all of the objects, but also sort them according to physical similarity, functional similarity, and overall similarity. Although the three groups did not differ significantly in their non-linguistic similarity judgments, they produced complex naming patterns that clearly disclosed distinct ways of partitioning the same referential territory for communicative purposes (Table 3.3). For example, of the 60 objects, 16 were preferentially called *bottle* in English, but there was not a matching lexical category in either Spanish or

Table 3.3. English, Argentinian Spanish, and Mandarin Chinese names for 60 common household containers.

English	N	Spanish	N	Chinese	N
jar	19	frasco	28	ping2	40
bottle	16	envase	6	guan4	10
container	15	bidón	6	tong3	5
can	5	aerosol	3	he2	4
jug	3	botella	3	guan3	1
tube	1	pote	2		
box	1	lata	2		
		tarro	2		
		mamadera	2		
		gotero	1		
		caja	1		
		talquera	1		
		taper	1		
		roceador	1		
		pomo	1		

Note: The numbers after the Chinese words indicate lexical tones.
From Malt et al. (2003, p. 25).

Chinese. Instead, those 16 objects fell into 7 smaller Spanish categories, and 13 of them were subsumed within a larger Chinese category that also included all 19 of the objects called *jar* plus 8 of the 15 objects called *container*. The fact that the various linguistic categories contrasted quite radically, whereas the non-linguistic ones did not, suggests that the former transcend the purely physical and functional properties of the designated objects and reflect other factors as well. According to Malt et al. (1999, 2003), such factors may include the overall salience of the container domain in a community, the uses of particular types of containers, their time of appearance, and whether the morphology of a language facilitates the relatively fine-grained differentiation of objects. This last factor is illustrated by Spanish, which allows speakers to easily form new names for containers by adding suffixes to roots. For example, *talc + era = talquera*, which denotes a container for dispensing talc (for additional insights drawn from Icelandic, see Whelpton et al., 2015).

Several other investigations have concentrated more narrowly on the cross-linguistic treatment of "dishes." Extending earlier work by Kronenfeld et al. (1985), Pavlenko and Malt (2011) compared the naming of 60 drinking vessels in English and Russian. As shown in Table 3.4, all of the objects were labeled with just three words in English—*cup, glass,* and *mug*—but they elicited no less than 10 terms in Russian. Moreover, the latter categories did not simply subdivide the former; instead, the two naming patterns criss-crossed in complex ways that reflected variation involving the relative importance of multiple conceptual features—most notably, shape, size, material, and function. The greatest overlap was for vessels that have vertical sides, a

Table 3.4. English and Russian names for 60 drinking vessels.
(A) Linguistic categories for English speakers and their composition
in terms of Russian speakers' dominant names. (B) Linguistic
categories for Russian speakers and their composition in terms
of English speakers' dominant names.

A

English

Name	N	Russian composition
cup	26	14 stakan, 7 chashka, 2 riumka, 1 kruzhka, 1 lozhka, 1 piala
glass	19	7 stakan, 4 fuzher, 4 riumka, 3 bokal, 1 vaza
mug	15	8 kruzhka, 4 chashka, 2 stakan, 1 kuvshin

B

Russian

Name	N	English composition
stakan	23	14 cup, 7 glass, 2 mug
chashka	11	7 cup, 4 mug
kruzhka	9	8 mug, 1 cup/mug
riumka	6	4 glass, 2 cup
fuzher	4	4 glass
bokal	3	3 glass
kuvshin	1	1 mug
lozhka	1	1 cup
piala	1	1 cup
vaza	1	1 glass

From Pavlenko & Malt (2011, p. 27).

wide bottom, and a handle, and that are intended mainly for hot drinks. The dominant English term for these containers was *mug*, and the dominant Russian term was *kruzhka*. The referential scopes of all the other terms, however, were much more language-specific. English speakers used the word *cup* to name a large number of vessels that differed in the presence/absence of a handle, the material they were made of (e.g., ceramic, plastic, Styrofoam), and whether they were for hot or cold drinks. In contrast, these speakers restricted the word *glass* to containers that were composed of glass; such objects, however, still varied with regard to the presence/absence of a stem and whether they were for alcoholic drinks, like wine, or non-alcoholic drinks, like water. Turning to Russian, the broadest category consisted of objects denoted by the term *stakan*, but while these containers were composed of a variety of materials and could be used for either hot or cold drinks, they were limited in shape to tall, tapered vessels without handles. Most of the other Russian terms denoted more circumscribed categories of containers. For instance, *chashka* was used to label small vessels that had handles and were for hot drinks; *fuzher* and *bokal* were used to name tall vessels, with or without stems, for alcoholic drinks; and *riumka* was used to refer to small vessels, with or without stems, for hard liquor. The remaining Russian terms in Table 3.4—*kuvshin, lozhka, piala,* and *vaza*—appeared to have less currency, since they were employed with low consensus for just one object apiece.

More recently, a research team led by Asifa Majid administered to speakers of 12 Germanic languages a standardized naming task that used as stimuli 67 color photographs of familiar household dishes (Majid et al., 2015). Even though the 12 languages have shared histories, their speakers displayed many differences regarding the lexical categorization of the very same objects. The average number of separate terms that speakers generated to label the containers was 39; the range, however, extended from a low of just 19 (Faroese) to a high of 71 (Schwyzerdütsch). Some of the more specific findings are illustrated in Table 3.5, which shows how the six drinking vessels portrayed at the top elicited both convergent and divergent naming patterns across the 12 languages. The most common strategy, exemplified by speakers of Norwegian, Icelandic, Luxembourgish, German, and Schwyzerdütsch, was to make the following three-way distinction: one term for the four small-to-medium-sized cups and mugs, a second term for the large mug, and a third term for the tall plastic cup. Against this background of similarity, however, many contrasts were observed between the other languages. Faroese speakers used just one word to describe all six vessels. Speakers of Belgian Dutch, Frisian, and Danish employed two words but drew the boundary between them at different points along the continuum of containers. Swedish and English speakers made three-way distinctions that differed not only from the common

Table 3.5. Naming patterns for drinking vessels across 12 Germanic languages. A color version is in the color plates section.

Faroese	koppur					
Dutch (BE)	tas					beker
Frisian	kopke			beker		
Danish	kop				krus	
Norwegian	kopp				krus	glass
Icelandic	bolli				krús	glas
Luxembourgish	Taass				Béierkrou	Becher
German	Tasse				Krug	Becher
Schwyzerdütsch	tassli				humpè	bächèr
Swedish	kopp			mugg		glass
English	cup			mug		cup
Dutch (NL)	kopje		kom	mok		beker

Note: Capitalization of the nouns in German and Luxembourgish follow the conventions of those languages' writing systems.

From Majid et al. (2015, p. 14).

Table 3.6 Mohawk (Iroquoian, Canada) tool words derived from verbal descriptions of how the designated objects are typically used.

Mohawk Word	English Transliteration	English Word
iehiatónhkhwa'	'one writes with it'	pen, pencil
iontekhwakon'onhstáhkhwa'	'one makes food tasty with it'	ketchup
ienonhsohare'táhkhwa'	'one floor washes with it'	mop
ienon'tawerontáhkhwa'	'one pours milk with it'	milk pitcher
ietsi'tsaráhkhwa'	'one puts flowers in with it'	vase
ionnitskaráhkhwa'	'one fixes a place to lie down with it'	sheets
iontenawirohare'táhkhwa'	'one tooth washes with it'	toothbrush
iontenonhsa'tariha'táhkhwa'	'one heats the house with it'	heater
iontkahri'táhkhwa'	'one plays with it'	toy
iontkonhsohare'táhkhwa'	'one face washes with it'	face cloth
teiehtharáhkhwa'	'one talks with it'	telephone
teionrahsi'tahráhkhwa'	'one sets one's feet up with it'	footstool
iehwistaráhkhwa'	'one inserts money with it'	wallet
tehatitstenhrotáhkhwa'	'they stand stones with it'	cement
iakehiahráhkhwa'	'one remembers with it'	souvenir

From Mithun (2004, p. 135).

one mentioned earlier, but also from each other. And finally, speakers of Netherlands Dutch carved the referential space into four separate categories.

Taken together, these studies indicate that the concepts encoded by container terms are remarkably complex and cross-linguistically variable, reflecting unique combinations, breakdowns, and weightings of myriad physical, functional, and cultural dimensions. Indeed, the semantic subtlety of these terms explains why it sometimes takes children up to 12 years to achieve an adult level of competence with them (Andersen, 1975; Ameel et al., 2008). More generally, the studies just discussed have broader implications for the conceptual domain of artifacts, since they suggest that, as Malt and Majid (2013, p. 598) put it, "the world seems to provide even less structure here than it does in the case of plants and animals."

Apart from the work on container terms that we just reviewed, not much systematic typological research has focused on the linguistic encoding of artifacts. It is worth mentioning, however, that some languages employ an interesting strategy of creating words for tools by explicitly specifying the customary functions of the designated objects. For instance, in Mohawk (Iroquoian, Canada), when the verb *iehiatón* "write" is combined with the instrumental suffix *-hkw* "with," the result is a noun that refers to a pen or pencil but literally means "one writes with it." The 15 tool words shown in Table 3.6 illustrate how productive this word-formation pattern is.[1] In addition, it is

---

[1] A comparable pattern is used to create place names—e.g., a church is "the place one prays with," a restaurant is "the place one dines with," a bank is "the place one lays money with," and a funeral home is "the place one lays bodies with."

notable that, through a process of grammaticalization, the suffix -*hkw* "with" derived historically from a verb meaning "pick up." These conceptual connections not only make obvious sense, since people usually pick up tools before using them, but may also be mirrored in the brain by close functional-anatomical relations between tool and hand representations, as described below.

Neurobiology

Ever since the mid-1980s, object concepts have been a major focus of research in cognitive neuroscience, and by far the greatest amount of work has concentrated on the domains of plants, animals, and artifacts. Much has been learned about the cortical underpinnings of these three conceptual domains by carefully investigating activation patterns, deficit-lesion correlations, and processing dynamics (for reviews, see Capitani et al., 2003; Gainotti, 2006; Martin, 2007; Mahon & Caramazza, 2009; Clarke, 2015; Contini et al., 2017). Moreover, this bounty of data has led to a rich array of theoretical frameworks that continue to be debated and refined (Mahon & Caramazza, 2011; Chen & Rogers, 2014; Clarke & Tyler, 2015). It is striking, however, that throughout this large literature there are very few references to the sorts of typological findings described above regarding cross-linguistic, and more broadly cross-cultural, similarities and differences in the representation of these kinds of objects. Our aim here is therefore to explore some of the ways in which such findings can inform this branch of cognitive neuroscience. Before proceeding with this exploration, though, we will first survey the most salient neuroscientific issues.

Many fMRI studies have directly compared the activation patterns associated with the processing of concepts for animals and tools, the latter category being the subdomain of artifacts that has received the most attention from neuroscientists. These studies have generally found that the two kinds of concepts differentially engage the following neural networks, which are depicted in Figure 3.2 (for reviews and meta-analyses, see Martin, 2007; Chouinard & Goodale, 2010; Ishibashi et al., 2016):

- animal concepts:
  - lateral fusiform gyrus (latFG), involved in category-related shape perception
  - posterior superior temporal sulcus (pSTS), involved in biological motion perception
- tool concepts:
  - medial fusiform gyrus (medFG), involved in category-related shape perception
  - posterior middle temporal gyrus (pMTG), involved in mechanical motion perception
  - anterior intraparietal sulcus (aIPS) and supramarginal gyrus (SMG), involved in reaching, grasping, and manipulating
  - ventral premotor cortex (vPMC), involved in storing and executing hand-related motor programs.

Interestingly, the nodes comprising each of these networks are physiologically integrated even during rest, as manifested by tightly correlated fluctuations of spontaneous activity (Stevens et al., 2015; for related functional connectivity studies that are especially pertinent to the tool network, see Almeida et al., 2013; Mahon et al., 2013;

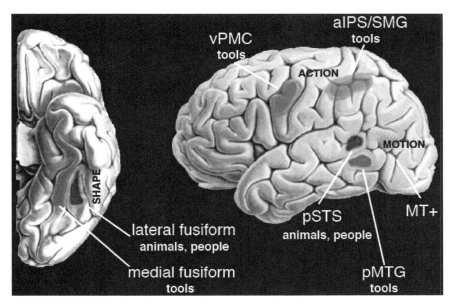

Figure 3.2. Neural networks differentially engaged during the processing of concepts for animals and tools in fMRI studies. Left panel: Ventral surface of left hemisphere. Right panel: Lateral surface of the left hemisphere. A color version is in the color plates section.
Abbreviations: pSTS = posterior superior temporal sulcus; pMTG = posterior middle temporal gyrus; aIPS = anterior intraparietal sulcus; SMG = supramarginal gyrus; vPMC = ventral premotor cortex. Modified from a figure kindly provided by Alex Martin.

Garcea & Mahon, 2014). Moreover, both networks are sensitive to contextual cues for (in)animacy (Martin & Weisberg, 2003; Wheatley et al., 2007), and the one that is specialized for animate stimuli can even detect the "aliveness" of real versus toy human and dog faces (Looser et al., 2013).

Unfortunately, much less functional imaging work has explored the neural substrates of plant concepts. It is noteworthy, however, that words for fruits and vegetables have been found to engage a circuit that includes ventral temporal areas linked with shape and color perception, motor areas linked with mouth actions, and orbitofrontal areas linked with rewarding tastes and smells (Price et al., 2003; Goldberg et al., 2006a, 2006b; Hwang et al., 2009; Carota et al., 2012).

Additional insight into the cortical organization of concepts for animals, tools, and fruits/vegetables comes from neuropsychological studies with brain-damaged patients who display semantic impairments that are much worse for some categories of objects than others (for reviews, see Mahon & Caramazza, 2009; McCarthy & Warrington, 2016). As shown in Figure 3.3, each of the three conceptual domains considered here can be disproportionately, or even selectively, impaired relative to the others. The most common pattern, however, is for knowledge of the two categories of living things—i.e., animals and fruits/vegetables—to be disrupted significantly more than knowledge of the one category of nonliving things—i.e., tools. With respect to lesion sites, category-related semantic deficits for animals and fruits/vegetables usually arise from either

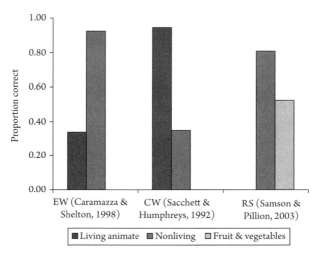

Figure 3.3. Representative brain-damaged patients who exhibit selectively impaired naming of particular kinds of objects: animals (left), artifacts (middle), and fruits/vegetables (right). A color version is in the color plates section.
From Chen & Rogers (2014, p. 328).

left-hemisphere or bilateral damage to the ventral temporal lobes, which, as mentioned earlier, have been implicated in form and color perception (for a review, see Gainotti, 2006). In sharp contrast, category-related semantic deficits for tools most often result from damage to the components of the tool network that have been implicated in mechanical motion perception and arm/hand actions, these being the left pMTG (e.g., Tranel et al., 1997a; Campanella et al., 2010), the left inferior parietal lobule (e.g., Mahon et al., 2007; Martin et al., 2016), and the left ventral premotor cortex (e.g., Reilly et al., 2011; Dreyer et al., 2015). In addition, tool concepts can be impaired by damage to the long-distance fiber tracts that interconnect these regions (Bi et al., 2015).

These sorts of findings, among many others (some of which are described in the following), have been interpreted most frequently from the very different perspectives of two competing theoretical frameworks. One approach is closely tied to the view that, as discussed in detail in Chapter 2, concrete concepts are grounded in modal systems for perception, action, and emotion, such that their online processing often involves the partial reconstruction of sensory, motor, and affective states. According to this account, the main reason why different domains of object concepts appear to be represented by different networks of brain regions is because they depend on different mixtures and weightings of modal features (Tranel et al., 1997b; Vinson & Vigliocco, 2008; Gainotti et al., 2009, 2013; Hoffman & Lambon Ralph, 2013; Binder et al., 2016). A variety of additional factors, however, may also influence the neural regionalization of different domains of object concepts, as summarized in the following passage from an important paper by Chen and Rogers (2014, pp. 340–341; note that all of these factors are elaborated in that paper):

> Impairments to knowledge about animals, or greater functional activation in response to animals, may arise because (1) animals rely more on visual or other perceptual information, (2) animal representations are more semantically or visually crowded, (3) animals are generally less familiar overall, (4) animals are more visually complex,

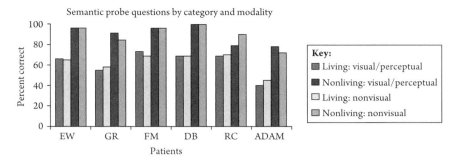

Figure 3.4. Representative brain-damaged patients who have significantly greater difficulty answering questions about living versus nonliving things regardless of whether those questions focus on visual/perceptual or nonvisual features. A color version is in the color plates section. From Mahon & Caramazza (2011, p. 98).

(5) rely more on high spatial-frequency information for differentiation, (6) require greater feature integration, and (7) have fewer 'semantically relevant' properties than artifacts. Impairments to knowledge about artifacts, or greater functional activation in response to artifacts, may arise because (1) artifact knowledge is typically acquired later in life, (2) such knowledge, especially for manipulable objects, depends more upon functional or praxic representations, or (3) artifacts have more individuating and fewer shared properties.

The other approach maintains that the primary reason why the conceptual domains of animals and tools—and also, to some extent, fruits/vegetables—dissociate from each other in functional imaging and neuropsychological studies is because they are subserved by separate circuits that were naturally selected during hominin evolution to represent these particular kinds of objects (Caramazza & Shelton, 1998; Caramazza & Mahon, 2003; Mahon & Caramazza, 2009, 2011). One source of empirical support for this adaptationist view comes from case studies of brain-damaged patients who, as shown in Figure 3.4, have significantly greater difficulty answering questions about living than nonliving things regardless of whether those questions focus on perceptual or nonperceptual features. Because these patients' deficits cannot easily be reduced to problems involving knowledge or processing of visual object properties, they may constitute genuinely domain-specific impairments. Additional evidence for the existence of innately specialized circuits for animal and tool concepts comes from an fMRI study which found that the category-related ventral temporal activity patterns exhibited by sighted individuals—namely, greater responses to words for animals in the latFG, and greater responses to words for tools in the medFG—is also exhibited by congenitally blind individuals, thereby demonstrating that visual experience is not necessary for the architecture to develop (Mahon et al., 2009).[2]

---

[2] In this connection, it is also notable that the fusiform gyrus has at least four cytoarchitectonically segregated sectors—two lateral and two medial—that are presumably established by genetic programming (Weiner & Zilles, 2016).

Which of these two theoretical frameworks has the greatest explanatory coherence continues to be debated (e.g., Gainotti, 2013; Chen & Rogers, 2014, 2015), and we will certainly not attempt to resolve the ongoing controversy here. Instead, we will explore some of the ways in which the typological data reviewed earlier bear on both viewpoints, as well as on several other issues involving the neural correlates of object concepts. We will begin by concentrating on concepts for living things and then turn to concepts for tools and other artifacts.

First of all, the domain-specific account espoused by Caramazza and colleagues is consistent with, and hence receives further support from, some of the cross-cultural and developmental data in the ethnobiology literature. Most notably, Atran and Medin (2008, pp. 63–119) hypothesize that "there is a naturally selected set of cognitive processes targeted on the biological world," and they bolster their argument with a wide range of evidence, including the universality of taxonomic hierarchies in plant and animal classification systems, the privileged yet experience-dependent status of the generic taxonomic level for purposes of categorization and reasoning, and—perhaps most compelling of all—the capacity of young children to base their causal expectations about organisms not on superficial perceptual properties, but rather on hidden teleological essences that they intuitively posit. This peculiarly essentialistic form of cognition is applied only to living things; it does not extend to tools and other artifacts (Sloman & Malt, 2003). But even though it seems to reflect an innately specialized aspect of ethnobiological thinking, its implementation in the brain remains quite mysterious, since it has not yet been investigated by cognitive neuroscientists.

Another important point is that all of the neuroscientific research that has been conducted so far on object concepts has involved people in WEIRD societies—i.e., societies that are Western(ized), educated, industrialized, rich, and democratic (Henrich et al., 2010). As indicated earlier, whereas most people in traditional foraging societies possess extensive generic-level knowledge about the local flora and fauna, most people in WEIRD societies do not; in fact, even though the latter people are just as neurologically intact as the former, they suffer from a modern malady called "nature-deficit disorder," since they have relatively little contact with and understanding of the natural world (Louv, 2008). This is probably why, as noted in the quotation from Chen and Rogers (2014), animals tend to be rated as less familiar, on average, than tools. It also explains the strange makeup of plant and animal stimuli in most neuroscientific studies of ethnobiological knowledge. These stimuli have usually been selected so that people in WEIRD societies can recognize and name them at the generic level, but close inspection quickly reveals that they form a motley assortment of species, many of which are not indigenous to the research participants' environment—unless, of course, one counts the grocery store in the case of plants and the zoo in the case of animals. For instance, the animal stimuli in functional imaging and neuropsychological experiments often include species like camels, pandas, giraffes, and crocodiles, which people in WEIRD societies rarely if ever see directly, but learn about instead from books, television shows, and the like.

How might the richly differentiated ethnobiological knowledge displayed by people in foraging societies be implemented in their brains? The neural networks for animals and fruits/vegetables that we discussed earlier presumably have the same basic organization across all humans, but their representational spaces may be more intricately partitioned in foragers. In addition, these individuals may have more highly developed circuitry mediating the interplay between two ventral temporal regions that have recently been implicated more in the generic-level processing of living than nonliving things—specifically, the latFG, which we have already encountered, and the perirhinal cortex, which resides in the anteromedial temporal lobes. In short, convergent data from fMRI and deficit-lesion correlations suggest that these two cortical areas operate synergistically to enable the discrimination and recognition of objects that have many shared visual features but few idiosyncratic ones—conceptual characteristics that are more common among living than nonliving things (Tyler et al., 2013; Clarke & Tyler, 2014; Wright et al., 2015; for a review, see Clarke & Tyler, 2015). It therefore seems quite likely that these two brain regions are heavily recruited by, say, members of the Hanunóo society in the Philippines, who are able to classify 956 generic plant species and 461 generic animal species in their own geographical territory (see again Tables 3.1 and 3.2).

It is also worth considering the neurobiological implications of cross-cultural variation in how people sort plants and animals according to similarity. For instance, we noted earlier that while American undergraduates generally group small songbirds together with large game birds, speakers of Itza' (Mayan, Mexico) tend to treat them differently, since the former birds are less important to them than the latter (Atran & Medin, 2008). These contrasting behavioral judgments must have contrasting cortical underpinnings, and it would be possible, at least in principle, to investigate them by employing the fMRI technique of representational similarity analysis. Interestingly, a recent study used this approach to show that the ventral temporal activity patterns evoked by pictures of different animal species are anatomically arrayed along a lateral-to-medial continuum of decreasing animacy: mammals (e.g., squirrel monkeys and ring-tailed lemurs) are relatively lateral; insects (e.g., ladybird beetles and luna moths) are relatively medial, much like inanimate objects; and birds (e.g., yellow-throat warblers and mallard ducks) are in between (Connolly et al., 2012; see also Sha et al., 2015). This cortical topography was not only consistent across the participants, but also reflected their behavioral similarity judgments. In the current context, however, what matters most is that these participants were all drawn from the Dartmouth College community. Would Itza' speakers yield somewhat different results, especially if the stimuli included the kinds of animal species that they and American students sort in systematically different ways?

As a final observation about the relevance of ethnobiological data to cognitive neuroscience, it is worth reiterating that because foraging societies maintain intimate interactions with their natural environments, their plant and animal classification systems routinely take into account the cultural utility of the designated categories; moreover, they do so at all taxonomic levels, from supra-generic through generic to sub-generic. Most of the neuroscientific research on plant and animal concepts, however, has adopted the very different perspective of people in WEIRD societies, and this has undoubtedly influenced what has and has not been discovered about the implementation of these concepts in the brain. For example, as noted earlier, although fruit/vegetable concepts often get relatively high ratings for functional features and tend to engage mouth-related motor regions, animal concepts are usually rated quite low for functional features and do not seem to depend on frontoparietal circuits for object-directed action. These negative findings for animal concepts, however, may be due in part to the fact that people in WEIRD societies rarely interact with the kinds of animals that are used as experimental stimuli. Perhaps more positive results would emerge if members of foraging societies were tested with the kinds of animals that they deal with on a regular basis.

Lastly, what about concepts for tools and other artifacts? In the cognitive neuro-science literature on this topic, there is a widespread but largely implicit assumption that people use the same tool concepts for both linguistic and non-linguistic purposes. To be sure, some research does seem to support this position. For instance, in an influential fMRI study, Chao et al. (1999) found that the tool network depicted in Figure 3.2 was engaged not only when participants performed two linguistic tasks (naming pictures of tools, and deciding whether words for tools denoted kitchen devices), but also when they performed two non-linguistic tasks (passively viewing pictures of tools, and making comparative judgments about pictures of tools). However, it is clear from the foregoing review of typological data that the meanings of words for tools and other artifacts vary greatly across languages. Hence it is likely that these meanings differ, at least somewhat, from the tool concepts that people use in various non-linguistic contexts. As we saw earlier, direct evidence for this view comes from Malt et al. (1999, 2003), who found that although speakers of three different languages named the same set of 60 containers in radically different ways, they sorted those objects according to physical, functional, and overall similarity in essentially identical ways. It is important to realize, though, that the nature of the relation between linguistic and non-linguistic concepts is a very complex and intellectually challenging issue, one that we will refrain from tackling head-on until Chapter 6. Here, the main point is simply this: A comprehensive account of the neural substrates of concepts for tools and other artifacts must ultimately address cross-linguistic similarities and differences in the lexical encoding of this semantic domain.

By way of closing this section and transitioning to the next, let's return briefly to Mohawk (Iroquoian, Canada), which exemplifies the intriguing strategy of referring to tools by explicitly specifying how they are typically handled. As described earlier, all of the tool words in Table 3.6 derive from the attachment of an instrumental suffix meaning "with" (but originally meaning "pick up") to an action verb (or a verb-noun pair) that indicates the conventional use of the designated object. This semantically transparent approach to forming tool words may have a strong neurobiological foundation. In particular, a recent fMRI study by Bracci et al. (2016; see also Striem-Amit et al., 2017) showed that all of the cortical nodes comprising the tool network respond not just to pictures of tools, but also to pictures of the principal body part that people use to manipulate them—namely, hands. Further investigation with multivariate pattern analysis revealed that within all of the key regions the specific activity patterns evoked by the two types of objects differed significantly. But it is noteworthy that the experiment was conducted in the United Kingdom, presumably with English speakers. This raises a provocative question: Might the functional-anatomical relations between tool-related and hand-related activity patterns turn out to be even tighter if a similar study were done with Mohawk speakers?

BODY PARTS

Typology

From the perspective of semantic typology, human body parts constitute an especially interesting conceptual domain. The reason is simple: Holistically, the human form has more or less the same objectively measurable organization in all societies worldwide, so if there are any cross-linguistic differences in its lexical-semantic segmentation, they must reflect cultural or environmental factors. During the past few decades, an increasing amount of typological research has focused on this topic, and the results clearly show that while there are certainly some constraints on the cross-linguistic conceptualization of body parts, there is also a great deal of diversity (Brown, 1976, 2005a, 2005b; Andersen, 1978; Witkowski & Brown, 1985; Heine, 1997a; Enfield et al., 2006; Wierzbicka, 2007; Majid, 2010; Majid & van Staden, 2015).

Body part terms encode complex semantic structures that have four main components: (1) information about the typical shape of the designated part; (2) information about the location of the designated part within the hierarchical spatial organization of the human form; (3) information about the characteristic function(s) of the designated part; and (4) information about the cultural associations of the designated part. Virtually all of the typological work on body part terms, however, has concentrated on the first component, which is logical, since it is probably the most important one.

Given that the human body is a single object with a continuous surface, the purpose of a mereological nomenclature is to allow speakers to refer to spatially delimited body segments. Current evidence suggests that, cross-linguistically, a common principle of body segmentation is visual discontinuity. For instance, most languages rely on the visual discontinuities of joints to distinguish between different parts of the limbs (e.g., upper arm, forearm, hand, finger). The presence of a salient discontinuity, however, does not ensure that a language will use it as the basis for separate terms.

For instance, Brown (2005a) found that in a global sample of 617 languages, only 389 (63%) have separate terms for arms and hands. Consistent with a previous study by Witkowski and Brown (1985) that involved a smaller sample, he also found that languages that do make this distinction tend to be located in non-equatorial zones where cold weather is frequent. Given this correlation with lattitude and, by extension, temperature, he proposed that because societies in these regions are more likely to wear clothes that increase the salience of the arm-hand boundary (e.g., gloves, mittens, and long sleeves ending at the wrist), they may be more inclined to develop separate terms for arms and hands. This is a plausible hypothesis, but it has not yet been rigorously tested. Another possible account of the typological data, one that also requires further investigation, is that languages that collapse the arm/hand distinction may be sensitive to the fact that these body segments usually move together when we execute upper limb actions (Majid & van Staden, 2015). In such languages, the single term for arm+hand may therefore be grounded more in the motor system than the visual system (consistent with work by de Vignemont et al., 2009).

More detailed typological insights about similarities and differences between body partonomies emerged from a pioneering project in which 10 fieldworkers gathered data from 10 genealogically and geographically diverse languages by using the same standardized methods (for an overview, see Enfield et al., 2006, which introduces a special issue of *Language Sciences* devoted to this project). Here are some representative results involving just the limbs.[3] Lavukaleve (Central Solomon, Solomon Islands) lacks distinct terms for arms and legs, employing instead a single term for both (analogous to the English word *limb*), and while it does have a separate term for feet, it lacks a corresponding term for hands (Terrill, 2006). Savosavo (Central Solomon, Solomon Islands) has different terms for arms and legs, but both of them cover the entirety of these limbs, with no other words that denote just hands or just feet (Wegener, 2006). Yélî Dnye (isolate, Papua New Guinea) treats upper limbs the same way as Savosavo, with a single term for arms and hands, but it treats lower limbs differently, since it has one term for the thigh and another for the calf and foot, thus respecting the knee discontinuity but ignoring the ankle discontinuity (Levinson, 2006). Jahai (Mon-Khmer, Malaysia) prefers specificity over generality, since it has different terms for the upper arm, forearm, and hand, as well as different terms for the thigh, calf, and foot, but no terms for whole arms or whole legs (Burenhult, 2006). Finally, Tidore (West Papuan, Indonesia) displays yet more peculiarities, since it has one term that covers the upper part of the thigh, and another term that covers the lower part of the thigh, the calf, and the foot, thus drawing a category boundary in the absence of a corporeal discontinuity (van Staden, 2006).

These cross-linguistic findings, among many others, show that even though body partonomies are strongly influenced by natural discontinuities in the human form, they vary greatly with regard to which ones they use as the basis for lexical-semantic distinctions.

Neurobiology

It is well-established that a critical brain region for explicitly coding the shapes of body parts is the extrastriate body area (EBA), which resides in the lateral occipitotemporal cortex (for reviews, see Peelen & Downing, 2007; Downing & Peelen, 2011, 2016). This region responds to body parts regardless of personal identity, emotional expression, movement pattern, and action goal; it generalizes across visual and haptic modalities; and it even detects body parts in silhouettes, cartoons, and stick figures. These representational capacities would appear to make the EBA well-suited to process the shapes of body parts for both perceptual and conceptual purposes, and there is some evidence that supports this possibility—not a lot, but some.

In a recent fMRI study, Bracci et al. (2015) found that the EBA represents visually presented body parts in a roughly topographic manner, as shown in Figure 3.5 (see also Orlov et al., 2010; Weiner & Grill-Spector, 2013). In addition, by using representational similarity analysis, they discovered that the different activity patterns evoked by different body parts fell into three clusters: one for body parts used as effectors (arms, hands, legs, and feet); another for non-effector body parts (chests and waists); and a third for face parts (upper faces and lower faces). Interestingly, this neural similarity

---

[3] These cross-linguistic studies also investigated other regions of the body, such as parts of the torso and parts of the head.

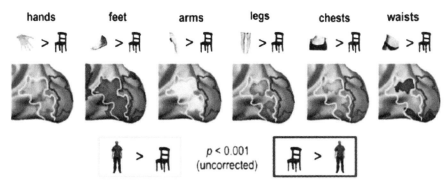

Figure 3.5. Example stimuli, experimental contrasts, and imaging results from Bracci et al.'s (2015) fMRI study of the representational topography of the extrastriate body area in the left lateral occipitotemporal cortex. The yellow outline in each brain image shows the boundaries of the region of interest defined by the contrast between pictures of whole persons and pictures of tools, and the blue outline shows the boundaries of the region of interest defined by the opposite contrast. Activation patterns associated with particular body parts, relative to chairs, are shown in different colors. A color version is in the color plates section.
From Bracci et al. (2015, p. 12979).

structure was largely consistent with a putative semantic similarity structure that the researchers derived from the co-occurrence frequencies of English body part words in texts. Bracci et al. (2015) suggest that the three-way organization of body part representations that emerged in both analyses may be, to some extent, functionally based, since limb parts are necessary for a host of non-social physical actions, whereas face parts are more important for conveying social information.

Are the shape specifications of body part terms represented in or near the EBA? Despite the tremendous interest in embodiment that has pervaded the behavioral and brain sciences in recent years, very little research has directly addressed this question, and the answer is still unclear. There are, however, a few suggestive findings. A PET study found that, relative to the silent naming of animals, faces, and maps, the silent naming of both body parts and tools engaged the left posterior inferior/middle temporal cortex, just anterior to the EBA (Gorno-Tempini et al., 2000). And a subsequent fMRI study revealed activity in the same territory during a complex task involving reading, covert speaking, and semantic comparison of body part terms, but not during a comparable task in which the words denoted fruits, birds, and articles of clothing (Goldberg et al., 2006a). In addition, although the available neuropsychological data indicate that knowledge of body part terms is remarkably resistant to impairment (Kemmerer & Tranel, 2008), some of the patients who have been reported to display such deficits suffered lesions that were in or near the EBA (Turnbull & Laws, 2000; Schwoebel & Coslett, 2005; Kemmerer & Tranel, 2008; for other cases about whom less is known regarding the precise lesion locations, see Hillis & Caramazza, 1991; Laiacona et al., 2006).

For instance, Figure 3.6 portrays the brain of an English-speaking stroke patient whose lesion affected much of the left occipitotemporal territory, including the EBA (Kemmerer & Tranel, 2008). This patient, referred to as case 2890, correctly named 93% of plants, animals, tools, and vehicles, but correctly named only 77% of body

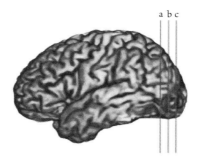

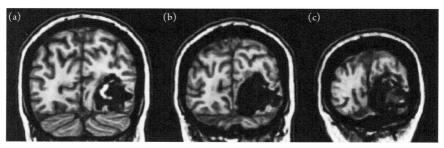

Figure 3.6. Lesion site of a patient with selectively impaired naming of body parts. The lesion is shown in a magnetic resonance (MR) scan obtained 1.5 years after lesion onset, reconstructed in standard brain space. The left hemisphere lateral perspective is shown, along with coronal cuts (black lines, a–c) that depict the cortical and white matter extent of lesion (with left hemisphere on the right). The lesion encompasses the left extrastriate body area (EBA). From Kemmerer & Tranel (2008, p. 618).

parts on his own body, on the examiner's body, and in isolated pictures. Moreover, he achieved a score of just 55% on a task that required him to judge which of three body part terms metaphorically describes a particular part of an inanimate object shown in a photograph. Here are some examples, with the correct term underlined: the *teeth/claws/face* of a comb; the *head/back/foot* of a hammer; the *arm/leg/foot* of a chair; the *mouth/nose/face* of a cave; the *nose/head/foot* of an airplane. Consistent with this finding, a recent fMRI study discovered that, relative to the comprehension of baseline sentences (e.g., *He is under her control*), the comprehension of sentences containing limb-related body part metaphors (e.g., *He is under her thumb*) engaged an anterior sector of the left EBA that was functionally localized as being limb-specific (Lacey et al., 2017).

There are, however, some complications. Even though case 2890 was significantly impaired at naming body parts and processing body part metaphors, he performed between 87% and 100% correct on six tasks that probed his understanding of body part terms in various ways. And even though Lacey et al. (2017) found that the EBA responded significantly more to limb-related metaphors than to semantically matched control sentences, they also found that the EBA did not respond significantly more to sentences with literal uses of body part terms (e.g., *His feet were small*) than to sentences without them (e.g., *His chair was small*). These discrepancies highlight the need for more research on the neural substrates of body part terms, certainly with respect to their shape specifications, and perhaps also with respect to their other semantic components (Kemmerer & Tranel, 2008).

As this field of inquiry moves forward, it would be prudent for investigators to take into account the sorts of typological differences in body partonomies described earlier. By doing so, they would not only be able to keep their own conceptual biases in check, but would also have an opportunity—in principle if not in practice—to directly explore the cortical underpinnings of contrasting mereological systems. For example, consider once again the cross-linguistic segmentation of limbs. Most, if not all, of the languages that cognitive neuroscientists are familiar with have separate terms for arms and hands, so it is tempting to take this distinction for granted and assume that it is a lexical-semantic universal. We have seen, however, that according to current estimates roughly a third of the world's languages lack an independent term for hands. Likewise, people are naturally inclined to suppose that languages everywhere segment the lower limbs in pretty much the same way, but we have seen that there are actually many different lexicalization patterns. Each of these unique systems must somehow be implemented in the brains of the speakers, but as yet very little is known about how this is done, or about how the language-specific representation of body parts relates to the non-linguistic representation of them.

SPLIT POSSESSION

Typology

All languages have formal devices for marking various types of possessive relationships, but there is substantial cross-linguistic diversity regarding what kind of entity may be the "possessor" and what kind may be the "possessed." Here we will restrict our focus to the nature of the possessed entity.

It turns out that English uses the same suffix to signal the possession of all kinds of entities, including body parts (e.g., *Bill's foot*), consanguineal kin (e.g., *Bill's mother*), affinal kin (e.g., *Bill's wife*), and ownable objects (e.g., *Bill's pen*). Many other languages, however, use different devices to indicate the possession of different sets of entities, and it is clear that these grammatical contrasts are semantically motivated (Nichols, 1988; Chappell & McGregor, 1995; Velazquez-Castillo, 1996; Heine, 1997b; Stolz et al., 2008; Dixon, 2010a, 2010b; Aikhenvald & Dixon, 2013). For example, as shown in Table 3.7, Dyirbal (Pama-Nyungan, Australia) uses one possession-marking device for body parts and another for consanguineal kin, affinal kin, and ownable objects. Typologists sometimes call the first type of possessive relationship "inalienable" and the second type "alienable," but it is generally understood that, as indicated by some of the other patterns in Table 3.7, inalienability is actually a continuum of conceptualized closeness between the possessor and the possessed, with different languages drawing a grammatical-semantic boundary (or sometimes two or more such boundaries) at different points along the scale. Thus, Lango (Nilotic, Uganda) treats consanguineal kin as being just as inalienable as body parts, and Amele (Gum, Papua New Guinea) extends its inalienable possession-marking device to encompass affinal relations as well. In an interesting twist, Ewe (Kwa, Ghana) groups body parts together with ownable objects, and consanguineal

Table 3.7. Cross-linguistically contrasting distributions of four sets of entity-denoting words across different possessive constructions in six languages.

Sets of Words	Different Semantically Based Possession-Marking Devices in Different Languages					
	English	Dyirbal	Lango	Amele	Ewe	Tachelhit
body parts (e.g., *foot*)	x	x	x	x	x	x
consanguineal kin (e.g., *mother*)	x	y	x	x	y	y
affinal kin (e.g., *wife*)	x	y	y	x	y	y
ownable objects (e.g., *pen*)	x	y	y	y	x	z

Note: For each language, different letters (x, y, z) indicate different possession-marking devices. Hence, across the six languages, different combinations of letters for the four sets of words reveal convergent and divergent coding patterns.
Adapted from Dixon (2010a, pp. 5–6, and 2010b, Chapter 16).

kin together with affinal kin, for grammatical-semantic purposes. Finally, Tachelhit (Berber, Morocco) has three devices—one for body parts, another for both types of kin, and a third for ownable objects.

A number of other systems have also been documented. For instance, Dakota (Siouan, North and South Dakota) has separate possession-marking devices for the following categories of objects: body parts construed as being particularly subject to willpower (e.g., mouth, eye, hand); other body parts (e.g., nose, ribs, lungs); both consanguineal and affinal kin; and ownable objects (Dixon, 2010b, p. 282). Remarkably enough, the languages in the Great Andamanese family (Andaman Islands) go even farther by using seven distinct possessive morphemes to partition the body into seven distinct zones (Abbi, 2011):

- mouth-related parts (e.g., tongue, palate, throat)
- major external and face-related parts (e.g., arm, nose, ear)
- leg-related parts (e.g., leg, ankle, heel)
- rounded parts and sexual organs (e.g., buttocks, pelvis, testicles)
- extreme ends (e.g., hand, nail, armpit)
- internal organs (e.g., kidney, liver, pancreas)
- external products (e.g., hair, sweat, breath).

It is also worth mentioning that this complex division of body parts has many other manifestations in the Great Andamanese languages; in fact, it may qualify as a "semplate" (Levinson & Burenhult, 2009), since it shapes the meanings and morphosyntactic patterns of nouns, verbs, adjectives, and adverbs in ways that are, according to Abbi (2011, p. 786), "governed by the specifics of the Andamanese culture and society."

Neurobiology

Taken together, these similarities and differences in possession-marking patterns show that systematically organized categories of objects can be identified across languages by investigating the ways in which this particular conceptual sphere is grammatically encoded. It is important to realize that each of the language-specific categories described above is in fact defined according to both grammatical and semantic criteria. But even though these categories are presumably represented in the brains of the speakers, their precise neural substrates are, for the most part, unknown.

Now, we noted earlier that one of the word classes that is cross-linguistically quite sensitive to possessive constructions—namely, body part terms—has already received some attention in cognitive neuroscience; however, we saw that the cortical underpinnings of these terms are still unclear. Hopefully, greater concern in the future about the grammatically relevant semantic properties of words will lead to more in-depth studies of the neurobiology of body part terms—studies that may take into account the complex relationships between these terms, the kinds of possessive constructions they occur in, and perhaps also the multisensory mechanisms that generate the experience of body ownership in the brain (for further discussion, see Kemmerer, 2014a).

NOMINAL CLASSIFICATION SYSTEMS

The goal of this last, and longest, section of the chapter is to explore some ways in which typological research on nominal classification systems can potentially illuminate and constrain neuroscientific research on object concepts.[4] As described in detail below, these are specialized semiotic systems in which a noun that designates a kind of object is frequently, or in some languages obligatorily, produced in conjunction with another element, often referred to as a classifier, that provides a more general level of categorization according to one of several conceptual criteria (for reviews, see Allan, 1977; Craig, 1986; Senft, 2000; Aikhenvald, 2000, 2006, 2017; Grinevald, 2007; Seifart, 2010; Contini-Morava & Kilarski, 2013; see also Fedden & Corbett, 2017). To take a few simple examples, in striking contrast to English and other European languages, in many languages around the world speakers must explicitly indicate such things as that an apple has a spherical form, that a tent is a habitable place, and that a pheasant is a type of bird.

The main argument that we will develop is that any viable theory of the neural substrates of object concepts must be able to accommodate the full range of cross-linguistic similarities and differences among nominal classification systems. On the one hand, we will see that some of the semantic parameters underlying the topographic organization of object concepts in the brain correspond remarkably well

---

[4] The bulk of this section is drawn from Kemmerer (2017a). See also the commentaries by Croft (2017), Bi (2017), Shay et al. (2017), Barsalou (2017), and Pecher and Zwaan (2017), as well as the response by Kemmerer (2017b).

with the most common semantic parameters underlying the linguistic representation of object concepts in nominal classification systems. These parameters involve, most prominently, animacy and related properties, shape and related properties, size, constitution, and interaction/function. On the other hand, we will also see that the neural substrates of object concepts are likely to be strongly influenced by language-specific factors, since many nominal classification systems have elements with unusual meanings that seem to reflect culturally idiosyncratic concerns. Some examples include classifiers for (1) female deities; (2) objects that consist of many fibers with the same orientation, like eyelashes and certain kinds of skirts; (2) objects that are roundish but flat on one side, like hats and masks; (3) loop-shaped objects that are worn, like garlands and necklaces; (4) objects that are deliberately broken, like biscuits; and (5) edible objects that are swallowed whole, like pills. In addition, we will see that another explanatory requirement for neuroscientific frameworks comes from languages in which the shapes of many objects are specified not by nouns, but rather by the classifiers they happen to combine with.

We will begin with a concise overview of the major types of nominal classification systems, based on grammatical factors. Then, after a brief transition, we will turn to the central issues, which involve the semantic parameters mentioned above. For each parameter (or set of parameters), we will first discuss a variety of cross-linguistically common and rare semantic distinctions, and then we will consider their possible neural underpinnings in the context of relevant research on how categories of object concepts are implemented in the brain. Finally, we will step back from the minutiae in order to make some final observations about the big picture.

Grammatically defined subtypes

The wide range of phenomena that fall under the rubric of nominal classification share the following core properties, according to Seifart (2010, p. 719), whose account draws heavily on McGregor's (2002) notion of "grammatical superclassification":

- Nouns collocate in well-defined grammatical environments with classificatory elements (these may be free forms, clitics, affixes, etc., and they may also occur elsewhere).
- The number of classificatory elements is larger than one but significantly smaller than the number of nouns.
- Classificatory elements show different patterns of collocation with nouns, i.e., they impose a classification (some overlap is allowed; prototypically, there is a relatively equal division of the nominal lexicon by classificatory elements).
- At least a substantial subpart of nouns are classified in this way.

This broad definition encompasses not only classifier systems, which are the main topic of interest here, but also noun class systems, which are germane as well. These different types of nominal classification are usually distinguished from each other by the following grammatical criteria: first, the presence or absence of agreement sets agreeing noun class systems apart from non-agreeing classifier systems; and second, the morphosyntactic locus of the classificatory element allows multiple kinds of classifier systems to be identified and characterized separately, including noun classifiers, numeral classifiers, possessive classifiers, verbal classifiers, locative classifiers, and deictic classifiers (Aikhenvald, 2000; Grinevald, 2000). This typology is briefly outlined below.

Noun classes

Noun class systems subsume what are traditionally called gender systems. They are defined by the fact that the nouns in a given class require other constituents (e.g., articles, adjectives, verbs) to be overtly marked for grammatical agreement with them, typically by means of affixes, clitics, or base modification. Noun classes are the most common kind of nominal classification, existing in up to half the world's languages. Although most languages with such systems have fewer than five noun classes, some have up to several dozen, most notably in parts of Africa, Australia, and Papua New Guinea. Because noun class systems are highly grammaticalized, the assignment of nouns to classes is often determined by a combination of phonological, morphological, and semantic factors. The pertinent semantic factors can sometimes be rather difficult to discern, but careful analysis usually reveals that they involve animacy, sex, and humanness, as well as shape, size, and other physical properties, especially in languages with large systems. For instance, the 18 noun classes in Bukiyip (Arapesh, Papua New Guinea) are partly phonologically based, but four of the classes contain animate nouns—specifically, males, females, nonhuman animates, and personal names—and the other 14 classes contain inanimate nouns that are differentiated according to various physical properties of the referents (Aikhenvald, 2000, p. 276).

Noun classifiers

Noun classifiers are usually independent morphemes that appear next to the noun, but in some languages they are realized as affixes. Semantically, the relationship between a noun classifier and the noun it combines with is sometimes described as generic-specific, since the classifier serves to categorize the meaning of the noun. For instance, as Dixon (1982, p. 185) points out, in Yidiny (Pama-Nyungan, Australia) "one would not generally say . . . 'the girl dug up the yam', or 'the wallaby is standing by the black pine'; it is more felicitous to include generics and say 'the person girl dug up the vegetable yam', or 'the animal wallaby is standing by the tree black pine.'" Noun classifier systems are found in many Australian languages, Western Austronesian languages, Tai languages, and Mayan languages. Such systems vary greatly in size, with some having as few as two members and others having as many as several hundred. Relatively large systems tend to express conceptual contrasts along a wide range of dimensions, including the social, physical, and interactional/functional aspects of objects.

Numeral classifiers

In languages with numeral classifier systems, when a speaker refers to a certain number of entities of a certain type, he or she often—or, in some languages, always—uses a special construction that includes not only the appropriate numeral and noun, but also the appropriate numeral classifier, which provides more general information about what is being counted. For example, to refer to three pencils in

Minangkabau (Austronesian, Sumatra), one would say *tigo batang pituluik*, where the first word, *tigo*, is a numeral meaning "three," the last word, *pituluik*, is a noun meaning "pencil," and the intervening word, *batang*, is a numeral classifier meaning "elongated object" (Gil, 2005). Like noun classifiers, numeral classifiers are usually independent morphemes; sometimes, however, they are manifested as affixes. Regarding global distribution, languages with numeral classifier systems are markedly concentrated around the Pacific Rim, including East and Southeast Asia, the Indonesian archipelago, Oceania, Mesoamerica, and the western parts of North and South America. The semantic distinctions captured by numeral classifier systems are quite heterogeneous, but they tend to involve animacy, humanness, shape, size, and spatial arrangement. It is also noteworthy that numeral classifiers are often divided into two subtypes: sortal classifiers, which describe inherent aspects of objects for the purpose of categorization; and mensural classifiers, which describe temporary aspects of objects for the purpose of measurement. Aikhenvald (2000, p. 115) illustrates this distinction with reference to Tzeltal (Mayan, Mexico): "the noun *lagrio* 'brick' is used with just one sortal classifier *pech* 'rectangular, non-flexible object'; [but] when counted it can occur with several different mensural classifiers depending on the arrangement: classifier *latz* is used to refer to a stack of bricks, *chol* to aligned bricks, and *bus* is used for a pile of bricks."[5] Finally, like noun classifier systems, numeral classifier systems vary substantially in size, from relatively few members to several hundred.

Possessive classifiers

Possessive classifiers are less common than the preceding kinds of classifiers. They occur exclusively in possessive constructions and break down into three subtypes, although the boundaries between them are somewhat fuzzy. First, relational classifiers categorize the ways in which possessors interact with certain possessed objects—e.g., eating, drinking, wearing, occupying, etc. These classifiers are found in some Oceanic, Micronesian, and Austronesian languages. For instance, Boumaa Fijian (Oceanic, Fiji) has two different classifiers for objects that are consumed: *'e-* applies to anything that undergoes a change of state as it is being consumed (e.g., a piece of meat that is chewed), whereas *me-* applies to anything that does not (e.g., a pill that is swallowed whole). Second, possessed classifiers tend to characterize owned objects in terms of their animacy and/or physical properties—e.g., shape, size, consistency, etc. These classifiers have been documented in some languages of North America, South America, Africa, and China. A good illustration is Panare (Carib, Venezuela), which has 21 such elements, including classifiers for animals, vehicles, and hunting weapons. Third, possessor classifiers distinguish between animate and inanimate possessors, but have been confirmed in only one language, namely Dâw (Makú, Brazil/Columbia).

---

[5] One might suppose that English expressions like *three sheets/wads/reams of paper* involve mensural classifiers, but Aikhenvald (2000, p. 116) presents several arguments against this view.

Verbal classifiers

Verbal classifiers appear on the verb, but they categorize a noun, typically either the intransitive subject or the transitive object. This is illustrated by the classifier *put*, which means "round object," in the following sentence in Waris (Waris, Papua New Guinea) (Aikhenvald, 2006, p. 467):

sa	*ka-m*	*put-ra-ho-o*
coconut	1SG-to	VERBAL.CL:ROUND-get-BENEFACTIVE-IMPERATIVE

"Give me a coconut" (literally "coconut to-me round.one-give")

Like possessive classifier systems, verbal classifier systems are relatively scarce, being restricted to some languages in Australia, Papua New Guinea, North America, and South America. However, such systems can contain up to several dozen items that characterize the meanings of nouns along the parameters of shape, consistency, interaction/function, and position.

Locative and deictic classifiers

The last two kinds of classifiers occur in spatial expressions. First, locative classifiers are fused with adpositions (i.e., prepositions or postpositions) and categorize the referent of the noun in terms of its physical properties, especially its form. Such systems are rare, found only in a few South American languages, and they are also rather small, usually with no more than five or six members. One of the most clear-cut cases is Palikur (North Arawak, Brazil), which has a remarkably rich set of 12 locative classifiers that distinguish between, among other categories, round objects, pointed objects, branched objects, flat objects, and vertically oriented one-dimensional objects. Second, deictic classifiers combine with demonstratives and categorize the referent of the noun in terms of its shape, configuration, orientation, movement, and visibility. Such systems have been identified in some North and South American languages, but, again, the inventories tend to be fairly small. For instance, Mandan (Siouan, North Dakota) has three deictic classifiers that derive from postural verbs and specify whether an object is standing, sitting, or lying.

Languages with multiple classification systems

Finally, it is important to note that many languages have more than one kind of nominal classification system. In fact, comparative studies have revealed a complex variety of combinations of systems, such that some languages have two, three, four, five, or even six sets of devices, with the particular types of devices in each combination differing considerably (Aikhenvald, 2000). The largest number of formally separate systems is probably in Palikur (North Arawak, Brazil; Aikhenvald & Green, 1998). This language has 3 noun classes, 19 numeral classifiers, 5 possessive classifiers, 11 verbal classifiers (one set for stative verbs and another for transitive verbs), and, as just mentioned, 12 locative classifiers. Several of these sets of devices overlap to some degree both phonologically and semantically, but each set is nonetheless grammatically distinct.

Transition to semantic parameters

Before proceeding to discuss the semantic aspects of nominal classification systems from both linguistic and neurobiological perspectives, four more preliminary points are in order. First, as shown by Gao and Malt (2009) with specific reference to Mandarin Chinese, for some classifiers the original semantic motivation for grouping certain nouns together has become opaque, so that what is left is just a seemingly arbitrary categorization of those nouns as purely linguistic forms. For other classifiers, however, the underlying semantic principles can still be discerned, sometimes quite clearly. Second, although some classifiers have just one straightforward meaning, others can be quite polysemous due to historical processes of semantic extension. For example, the Japanese numeral classifier *hon* prototypically covers long, thin, rigid objects such as candles, canes, and trees, but it also applies to a wide range of other phenomena, including hits in baseball, shots in basketball, rolls of tape, telephone calls, movies, and radio and television programs (Matsumoto, 1993). Third, in many languages with large classifier inventories, different classifiers can be used with the same noun to emphasize different facets of its meaning. This is nicely illustrated by Baniwa (North Arawak, Brazil), which allows speakers to combine the word for "bone" with any of several classifiers—e.g., for animate entities, vertical entities, or long entities—in order to convey a specific subjective construal of the designated object (Aikhenvald, 2007).[6] Fourth, and conversely, in some languages the link between a certain noun and a certain classifier is much more conventional. Thus, the word for "banana" might be associated with a classifier for oblong entities in a fixed way, so that speakers are always required to use that particular classifier with that particular noun, even in situations when the designated banana does not really have an oblong shape, as when, for instance, it has been squashed by someone's foot (Seifart, 2010).

With these points, as well as the foregoing background material, in mind, we turn now to the major semantic parameters of nominal classification systems. In each of the following subsections, the discussion begins by reviewing some cross-linguistically frequent and infrequent semantic distinctions involving the given parameter (or set of parameters), and then it considers the relevance of those findings to cognitive neuroscience, with an eye toward showing that the category-level representation of object concepts in the brain is influenced by both universal tendencies and cultural idiosyncrasies. The specific parameters included here, and the linguistic data associated with them, are based largely, but not entirely, on information provided by Frawley (1992), Aikhenvald (2000), and Grinevald (2007).

---

[6] Another good example is Burmese (Tibeto-Burman, Myanmar), in which, depending on which classifier is used, a river can be construed as a place (e.g., a destination for a picnic), a line (e.g., on a map), a section (e.g., a fishing area), a connection (e.g., between two villages), a sacred object (e.g., in mythology), or a conceptual unit (e.g., in a conversation about rivers in general) (Becker, 1975).

Animacy and related properties

Typology

Across the world's languages, animacy is one of the most grammatically significant semantic parameters, with well-attested influences on subject-verb agreement, word order, case marking, transitivity, pronoun systems, and, of greatest importance here, nominal classification systems (Comrie, 1989; Whaley, 1997). Linguistic animacy does not always correspond, however, to biological animacy, and there is some cross-linguistic diversity in how this category is demarcated. For example, some languages treat fish and insects as animate, whereas others do not. Moreover, the nominal classification systems of many languages are sensitive not just to animacy, but to several related properties as well, including humanness, rationality, sex, age, kinship, social status, and various culture-specific concerns. As shown below, these sorts of factors are manifested mainly in systems involving noun classes, noun classifiers, and numeral classifiers.

Three kinds of simple two-way conceptual contrasts have been reported. First, some languages have a nominal classification system that distinguishes between animate and inanimate entities. This basic distinction is found, for instance, in the noun classes of Siouan and Algonquian languages and in the numeral classifiers of Tai languages. Second, even more languages have a system that separates humans from nonhumans. This contrast appears, for instance, in the noun classifiers of Tzeltal (Mayan, Mexico), Yurok (Algic, California), and Minangkabau (Austronesian, Sumatra), as well as in the numeral classifiers of Ainu (isolate, Hokkaido), Khasi (Mon-Khmer, India), and Telugu (Dravidian, India). Third, in some Dravidian languages, such as Tamil, all nouns are again divided into two classes, but this time the distinction is between what are traditionally called rational and nonrational entities, with the former group being restricted to people, gods, and demons.

Animacy-related nominal classification systems with three- and four-way conceptual contrasts have also been documented. The most common three-way system distinguishes between humans, nonhuman animals, and inanimate entities. This is exemplified by the numeral classifiers in Indonesian (Frawley, 1992, p. 91):

se-orang　　　　　　　　　*mahasiswa*

one-NUM.CL:HUMAN　　　student

"one student"

se-ekor　　　　　　　　　　*kuda*

one-NUM.CL:ANIMAL　　　horse

"one horse"

se-buah　　　　　　　　　　*buku*

one-NUM.CL:INANIMATE　　book

"one book"

It is noteworthy, however, that what falls into the animal category varies across languages—for instance, Achagua (North Arawak, Brazil) restricts its animal classifier to mammals. Turning to four-way systems, they often add a category for plants. This is illustrated by the numeral classifier inventories of some Mayan languages, such as Chol (Mexico): *tyikil* "human," *kojty* "animal," *tyejk* "plant," and *p'ejl* "inanimate thing" (Hopkins, 2012, p. 412).

Finally, there are other kinds of nominal classification systems that exhibit much greater conceptual complexity with regard to animacy and related properties. For instance, some languages, like Bahwana (North Arawak, Brazil), have different classifiers for different groupings of animals. The distinctions that are drawn, however, are inconsistent across languages and do not match well with biological taxonomies. A more frequent approach to expanding a system is to subcategorize humans according to sex, age, kinship, social status, and culture-specific criteria. This is illustrated by Mayan languages of the Kanjobalan branch, like Jacaltec (Mexico), which has 24 noun classifiers that Craig (1986, p. 245) divides into two subsystems, one for social interaction and another for physical and functional interaction, as shown in Table 3.8. It also bears mentioning that some Australian languages have social status noun classifiers with specialized, culturally idiosyncratic meanings like "initiated man." Similarly, the nominal classification systems of East and Southeast Asian languages tend to make many contrasts involving social status.

Neurobiology

The fact that animacy is one of the most frequently manifested semantic parameters of nominal classification systems converges remarkably well with the fact that animacy is also one of the strongest determinants of the organization of object concepts in the brain. Earlier in this chapter we noted that, according to numerous fMRI studies, animal concepts tend to activate the lateral fusiform gyrus (involved in category-related form perception) and the posterior superior temporal sulcus (involved in biological motion perception), whereas tool concepts tend to activate the medial fusiform gyrus (involved in category-related form perception), the posterior middle temporal gyrus (involved in mechanical motion perception), the inferior parietal lobule (involved in reaching, grasping, and manipulating), and the ventral premotor cortex (involved in storing and executing hand-related motor programs) (see Figure 3.2 and the associated text). We also saw that the two largest domains of object concepts—namely, living and nonliving things—can be impaired independently of each other by focal lesions. These considerations, among others, support the hypothesis that the meanings of nominal classifiers for animate and inanimate entities are neurobiologically grounded at least partly in these cortical networks.

There is, however, an intriguing complication that we touched on briefly in our previous discussion of ethnobiological knowledge, and that warrants greater attention here. On the one hand, by using representational similarity analysis, some fMRI studies have found that in the ventral temporal cortex the multivoxel activity patterns triggered by animate and inanimate entities are distinct in the manner described earlier, with animate entities engaging mainly the lateral fusiform gyrus and inanimate entities engaging mainly the medial fusiform gyrus (e.g., Mur et al., 2013). Moreover, these functional-anatomical associations persist even when exemplars of the two categories are matched for shape—e.g., a coiled snake and a coiled rope—which suggests that although the ventral temporal cortex has historically been regarded as representing

Table 3.8. Noun classifiers in Jacaltec (Mayan, Mexico), together with English translations of their meanings.

Subsystem I: Social Interaction

Cumam	Male deity
Cumi7	Female deity
Ya7	Respected human
Naj	Male non-kin
Ix	Female non-kin
Naj ni7an	Young male non-kin
Ix ni7an	Young female non-kin
Ho7	Male kin
Xo7	Female kin
Ho7 ni7an	Young male kin
Xo7 ni7an	Young female kin
Unin	Infant

Subsystem II: Physical and Functional Interaction

No7	Animal
Metx'	Dog
Te7	Plant
Ixim	Corn
Tx'al	Thread
Tx'an	Twine
K'ap	Cloth
Tx'otx'	Soil/dirt
Ch'en	Rock
Atz'am	Salt
Ha7	Water
K'a7	Fire

From Craig (1986, p. 245).

primarily the forms of objects (as well as their colors and textures; for a review, see Kravitz et al., 2013), it also captures form-independent categorical distinctions (Bracci & Op de Beeck, 2016; Proklova et al., 2016; see also Kaiser et al., 2016; Bracci et al., 2017). On the other hand, several other fMRI studies have also employed representational similarity analysis to challenge the notion that animate and inanimate entities are sharply dissociated in the fusiform gyri, and to suggest instead that they are encoded in a more continuous manner along the lateral-to-medial axis (Connolly et al., 2012; Sha et al., 2015). More specifically, these studies compared the ventral temporal activity patterns evoked by pictures of many different kinds of objects, including humans, primates, quadruped mammals, birds, fish, invertebrates, and tools. Although they replicated the often-reported coarse-grained finding that high-animacy species (e.g., humans and chimpanzees) are represented mainly in the lateral fusiform gyrus whereas inanimate artifacts (e.g., hammers and keys) are represented mainly in the medial fusiform gyrus, they also discovered a more fine-grained functional topography that seems to reflect an animacy gradient, with intermediate-animacy species (e.g., pelicans and stingrays) falling roughly in the middle and low-animacy species (e.g., ladybugs and lobsters) patterning much like inanimate artifacts.

It is essential to realize, though, that Connolly et al.'s (2012) and Sha et al.'s (2015) participants did not speak a language with a nominal classification system that regularly requires its users to explicitly distinguish between animate and inanimate entities. Given that some neuroscientific studies have shown that language-specific semantic distinctions can influence visual perception (Thierry et al., 2009; Athanasopoulos et al., 2010; Boutonnet et al., 2013; see Chapter 6 of this volume for details), it is possible that if studies like those by Connolly et al. (2012) and Sha et al. (2015) were conducted with speakers of a language with animate and inanimate classifiers, a clearer contrast between these two types of objects would be found in the ventral temporal cortex. After all, for such speakers this categorical division must be easy to "read out" from perceptual data, and computational models of visual processing suggest that the most efficient way to extract important pieces of information that are "tangled together" at early stages of the ventral stream is to create anatomically separate representations of them at later stages (for a review, see Grill-Spector & Weiner, 2014). In this connection, it is worth reiterating that languages with classifiers for animate and inanimate entities vary in terms of where exactly they "draw the line" between these two categories. For instance, fish and insects qualify as animate in some languages but not in others. This suggests that cross-linguistic diversity along the semantic parameter of animacy may correspond to neurotopographic diversity in the detailed ventral temporal representation of objects, such that within the relevant parts of this cortical territory there may be some degree of cultural influence on how columns of neurons are clustered together to form representationally similar patches, or complex mosaics of such patches, that capture the language-specific categories of animate and inanimate entities.

The same line of thinking can also be applied to the human/nonhuman distinction. Although some fMRI studies have identified this distinction in the representational geometry of the ventral temporal cortex (Kriegeskorte et al., 2008; Jozwik et al., 2016), others have failed to find it (Connolly et al., 2012; Mur et al., 2013; Sha et al., 2015). Once again, however, it is not unreasonable to suppose that this conceptual contrast would be more consistently and robustly observed in the ventral temporal cortex of people whose language requires them to routinely encode it with classifiers.

Another interesting point involves the nominal classificatory distinction that some Dravidian languages, like Tamil, make between rational and nonrational entities. From a neuroscientific perspective, this distinction is thought-provoking because it is closely related to a recent fMRI study by Shultz and McCarthy (2014). These researchers first noted that perceptual cues for animacy include not only shape features (e.g., faces and other body parts) and motion features (e.g., self-propulsion), but also, and perhaps more importantly, rational goal-directed behaviors, which are "purposeful and efficient given the constraints of the surrounding environment" (Shulz & McCarthy, 2014, p. 115; see also Gergely & Csibra, 2003; Martin & Weisberg, 2003). Then they showed that the lateral fusiform gyrus responds more strongly when participants watch movie clips of rational versus irrational behaviors of human avatars, even when the surface features of the avatars are identical. These findings suggest that, as with the meanings of animate/inanimate and human/non-human classifiers, the meanings of rational/nonrational classifiers may depend in part on the ventral temporal cortex.

Finally, what about the fact that some languages have nominal classification systems that subcategorize people according to such factors as sex, age, kinship, social status, and culture-specific criteria? Surprisingly, most of these aspects of person perception and cognition have not received much attention in the cognitive neuroscience literature. There is some fMRI evidence that both the occipital face area and the fusiform face area contribute to both male/female and young/old discriminations (Wiese et al., 2012), but the underlying representations and computations have not yet been probed. Similarly, the neural basis of kinship knowledge remains largely if not entirely unexplored—a gap that is also relevant to grammatical-semantic splits involving possession, as indicated earlier. In contrast, the neural substrates of social status judgments have recently begun to be addressed, and they appear to include the intraparietal sulcus (for coding status on a scale of magnitude), the dorsolateral prefrontal cortex (for coding status as a social norm), the ventromedial prefrontal cortex (for coding status relative to value and reward), and the amygdala (involved in emotion and personal relevance) (for a review, see Watanabe & Yamamoto, 2015; see also Munuera et al., 2018). These findings invite the inference that the meanings of classifiers for various social ranks, like the Jacaltec category of "respected humans," may be supported by some of the brain regions just mentioned, perhaps in concert with the anterior temporal lobes, which have been implicated more generally in social concepts (for a review, see Olson et al., 2013), and which may therefore also subserve the meanings of more culture-specific notions, like "initiated man."

Shape and related properties

Typology

Another semantic parameter that is quite common across nominal classification systems is shape, which involves the extension of objects in space. More precisely, shape can be characterized in terms of the following geometric properties:

- dimensionality: one-dimensional (1D), two-dimensional (2D), or three-dimensional (3D)
- axis: straight or curved
- cross-section: straight or curved
- termination: truncated, rounded, or pointed
- aspect ratio: relations between height, width, and depth
- interior: solid or hollow.

Schematic shapes defined according to these basic properties are encoded most often by noun classes, numeral classifiers, and verbal classifiers; they are sometimes also expressed by possessive classifiers, locative classifiers, and deictic classifiers, but rarely if ever by noun classifiers. Although the properties just described may be considered primary for the specification of shapes, they are frequently combined with the following additional properties:[7]

- consistency: rigid or flexible
- orientation: vertical or horizontal
- size: large or small
- boundedness: delimited or nondelimited.

It is also noteworthy that an object's shape may be linked with its function (e.g., concave objects make useful containers), and these connections are sometimes captured by nominal classification systems.

In many languages with masculine and feminine noun classes, the assignment of genders to non-sex-differentiated inanimate referents is based predominantly on their physical attributes, with shape playing a major role, often in conjunction with orientation, solidity, and size (for a detailed discussion, see Aikhenvald, 2012). It is common, for instance, to find that long and/or straight objects are treated as masculine, whereas round ones are treated as feminine—a pattern exemplified by Alamblak (Sepik, Papua New Guinea), Khwe (Central Khoisan, Namibia), and Tiwi (Australian, North Australia). Similarly, vertical objects tend to be assigned the masculine gender and horizontal ones the feminine gender, as in Manambu (Ndu, Papua New Guinea). Another set of associations, illustrated by Katcha (Kordofanian, Sudan), is that solid objects are masculine while hollow, deep, or concave ones are feminine. Size is also an important semantic factor in numerous noun class systems, but this is not discussed until the next subsection.

Turning to languages with various kinds of classifier systems, it is well-established that the most frequently encoded shape distinctions correspond to the major dimensional outlines of objects—namely, 1D vs. 2D vs. 3D. This three-way contrast has developed independently in many classifier systems around the world. Moreover, the relevant classifiers tend to derive historically from nouns that specify the kinds of botanical entities that human communities encounter and handle most often. In particular, classifiers for saliently 1D entities (e.g., vines and spears) tend to derive from nouns for tree trunks or sticks; classifiers for saliently 2D entities (e.g., plates and blankets) tend to derive from nouns for leaves; and classifiers for saliently 3D entities (e.g., eggs and boxes) tend to derive from nouns for fruits.

In some languages shape-related numeral classifiers serve an important unitizing function for the nouns they combine with. This is because most of the nouns for inanimate entities in these languages are, from a grammatical-semantic perspective,

---

[7] Another property related to shape involves the temporary arrangement/configuration of an entity or set of entities. This property is central to the meanings of numeral classifiers of the mensural subtype, and systems of such classifiers can be very complex, as shown, for instance, by Berlin's (1968) photographic essay illustrating the subtle semantics of dozens of elements in Tzeltal (Mayan, Mexico). Here, however, we will set aside the conceptual intricacies of these kinds of classifiers. On the other hand, we will consider the meanings of numeral classifiers of the sortal subtype, since they often involve the inherent shape properties of entities and hence are more relevant to object categorization.

essentially mass nouns. For instance, in Yucatec (Mayan, Mexico) the word *ha'as* has a very general meaning—something like "banana stuff"—and its specific interpretation in a given context depends on the numeral classifier that the speaker happens to choose, as shown on the left side of Table 1.3 in Chapter 1. Orthogonally, when the same numeral classifier is applied to different nouns, it performs more or less the same kind of geometrically specified unitizing role, as shown on the right side of that table.

Many shape-related classifier systems go beyond the simple 1D vs. 2D vs. 3D distinctions by including elements that encode interactions between dimensionality and some of the other properties mentioned earlier. For instance, Southern Haida (Haida, British Columbia) not only has three 1D verbal classifiers—one for long, narrow, rigid objects (e.g., canes and needles), another for long cylindrical objects (e.g., bottles and pipes), and a third for long flexible objects (e.g., ropes and belts)—but also has two 3D verbal classifiers—one for fairly spherical objects (e.g., clams and stones) and another for objects that are roundish but flat on one side (e.g., hats and masks). Similarly, Burmese (Tibeto-Burman, Myanmar) has two 2D numeral classifiers—one for thin flat objects (e.g., carpets and slices of bread) and another for *very* thin flat objects (e.g., leaves and sheets of paper).

Moving deeper into the semantic domain of shape, it is interesting that while some classifier meanings are not as common as those that are strongly anchored in dimensionality, they are nevertheless found in many unrelated languages. Some prominent examples in the literature are classifiers for straight things, curved things, pointed things, vertical things, horizontal things, hollow things, ring-like things, and holes.

Taking this line of thinking one step further, some languages have shape-related classifiers whose meanings appear to be so idiosyncratic that they may reflect culture-specific spatial concepts, or what Aikhenvald and Green (1998, p. 465) call "ethnogeometry." Here are five examples. Minangkabau (Austronesian, Sumatra) has a numeral classifier for rolled objects. Akatek (Mayan, Mexico) has a numeral classifier for bent or half-circle-shaped objects. Burmese (Tibeto-Burman, Myanmar) has a numeral classifier for loop-shaped objects that are worn. Southern Haida (Haida, British Columbia) has a verbal classifier for long teardrop-shaped objects. And Palikur (North Arawak, Brazil) has matching numeral, verbal, and locative classifiers for objects that split and branch out from a central axis.

To round out this discussion of the semantics of shape-related classifiers, it is instructive to see a large set of elements from a single language. Table 3.9 therefore provides rough glosses of 20 of the 66 shape-related classifiers in Miraña (Witotoan, Peru/Columbia), together with descriptions of some of the objects that they apply to (Seifart, 2005). The 20 classifiers shown here are among those whose meanings most clearly and purely pertain to shape. All of the classifiers in Miraña occur in diverse morphosyntactic contexts and hence do not easily fit into the taxonomy sketched earlier (Seifart, 2009), but this is not important here, since what matters for present purposes is that the classifiers encode a remarkably wide range of geometric structures. In fact, the whole system is so rich that, according to a recent psycholinguistic study, its regular use by Miraña speakers leads them to become conceptually more attuned to object shape than not only English speakers but also monolingual Spanish speakers who live in the same environment (Perniss et al., 2012).

Table 3.9. The meanings of 20 of the 66 shape-related classifiers in Miraña (Witotoan, Columbia/Peru), together with examples of the objects they apply to.

Meaning of Classifier	Sample Nouns
1. thin and relatively long and pointed	fishing rod, arrow, pear apple fruit
2. thin and of medium length	walking stick, candle, pestle
3. thin and small, spine-like	thorn, pointed broken branch, quills of some fish
4. large, slender, and upright	tree trunk, pole, pillar
5. flat and rigid, with at least one straight edge	paddle, ladder, knife
6. very flat	flat pan, flat brick, flattened prey animal in a trap
7. flat platform	raft, grill, floor of a house
8. flat and round	wheel, plate, lid
9. round protuberance	neck of a tree, signal drum
10. small and spherical	eye, pebble, small ball
11. oblong	nose, beehive, banana
12. curved	curve in a river, curve of a stick, curve of a brow
13. tubular	rifle, cigarette, mouth
14. bottle-shaped container	bottle, salt container, boot
15. cylindrical container with open top	coca powder container, manioc starch container
16. deep container	basket, hammock, lagoon
17. hole	shoe, cave, hole of a blowgun (not a hole in the ground)
18. shallow hole	navel, vagina, shallow hole in ground
19. a number of fibers with the same orientation	skirt (of fibers), eyelashes, tail of certain monkey species
20. very uneven and twisted	highly twisted candle

From Seifart (2005, pp. 86–94).

Neurobiology

As indicated earlier, a few recent fMRI studies found that in certain areas of the ventral temporal cortex, objects are organized and represented partly according to form-independent categories like animate vs. inanimate (Bracci & Op de Beeck, 2016; Proklova et al., 2016). In the current context, however, what is especially interesting is that the very same studies also discovered that in certain overlapping and adjacent areas, objects are organized and represented partly according to form-dependent categories like round vs. long and thin. Such categories clearly bear a striking resemblance to those that tend to be encoded by shape-related classifiers, which raises the possibility that the latter categories are subserved by the ventral temporal cortex as well, at least to a large extent.

A theoretical framework that can provide some leverage here is the "geon" approach to visual object recognition developed by Irving Biederman and his colleagues

(Biederman, 1987, 1995, 2013; Hummel & Biederman, 1992). Geons are relatively simple yet highly distinctive shapes defined in terms of the same properties mentioned at the outset of the overview of shape-related classifiers. Some examples include bricks, wedges, cylinders, and cones, which can vary with regard to size, aspect ratio, degree of curvature, etc. With a small number of basic geon configurations and a small number of spatial relations between them, one can generate the minimal contours of several *billion* two- or three-part objects, such as a flashlight, a briefcase, a mug, a pail, and a lamp (Figure 3.7). An important virtue of geons, and of complex objects composed of them, is that their shapes are viewer-invariant, due to their being based on "non-accidental" properties like straightness, symmetry, and parallelism that do not change with orientation in depth. In other words, each geon can be distinguished from the others from almost any perspective, the main exception being "accidents" at certain restricted angles, as when an end-on view of a cylinder could be mistaken for a sphere or circle. Thus, the structures of geons are perceptually significant because they offer a solution to the inverse optics problem—i.e., the problem that any image on the retina could in principle be produced by an infinite number of real-world objects.

Returning to the brain, Biederman (2013) argues that the non-accidental shape properties of objects are captured by neuronal populations at intermediate stages of the ventral stream, and that conjunctions of such properties, which represent whole geons and spatially integrated combinations of them, are captured by neuronal populations at later stages. Evidence supporting these proposals comes not only from the fMRI studies mentioned earlier (namely, Bracci & Op de Beeck, 2016, and Proklova et al., 2016), but from many other investigations as well. For instance, several fMRI studies suggest, first, that both ventral and lateral sectors of the occipitotemporal cortex are sensitive to non-accidental shape properties (Kim & Biederman, 2012), and second, that the posterior fusiform cortex plays a key role in representing the geons that categorize the parts of multicomponent objects, like the wings of an airplane (Hayworth & Biederman, 2006; see also Erdogan et al., 2016). In addition, a growing number of single-cell recording studies in macaques suggest that a substantial proportion of inferotemporal (IT) neurons are tuned to various kinds of geon-like stimuli. Here are

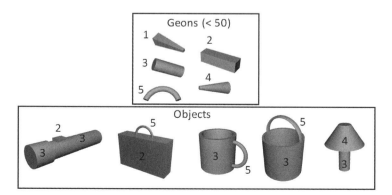

Figure 3.7. With a small number of geons and a small number of geon-pair relations (e.g., top-of, larger-than), several billion two- and three-part objects can be generated.
This figure was kindly provided by Irving Biederman.

three examples. Tanaka (2003) observed that many IT cells respond preferentially to only moderately complex geon-like shapes (sometimes with certain colors and/ or textures), and that neighboring columns of such cells have comparable stimulus selectivities (Figure 3.8). Similarly, Kayaert et al. (2005b) identified many IT cells whose firing rates were significantly modulated by a change from one regular geon-like shape to another (e.g., from a circle to a square), but not by a change from one irregular non-geon-like shape to another (see also Kayaert et al., 2005a). And finally,

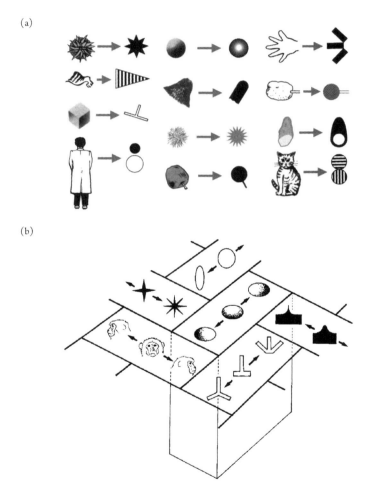

Figure 3.8. Stimulus selectivities and columnar arrangements of shape-sensitive cells in the macaque inferotemporal (IT) cortex. (a) Examples of reduction determination of optimal features for 12 IT cells. The images to the left of the arrows represent the original versions of the most effective object stimulus, and those to the right of the arrows represent the critical features determined by reduction. (b) Schematic drawing of the columnar organization of IT cells. Stimulus parameters are continuously mapped across the cortical surface such that clusters of adjacent columns represent different but closely related features. A color version is in the color plates section.
From Tanaka (2003, pp. 91, 96).

by using cutting-edge data processing techniques, Baldassi et al. (2013) found that IT cells are functionally organized as clusters that represent geon-like shapes such as starry objects, horizontally elongated objects, vertically elongated objects, and round objects—all of which, interestingly enough, are often encoded by shape-related classifiers.

Taken together, these considerations bolster not only the hypothesis that the schematic spatial concepts encoded by shape-related classifiers reside primarily in the ventral temporal cortex, but also the related hypothesis that they correspond, in some if not many cases, to geons. If correct, the latter hypothesis implies that languages with shape-related classifiers tap directly into some of the most important perceptual building blocks of object recognition. At the same time, however, it also raises new and difficult questions, perhaps the most pressing of which is this: Given the semantic diversity of shape-related classifiers (e.g., see again Table 3.9), which ones might legitimately be said to encode geons, and which ones might not? Answering this question would probably require further empirical and theoretical research on the nature of geons, including more work on the extent to which they are universal vs. culturally modifiable representations (for an initial inquiry, see Lescroart et al., 2010). It might also be beneficial, though, to approach this topic from the other direction—i.e., from the vantage point of the literature on nominal classification systems. After all, if the meanings of some shape-related classifiers do in fact reflect geons, it is reasonable to suppose that they would be among the most frequently manifested ones across the world's languages. Conversely, those shape-related classifier meanings that are much less common, or even culture-specific, may be less likely to reflect geons. My aim here is not to resolve these issues—far from it—but to simply suggest that a great deal could be gained by exploring more carefully the relationship between classifiers and geons, especially in connection with the functional topography of the ventral temporal cortex.

This brings us to a final point, which is, in short, that shape-related classifier systems are quite relevant to contemporary research on the neural substrates of object concepts. It is widely acknowledged that shape is an important aspect of such concepts (e.g., Tranel et al., 1997b; Vinson & Vigliocco, 2008; Gainotti et al., 2009, 2013; Hoffman & Lambon Ralph, 2013; Binder et al., 2016). But there is nevertheless a tendency to treat particular shape features, and relatively simple geometric configurations, as mere bridges to more complex meanings. For instance, in their recent attempt to explain how object concepts are organized and represented in the ventral temporal cortex, Jozwik et al. (2016) conclude that features like "round," "pear-shaped," "straight," "rectangular," and "branched" are just stepping stones toward what they regard as genuine semantic structures. As indicated earlier, however, in many languages these sorts of shape specifications are full-fledged concepts in their own right, encoded by classifiers that speakers habitually use in everyday discourse to impose a high level of categorical order on the intra-linguistic world of nouns and, by extension, the extra-linguistic world of objects. More generally, it is probably not a fluke that dimensionality—i.e., the three-way contrast between saliently 1D, 2D, and 3D objects—plays a major role in shape-related classifier systems all over the world; indeed, the remarkable prominence of this semantic factor suggests that it may reflect a fundamental aspect of object perception and cognition, one that warrants more attention from neuroscientists. It is also far from trivial that numerous shape-related classifier meanings are cross-linguistically rare, since this entails that their neural implementations are likewise unusual and, to a large degree, culturally influenced. To take yet another example, in Tariana (North Arawak, Brazil) the words *dina* "feather" and *papera* "paper" are not just nouns for certain kinds of objects; they also fall under the conceptual rubric of "leaf-like" things, since they both take the classifier *phe*, which encompasses a wide range of such entities (Aikhenvald, 1994). The upshot is that neuroscientists will have to take these sorts of schematic meanings into account if their ultimate aim is to achieve a comprehensive understanding of how object concepts are realized in the brain.

Size

Typology

Another interesting semantic parameter of nominal classification systems is size. As stated earlier, size plays an important role in many languages with noun class systems that have a conceptually motivated binary distinction between masculine and feminine gender (for a detailed discussion, see Aikhenvald, 2012). Not surprisingly, there is a strong tendency for these languages to treat relatively large things as masculine and relatively small ones as feminine. Such associations are manifested, for instance, in many of the Sepik languages spoken in Papua New Guinea (e.g., Iatmul, Gala, and Sare) as well as in many of the Omotic languages spoken in Ethiopia (e.g., Wolaitta, Sheko, and Dizi). A few languages, however, have been found to display the opposite associations, treating relatively large things as feminine and relatively small ones as masculine. These unusual patterns are present, for instance, in Yonggam (Ok, Papua New Guinea) and Hamar (Omotic, Ethiopia).

Contrary to many familiar European languages, such as German, in some of the languages just mentioned (among others), nouns for nonhuman animate and inanimate objects do not have fixed gender assignments; instead, whether they are regarded as masculine or feminine depends on whether the size of the particular entity being referred to in the given situation is big or little relative to what would ordinarily be expected for that general type of object. As an illustration, Aikhenvald (2012, pp. 58–59) quotes the following observations of an expert on Sare: "With regard to the size of things like houses, canoes, and containers, it is the capacity of the referents of these nouns to hold persons or things that determines what gender the noun takes. If a house, for instance, has space enough only for a single family (parents, children and grandparents), then it would normally be described as a small house, thus taking the feminine gender. If, on the other hand, the house has a capacity for several families, then it would normally be described as a big house and be accorded the masculine gender."

Essentially the same principle is also employed by Manambu (Ndu, Papua New Guinea), but this language takes it even farther, as shown in Figure 3.9. The genders of adult humans are, of course, determined by sex, but those of children and babies are sometimes based on size, such that relatively large individuals are treated as masculine and relatively small ones as feminine. The genders of higher nonhuman animate entities, such as dogs and pigs, are determined by species-specific scales of size, which is to say that within a certain species big individuals are assigned masculine gender, whereas little ones are assigned feminine gender. In a similar fashion, the

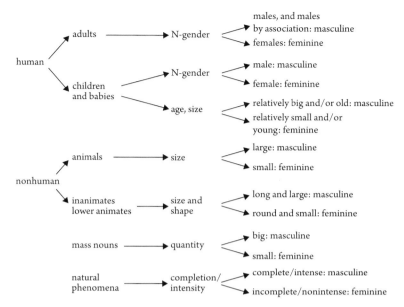

Figure 3.9. Gender assignment in Manambu (Ndu, Papua New Guinea). See the main text for details. "N-Gender" = natural gender.
Adapted from Aikhenvald (2012, p. 53).

relative within-species sizes of the members of lower nonhuman animate entities, such as reptiles and insects, usually dictate their gender; sometimes, however, the typical shape of the species overrides size as the key factor—e.g., crocodiles are masculine because they are long and thin, whereas turtles are feminine because they are round. Turning to inanimate entities, the genders of mass substances are determined by quantity—e.g., a large pool of blood is masculine, whereas a small one is feminine. And the genders of natural phenomena are determined by extent or intensity—e.g., a very dark night and a very strong wind are masculine, whereas a moonlit night and a light breeze are feminine.

Finally, although the semantic parameter of size is quite relevant to noun class systems, it is not often seen in the various types of classifier systems, with just one exception, namely numeral classifiers. In these systems, however, size is rarely expressed independently of other semantic parameters; instead, it usually clusters with shape and/or dimensionality. For instance, Baniwa (North Arawak, Brazil) has two numeral classifiers for holes or openings of different sizes: *yawa* covers large ones (e.g., a doorway), and *wa* covers small ones (e.g., a person's mouth).

Neurobiology

The role of size in the cortical implementation of object concepts has not received much attention, but a few recent studies have begun to address this topic (Konkle & Olivia, 2012; Konkle & Caramazza, 2013; Borghesani et al., 2016; Chiou & Lambon Ralph, 2016). As shown in Figure 3.10, there is some evidence that size interacts with

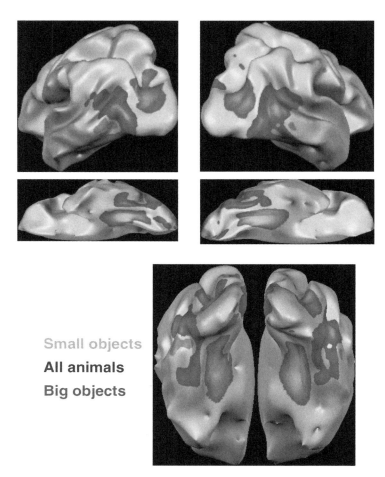

Figure 3.10. Three-way preference maps for animals (purple), large inanimate objects (blue), and small inanimate objects (orange), displayed on partially inflated caudal/lateral (top) and ventral (middle and bottom) surfaces of the right and left hemispheres. Regions activated by animals, regardless of size, include the lateral portion of the ventral temporal cortex and the pSTS/pMTG. Regions activated by large inanimate objects (e.g., ladders and tractors) include the medial portion of the ventral temporal cortex and a posterior sector of the lateral occipitotemporal cortex. And regions activated by small inanimate objects (e.g., coffee cups and calculators) include a ventral temporal area lateral to the one for animals, as well as several parietal and premotor/prefrontal areas (the latter not shown here). A color version is in the color plates section.
From Konkle & Caramazza (2013, p. 10239).

animacy in a complex manner that yields a tripartite division in the ventral stream between animals, large inanimate objects, and small inanimate objects. Consistent with the studies reviewed earlier, animals preferentially activate the lateral portion of the ventral temporal cortex, together with some nearby regions in the pSTS/pMTG. Moreover, large animals (e.g., bears and giraffes) are *not* anatomically segregated from small ones (e.g., rabbits and parrots). In contrast, inanimate objects seem to be partitioned according to size, with large ones (e.g., ladders and tractors) being subserved by both the medial portion of the ventral temporal cortex and a posterior sector of the lateral occipitotemporal cortex, and small ones (e.g., coffee cups and calculators) being subserved by a ventral temporal area lateral to the one for animals, together with several parietal and premotor/prefrontal areas (for similar results, see Mahon et al., 2007). The reason for this tripartite scheme is not clear, but Konkle and Caramazza (2013, p. 10241) suggest that it may reflect behavioral factors: "the size of an inanimate object causally influences how we interact with it (with our hands or whole body), whereas for animals, our primary interactions are not related to real-world size."[8]

These findings and ideas are certainly interesting, but they provide only partial insight into the neural underpinnings of how the semantic parameter of size is most often manifested in nominal classification systems. This is because the fMRI studies by Konkle and colleagues focused on the *average* sizes of objects. In languages like Sare and Manambu, however, such knowledge only takes speakers half-way toward competent use of gender, since the *average* size of, say, coffee cups merely constitutes the standard against which the *actual* size of a particular cup must be mentally measured so that the object can be treated as either masculine (if relatively large) or feminine (if relatively small). In other words, what is conceptually important for speakers of these languages (and of others like them) is not whether cups in general tend to be large or small compared to, say, ladders, but instead whether a specific cup being referred to on a specific occasion happens to be large or small *for a cup*. Moreover, this kind of judgment must be made routinely not only for inanimate objects, but also for animate ones.

At the level of large-scale neural networks, it is reasonable to suppose that speakers store long-term conceptual knowledge about the average sizes of objects in the category-specific cortical zones identified by Konkle and Caramazza (2013) and perhaps also in a higher-order ventrolateral sector of the anterior temporal lobe (ATL; Chiou & Lambon Ralph, 2016). In addition, there is evidence that the visual perception of the actual size of an object relies on neuronal populations in area V4 that integrate signals about the distance of the object with signals about the extent of its retinal projection (Tanaka & Fujita, 2015). So, taking both of these factors into account, it may be that when a speaker figures out what gender to assign to a particular noun on a particular occasion, he or she first compares the *actual* size of the designated object—computed in V4—with the *average* size of that general type of object—retrieved from the appropriate category-specific and ATL regions—and then determines whether the former magnitude is greater than or less than the latter. It is also noteworthy that the magnitude comparison process may depend on the intraparietal sulcus (Cohen Kadosh et al., 2005). Overall, this proposal is admittedly quite speculative and simplistic, but hopefully it points, if only in a vague way, to the kind of neurobiological explanation that would need to be fleshed out in order to accommodate the data from languages like Sare and Manambu.

---

[8] Another possibility is that neural responses in the medial portion of the ventral temporal cortex may be driven by highly contextualized objects, since large non-manipulable man-made objects tend to be found in particular places (Bar & Aminoff, 2003). I thank Brad Mahon for pointing this out.

Constitution

Typology

Some nominal classification systems include physical constitution, or material makeup, as a semantic parameter for grouping nouns—and, by extension, the objects they denote—into categories. This kind of information is specified mainly by numeral classifiers, but it is sometimes also expressed by noun classifiers and verbal classifiers. Here are a few representative examples from the realm of numeral classifiers. Many languages have a classifier for things made of wood—e.g., Akatek (Mayan, Mexico), Kilivila (Austronesian, Trobriand Islands), and several Tai languages. Similarly, many languages have a classifier for liquids—e.g., Akatek, Nambiquara (Nambiquaran, Brazil), and Baniwa (North Arawak, Brazil). Other constitution-based categories that tend to be encoded, albeit less often, are things made of stone (e.g., Akatek), things made of cloth (e.g., Baniwa), and things made of metal (e.g., Palikur, North Arawak, Brazil). Categories that seem to be encoded more rarely include powder-like things (e.g., Nambiquara) and excrement (e.g., Baniwa), the latter being culturally special "because of the importance of identifying animal droppings when hunting game" (Aikhenvald, 2000, p. 290).

Neurobiology

As with the previously discussed semantic parameters, this one is closely tied to the ventral stream. In particular, several fMRI studies suggest that the material properties of objects, as inferred from their visually perceived textures, are recognized primarily in a constellation of medial occipitotemporal regions (Cant & Goodale, 2007, 2011; Cant et al., 2009; Cavina-Pratesi et al., 2010a, 2010b; Hiramatsu et al., 2011; Jacobs et al., 2014). Interestingly, these cortical regions are more sensitive to the physical constitutions than the geometric forms of unfamiliar "nonsense" objects that appear to be made of substances such as wood, stone, cloth, metal, glass, or ceramic. And in keeping with these differential activity patterns, damage to the medial occipitotemporal territory, especially in the posterior collateral sulcus, impairs visual judgments of the physical constitutions but not the geometric forms of objects (Cavina-Pratesi et al., 2010a, 2010b). Furthermore, according to one fMRI study that employed representational similarity analysis, the activity patterns elicited by different kinds of materials cluster in ways that match the participants' subjective perceptual groupings of those materials (Hiramatsu et al., 2011). For instance, three similarity-based sets are as follows: (1) wood, bark, and stone; (2) metal, glass, and ceramic; and (3) cloth, fur, and leather. Another notable point is that the physical constitutions of objects can be sensed and categorized not only by sight but also by touch, and there is evidence that certain cortical areas in both the visual system and the somatosensory system are jointly engaged in a multimodal manner by the perception of textured objects even when these objects are experienced through just one or the other input modality (Stilla & Sathian, 2008; Jacobs et al., 2014).

By combining all of these findings with additional data suggesting that object concepts are grounded in sensorimotor systems (see Chapter 2), one can reasonably suppose that the meanings of constitution-related classifiers depend at least partly on some of the same medial occipitotemporal areas—and perhaps also some of the same parietal and insular areas—that have been implicated in the visual and tactile recognition of different kinds of materials. In addition, it is worth emphasizing that if this proposal is on the right track, the relevant neurocognitive representations may be very deeply entrenched for the human communities whose languages contain constitution-related classifiers. This is because classifiers, including those that are culturally distinctive, tend to be employed quite frequently in ordinary speech.

Interaction/Function

Typology

The fifth and final semantic parameter to be discussed here is interaction/function. In many nominal classification systems, the criteria for categorizing nouns include the ways in which people typically use the designated objects to achieve certain goals. Such information is often encoded by noun classifiers, numeral classifiers, and possessive classifiers; it is sometimes also encoded by verbal classifiers, but never by locative or deictic classifiers, and only rarely by noun classes.

Some interaction/function-based categories of objects show up quite often in the meanings of classifiers. This was clearly demonstrated by Carlson and Payne (1989), who compared the meanings of possessive classifiers in 14 languages from Oceania and found the following distribution, in decreasing order of frequency: edible objects (14), drinkable liquids (12), animals (8), vehicles (6), habitable places (5), captured game (4), earrings (4), garlands (4), islands (4), plants (3), sheets (2), and pillows (2).

Narrowing the focus to particular languages, however, almost always reveals classifiers that encode more unusual, sometimes even culture-specific, interaction/function-based categories of objects. This is nicely illustrated by the extinct language Kipeá-Kariri (isolate, Brazil), which had a system of 12 possessive classifiers that specified different ways in which possessed objects could be handled by their possessors. Foods were categorized not only according to how they were prepared— by roasting (*upodó*), boiling (*udé*), or allowing to mature at home (*ubó*)—but also according to how they were acquired—by gathering wild plants (*uaprú*), raising animals (*enkí*), cultivating manioc (*uanhí*), or cultivating other plants (*udjé*). Nonconsumable items were also categorized according to how they were acquired—by sharing with others (*ukisí*), obtaining as booty (*boronunú*), obtaining as a gift (*ubá*), or finding/ creating independently (*e*). Some of these classifiers are shown below in connection with the same noun, *sabuka* "fowl" (Aikhenvald, 2000, p. 135):

dz-upodó	*do*	*sabuka*
1SG-CL:ROASTED	POSS	fowl
"my fowl (roasted)"		

dz-udé	*do*	*sabuka*
1SG-CL:BOILED	POSS	fowl
"my fowl (boiled)"		

dz-ukisí	*do*	*sabuka*
1SG-CL:SHARING	POSS	fowl
"my fowl (that was my share)"		

dz-ubá		*do*	*sabuka*
1SG-CL:GIFT		POSS	fowl

"my fowl (that was given to me)"

Here are a few more examples of interesting interaction/function-based categories of objects that are sometimes captured by nominal classification systems. Yagua (Peba-Yagua, Peru) has one noun class marker, *ray*, for cutting tools (e.g., knives and machetes) and another, *roo*, for piercing tools (e.g., needles and spears). Minangkabau (Austronesian, Sumatra) has a numeral classifier, *gagang*, for tools with handles. Tinrin (Austronesian, New Caledonia) has a possessive classifier, *hwiie*, for foods that must be chewed. And Imonda (Waris, Papua New Guinea) has a verbal classifer, *pui*, for objects that are deliberately broken (e.g., biscuits).

Neurobiology

The category-level organization of object concepts in the brain is strongly influenced by both interactional and functional factors, but in different ways. This is not surprising, since objects that are manipulated similarly do not always serve similar purposes (e.g., a piano keyboard and a computer keyboard), and conversely, objects that serve similar purposes are not always manipulated similarly (e.g., a match and a lighter). Research on the neural substrates of these two aspects of object concepts has been growing, and evidence that interactional features depend on inferior parietal and premotor regions, whereas functional features depend on anterior temporal regions, comes from several sources, including fMRI (e.g., Boronat et al., 2006; Canessa et al., 2008), neuropsychology (e.g., Sirigu et al., 1991; Buxbaum & Saffran, 2002), and transcranial magnetic stimulation (e.g., Ishibashi et al., 2011; Pelgrims et al., 2011). In addition, a recent fMRI study suggests that functional features of object concepts also recruit medial temporal regions (Chen et al., 2016a).

Findings like these provide a plausible neurobiological foundation for the meanings of classifiers that specify interaction/function-based categories of objects. For instance, we noted earlier in this chapter—specifically in connection with the cortical underpinnings of plant concepts—that reading English nouns for various foods engages motor areas for mouth movements (Carota et al., 2012), and this is relevant here because it supports the hypothesis that the meanings of classifiers for edible objects and drinkable liquids are also grounded partly in these brain regions. More generally, however, what matters most in the current context is this: The neural networks that underlie the interactional and functional features of object concepts must be flexible enough to accommodate not only the sorts of categories that are commonly encoded by classifiers—e.g., those involving consumption, transportation, and habitation—but also the sorts that are encoded much less frequently—e.g., those involving entities that are cooked in certain ways, acquired in certain ways, and incised in certain ways.

Final remarks

In this section we have viewed object concepts through the lens of languages with nominal classification systems. Speakers of such languages routinely categorize objects at two taxonomic levels—indicating, for instance, that a particular entity is not just a pencil but an elongated thing. According to the available typological data, the semantic scaffolding that guides and constrains the development of nominal classification systems consists of a fairly restricted set of parameters—most prominently, animacy and related properties, shape and related properties, size, constitution, and interaction/function. In addition, some of these parameters tend to be associated more with certain syntactic types of classificatory elements than others, which suggests that the cognitive toolkit underlying nominal classification systems includes preferences, albeit rather loose ones, regarding the mapping between meaning and form. At the same time, however, typological studies have also revealed a tremendous amount of diversity in the manifestation of nominal classification systems. Such systems vary greatly with respect to which of the possible semantic parameters are incorporated, how those parameters are syntactically realized, and how many classificatory elements are present in the inventory. Furthermore, although some semantic distinctions along certain parameters are frequently found in systems all over the world, many others are relatively rare and hence may reflect culture-specific ways of categorizing the intra-linguistic realm of nouns and, by extension, the extra-linguistic realm of objects. Thus, by adopting a global, species-wide perspective, this branch of semantic typology provides a wealth of information about both the similarities and the differences in how humans structure the conceptual domain of objects for communicative purposes. This information is clearly quite relevant to cognitive neuroscience because it can be construed as a rich set of behavioral findings that must be accommodated by current theories about the organization and representation of concepts in the brain.

We have seen that almost all of the key semantic parameters that enter into nominal classification systems can be aligned with previously documented functional-anatomical dimensions of the ventral stream of object processing. It is therefore reasonable to suppose that this cortical infrastructure underlies the conceptual scaffolding that, as just mentioned, serves as the universal foundation for assembling nominal classification systems. This proposal is consistent with Christiansen and Chater's (2008, 2016) well-supported claim that languages are "shaped by the brain," and it also seems quite plausible as an overarching hypothesis, but several issues require deeper consideration.

People who use languages with nominal classification systems must coordinate two explicitly coded levels of object categorization that differ in granularity, and they must do so accurately and habitually on the brief time scale of spoken noun-phrases and clauses. This raises the question of how, for a given semantic parameter, these two levels of representation are related to each other across the expanse of ventral temporal cortex. One possibility, which is based on the account of object categorization put forth by Grill-Spector and Weiner (2014), is that the different levels may be organized as spatially superimposed hierarchies, such that the kind of high-level information encoded by a classifier (e.g., animate) may be represented within a particular cortical territory at the relatively coarse scale of centimeters, and the kind of lower-level information encoded by an adjacent noun (e.g., dog) may be represented within that same territory at a finer scale of millimeters. In line with Grill-Spector and Weiner's (2014) ideas, which level of representation is accessed for readout during online language processing may shift from moment to moment through the dynamic operation of a top-down gating mechanism. This approach is not without merit, but there is also evidence that while posterior regions of the ventral temporal cortex contribute to all levels of object categorization, increasingly anterior regions are recruited for increasingly specific levels (e.g., Rogers et al., 2006; Patterson et al., 2007; Clarke, 2015). In addition, neuropsychological studies have shown that basic and superordinate levels of object categorization can be impaired independently of each other (for a review, see Marques, 2007). Taken together, these findings suggest that, on average, the meanings of basic-level nouns may be neurally represented more anteriorly than those of comparatively schematic classifiers. Interestingly, this view predicts that speakers of classifier languages who suffer from semantic dementia should typically lose their knowledge of nouns before their knowledge of classifiers, because the atrophy that characterizes this disease affects the anterior sectors of the temporal lobes before it spreads to more posterior sectors (Bright et al., 2008). This prediction could be tested by focusing on Mandarin Chinese, a language that not only has a well-described nominal classification system (Gao & Malt, 2009), but is also spoken by roughly 900 million people, making research participants easier to obtain than for many of the more remote classifier languages around the world.

Lastly, it is worth emphasizing that while cognitive neuroscientists have traditionally concentrated on just a few domains of object concepts—especially plants, animals, artifacts, and body parts, as discussed earlier—nominal classification systems often contain much larger sets of such categories, with inventories that sometimes reach into the hundreds. As a refresher, here are some examples from the preceding survey, restricted to categories involving the semantic parameter of shape and related properties: rigid rectangular objects; long cylindrical objects; thin flat objects; thin spine-like objects; ring-like objects; hollow objects; pointed objects; twisted objects; stretchable objects; objects that are roundish but flat on one side; and objects that split and branch out from a central axis. Of course, the simple fact that some languages have classifiers for dozens of such categories entails that the people who produce and comprehend them on a regular basis must have robust and clearly differentiated neural representations of their meanings. As argued earlier, these representations are presumably implemented, for the most part, in the ventral temporal cortex, but the nature of their functional-anatomical arrangement is completely unknown. Although this arrangement will undoubtedly be difficult to elucidate, some progress could potentially be made by focusing, once again, on Mandarin Chinese, for the same reasons indicated earlier. Indeed, this would be an excellent opportunity for researchers to begin to connect the remarkable advances that have occurred in neuroimaging technology, such as the development of sophisticated kinds of multivariate analysis, with the impressive discoveries that have been made in the parallel field of semantic typology, such as the insights about nominal classification systems reviewed above.

CONCLUSION

The world is full of objects, and it is tempting to suppose that all languages represent them in comparable ways. For instance, the concepts encoded by the English nouns *cup* and *hand* seem so natural and self-evident that it is hard to imagine why any language wouldn't lexicalize them. Extensive typological research has shown, however, that while there are certainly many cross-linguistic similarities in the enormous semantic realm of objects, there are also numerous differences. The purpose of this chapter has been to describe some of these typological findings and explore their connections with cognitive neuroscience.

With regard to cross-linguistic similarities in the treatment of objects, the most obvious reason why they are relevant to cognitive neuroscience is because at least some of them are likely to reflect built-in biological constraints on human conceptualization. For instance, languages everywhere categorize plants and animals in terms of multilevel taxonomies, and these taxonomies may derive from the innate functional-anatomical organization of the ventral occipitotemporal stream, which, according to one influential line of work, represents living things with increasing specificity as processing moves forward. In the same vein, languages with complex nominal classification systems usually draw upon a limited set of semantic parameters, and these parameters appear to stem from some of the most deep-seated and well-established cortical dimensions of object representation. These examples illustrate how semantic typology can contribute to cognitive neuroscience by revealing cross-linguistic tendencies in the lexical and grammatical encoding of objects that converge with, and thereby lend credence to, contemporary theories about the implementation of object concepts in the brain. But an equally if not more valuable benefit of semantic typology is that it can disclose aspects of object representation that are cross-linguistically common, and hence conceptually important, but nonetheless neglected in cognitive neuroscience. This is nicely exemplified by the major role that dimensionality—or, more precisely, the three-way contrast between saliently 1D, 2D, and 3D objects—plays in shape-related classifier systems worldwide. As noted earlier, although this aspect of object representation has been studied in detail by typologists, it has not received much attention from neuroscientists.

Turning to cross-linguistic, and more broadly cross-cultural, differences in the treatment of objects, we have seen that they, too, have significant implications for cognitive neuroscience. Here are some of the most striking examples elaborated earlier. First, virtually all of the neuroscientific research on plant and animal concepts has been conducted with people in industrialized societies whose ethnobiological knowledge is actually quite impoverished relative to the historical standard for our species, which is epitomized by people in foraging societies. Second and third, different languages partition the lexical-semantic spaces of both artifacts and body parts into crosscutting categories, with likely consequences for the representational geometries of both the tool network and the cortical territory in and around the EBA. Fourth, some languages use distinct possession-marking devices for distinct domains of objects, but the neural substrates of these grammatical-semantic contrasts are still largely unknown. Fifth, many languages with richly developed nominal classification systems require their speakers to habitually categorize objects in ways that seem to be culturally idiosyncratic; however, the cortical underpinnings of these sorts of concepts remain mysterious. Finally, many of these languages also require their speakers to represent and package information about the shapes of objects in a manner that is, compared to English, rather unusual, since this information is not encoded in much if any detail by the vast majority of nouns, but is instead encoded in a fairly schematic fashion by numeral classifiers (and by dispositional predicates, as described in Chapter 1). Now, to be sure, some valuable neuroscientific work has been done on the somewhat related count/mass distinction in English and in a few other languages with similar contrasts

(Semenza et al., 1997; Borgo & Shallice, 2003; Garrard et al., 2004; Bisiacchi et al., 2005; Taler et al., 2005; Crutch & Warrington, 2007; Herbert & Best, 2010; Fieder et al., 2014, 2015). But most of this work has focused more on the morphosyntactic than the semantic aspects of the distinction, and the far more intriguing sorts of phenomena found in classifier systems have only just begun to be investigated from a neuroscientific perspective (Zhou et al., 2010; Chou et al., 2012, 2014).[9] Thus, as with the other topics mentioned above, the field is wide open.

[9] A qualification: Neurolinguistic research on classifier constructions in American Sign Language and British Sign Language has actually been growing (Emmorey et al., 2002, 2005, 2013; MacSweeney et al., 2002; Atkinson et al., 2005; Hickok et al., 2009), but this literature has largely been neglected by the branch of cognitive neuroscience that concentrates on conceptual knowledge.

4

ACTIONS

Linguistic signs do not reflect the way of the world. They portray it.
—N. J. Enfield (2015b, p. 110)

INTRODUCTION

As with object concepts, action concepts have been intensively investigated in both semantic typology and cognitive neuroscience. In the former field, researchers have been documenting, with increasing sophistication, a wide range of cross-linguistic similarities and differences in the lexical and grammatical encoding of actions. And in the latter field, researchers have been probing not only the neural networks that subserve the meanings of action verbs, but also the complex relationships between those networks and the ones that underlie the observation and execution of various kinds of behavior. For many years, however, these two lines of inquiry have been pursued, for the most part, independently of each other and with very little cross-talk, let alone cross-fertilization. The purpose of this chapter is therefore to explore some points of potential contact between them, with special emphasis on how typological findings about action concepts can inform neuroscientific work on their cortical implementation. Because common representational patterns in the cross-linguistic treatment of actions are likely to reflect fundamental properties of this intricate semantic sphere, they provide neuroscientists with important "targets" to search for in the brain. And because less frequent and downright rare patterns reveal the scope of cultural variation, they show neuroscientists how much conceptual diversity must ultimately be accommodated by any comprehensive brain-based theory.

The first section concentrates on motion events—a rich conceptual arena that has been studied in depth in semantic typology and has also received considerable attention in cognitive neuroscience, but with negligible communication between the two approaches. Then the next section discusses events of cutting, breaking, and opening—three closely related realms of regular human activity that have been the focus of dedicated cross-linguistic projects, but have only just begun to be carefully investigated from a neuroscientific perspective. After that, we turn to events of putting and taking—symmetrical everyday behaviors that have recently been explored in semantic typology, but have largely been ignored in cognitive neuroscience. Finally, the last two sections deal with serial verb constructions and verbal classification systems—two well-established strategies of action representation that are quite different from those adopted by English, but that must be taken seriously by any neuroscientific account of conceptual knowledge that aims for complete cross-linguistic coverage.[1]

MOTION EVENTS

Typology

As noted in Chapter 1, the linguistic representation of motion events has been one of the hottest areas of typological research for nearly 40 years (Talmy, 1985, 1991, 2000; Matsumoto, 2003; Slobin, 2004, 2006; Levinson & Wilkins, 2006a; Filipović, 2007b; Beavers et al., 2010; Croft et al., 2010; Imbert, 2012; Goschier & Stefanowitsch, 2013; Levin & Rappaport Hovav, in press; see also the references in footnote 1 of Slobin et al., 2014). Here, however, we will restrict our attention to findings that are especially pertinent to contemporary research on the neural substrates of action concepts.

According to the classic framework developed by Leonard Talmy (1985, 1991, 2000), a motion event has four fundamental conceptual components: (1) the *figure*, which is the entity that moves, such as a person, animal, or inanimate object; (2) the *path*, which is where the figure moves relative to its external frame of reference, such as into, onto, or over something; (3) the *manner*, which is how the figure moves relative to its internal frame of reference, such as climbing, crawling, or hopping; and (4) the *ground*, which is an entity that serves as a landmark for determining the path, such as the source or goal of motion. For example, in a playful situation in which a little girl somersaults down a hill, the figure is the girl, the path of motion is her downward trajectory, the manner of motion is somersaulting, and the ground is the hill.

Although languages worldwide distinguish between these four basic components of motion events, they vary in how they preferentially encode them. Following Talmy's lead, most of the typological research on this topic has involved sorting languages according to how the path component is lexicalized, since it specifies translocation and is therefore often regarded as the central element of a motion event. Several language types have been distinguished (Talmy, 1985, 1991, 2000; Slobin, 2004; Levinson & Wilkins, 2006b), but the two that have been studied most intensively are as follows: *satellite-framed languages* (henceforth S-languages) in which path is encoded by a so-called satellite[2] to the verb, and manner is encoded by the verb itself; and *verb-framed languages* (henceforth V-languages), in which path is encoded by the main verb, and manner is encoded by an adverbial adjunct in a syntactically subordinate clause. S-languages include Mandarin Chinese, Russian, Warlpiri (Pama-Nyungan, Australia),

---

[1] Due largely to space limitations, several other grammatically oriented aspects of action representation are not included here, such as voice phenomena (e.g., Shibatani, 2006), causality (e.g., Wolff et al., 2010), and argument-structure and tense-aspect constructions (e.g., Croft, 2012; Malchukov & Comrie, 2015).

[2] The term "satellite" is defined quite broadly as "any constituent other than a nominal complement that is in a sister relation to the verb root" (Talmy, 1991, p. 486). It therefore encompasses such diverse elements as verb particles in English, separable and inseparable verb prefixes in German, verb prefixes in Russian, non-head "versatile verbs" in Lahu (Sino-Tibetan, Southwestern China), incorporated nouns in Caddo (Caddoan, South-central United States), and polysynthetic affixes around the verb root in Atsugewi (Hokan, Northern California).

and Ojibwa (Algonquian, Canada), as well as the Finno-Ugric family and most of the Indo-European family, excluding Romance. V-languages, on the other hand, include Japanese, Tamil (Dravidian, India), Arrernte (Pama-Nyungan, Australia), and Nez Perce (Sahaptian, Northwestern United States), as well as the Polynesian and Semitic families, most of the Bantu and Mayan families, and the Romance subfamily of Indo-European.

In S-languages both manner and path are preferentially expressed within a monoclausal grammatical construction, as in the English sentence *I limped into the house* (Table 4.1). The conceptual component of manner is easily accessible for encoding because it is realized as the main verb. After all, every sentence requires a main verb, and with respect to the number of lexical items that a speaker must retrieve, it is just as economical to produce a manner-specific verb like *run* as it is to produce a manner-neutral verb like *go*, so speakers of S-languages effectively get manner "for free" (Slobin, 2003, p. 162). As a result, speakers of S-languages make abundant—one could even say habitual—use of manner verbs in descriptions of motion events, and historically this has led S-languages to develop large lexicons in which the semantic field of manner is intricately partitioned.

In English, for instance, this complex psychological space is divided into distinct categories by well over 100 verbs that vary in terms of visual pattern, motor pattern, intention, emotion, and social significance, leading to numerous clusters of lexical items that encode subtly different kinds of rapid motion (e.g., *dash, charge, trot, sprint*), leisurely motion (e.g., *amble, drift, stroll, mosey*), furtive motion (e.g., *creep, sneak, tiptoe, sidle*), smooth motion (e.g., *glide, slide, slink, slip*), awkward motion (e.g., *limp, lurch, stagger, stumble*), and so forth (Levin, 1993; Slobin, 2000). The meanings of some of these verbs are so specialized that it is hard to find equivalents in other languages. For instance, as noted by Snell-Hornsby (1983), English distinguishes between *scuttle, scurry, scamper*, and *scramble*, but German—another S-language that is genealogically related to English—has no exact matches for these verbs; conversely, German is more elaborate than English with regard to subtypes of firm, heavy walking, as indicated by the finely contrasting verbs *stapfen, stiefeln, trampeln*, and *stampfen*.

The way that S-languages encode motion events also allows speakers to describe paths in detail because, as Berman and Slobin (1994, p. 118) point out, "the syntax makes it possible to accumulate path satellites to a single verb, along with prepositional phrases that add further specification." In fact, it is not uncommon for speakers of S-languages to produce monoclausal descriptions of motion events in which the manner component, expressed by a verb, is tightly integrated both semantically and syntactically with a complex path that consists of several subtrajectories and is expressed by a series of particles and prepositional phrases, as in *The deer threw them off over a cliff into the water* (Berman & Slobin, 1994, p. 118) and *They decided to walk outside the house down to the back of the garden out into the bit of a forest there* (Slobin, 2004, p. 239).

Like S-languages, many V-languages also have a monoclausal intransitive motion construction in which manner is realized as a verb and path as a satellite; however, the expressive range of this construction is typically much narrower in V-languages than S-languages. In particular, the construction can only be used to represent motion events if the path is continuous and uninterrupted (comparable to the English phrase *run toward/away from a building*). If instead the path culminates in the crossing of some kind of boundary, then information about the specific nature of the path cannot

Table 4.1. The lexicalization of motion events in satellite-framed and verb-framed languages (abbreviated as S- and V-languages).

	S-Languages (e.g., English)				V-Languages (e.g., French)			
Lexical and clausal packaging	figure	MANNER	PATH	GROUND	FIGURE	PATH	GROUND	MANNER
	[SUBJECT	VERB	SATELLITE	OBJECT]CLAUSE	[SUBJECT	VERB	OBJECT]CLAUSE	[ADVERB]CLAUSE
	I	limped	into	the house	Je	suis entré	dans la maison	en boitant
					I	am entered	in the house	in limping
					I	entered	the house	limping
Manner granularity	Many fine-grained manner distinctions				Few fine-grained manner distinctions			
Path granularity	Many subtrajectories of complex paths				Few subtrajectories of complex paths			
Rhetorical style	Both manner and path usually expressed				Manner frequently omitted			
Sample languages	Mandarin Chinese, Russian, Warlpiri, Ojibwa, the Finno-Ugric family, and most of the Indo-European family (excluding Romance)				Japanese, Tamil, Arrernte, Nez Perce, the Polynesian and Semitic families, most of the Bantu and Mayan families, and the Romance subfamily of Indo-European			

Generalizations about manner granularity are from Slobin (2000, 2003, 2004). Generalizations about path granularity are from Slobin (1996, 2004). Generalizations about rhetorical style are based on elicited narratives analyzed in Berman and Slobin (1994) and Strömqvist and Verhoeven (2004).

be encoded in the form of a satellite (as in *run into/out of a building*) but must rather be encoded more prominently as a main-clause verb, forcing the manner component to be shifted to adjunct status, often in an optional subordinate clause (as in *enter/exit*[3] *a building running*) (Aske, 1989; Slobin & Hoiting, 1994). Due to this grammatical-semantic constraint, the latter biclausal construction, which is illustrated by the French example in Table 4.1, has a greater frequency of usage than the former monoclausal construction, as shown by quantitative analyses of narrative data (Berman & Slobin, 1994; Strömqvist & Verhoeven, 2004).

Path is highly codable in the biclausal construction because it is mapped onto the main verb slot; however, manner is "costly" to produce since it requires generating a separate clause, and for this reason it is sometimes omitted entirely (Slobin, 2003, p. 162). A historical consequence of this downgrading of manner information is that the manner-verb lexicons of V-languages are generally not as densely differentiated as those of S-languages. For instance, Spanish *escabullirse* does not distinguish between *glide, slide, slip*, and *slither*, and French *bondir* does not distinguish between *jump, leap, bound, spring*, and *skip* (Slobin, 2000, 2003). It is also noteworthy that with regard to path information, while S-languages allow successive segments of complex paths to be encoded compactly in conjoined prepositional phrases (e.g., *The frog crawled out of the jar and through the window into the woods*), the boundary-crossing constraint in V-languages frequently forces speakers to devote a separate clause to each segment of a complex path (comparable to the English sentence *The frog exited the jar, passed through the window, and entered the woods*). Such clausal chains are apparently dispreferred, however, since they are exceptionally rare in both oral narratives and literary novels (Slobin, 2004, 2006).

The example sentences given above about a frog, a jar, a house, a garden, a forest, a deer, and a cliff all come from what are affectionately referred to as "frog stories" in the typological literature on motion events. These stories are based on a wordless picture book for children called *Frog, Where Are You?* (Mayer, 1969), which portrays in black-and-white drawings the adventures of a boy and his dog as they wander through a forest searching for his pet frog who escaped from a jar during the night while he was sleeping. This book has been used to elicit oral narratives (i.e., frog stories) from speakers of over 70 languages and 13 language families worldwide, and some of the most important discoveries about the contrasts between S- and V-languages, especially with regard to the encoding of motion events, derive from these investigations (Berman & Slobin, 1994; Strömqvist & Verhoeven, 2004; Levinson & Wilkins, 2006a).[4]

Consider, for instance, the picture shown in Figure 4.1. To get a sense of the context, the picture immediately preceding this one portrays two simultaneous situations: first, the boy is straddling a branch of the tree and peering into the hole, presumably looking for the runaway frog; and second, the dog has just knocked down a beehive from another tree, and the bees are starting to swarm. Now, in the current

---

[3] Most of the pure path verbs in English (e.g., *enter, exit, ascend, descend*) derive from Latin, a Romance V-language.

[4] All of the drawings comprising *Frog, Where Are You?* are reproduced in Berman and Slobin (1994) and Strömqvist and Verhoeven (2004).

-12-

Figure 4.1. The emergence of the owl in *Frog, Where Are You?*
From Mayer (1969).

scene, one can infer that the owl has suddenly emerged from the hole, causing the boy to fall; in addition, the bees are chasing the dog. From a typological perspective, what is most interesting about this scene is that speakers of S- and V-languages tend to describe the emergence of the owl in quite different ways (Slobin, 2004). In particular, as shown in Table 4.2 and Figure 4.2, S-language narrators of all ages often describe this event by combining a manner verb with a path satellite, as in the expressions *fly out*, *jump out*, and *pop out*, whereas V-language narrators of all ages almost always describe it by using a single path verb meaning "exit," without any additional information about the specific way in which the owl left the hole.

The greater salience of manner of motion in S-languages than V-languages can also be seen in several other natural and experimental contexts, such as spontaneous conversation, creative writing, newspaper reporting, naming videoclips of motion events, and speeded fluency—that is, listing as many motion verbs as possible in one minute (Slobin, 2000, 2003). For instance, this discrepancy between the two language types is clearly manifested in translations of novels and other forms of discourse. As a case in point, Slobin (2000) considers a dramatic episode in J. R. R. Tolkien's *The Hobbit* when some dwarves flee into trees in order to save themselves from an attacking horde of wolves. Tolkien describes the event with an English expression that combines a vivid manner verb with a path particle, *scramble up*, and Slobin observes that translations into other S-languages use equally graphic expressions: Dutch *omhoogklauteren*, Russian *vs-karabkat'sja*, and Serbo-Croatian *pentrati-se*. In sharp contrast, V-language translations use neutral verbs of climbing: Spanish *trepar*, French *grimper*, Turkish *trmanmak*, Italian *arrampicarsi*, and Hebrew *le-tapes*. The Portuguese version even omits manner entirely, using just the pure path verb *subir* "ascend."

Table 4.2. Examples of oral descriptions of the emergence of the owl in Figure 4.1 from speakers of (A) S-languages and (B) V-languages. The former speakers often combine manner verbs with path satellites, whereas the latter speakers almost always use a single path verb meaning "exit," with no information about manner (see also Figure 4.2).

A. S-languages

English

   An owl popped out.

German

   ... *weil*   *da*   *eine Eule plötzlich* <u>*raus-flattert*</u>.
   ... because there an owl suddenly out-flaps.

Dutch

   ... *omdat*   *er*   *een uil* <u>*uit-vliegt*</u>.
   ... because there an owl out-flies.

Mandarin Chinese

   <u>*Fē*</u> <u>*chu*</u> *yī zhī máotóuyīng*.
   Fly out one owl.

Russian

   Tam <u>*vy-skočila*</u>   *sova.*
   There out-jumped owl.

B. V-languages

Spanish

   <u>*Sale*</u> *un buho.*
   Exits an owl.

French

   D'un   *trou de l'arbre* <u>*sort*</u> *un hibou.*
   From a hole of the tree exits an owl.

Turkish

   Oradan bir   *baykus* <u>*çikiyor*</u>.
   From there an owl exits.

Italian

   Da   *quest' albero* <u>*esce*</u> *un gufo.*
   From that tree exits an owl.

Hebrew

   <u>*Yaca*</u> *mitox*   *haxor yanšuf.*
   Exits from inside the hole owl.

Adapted from Slobin (2004, p. 224).

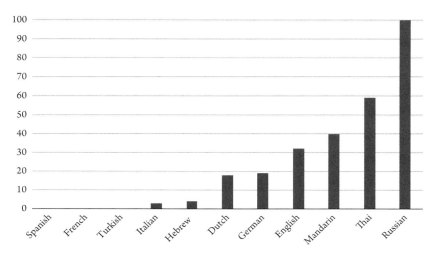

Figure 4.2. Percentage of narrators using a manner-of-motion verb to describe the emergence of the owl in oral frog stories. Spanish, French, Turkish, Italian, and Hebrew are V-languages; Dutch, German, English, Mandarin, Thai, and Russian are S-languages.
Note: As in the original figure from Slobin, Mandarin is treated here as an S-language, but its typological status has actually been quite controversial (Zheng, 2017).
Adapted from Slobin (2004, p. 225).

There is also ample evidence for the opposite phenomenon—that is, the amplification or insertion of manner features when translating from V- to S-languages. This occurs not only in literary fiction, but also in the socially more consequential domain of eyewitness testimony, where descriptions of motion events can be crucial in the characterization of crimes. Focusing on transcripts of eyewitness testimony conducted in Spanish, Filipović (2007a, 2009) analyzed 457 passages involving motion events and found that only 21% of them included manner verbs. Even though many of these descriptions were about highly dynamic events such as muggings, robberies, domestic violence, and manslaughter, the low proportion of manner verbs was predicted by the typological classification of Spanish as a V-language. Filipović (2007a, 2009) also discovered, however, that when these reports were translated into English, there was a strong tendency for details to be added regarding the manner in which key participants moved through the scenes. For instance, in one case the original Spanish document contained no explicit information whatsoever about how fast the events unfolded, but the English translation contained multiple uses of the verbs *run* and *chase*, thereby implying a rapid pace and encouraging inferences about the suspect's physical state and location (e.g., if he was running the whole time, he would probably be tired and would have covered a substantial distance). As Filipović (2009, p. 305) points out, the upshot is that "we could draw different conclusions about a described event from the Spanish original and its English translation." And this, needless to say, could have serious legal repercussions.

Turning to more carefully controlled experimental studies, several investigations have explored how speakers of different languages name videoclips of people moving in various ways. The first study of this kind was carried out by Malt et al. (2008, 2010), who asked speakers of two S-languages (English and Dutch) and two V-languages (Spanish and Japanese) to name the changing gaits of an actor who was filmed while locomoting on a treadmill as the angle and rate of motion increased. The researchers found that speakers of all four languages lexically distinguished between two basic gaits, walking and running, and they explained this consistency by noting that the distinction reflects a categorical biomechanical discontinuity: ". . . in walking, the legs are like a pendulum around a fulcrum point and one foot is always in contact with the ground. Running has an impact-and-recoil motion, and there is a point in each stride in which neither foot is in contact with the ground" (Malt et al., 2010, p. 38). Beyond these two basic gait types, however, there was considerable cross-linguistic diversity in the naming of other movement patterns. In keeping with previous studies demonstrating different degrees of manner salience in S- and V-languages, both English and Dutch speakers produced many fine-grained verbs for subtle subtypes of walking and running, but Spanish and Japanese speakers produced few, if any.

Similar results emerged in a subsequent experiment in which speakers of the same four languages named a wide range of expressive manners of locomotion performed by an actor (Malt et al., 2014). As in the treadmill study, all of the speakers distinguished between pendulum-based and bounce-and-recoil movements, but English and Dutch speakers were far more likely than Spanish and Japanese speakers to also discriminate between a number of more specialized kinds of movement patterns. For example, the videoclips that were named *hop, skip, jump*, or *leap* by English speakers were all named just *saltar* "jump" by Spanish speakers, corroborating once again the contrast between S- and V-languages that Slobin (2004, 2006) highlighted in his earlier analyses of spoken and written narratives.

In yet another study, Slobin et al. (2014) focused on two S-languages (English and Polish) and three V-languages (French, Spanish, and Basque [isolate, Spain]). Notably, the stimuli were not staged motion events performed by a single actor, as in Malt et al.'s (2008, 2010, 2014) experiments, but were instead completely natural motion events performed, for the most part, by anonymous agents in everyday life. In particular, the stimuli consisted of 34 mostly candid videoclips capturing a broad array of movement patterns, and speakers of each language were asked to describe them. Mirroring Malt et al.'s (2008, 2010, 2014) results, speakers of all five languages reliably distinguished between the two basic gaits of walking and running. In fact, when the researchers conducted a multidimensional scaling analysis to explore the similarities among all the naming responses, they found that the primary underlying dimension appeared to reflect velocity. This is revealed by the horizontal axis in Figure 4.3, since relatively slow gaits are toward the right and relatively fast ones are toward the left. Moreover, among the four main clusters of movement patterns that are circled and labeled in this figure, it is clear that one encompasses manners of walking and another encompasses manners of running. As for the other two clusters, one is restricted to quadrupedal "crawl" movements and the last consists of non-canonical gaits that break down into bounce-and-recoil "jump/leap/hop" movements and syncopated "skip/gallop/prance" movements.

Importantly, additional analyses indicated that even though all five languages partition the semantic space of manner of motion into the four clusters shown in Figure 4.3, they vary greatly in the extent to which they carve this space into more finely differentiated categories. As the researchers predicted, the two S-languages

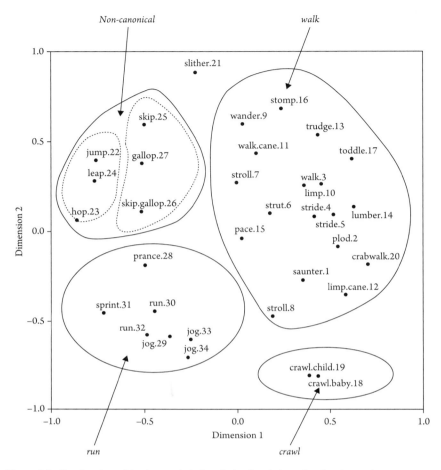

Figure 4.3. Results of a multivariate statistical analysis of pooled naming data for motion events, derived from speakers of two S-languages (English and Polish) and three V-languages (French, Spanish, and Basque [Isolate, Spain]). Videoclip names and numbers are mnemonics bestowed by the investigators, not labels produced by the participants. Within the plot, points represent videoclips, and distance indicates the likelihood of common labeling. Dimension 1 appears to reflect velocity, with slower gaits on the right and faster ones on the left. Dimension 2, however, is not readily interpretable. Four main clusters of movement patterns are circled and referred to with red labels and arrows.
From Slobin et al. (2014, p. 713).

turned out to have greater lexical-semantic granularity than the three V-languages, and this was manifested in many ways. To give just one illustrative example, English speakers produced a total of 16 expressions for subtypes of so-called "labored progress" (*bumble, creep, dawdle, drag feet, drag oneself, lumber, mope, plod, poke, shuffle, skulk, slouch, sulk, toddle, trudge,* and *wobble*), and speakers of the other S-language, Polish, produced seven such expressions. In contrast, speakers of the three V-languages produced far fewer expressions of this kind: four in French, three in Basque, and just one in Spanish. Such discrepancies provide further evidence that the semantic space of manner of motion is more richly subdivided in S- than V-languages. It is worth highlighting how this relates to some of the points made at the outset of Chapter 1, since one can infer that for speakers of S-languages manner of motion tends to be a well-developed domain of conceptual common ground that supplies cultural group-mates with an intricately organized, historically honed, and socially shared system for categorizing this particular realm of experience.[5]

Although Talmy's (1985, 1991, 2000) binary distinction between S- and V-languages has inspired a great deal of fruitful research, it has also been the subject of considerable debate. Slobin et al. (2014, footnote 1) provide a short but meticulous guide to the various problems that have arisen (see also Levinson & Wilkins, 2006b). Here we will briefly discuss just four issues before concluding this overview of the typology of motion events with a nod to another important observation by Talmy.

First, in some languages, such as Serbo-Croatian and Modern Greek, when people talk about motion events, they use satellite-framed and verb-framed constructions with more or less equal frequency (Filipović, 2007b; Soroli, 2012). Because neither lexicalization pattern is clearly dominant, these languages defy simple classification within Talmy's (1985, 1991, 2000) typology (for further discussion, see Beavers et al., 2010; Croft et al., 2010). Relatedly, the frog story data depicted in Figure 4.2 reveal variability in manner encoding between languages that are all classified as satellite-framed, and between languages that are all classified as verb-framed, suggesting that it may be a mistake to treat these two types of languages as being dichotomous; instead, it may be more accurate to regard them as lying on a continuum of manner salience (Slobin, 2004).

Second, other languages cannot easily be classified as either satellite-framed or verb-framed because grammatical categories of equal status represent both the path and manner components of motion events (Slobin, 2004). To accommodate these languages, a third type has been proposed—namely, *equipollently framed*—and several subtypes have been distinguished, as shown in Table 4.3. For example, in many Native American languages, such as those in the Hokan and Penutian families, verbs for motion events have a bipartite structure, with one morpheme expressing path and another expressing manner (DeLancey, 1989, 1996). In addition, numerous languages scattered around the globe have serial verb constructions in which the path and manner components of motion events are conveyed by consecutive verbs (Aikhenvald & Dixon, 2006; Bisang, 2009; Haspelmath, 2016). Finally, many Northern Australian languages have verbal classification systems in which motion events are represented by complex predicates that contain the following elements: a single generic verb with an austere meaning such as "go" or "come," and one or more so-called coverbs with more precise specifications of path and/or manner (Wilson, 1999; Schultze-Berndt,

---

[5] Slobin et al. (2014) also analyzed more elaborate motion descriptions across the five languages and found, somewhat surprisingly, that V-language speakers often conveyed manner information through various forms of modification. This result conflicts with many previous studies that, as mentioned earlier, focused on motion descriptions in other contexts, such as narratives. For present purposes, however, what matters most is that unlike V-language speakers, S-language speakers have at their disposal, and routinely employ, a large lexicon of motion verbs that encode prepackaged, conventionalized action concepts with the manner component directly incorporated.

Table 4.3. Three subtypes of equipollently framed languages in which the path and manner components of motion events are encoded by more or less equivalent grammatical forms.

Language Subtype	Schematic Event Packaging	Examples
Bipartite verbs	[path + manner]$_{verb}$	Algonquian, Athabaskan, Hokan, Klamath-Takelman, and Penutian families in North America
Verbal classification systems	path coverb + manner coverb + generic verb	Many languages in Northern Australia
Serial verb constructions	path verb + manner verb	Niger-Congo, Hmong-Mien, Sino-Tibetan, Tai-Kadai, Mon-Kmer, and Austronesian families, among others

Adapted from Slobin (2004, p. 249).

2000; McGregor, 2002). Incidentally, the latter two language types—i.e., those with serial verb constructions and those with verbal classification systems—are the topics of separate sections later in this chapter. (For responses to the notion of equipollently framed languages, see Talmy, 2009, 2016).

Third, there are also many languages, especially in Africa, East Asia, and Southeast Asia, that encode manner of motion not only in verbs, but also in accompanying or independently occurring sound-symbolic ideophones (Voeltz & Kilian-Hatz, 2001). Here are a few examples from Slobin (2004, p. 235):

- *gulukudu* "rush in headlong" (Zulu, Niger-Congo, South Africa)
- *minyaminya* "stealthily" (Ewe, Niger-Congo, Ghana)
- *kítíkítí* "at a stomp" (Emai, Niger-Congo, Nigeria)
- *widawid* "swinging the arms while walking" (Ilocano, Austronesian, Philippines)
- *dēngdēng* "tramping" (Mandarin Chinese)
- *tyôko-maka* "moving around in small steps" (Japanese).

Notably, ideophone inventories can be quite large. For instance, according to Slobin (2004, p. 251), "Westermann's (1930) grammar of Ewe gives examples of 37 ideophones that can be used with the verb [for] 'walk,' with the additional information that these forms can be reduplicated and can occur with high tone for diminutives and low tone to describe motions of large entities."

Fourth, some languages, especially in Australia and South America, have an unusual grammatical-semantic category of "associated motion" that does not fit readily into Talmy's (1985, 1991, 2000) typology. In general, this category is realized by affixes which indicate that the action specified by the verb occurs in the context of a concurrent, prior, or subsequent motion event with a particular direction in space. For instance, Arrernte (Pama-Nyungan, Australia) has inflections for no less than 14 kinds of associated motion, as shown in Table 4.4 (Wilkins, 2006). The occurrence of one such device is underlined in the following sentence:

Table 4.4. Types of "associated motion" in Arrernte (Pama-Nyungan, Australia).

Action and motion concurrent		Action and motion non-concurrent	
Deictically directed	Oriented	Go (-*alhe*)	Go back (-*alpe*)
-*intye* = do coming	-*nhe* = do past	-*ty.alhe* = go & do	-*ty.alpe* = go back & do
-*inty.alpe* = do coming back	-*ty.antye* = do upwards	-*rl.alhe* = do & go	-*rl.alpe* = do & go back
-*inty.alhe* = do coming through	-*ty.akerle* = do downwards	-*artn.alhe* = quickly do & go	-*artn.alpe* = quickly do & go back
-*irtne* = reversive: (a) do going back; (b) do back to	-*artn.akerle* = quickly do downwards		

Adapted from Wilkins (2006, p. 49).

. . . *ahelhe-ke*	*anteme*	*itne*	*irrpe-<u>ty</u>alpe-ke*
. . . ground-DATIVE	now	3.PL.SUBJ	enter-<u>GO.BACK&DO</u>-PAST.COMPLETIVE

. . . "they went back and now entered the ground" (literally "entered after having returned")

Interestingly, a recent analysis of 44 South American languages with associated motion affixes found that 22 have simple systems with just one or two markers, 12 have more complex systems with three to five markers, and 10 have very complex systems with six or more markers, the winner being Tacana (Takanan, Bolivia), which has 13 affixes for different kinds of associated motion (Figure 4.4; Guillaume, 2016).

Finally, let's wrap up this survey of the cross-linguistic representation of motion events by recapitulating an important point of Talmy's (1985, 1991, 2000) that we first encountered in Chapter 1. Although we have focused primarily on the different ways in which the path and manner components of motion events are lexicalized, it is worth noting that there is also typological variation regarding the lexicalization of the figure component. Of greatest significance, perhaps, is the fact that this component is not always encoded by a noun-phrase; instead, in some languages it is regularly encoded by a verb root. This is the case, for instance, in Atsugewi (Hokan, Northern California), a language that recently went extinct. Several examples of figure-incorporating Atsugewi verb roots are shown in Table 1.4 in Chapter 1, including the following: -*caq*- "for a slimy lumpish object (e.g., a toad, a cow dropping) to move/be-located"; -*swal*- "for a limp linear object suspended at one end (e.g., a shirt on a clothesline, a hanging dead rabbit) to move/be-located"; and -*staq*- "for runny icky material (e.g., mud, rotten tomatoes) to move/be-located." As illustrated in Table 4.5, in this language descriptions of motion events are built around verb roots like these, specifically by adding prefixes and suffixes that express other bits of information. Compared to English and other familiar European languages, this way of habitually packaging motion events for communicative purposes is quite unusual, and it may have implications for the branch of cognitive neuroscience that studies action concepts, as described below.

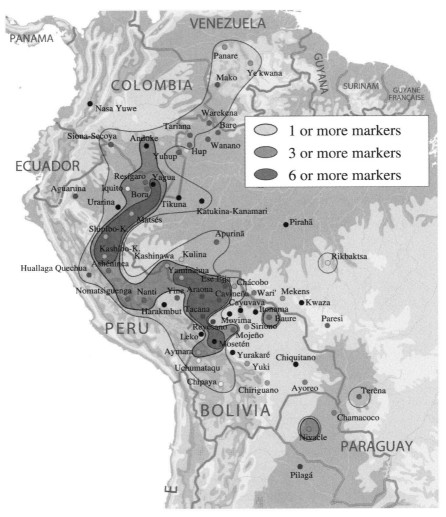

Figure 4.4. Geographical distribution of 44 South American languages with three different levels of complexity of "associated motion" systems. The colors of the circles for individual languages represent their genealogical affiliations. A color version is in the color plates section.
From Guillaume (2016, p. 112).

Neurobiology

The cortical underpinnings of action concepts, including those that are lexicalized by verbs, have received increasing attention from cognitive neuroscientists during the past few decades, especially in connection with the sorts of grounded theories of semantic knowledge that we covered in Chapter 2 (for reviews see Watson & Chatterjee, 2011; Gennari, 2012; Watson et al., 2013; Kemmerer, 2015a, 2015c, 2015d, 2015e; Quandt & Chatterjee, 2015). However, most of the experimental work on this topic has been heavily influenced by English and a few other languages, and has ignored the

Table 4.5. Descriptions of motion events in Atsugewi (Hokan, Northern California) are built around verb roots that encode the figure component. Two examples are provided, both of which involve the verb root *-staq-* "for runny icky material to move/be-located." For each example, the top four rows show, in descending order, the four linguistic units that are strung together to make up the sentence, and the bottom three rows show the complete sentence, its literal meaning, and a possible real-world referent event.

Linguistic Units	Sentence 1	Sentence 2
Inflectional affix set	'- *w*- -*a*' 3rd person subject, factual mood'	*s*- '- *w*- -*a*' 1st person subject, 3rd person object, factual mood'
Cause prefix	*ca*- 'from the wind blowing on the figure'	*cu*- 'from a linear object, moving axially, acting on the figure'
Figure-incorporating verb root	*-staq-* 'for runny icky material to move/be-located'	*-staq-* 'for runny icky material to move/be-located'
Path suffix	*-ict* 'into liquid'	*-cis* 'into fire'
Complete sentence	'-*w-ca-staq-ict-*ᵃ	*s-'-w-cu-staq-cis-*ᵃ
Literal meaning	Runny icky material moved into liquid from the wind blowing on it.	I caused it that runny icky material move into fire by acting on it with a linear object moving axially.
Possible real-world event	The guts blew into the creek.	I prodded the guts into the fire with a stick.

Adapted from Talmy (2000, p. 59).

typological literature on motion events that we just examined. It is therefore important to consider some of the ways in which the neuroscientific approach could potentially be enriched by taking into account the many insights that have emerged from the typological approach. To this end, we will now look closely at several brain regions that have been implicated not only in the observation and execution of human movement patterns, but also in their verbal encoding, and over the course of this discussion we will highlight a number of issues that warrant further investigation from a cross-linguistic perspective.

It is well-established that within the hierarchy of cortical structures comprising the human visual system, area MT+ (also known as V5 or hOc5) is the first site that is specialized primarily for motion processing (Zeki, 2015; see Figure 3.2 in Chapter 3 of this volume). It resides in the vicinity of the anterior occipital and lateral occipital sulci (Malikovic et al., 2007); it receives bottom-up input from multiple lower-level visual areas (Nassi & Callaway, 2006); and it overlaps the extrastriate body area (EBA), which responds preferentially to the sight of human bodies and body parts (Peelen & Downing, 2007; Downing & Peelen, 2011, 2016; see Figure 3.5 in Chapter 3 of this volume). The anatomical intersection of MT+ and the EBA has interesting functional consequences, since it allows the kinematics and the configurations of perceived body parts to be efficiently linked (Jastorff & Orban, 2009). Both MT+ and the EBA project forward to the posterior superior temporal sulcus (pSTS) and the posterior middle temporal gyrus (pMTG)—areas that process the complex visual motion patterns of humans, animals, and manipulable tools, even when they are presented as just point-light displays, i.e., stimuli that consist of illuminated dots that move like the major joints or axes of living or nonliving things (for reviews, see Beauchamp & Martin 2007; Grossman, 2008; Saygin, 2012; Giese, 2015; see also Grosbras et al., 2012, for a meta-analysis of functional neuroimaging studies). As shown in Figure 4.5, the lateral occipitotemporal cortex (LOTC) encompasses all of these areas—MT+, the EBA, the pSTS, and the pMTG—and different sectors of this large territory have been associated with different aspects of the perception, conceptualization, and verbal encoding of bodily actions (Lingnau & Downing, 2015).

In recent years, there has been growing evidence for the hypothesis that the LOTC represents the visual aspects of the manner of motion features of verb meanings. Much of this evidence comes from functional neuroimaging studies that have found

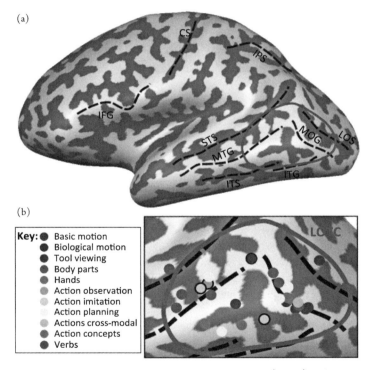

Figure 4.5. Approximate borders of the lateral occipitotemporal cortex (LOTC), and activation peaks within it. (a) Outline of the LOTC superimposed on the segmented and inflated left hemisphere of a single subject. (b) Outline of LOTC (red line), together with activation peaks reported in a variety of functional neuroimaging studies (for references, see Lingnau & Downing, 2015). Note that peaks do not reflect the typical spatial extent of activations, nor overlap among them. A color version is in the color plates section.

Abbreviations: CS = central sulcus; IFG = inferior frontal gyrus; IPS = intraparietal sulcus; STS = superior temporal sulcus; MTG = middle temporal gyrus; ITS = inferior temporal sulcus; ITG = inferior temporal gyrus; MOG = middle occipital gyrus; LOS = lateral occipital sulcus. From Lingnau & Downing (2015, p. 270).

significant engagement of this region, more strongly in the left than the right hemisphere, when people process the meanings of action verbs, relative to when they perform baseline tasks. For example, Kemmerer et al. (2008) used fMRI to investigate the neural substrates of the following five classes of English verbs, as defined by Levin (1993): Running verbs (e.g., *run, jog, sprint*), Hitting verbs (e.g., *hit, poke, jab*), Cutting verbs (e.g., *cut, slice, hack*), Speaking verbs (e.g., *yell, murmur, sing*), and Change of State verbs (e.g., *shatter, crumple, snap*). In our survey of the semantic typology of motion events, we emphasized cross-linguistic similarities and differences in the encoding of various styles of human locomotion, and for this reason it is worth noting that the class of so-called Running verbs in Levin's (1993) compendium actually has 124 members that capture a remarkably diverse range of locomotion categories, 20 of which were included in the fMRI study.[6] The main task involved making fine-grained discriminations among triads of verbs within each class—for instance, determining that *limp* is more like *trudge* than *stroll*—and the baseline task involved making similarity judgments about strings of meaningless characters in a peculiar font called Wingdings. Compared to the baseline condition, the five verb classes elicited widely distributed patterns of brain activity that differed from each other in many theoretically interesting ways. For present purposes, however, what matters most is that, as portrayed in Figure 4.6, all of them recruited the LOTC, with many complex combinations of overlapping activity in several sectors of this large cortical territory, as well as some intriguing instances of class-specific activity. Of greatest relevance in the current context is the discovery that (averaging across subjects) Running verbs uniquely engaged the lower bank of the mid-pSTS, as shown by the biggest red patch within the black oval marking the LOTC.[7] More generally, though, the multiple manifestations of class-specific activity in the LOTC suggest that the representational topography of this region may be organized at least partly according to different categories of action concepts.

It is also notable that a recent meta-analysis conducted by Watson et al. (2013) strongly supports the view that the LOTC plays a major role in the neural representation of action concepts. In particular, by pooling data from 29 different positron emission tomography (PET) and fMRI studies, these researchers were able to demonstrate that the LOTC is the region of maximal concordance not only among experiments that focused on the conceptual processing of action *images*, but also among experiments that focused on the conceptual processing of action *verbs*. Interestingly, the data revealed a gradient of increasing representational schematicity along the posterior-to-anterior axis of the LOTC, such that posterior areas were engaged significantly more by action images than action verbs, middle areas were engaged equally by both types of stimuli, and anterior areas were engaged significantly more by action verbs than action images. These results bolster the idea that the LOTC represents and perceptually grounds the visual manner of motion features of verb meanings.

---

[6] *Walk, amble, stroll, saunter, strut, march, stomp, limp, trudge, stagger, stumble, sprint, run, jog, skip, sneak, tiptoe, leap, jump,* and *hop.*

[7] See also Osaka (2009), who found that Japanese ideophones for manners of walking activated the left pSTS, relative to pseudowords matched for length. Thanks to Asifa Majid for directing me to this study.

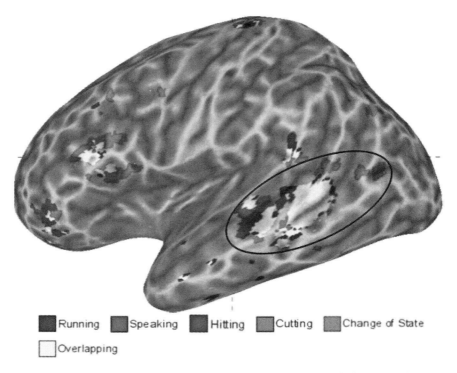

Figure 4.6. Activity patterns associated with semantic similarity judgments for five classes of English verbs—Running, Speaking, Hitting, Cutting, and Change of State—in the left lateral occipitotemporal cortex (LOTC), the approximate boundaries of which are marked by the black oval. Significant activations are rendered on the left hemisphere of a partially inflated 3D brain, color-coded according to verb class, with yellow patches indicating overlap of two or more classes. A color version is in the color plates section.
Previously unpublished figure based on data from Kemmerer et al. (2008).

The putative link between the LOTC and these aspects of verb meanings has been challenged, however, by two fMRI studies by Bedny et al. (2008, 2012). In the first study, they recorded subjects' brain responses to three sets of verbs—high motion (e.g., *to kick*), medium motion (e.g., *to bleed*), and low motion (e.g., *to think*)—and three sets of nouns—high motion (e.g., *the tiger*), medium motion (e.g., *the drill*), and low motion (e.g., *the rock*). They found that the activity levels in the LOTC were equally strong for all three sets of verbs and equally low for all three sets of nouns, and they interpreted these results as evidence that the LOTC does not really represent the visual manner of motion features of action verbs, but instead represents more abstract features that distinguish verbs in general from nouns in general. In the second study, they obtained essentially the same outcomes in a group of congenitally blind subjects and, not surprisingly, argued that the data reinforce the notion that the LOTC does not register the degree to which verbs convey visual motion patterns.

Problems still remain, however, because the results of Bedny et al.'s studies must somehow be reconciled with the results of two other lines of work. First, according to several neuropsychological studies that are discussed further below, brain-damaged patients with lesions affecting the LOTC are often impaired on tasks that require know-ledge of the concrete components of verb meanings, including their visual manner of motion properties. And second, contradicting Bedny et al.'s studies, many other fMRI studies have shown that the LOTC does in fact tend to respond significantly more to motion-related than non-motion-related expressions (Tettamanti et al., 2005; Deen & McCarthy, 2010; Saygin et al., 2010; Lin et al., 2011; Wallentin et al., 2011; Humphreys et al., 2013; Spunt et al., 2016). Here are a few examples. Wallentin et al. (2011) asked Danish-speaking subjects to simply listen to Hans Christian Andersen's famous fairy tale *The Ugly Ducking*, and found that the LOTC was significantly engaged when all of the clauses describing motion events were contrasted against all of the clauses describing non-motion events. In addition, Spunt et al. (2016) asked English-speaking subjects to make "how" and "why" judgments about event descriptions at different levels of abstraction (e.g., *cut vegetables—make a salad—get nutrients—be healthy*), and found that regardless of which type of judgment was required, the more concrete the phrases were, the more strongly the LOTC was activated.

Taking all of these considerations into account, one possibility is that the LOTC is innately predisposed to represent several different aspects of verb meaning, including visual manner of motion patterns as well as more schematic kinds of information. Data consistent with this view come from an fMRI study by Peelen et al. (2012) which showed that partially segregated sectors of the LOTC respond to action verbs like *walk* on the one hand and to purely stative verbs like *exist* on the other. (It is also likely that certain portions of the LOTC are sensitive to grammatical-semantic aspects of verbs and argument structure constructions, but we will not address this topic here; for useful references, see Grewe et al., 2007; Shetreet et al., 2007; Wu et al., 2007.) So, even though this large cortical territory does not receive normal visual input in con-genitally blind individuals, it may nevertheless serve as the default region for storing long-term records of whatever conceptual knowledge can be acquired through other senses about the idiosyncratic manner of motion patterns encoded by action verbs. Further research is needed to explore this issue in greater depth.

The hypothesis that the LOTC represents the visual manner of motion features of verb meanings predicts that damage to this region should impair the processing of such features, and several neuropsychological studies have provided supportive results (Aggujaro et al., 2006; Tranel et al., 2008; Kalénine et al., 2010; Kemmerer et al., 2012; Taylor et al., 2017). In one of the largest investigations to date, Kemmerer et al. (2012) administered the following battery of six standardized tasks to 226 brain-damaged patients with widely distributed lesions in the left and right hemispheres:

- Naming ($N = 100$ items): For each item, the participant is shown a photograph of an action, and the task is to orally name each one with a specific verb.
- Word-Picture Matching ($N = 69$ items): For each item, the participant is shown a printed verb together with two photographs of actions, and the task is to determine which action the verb describes.
- Word Attribute ($N = 62$ items): For each item, the participant is shown two printed verbs, and the task is to indicate which one designates a type of action that satisfies a certain value for a single attribute (e.g., more tiring; moving the hands in a circle; moving the hands up/down; etc.).

- Word Comparison (N = 44 items): For each item, the participant is shown three printed verbs, and the task is to determine which one is most different in meaning from the other two.
- Picture Attribute (N = 72 items): This task is analogous to the Word Attribute task, but the stimuli are photographs of actions instead of verbs.
- Picture Comparison (N = 24 items): This task is analogous to the Word Comparison task, but the stimuli are photographs of actions instead of verbs.

Of the 226 patients who were studied, 61 failed one or more of the six tasks. And although only four patients failed the entire battery, it is striking that one of them—namely, case 1808—had a highly focal lesion that was completely confined to the LOTC and underlying white matter, as shown in Figure 4.7. Moreover, group analyses were carried out to explore lesion-deficit relationships on a task-by-task basis in the 147 patients for whom brain scans were available, and it turned out that damage to the LOTC and underlying white matter was significantly associated with impaired performance on five of the six tasks (see Figure 4.13 later in this chapter). Overall, these findings from both the single case of 1808 and the larger group of patients constitute strong evidence that the LOTC is essential for representing the kinds of action concepts that tend to be encoded by verbs. And more specifically, they are consistent with the hypothesis that this region subserves the visual manner of motion features of such concepts.[8]

Let's turn now to the motor aspects of the manner of motion features of verb meanings. Because we have already discussed this topic in Chapter 2 (see the sections called "Modal systems" and "Flexible processing"), we will only consider it briefly here. The key point is that the relevant motor specifications of action verbs appear to depend largely on the precentral motor cortices (for reviews, see Kemmerer, 2015a, 2015c, 2015d, 2015e).[9] These brain regions are major components of the mirror neuron system, since they contribute to both the production and the perception of actions (for reviews and meta-analyses, see Van Overwalle & Baetens, 2009; Molenberghs et al., 2012; Avenanti et al., 2013; Rizzolatti et al., 2014; see also Figure 4.12 later in this chapter). And as shown in Figure 4.8, they also display what is frequently referred to as semantic somatotopy, since descriptions of leg/foot actions (e.g., *kick*), arm/hand actions (e.g., *pick*), and face/mouth actions (e.g., *lick*) tend to engage the corresponding effector-related dorsal, lateral, and ventral sectors of the classic motor homunculus. Moreover, these regions are typically ignited by action verbs within 200 msec of presentation, and when their normal operation is disrupted, either temporarily by TMS or chronically by lesions, the comprehension of action verbs is often affected. Such findings support the

---

[8] Because some of the tasks used static photographs of actions as stimuli, one might wonder if some of the patients who failed them had trouble perceptually inferring, rather than conceptually categorizing, the implied motion patterns. But while this might be true for a very small number of cases, it is unlikely to apply to a large proportion of them, since a separate neuropsychological study with 78 patients found that their performances on parallel static and dynamic action naming tasks were highly correlated (r = .91), with very few dissociations (Tranel et al., 2008).

[9] Parietal regions also contribute to some of the motor aspects of verb meanings, but we will not discuss them until later in this chapter.

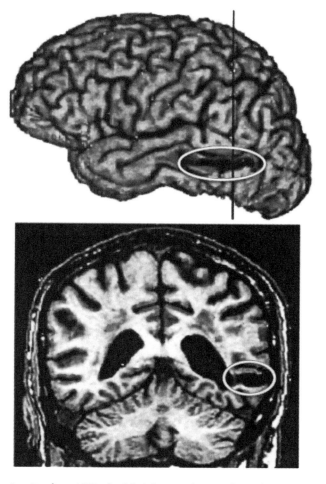

Figure 4.7. Lesion site of case 1808, who failed the entire battery of six tasks that, as described in the main text, evaluate knowledge of action concepts in a variety of linguistic and nonlinguistic ways. The damage, highlighted by the yellow circles, is restricted to the posterior portion of the left middle temporal gyrus and underlying white matter. The vertical line in the upper panel indicates the plane of the coronal section shown below, where the left hemisphere is depicted on the right side. A color version is in the color plates section.
From Tranel et al. (2003, p. 421).

view that understanding action verbs involves, to some extent, partially retrieving or reconstructing the motor programs that guide the execution of the designated types of behaviors (bearing in mind, of course, that this process is influenced by task, context, and individual differences, as described in Chapter 2).

It is worth emphasizing, however, that the activation peaks portrayed in Figure 4.8 are distributed quite broadly, with clusters that only loosely match the somatotopic layout of the motor homunculus (see also the similar plot in Carota et al., 2012). This variability has led some researchers (Fernandino & Iacoboni, 2010; Kemmerer

(a)

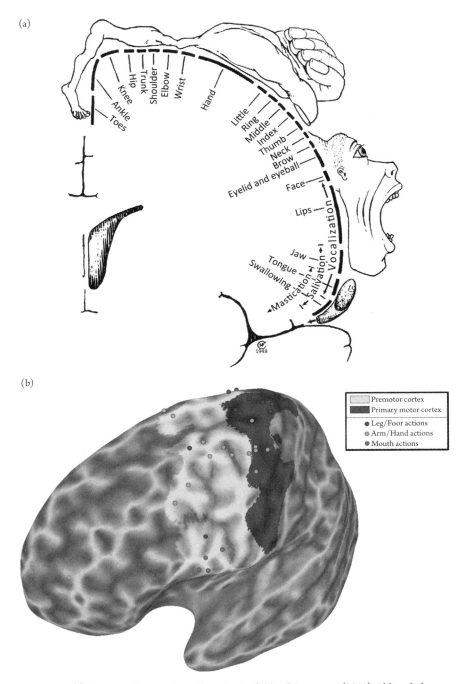

(b)

Figure 4.8. (a) The motor homunculus as drawn by Penfield and Rasmussen (1950). Although the drawing shows an orderly progression of body parts, the authors warned that there is actually extensive representational overlap. (b) Peak activations in the left precentral motor cortices reported by several fMRI studies that have investigated the motor features of verbs and sentences encoding leg/foot actions, arm/hand actions, and face/mouth actions (for references, see Kemmerer et al., 2012). Activations are plotted on a color-coded inflated 3D brain with definitions for the primary motor cortex (dark blue) and premotor cortex (yellow) from Mayka et al.'s (2006) Human Motor Area Template. A color version is in the color plates section.

(a): From Graziano (2009, p. 33); (b): From Kemmerer et al. (2012, p. 843).

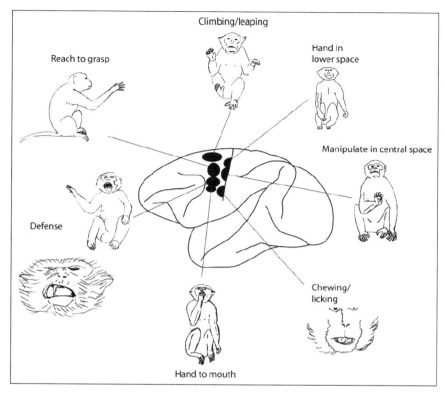

Figure 4.9. Action zones in the motor cortex of the macaque monkey. These categories of movement were evoked by electrical stimulation of the cortex on the behaviorally relevant timescale of 0.5 seconds. Images traced from video frames. Each image represents the final posture obtained at the end of the stimulation-evoked movement. Within each action zone in the motor cortex, movements of similar behavioral category were evoked. These findings suggest that the functional organization the motor cortex is influenced not only by the structure of the body, as shown in Figure 4.8a, but also by the structure of the behavioral repertoire.
From Graziano & Aflalo (2007, p. 243).

& Gonzalez-Castillo, 2010) to draw attention to the fact that although somatotopy has traditionally been regarded as the main organizational principle of the precentral motor cortices, another influential factor is actotopy, which involves the functional partitioning of cortical areas according to distinct categories of complex, well-learned behaviors. For instance, Graziano and Aflalo (2007) found that, as illustrated in Figure 4.9, the precentral motor cortices of the macaque monkey are divided into separate zones for ethologically important kinds of actions, such as climbing/leaping movements, reaching movements, hand-to-mouth movements, defensive movements, and central space/manipulation movements. In addition, Graziano (2016) points out that more recent research has yielded evidence for actotopy in the precentral motor cortices of other mammalian species, including humans. These intriguing findings suggest that at least some of the variability in activation peaks shown in Figure 4.8 could reflect differences in the kinds of complexly coordinated actions encoded by the verbs and sentences that were used as stimuli both within and across the studies.

The manner of motion features of verb meanings include not only visual and motor specifications, but also, in many cases, intentional, emotional, and social ones. We touched on this topic in our discussion of the typology of motion events, and it is worthwhile to address it again here by looking more closely at the Running verbs that were used in Kemmerer et al.'s (2008) fMRI study (see footnote 6 in this chapter). It is apparent that many of these verbs are associated with certain goals, feelings, and social situations. For instance, *amble* and *stroll* express calm, relaxed, and leisurely forms of walking; *strut* suggests an arrogant or conceited attitude; *march* brings to mind a military parade or political protest; *limp* and *trudge* convey effort, discomfort, and exhaustion; *stagger* and *stumble* both involve loss of control; *skip* connotes a light, playful, and carefree state of mind; and *sneak* and *tiptoe* imply stealth, that is, a desire not to be detected. The neural substrates of these sorts of intentional, emotional, and social specifications are not yet clear, but there are some hints that they include parts of the mentalizing network (also known as the theory of mind network). First of all, in Kemmerer et al.'s (2008) fMRI study, the class of Running verbs engaged not only the LOTC and a superior, putatively leg-related sector of the precentral motor cortices, but also the dorsomedial prefrontal cortex, which is a core node of the mentalizing network (see the meta-analysis by Schurz et al., 2014). In addition, Lin et al. (2015) found that the same region, as well as several other cortical components of the mentalizing network, responded more strongly to verbs for social actions than private actions (see also Lin et al., 2018). Finally, there is substantial evidence that the pSTS, which was heavily recruited by Running verbs (see Figure 4.6), represents not just the visual aspects of animate movement patterns, but also the hidden intentions that underlie them (e.g., Grèzes et al., 2004; Pelphrey et al., 2004; Schultz et al., 2004; Osaka et al., 2012).

How might the various neuroscientific issues that we have considered so far be further illuminated and perhaps taken in new directions by the typological findings that we reviewed earlier, specifically regarding cross-linguistic similarities and differences in the treatment of manner of motion? To begin with the most common lexicalization strategies, it is worth recalling that although detailed investigations of motion verb inventories have only been conducted for a handful of languages, translation equivalents of English *walk* and *run* have consistently been found in both S- and V-languages (Malt et al., 2008, 2010, 2014; Slobin et al., 2014). We noted earlier that the cross-linguistic prevalence of these two basic verbs is probably due to the fact that they encode the two most biomechanically stable gaits. We also saw that, according to a multidimensional scaling analysis, such verbs frequently serve to anchor clusters of other verbs for more specialized forms of walking and running (Slobin et al., 2014). Moreover, the same analysis revealed that, as shown in Figure 4.3, both S- and V-languages tend to have at least one verb for quadrupedal "crawl" movements, together with a variably sized set of verbs for non-canonical gaits encompassing bounce-and-recoil "jump/leap/hop" movements and syncopated "skip/gallop/prance" movements (Slobin et al., 2014). Because these cross-linguistic similarities reveal the most widely attested ways of carving up the semantic field of manner of motion, they provide cognitive neuroscientists with valuable clues about what to look for, at a relatively coarse level of granularity, in the cortical mapping of this domain. Indeed, such typological findings could potentially help to constrain and/or interpret future fMRI studies that use multivariate techniques, like representational similarity analysis (RSA), to explore the internal functional organization of brain regions that have already been implicated in the manner of motion features of verb meanings—in particular, the LOTC and precentral motor cortices.

Shifting to cross-linguistic diversity, we noted earlier that, according to several sources of data (e.g., frog stories, literary fiction, eyewitness testimony, and naming videoclips of actions), the conceptual space of manner of motion is more densely differentiated in S- than V-languages, ostensibly because information about manner is directly expressed by the main verb in languages of the former type, but is relegated to adjunct status in languages of the latter type (see again Table 4.1). In addition, we observed that many verbs in S-languages capture very subtle movement patterns that may, in some cases, be so idiosyncratic as to be unique to the given language. For instance, in Slobin et al.'s (2014) naming study, English speakers generated 16 separate expressions for subtypes of "labored progress," including some highly nuanced verbs like *bumble, dawdle, lumber*, and *plod*. Spanish speakers, on the other hand, produced just one—*arrastrar se* "drag self." We also saw that sound-symbolic ideophones in a variety of other languages often encode quite distinctive action concepts, such as *gulukudu* "rush in headlong" (Zulu, Niger-Congo, South Africa), *widawid* "swinging the arms while walking" (Ilocano, Austronesian, Philippines), and *tyôko-maka* "moving around in small steps" (Japanese). Typological differences of this nature are clearly relevant to cognitive neuroscience, since they suggest—one could even say imply— that, at a relatively fine level of granularity, the cortical representations of the manner of motion features of verb meanings vary greatly across cultures. In general, these representations are likely to be realized as more precisely and narrowly differentiated patterns of brain activity in populations of S-language speakers than in populations of V-language speakers. And more specifically, the complex and partly unique categorization systems of individual S-languages may be neurally implemented by equally rich and culture-specific representational geometries not only in the LOTC and precentral motor cortices, but perhaps also in certain sectors of the mentalizing network, such as the dorsomedial prefrontal cortex. As fMRI methods like RSA continue to improve, it should become increasingly feasible to test hypotheses like these.

Up to this point, we have focused exclusively on the neural substrates of the manner component of motion events. But what about the neural substrates of the path component? Unfortunately, very little research has addressed this question, and I am only aware of two studies that have been published so far, both of which involved fMRI and were carried out in Anjan Chatterjee's laboratory at the University of Pennsylvania. The first study found that when subjects watched videoclips of moving characters, manner information was, in keeping with the data reviewed earlier, processed primarily in the LOTC, whereas path information was processed primarily in the left inferior parietal lobule and the right superior parietal lobule—brain regions that are known to be important for spatial representation (Wu et al., 2008; see also Chapter 5 in this volume). The second study sought to determine whether similarly segregated activity patterns would occur when subjects made plausibility judgments about English phrases containing either manner verbs (e.g., *jump the stream*) or path prepositions (e.g., *into the stream*) (Quandt et al., 2015). As the researchers expected, manner verbs engaged the LOTC; however, contrary to their expectations, path prepositions did not engage any parietal areas. Hopefully, more attention will be devoted to this topic in the future. It would be interesting, for example, to compare manner verbs not with path prepositions, but rather with path verbs, so as to avoid confounds between semantic and grammatical categories. Although English has only a small number of pure path verbs, many other languages have larger inventories; indeed, this is most evident in V-languages, since they, by definition, preferentially encode the path component of motion events in verbs. Here, then, is an excellent opportunity for cognitive neuroscientists to use insights from semantic typology to shed more light on the cortical representation of motion events.

It is also instructive to return to our discussion of cross-linguistic diversity in the how the figure component of motion events is usually expressed. We have seen that although the vast majority of languages tend to map this component onto nouns, there are some—not a lot, to be sure, but some—that routinely map it onto verbs instead. For instance, Atsugewi (Hokan, Northern California) has myriad verbs the specify detailed physical features of the moving entity—e.g., -staq- "for runny icky material (e.g., mud, rotten tomatoes) to move/be-located" (see again Table 4.5 as well as Table 1.4 in Chapter 1). How do such languages bear on the branch of cognitive neuroscience that investigates action concepts? As indicated in Chapter 3, the physical features of objects, like shape and constitution, are subserved mainly by the ventral temporal cortex. But while it is widely believed that this large anatomical territory contributes much more to the meanings of nouns than verbs, this assumption fails to take into account rare languages like Atsugewi (Kemmerer, 2014b). In fact, it seems likely that in such languages the meanings of motion verbs rely crucially on the kinds of object representations that reside in the ventral temporal cortex.

Finally, it is important to consider some of the ways in which, cross-linguistically, the meanings of motion verbs may depend on the various transmodal cortical systems that we discussed in Chapter 2. We observed there that one of the most well-established functions of these systems is to integrate the anatomically distributed features of concepts; hence, it is reasonable to hypothesize that they perform such operations for the meanings of motion verbs, perhaps at several levels of integration. For instance, at a relatively low level, transmodal systems may serve to bind together—either comprehensively or in different combinations—the visual, motor, intentional, emotional, and social aspects of just the manner component of motion verbs. And at a more abstract level, they may capture, in highly schematic or distilled form, the three major kinds of semantic conflation classes that Talmy (1985, 1991, 2000) identified in his typological framework for characterizing motion verbs: [motion + manner], [motion + path], and [motion + figure]. If the componential structures of these three conflation classes are in fact captured by transmodal systems, their degree of neurocognitive entrenchment must vary across cultures, with the first one being dominant for speakers of S-languages, the second one being dominant for speakers of V-languages, both the first one and the second one having equal status for speakers of equipollently framed languages, and the third one being dominant for speakers of languages with figure-incorporating verbs. In addition, transmodal systems may carry out even more complex conjunctive operations during the processing of motion verbs, such as integrating the meanings of verb roots with the meanings of suffixes for different kinds of "associated motion" in languages like Arrernte (Pama-Nyungan, Australia; see again Table 4.4 and the associated text). As yet, neuroscientific research on transmodal systems has focused much more on their involvement in object concepts than action concepts, but it is notable that one of the main hubs—namely, the anterior temporal lobe (ATL)—has been heavily implicated in both verbal and nonverbal action concepts, according to several studies with semantic dementia patients (Bak & Hodges, 2003; Cotelli et al., 2006; Hillis et al., 2006; Yi et al., 2007; Bonner et al., 2009; Pulvermüller et al., 2009). Hopefully, interest in how transmodal systems contribute to the meanings of motion verbs in different types of languages will grow in the coming years and lead to new insights.

EVENTS OF CUTTING, BREAKING, AND OPENING

Typology

Three closely related domains of action that have recently been studied in semantic typology are often referred to as events of cutting, breaking, and opening (see especially Majid & Bowerman, 2007; Majid et al., 2007, 2008; see also Goddard & Wierzbicka, 2008). What these three arenas of human behavior have in common is that they all involve situations in which people cause objects to separate in various ways, either through an irreversible destruction of their material integrity, in the case of cutting and breaking events (e.g., slicing a carrot, shattering a window), or through a reversible disjunction of their parts, in the case of opening events (e.g., removing the lid from a saucepan).

At first glance, these sorts of actions may not seem to warrant special attention, but there are actually several reasons why they have received intensive cross-linguistic examination. For one thing, the fact that flaked stone cutting tools date back over 2.5 million years in the hominin fossil record suggests that we have an ancient and universal neurocognitive capacity for creating and using implements designed to incise objects (Semaw et al., 2003; Stout & Hecht, 2015). In addition, analyses of English and other languages have revealed syntactic differences between cutting and breaking verbs that appear to reflect semantic differences (Guerssel et al., 1985; Levin & Rappaport Hovav, 1995; for the most extensive typological study of this topic, see Bohnemeyer, 2007; see also Malchukov & Comrie, 2015). Furthermore, some intriguing hints that the conceptual domains of cutting, breaking, and opening are related to each other in complex ways come from the spontaneous speech errors of young children acquiring English, Mandarin Chinese, and K'iche' (Mayan, Mexico) (Pye et al., 1995; Bowerman, 2005). Examples include using the verb *cut* to describe a person breaking ice cubes into chips with a rolling pin, using the verb *open* to describe a person breaking the leg off a plastic doll, and using a core breaking verb in Mandarin (*duan4* "be.broken.crosswise [of a long thing]") or K'iche' (*q'upi:j* "break a hard thing") to describe a person cutting paper with scissors. Finally, early efforts to explore the fine-grained meanings of cutting, breaking, and opening verbs from a typological perspective obtained some striking initial evidence for cross-linguistic variation, as shown in Table 4.6 (Pye et al., 1995; Pye, 1996; see also Fujii, 1999).

Together, these considerations inspired the members of the Event Representation Project at the Max Planck Institute for Psycholinguistics to systematically study the verbal encoding of cutting, breaking, and opening events in the 28 genealogically and geographically diverse languages listed in Table 4.7, using as stimuli a standardized

Table 4.6. Partially mismatching applications of cutting and breaking verbs to four objects—a piece of cloth, a bubble, a plate, and a stick—in English, Garifuna (Maipurean, Honduras), and Mandarin (Sino-Tibetan, China).

	cloth	bubble	plate	stick
English	*tear/rip*	*pop*	*break*	
Garifuna	*teiriguana*	*bowguana*		*halaguana*
Mandarin	*noŋ4-puo4*			*noŋ4-duan4*

(From Majid et al., 2007, p. 135).

Table 4.7. List of 28 languages included in a typological study of cutting, breaking, and opening events.

Language	Affiliation	Location
Biak	Austronesia	Indonesia
Chontal	Isolate	Mexico
Dutch	Indo-European	Netherlands
English	Indo-European	UK, USA
Ewe	Niger-Congo	Ghana
German	Indo-European	Germany
Hindi	Indo-European	India
Jalonke	Niger-Congo	Guinea
Japanese	Isolate	Japan
Kilivila	Austronesian	Papua New Guinea
Kuuk Thaayorre	Pama-Nyungan	Australia
Lao	Tai Kadai	Laos
Likpe	Niger-Congo	Ghana
Mandarin	Sino-Tibetan	China
Miraña	Witotoan	Colombia
Swedish	Indo-European	Sweden
Tamil	Dravidian	India
Tidore	West Papuan	Indonesia
Tiriyó	Cariban	Brazil
Touo	Papuan Isolate	Solomon Islands
Turkish	Altaic	Turkey
Tzeltal	Mayan	Mexico
Yélî Dnye	Papuan	Rossel Island
Yukatek	Mayan	Mexico

Based on Majid et al. (2007, p. 138), and Majid et al. (2008, p. 238).

battery of 61 short videoclips depicting various kinds of separations (Majid & Bowerman, 2007). Although these researchers were well aware that their stimuli would necessarily be influenced by their own partially implicit assumptions about the conceptual domains under investigation, they made a concerted effort to create a broad assortment of scenes that differed in ways which, according to preliminary work, were likely to reflect the semantic parameters that are most relevant to cross-linguistic representation. Thus, they manipulated the physical properties of the affected objects (e.g., stick, rope, cloth, plate, pot, hair, food items), the types of tools that were employed (e.g., hand, knife, machete, scissors, hammer), the manners in which the actions were executed (e.g., once or repeatedly, calmly or intensely), and whether the separations could be partly or completely reversed (e.g., peeling a banana, opening a book).

As described below, careful scrutiny of the naming data revealed an intricate tableau of patterned cross-linguistic variation in the referential scopes of verbs for cutting, breaking, and opening events. On the one hand, several multivariate statistical analyses of the entire dataset disclosed a small set of underlying dimensions that appear to shape the ways in which languages subdivide these conceptual domains. On the other hand, a tremendous amount of diversity still emerged, as shown rather dramatically by the discovery that the number of distinct verbs that consultants in each language produced to name the 61 clips ranged from a remarkably low minimum of just three in Yélî Dnye (Papuan, Rossel Island) to an amazingly high maximum of 23 in Tzeltal (Mayan, Mexico). The three verbs in Yélî Dnye were *chaa* "coherent severance with the grain," *châpwo* "coherent severance against the grain," and *pwââ* "incoherent severance regardless of grain"—distinctions that may strike us as being rather exotic, but that actually accord quite well with what Levinson (2007, p. 216) describes as "a material culture based on fibers and the relatively recent introduction of steel cutting tools." In contrast, most of the 23 verbs that Tzeltal speakers used have very specific meanings, such as the following: *jaw* "cut/break something so that it falls open in two halves"; *jep* "cut/break something into two vertical halves"; *sew* "cut a round or bulky soft thing across its long axis"; *sil* "cut something into slivers along its long axis"; *putz'* "partially separate a long thing so that it is not fully broken"; and *woch'* "break into the interior of something" (Brown, 2007).

The purpose of the statistical analyses mentioned above was to determine the degree to which the 61 stimuli are treated similarly across the 28 languages, with similarity being measured in terms of which clips tend to be named, and hence grouped together, with the same verbs (Majid et al., 2007, 2008). The first analysis showed that, at the level of the whole sample, although speakers frequently used certain verbs to name multiple cutting and/or breaking actions, they rarely applied those verbs to opening actions as well. This suggests that events of cutting and breaking generally hang together as a composite class, most likely because they all involve material destruction. Conversely, events of opening seem to stand apart as a fairly independent class, since they all involve reversible separation.[10]

---

[10] The first analysis also revealed that the clips depicting "peeling" actions (peeling an orange and peeling a banana) and "taking apart" actions (pulling a chair back from a table and pulling apart two nested paper cups) ended up falling in between the "cutting and breaking" and "opening" clusters, although the two "peeling" stimuli were closer to the "cutting and breaking" cluster than to the "opening" cluster.

This is definitely a valuable finding, but it is also noteworthy that, at the level of individual languages, two intriguing exceptions were found, both of which are reminiscent of the developmental errors described earlier in which English-speaking children overextend the verb *open* to cut/break-type situations (Bowerman, 2005). First, Kuuk Thaayorre (Pama-Nyungan, Australia) has a verb, *thuuth*, that covers actions in which an agent separates a long thing from a base by means of an instantaneous outward pulling force (Gaby, 2007). Crucially, such actions include not only cutting/breaking events like plucking an eyebrow or yanking a string so that it snaps, but also opening events like removing the lid of a teapot or taking the cap off a pen. Second, in Tidore (West Papuan, Indonesia) the verb *hoi* denotes certain actions in which an agent separates part of an object from the whole (van Staden, 2007). In the current context, what's most relevant is that this verb groups together such otherwise disparate events as decapitating a fish and opening a jar. Both of these peculiar verbs, *thuuth* and *hoi*, imply that even though the psychological spaces of cutting/breaking events and opening events are usually segregated, the boundaries between them are by no means strict.

Another statistical analysis focused on just the data for cutting and breaking events, and it identified three underlying dimensions, illustrated in Figure 4.10, that collectively account for nearly half of the cross-linguistic variance in naming responses. None of these dimensions is explicitly labeled in any of the languages; instead, they form an ineffable semantic framework, a kind of covert conceptual trellis, that both

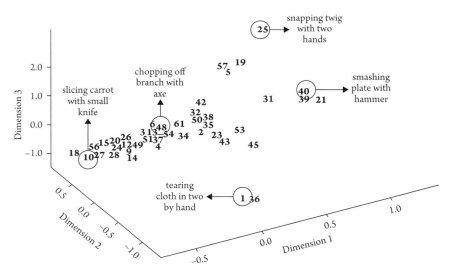

Figure 4.10. Results of a multivariate statistical analysis of pooled naming data for cutting and breaking events, derived from speakers of the 28 languages listed in Table 4.7. Videoclip descriptions and numbers are mnemonics bestowed by the investigators, not labels produced by the participants. Within the plot, points represent videoclips, and distance indicates the likelihood of common labeling. Dimension 1 appears to reflect the predictability of the locus of separation in the affected object. Dimension 2 distinguishes the two tearing events from all of the others. And Dimension 3 distinguishes between smashing events and snapping events.
From Majid et al. (2007, p. 143).

guides and limits the ways in which individual languages categorize the relevant sorts of actions.

Dimension 1 is a continuous variable that can be characterized in terms of the *predictability of the locus of separation* in the affected object. The "high predictability" end of this continuum is toward the left along the pertinent axis in Figure 4.10, and most of the cutting events are clustered here because they often involve an agent incising an object in a controlled manner by using a sharp instrument, as in clip 10, which shows a person slicing a carrot with a small knife. In contrast, the "low predictability" end is toward the right, and most of the breaking events are clustered there because they often involve an agent destroying an object in an imprecise manner by using a blunt instrument, as in clip 40, which shows a person smashing a plate with a hammer. Importantly, Majid et al. (2007, 2008) found that languages tend to have different verbs for designating events at the extreme ends of Dimension 1. In other words, most languages lexically distinguish between ideal instances of cutting and breaking events.

The researchers also found, however, that languages vary greatly in their categorization of events at more intermediate positions along Dimension 1. Consider, for instance, the following three events, which are distributed from left to right along the spectrum of predictability: slicing a carrot with a knife (clip 10); cutting a carrot with a karate-chop hand movement (clip 32); and snapping a stick into two separate pieces (clip 19). The key question is how the second, intermediate event is treated cross-linguistically. Speakers of Chontal (isolate, Mexico) adopt one strategy, which is to refer to this event with the same verb that they use to name the first event, and apply a different verb to the third event (O'Connor, 2007). Speakers of Hindi (Indo-European, India), however, adopt the opposite approach, which is to use one verb to group the second event together with the third, and another verb to designate just the first (Narasimhan, 2007). Meanwhile, speakers of Jalonke (Niger-Congo, Guinea) opt for maximal differentiation, applying distinct verbs to all three events (Lüpke, 2007). Interestingly, it appears that none of the languages in the sample assigns the first and third events to one category and the second event to a different category. But this clearly makes sense, because such a strategy would violate the continuum of predictability.

To get an even better understanding of the breadth of cross-linguistic diversity that emerged in connection with Dimension 1, here are a few more examples (among many others that could easily be adduced). Dutch (Indo-European, Netherlands) has distinct verbs for cutting with a knife and cutting with scissors (Majid et al., 2007). Tidore (West Papuan, Indonesia) has distinct verbs for cutting with a large knife, cutting with a small knife, and cutting with scissors (van Staden, 2007). Lao (Tai Kadai, Laos) has distinct verbs for cutting with a placed blade and cutting with a moving blade (Enfield, 2007b). And Sranan (Creole, Surinam) has distinct verbs for separation events that produce clean fractures and those that produce messy ones, regardless of what kind of tool is used (Essegbey, 2007).

Compared to Dimension 1, Dimension 2 is much less consequential, since it simply reveals that the two clips showing an agent tearing cloth tend to be named differently than the other 59 clips. More precisely, this dimension derives from the fact that 10 of the 28 languages in the sample turned out to have a single verb that speakers applied exclusively to these two events. But what about the remaining 18 languages? All of them were found to have more general verbs that speakers used to group the two tearing events together with other events, albeit in variable ways. In one pattern, for instance, speakers of Sranan (Creole, Surinam), Tiriyó (Cariban, Brazil), and Yucatec (Mayan, Mexico) used the same verb to name not only the two events in which a piece of cloth is torn, but also two other events in which a piece of cloth is separated by a karate chop and a hammer blow (Majid et al., 2008). Furthermore, in an even broader grouping, speakers of Otomi (Otomanguean, Mexico) used just one verb to describe all sorts of separations of cloth, yarn, and rope by means of a knife, a chisel, a pair of scissors, or the agent's bare hands (Palancar, 2007).

Lastly, as indicated by the vertical axis in Figure 4.10, Dimension 3 distinguishes between two subsets of events that have, according to Dimension 1, a poorly predictable locus of separation: first, those that involve smashing things; and second, those that involve snapping them. The smashing cluster includes events in which an agent breaks a hard object into many fragments with a sudden blow, as in clip 40, which shows a person smashing a plate with a hammer. In contrast, the snapping cluster includes events in which an agent breaks a long, thin, rigid object into just two pieces, as in clip 25, which shows a person snapping a twig with two hands. As with Dimensions 1 and 2, however, cross-linguistic variation was observed for Dimension 3. Whereas speakers of some languages, like Ewe (Niger-Congo, Ghana) and Lipke (Niger-Congo, Ghana), reliably used distinct verbs to name smashing and snapping events (Ameka & Essegbey, 2007), speakers of other languages, like Hindi (Indo-European, India) and Tamil (Dravidian, India), consistently applied a general break-type verb to both clusters of clips (Narasimhan, 2007). Moreover, English speakers alternated between these two approaches, with some consultants using the specific verbs *smash* and *snap* and others using the more general verb *break* (Majid et al., 2008).

Now let's step back from all of these details and briefly review the main results of this typological investigation. First of all, languages tend to treat cutting and breaking events as a composite class that stands apart from opening events, most likely because the former events involve material destruction whereas the latter involve reversible separation. In addition, languages tend to categorize cutting and breaking events in recurrent ways that reflect a skeletal conceptual framework defined in terms of three primary dimensions. Dimension 1 distinguishes events according to the predictability of the locus of separation in the affected object, with cutting events falling toward the high end of the spectrum and breaking events falling toward the low end. Dimension 2 distinguishes events of tearing from all others. And finally, among breaking events— i.e., those in which the locus of separation is only weakly predictable—Dimension 3 distinguishes events of smashing from events of snapping. Another critical finding, however, is that even though there is substantial agreement across languages in the major dimensions along which cutting and breaking events are categorized, there is also a great deal of diversity in both the number of distinctions that are made and the placement of their boundaries.

To reinforce this important point about cross-linguistic variation, we will conclude by taking a quick look at some illuminating data from two other studies. First, Heath and McPherson (2009) argue that the Dogon languages—of which there are about 20 spoken in east-central Mali, West Africa—have a lexicalization strategy for action verbs that reflects a "cognitive set" of profiling manner and/or process rather than result and/or function. This strategy is manifested in many domains of action verbs, including those for breaking events, as shown in Table 4.8, which lists some

Table 4.8. A sample of breaking verbs in Jamsay (Dogon, Mali), organized as subclasses.

(a) break cleanly	
pé:ré	'break in half (long object, e.g., stick, bone, brick)'
	'break (cigarette), break apart (two joined objects)'
(b) break into pieces	
bèrèwé	'dismember (something) into pieces'
pójó	'granulate (something), break up, cause to crumble'
pógójó	'cause to explode, detonate'
(c) pick or break off an extremity or appendage	
pémé	'pick (grains, plant sprouts) one at a time by hand'
pó:	'pick (e.g., mangoes) one by one'
	'pick (fruit) from tree or plant'
	'pick (peanut pods)'
pé:	'break off (a protrusion on a stone, with a hammer)'
pújúró	'pick (cotton)'
pállá	'break (something soft, e.g., meat, bread) into pieces by hand'
Péllé	'break or cut off (a piece of something flat, e.g., fabric, leaf, paper)'
	'pick off, pull or break off (e.g., a leaf) by hand'
	'pick off (a small piece of a leaf, etc.) by hand'
púlló	'pull off (fruit, by pulling down with hooked pole)'
	'pick (peanut pods)'
	'snap, break (string, by pulling or biting)'
káráwá	'break off a piece of (something)'
túmúrⁿó	'break or cut off the end of (stick, arm, leg)'
téné	'break off, prune (flowering stem of onion, at its base, so the bulb will grow well'
(d) pick or strip off (many at once)	
tóró	'(somebody) strip off (leaves or fruits, from a branch, in one action)'
léréwé	'(animal) skim off (leaves, from a branch)'

From Heath & McPherson (2009, p. 47).

items from Jamsay, a representative Dogon language. Although the English glosses are, as the authors admit, rather simplistic, it is apparent that many of these verbs do in fact encode very idiosyncratic action concepts that focus on subtly different ways of irreversibly detaching or fragmenting objects—e.g., *pémé:* "pick (grains, plant sprouts) one at a time by hand"; *pállá* "break (something soft, e.g., meat, bread) into pieces by hand"; and *púlló* "pull off (fruit, by pulling down with hooked pole)."

The second study that warrants attention is Bowerman's (2005) brilliant comparison of English and Korean verbs for various kinds of opening events. As depicted in Figure 4.11, these two languages partition the same conceptual space in radically different ways, since English has a single generic verb, namely *open*, that groups together a wide range of events, whereas Korean has a whole arsenal of highly specific

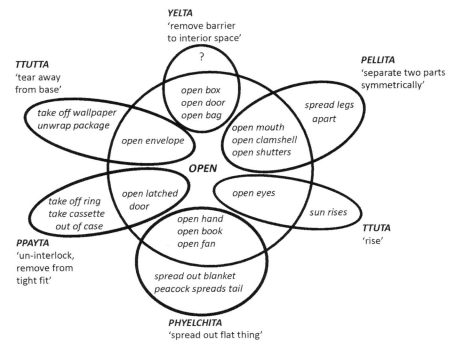

Figure 4.11. Cross-cutting classifications of opening events in English and Korean. Adapted from Bowerman (2005, p. 227).

verbs that distinguish between a variety of fine-grained categories—e.g., *pellita* "separate two parts symmetrically," which applies not only to opening one's mouth but also to spreading one's legs apart; *ttutta* "tear away from base," which applies not only to opening an envelope but also to taking off wallpaper; and *phyelchita* "spread out flat thing," which applies not only to opening a book but also to spreading out a blanket. As Bowerman (2005, p. 226) observes, "the conceptual glue that unifies, for example, 'opening a door,' 'opening the mouth,' 'opening an envelope,' and 'opening a book' for speakers of English seems to be missing [in Korean], and the domain is parceled out among a number of crosscutting categories that emphasize different aspects of the events."

Neurobiology

Because the conceptual domains of cutting, breaking, and opening are rather narrow, it is not surprising that, at least so far, only a few neuroscientific studies have explored them. However, there is now a large neuroscientific literature on the more general topic of object-directed arm/hand actions in peripersonal space, and it is quite relevant here, since the specific kinds of events that we are concerned about (especially cutting events) fall under this rubric. We will therefore begin by discussing the neural substrates of the observation, execution, and conceptualization of object-directed actions, including those that involve tool use. Then, after laying this foundation, we

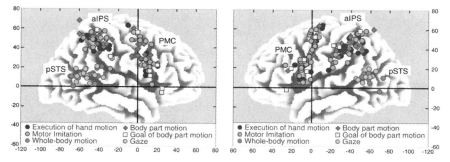

Figure 4.12. Peak activations from fMRI studies of the human mirror neuron system, plotted according to Talairach *y*-*z* coordinates. The posterior superior temporal sulcus (pSTS) is engaged during the visual perception of whole-body motion (green circles) and gaze direction (yellow circles), whereas the premotor cortex (PMC) and anterior intraparietal sulcus (aIPS)—which constitute what are traditionally regarded as the two main components of the mirror system—are recruited during the execution of hand actions (dark blue circles), the imitation of hand actions (light blue circles), the observation of hand, mouth, and foot actions (green diamonds), and the understanding of the immediate goals of perceived actions (red squares). A color version is in the color plates section. From Van Overwalle & Baetens (2009, p. 576).

will turn to the small but interesting set of studies that have concentrated on the cortical underpinnings of cutting, breaking, and opening events. Finally, we will conclude by considering how the typological findings described above provide a valuable cross-linguistic database that can potentially inspire and constrain further neuroscientific research on these conceptual domains.

It is well-established that, as shown in Figure 4.12, seeing people perform various kinds of object-directed arm/hand actions engages not only the LOTC, but also certain parietofrontal circuits that are essential for planning and executing the same kinds of behaviors (for meta-analyses, see Van Overwalle & Baetens, 2009; Caspers et al., 2010; Molenberghs et al., 2012). Because these circuits directly map observed actions onto the most closely matching motor programs in the perceiver's behavioral repertoire, they constitute the heart of the human mirror neuron system (for a review, see Rizzolatti et al., 2014). The literature on this system is much too complex to delve into here, but it's worth noting that despite a substantial amount of controversy (Hickok, 2014), there is mounting evidence that the system doesn't just respond to perceived actions, but actually facilitates and deepens their recognition and understanding (e.g., Avenanti et al., 2013; Urgesi et al., 2014; Palmer et al., 2016; Binder et al., 2017; Panasiti et al., 2017; see also Kemmerer, 2015d).

In this connection, let's return to the neuropsychological study by Kemmerer et al. (2012) that we first encountered in the previous section on motion events. Recall that these researchers investigated lesion-deficit relationships in 147 patients who were given six tasks that evaluated their knowledge of action concepts in a variety of verbal and nonverbal ways. Although these tasks did not employ a carefully controlled set of concepts for object-directed arm/hand actions, over two-thirds of the items did include concepts of this nature, exemplified by verbs like *scoop, fasten, load, wipe, polish, slap, punch, lift, fold, knit, scribble, whittle,* and *carve*. For this reason, it is especially interesting that, as shown in Figure 4.13, poor performance on four to six tasks

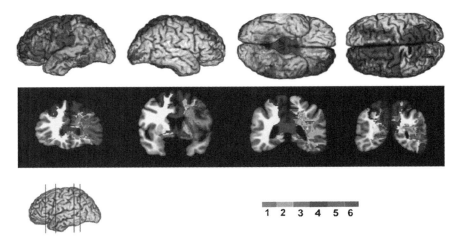

Figure 4.13. Lesion-deficit relationships in 147 brain-damaged patients who were given six tasks that evaluated their knowledge of action concepts in a variety of verbal and nonverbal ways. The color coding indicates, for every voxel, the total number of tasks for which poor performance was significantly related to damage at that site, according to a statistical mapping analysis. Dark gray shading indicates regions where there was insufficient data to obtain reliable results. Upper tier: From left to right, left lateral, right lateral, ventral, and dorsal views of the cortex. Lower tier: Four coronal sections along the planes indicated by the vertical lines on the brain shown below. A color version is in the color plates section.
From Kemmerer et al. (2012, p. 836).

was significantly linked with damage not only in the left LOTC (more specifically, the left pMTG/pSTS), but also in several sectors of the left parietofrontal circuits that comprise the mirror neuron system—in particular, the supramarginal gyrus (SMG), the inferior frontal gyrus (IFG), hand-related parts of the ventral premotor cortex (vPMC), and the white matter fiber tracts that interconnect these regions. Although the precise nature of the relationship between semantic cognition and the mirror neuron system is still unclear (for some preliminary proposals, see Kemmerer & Gonzalez-Castillo, 2010), these findings support the hypothesis that, in keeping with the sorts of grounded theories reviewed in Chapter 2, many concepts for object-directed arm/hand actions do depend on some of the same relatively high-level sensorimotor mechanisms that underlie the perception and production of such behaviors.

It is also worth highlighting the fact that many of the action concepts that were included in the six tasks imply the skilled use of tools (e.g., hammers, saws, forks, knives, spoons, needles, brushes, etc.). This is important because the pMTG, SMG, and vPMC have all been associated with various aspects of tool knowledge. Space limitations preclude a detailed summary of the vast literature on this topic, but one well-motivated approach, offered by Ramayya et al. (2010), is illustrated in Figure 4.14 and briefly described below (for other perspectives, see Johnson-Frey, 2004; Lewis, 2006; Binkofski & Buxbaum, 2013; van Elk et al., 2014; Reynaud et al., 2016; see also Figure 3.2 in Chapter 3). Besides representing some functional features of tools (Goldenberg & Spatt, 2009), the pMTG may store long-term records of their visual motion patterns (Beauchamp & Martin, 2007), and in a similar fashion it may also contribute to the

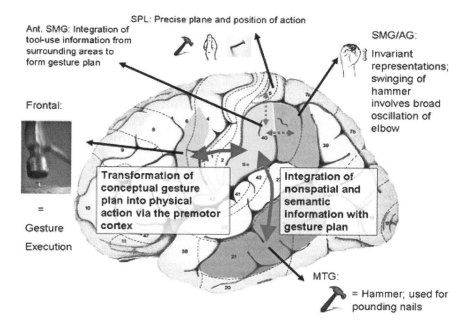

SPL: Precise plane and position of action

Ant. SMG: Integration of tool-use information from surrounding areas to form gesture plan

SMG/AG: Invariant representations; swinging of hammer involves broad oscillation of elbow

Frontal:

Transformation of conceptual gesture plan into physical action via the premotor cortex

Integration of nonspatial and semantic information with gesture plan

= Gesture Execution

MTG:

= Hammer; used for pounding nails

Figure 4.14. A neurobiological model of tool use. Following the abbreviation of each cortical area is a brief description of its putative function. Also, the solid, curved, double-headed arrows indicate long-distance fiber tracts, and their putative functions are briefly described in the adjacent boxes. A color version is in the color plates section.

Abbreviations: MTG = middle temporal gyrus; SMG = supramarginal gyrus; AG = angular gyrus; SPL = superior parietal lobule.

From Ramayya et al. (2010, p. 510).

preparation of tool-related actions by predicting their dynamic appearances (Gallivan et al., 2013; Tarhan et al., 2015). The posterior SMG, extending into the angular gyrus (AG), may contain invariant representations of proper tool use (e.g., swinging a hammer requires a broad oscillation of the elbow), and the anterior SMG may integrate these representations with those from the pMTG (and from other regions as well) to form multimodal gesture plans that specify how certain tools should be manipulated to causally affect target objects in certain ways (Vingerhoets, 2008; Orban & Caruana, 2014; Watson & Buxbaum, 2015; Chen et al., 2018; see also van Dam et al., 2012). Finally, the vPMC may convert these gesture plans into physical arm/hand motor programs for grasping and wielding tools appropriately (Saygin et al., 2004; Kan et al., 2006).

With these considerations in mind, let's shift to the small number of neuroscientific studies that have investigated the cortical underpinnings of cutting, breaking, and opening events. First of all, in the previous section on motion events, we discussed an fMRI study by Kemmerer et al. (2008) that aimed to elucidate how five classes of English verbs, as defined by Levin (1993), are implemented in the brain. In that section we concentrated on the class of Running verbs, but here we will focus on two other classes—namely, Cutting verbs and Change of State verbs. The experiment included 20 verbs of each type, and it is notable that 11 of the Change of State verbs belonged to the Breaking subclass.[11] As mentioned earlier, the task required close attention to subtle similarities and differences between the verbs in each class, since participants had to make fine-grained discriminations among triads of items—for instance, determining that *hack* is more like *chop* than *carve*, or that *tear* is more like *rip* than *crack*.

Based on grounded theories of conceptual knowledge, the researchers predicted that because Cutting verbs denote various kinds of object-directed arm/hand actions involving sharp instruments, they should engage some of the brain regions described above in relation to Figures 4.12, 4.13, and 4.14. As shown by the widely distributed cyan patches in Figure 4.6, this prediction was confirmed, since these verbs uniquely activated multiple parts of the LOTC, a potentially tool-related sector of the AG (similar to the one found by Ebisch et al., 2007), a cluster of voxels in the vPMC, and several large portions of the IFG. Furthermore, because Cutting verbs entail that the target objects are incised in certain ways (e.g., compare the outcomes denoted by *slit*, *gouge*, and *dice*), the researchers also predicted that they would activate at least one of the many ventral temporal regions that, as discussed in Chapter 3, represent the forms of entities, and this too was confirmed, since a small patch of the fusiform cortex did turn out to be engaged (though this is not visible in Figure 4.6). Actually, it is rather surprising that this activation wasn't more extensive, for the following reason. After surveying approximately 1,900 English verbs that either require or allow the thematic role commonly known as "instrument," Koenig et al. (2008, p. 175) concluded that these verbs "constrain the end states of the situations they describe more than they constrain the agent's initial activity."

With regard to Change of State verbs, although they activated the IFG, they did not recruit the more central parietofrontal circuits associated with object-directed arm/hand actions. Kemmerer et al. (2008) argue, however, that this makes sense because, strictly speaking, their most basic event structure template consists of a single-argument predicate which indicates that an entity shifts from one state or condition to another, as expressed by intransitive sentences like *The glass broke, The plate shattered*, and *The twig snapped* (Pinker, 1989; Levin & Rappaport Hovav, 1995; Kuno & Takami, 2004). Now, it is true that of the 20 Change of State verbs that were used in the fMRI study, a total of 15, including the 11 in the Breaking subclass, can also occur in transitive sentences with agentive subjects—i.e., sentences like *She broke the glass, She shattered the plate*, and *She snapped the twig*.[12] But this reflects the addition of a causal semantic component through a process that is sometimes called "template augmentation" (Rappaport Hovav & Levin, 1998; see also Dixon, 2000; Van Valin, 2005). Moreover, the idiosyncratic semantic features of these verbs do not indicate the particular kind of action that the agent executes to alter the state of the affected object; instead, they focus on different

---

[11] The 20 Cutting verbs were *snip, clip, cut, hack, scrape, scratch, slash, slit, gouge, gash, chop, dice, mince, grate, shred, slice, carve, grind*, and *sever*. The 11 verbs that fell within the Breaking subclass of the Change of State class were *break, shatter, smash, chip, crack, fracture, split, snap, rip, tear*, and *crumble*. And the other 9 Change of State verbs were *bend, fold, crease, crumple, bloom, blossom, sprout, wilt*, and *wither*.

[12] These are the kinds of sentences that English speakers might produce to describe some of the videoclips of breaking events in Majid and Bowerman's (2007) typological study.

types of object transformation.[13] For these reasons, Kemmerer et al. (2008) predicted that Change of State verbs would engage primarily the motion-related LOTC together with a shape-related ventral temporal area, and both of these expectations were met. Indeed, the specific ventral temporal region that was activated by these verbs was also activated by Cutting verbs, which supports the idea that it represents the various kinds of separations and fragmentations encoded by these two verb classes.

So far, no neuroscientific studies have directly investigated the linguistic representation of opening events; however, a recent fMRI study by Wurm and Lingnau (2015) used multivariate pattern analysis to examine the cortical underpinnings of different levels of generalization in action understanding, and because it focused specifically on the observation of opening events, it is quite pertinent here. While being scanned, the participants watched videoclips of a person opening and closing not only two kinds of bottles (one with a screw-cap requiring a twisting movement, and another with a cork requiring a pull/push movement), but also two kinds of boxes for cosmetics (again, one with a lid requiring a twisting movement, and another with a lid requiring a pull/push movement), and they pressed a button whenever an action was followed by an additional step, like moving, tilting, or lifting the object. The researchers then employed a clever method to find the brain regions that distinguish between opening and closing actions at different levels of generalization, from very concrete, to intermediate, to more abstract. To identify the neural substrates of the concrete level of understanding, they first trained a computer program called a "classifier" to discriminate between the activity patterns associated with opening and closing a specific bottle, and then they tested it with other trials involving the very same bottle. To identify the neural substrates of the intermediate level of understanding, they used the same classifier, but tested it with trials involving the second bottle. And to identify the neural substrates of the abstract level of understanding, they used the same classifier again, but tested it with trials involving a box. The main results were as follows. At the concrete level, opening and closing actions could be discriminated with a significant degree of accuracy by multivoxel activity patterns not only in the LOTC and SMG, but also in the vPMC; however, at the intermediate and abstract levels, they could only be discriminated by patterns in the LOTC and SMG.

Wurm and Lingnau (2015, p. 7727) argue that these findings "undermine" theories which maintain that the precentral motor cortices contribute to high-level action understanding. However, such a sweeping interpretation seems much too strong. As discussed earlier, numerous studies employing diverse brain mapping techniques have provided convergent evidence that these frontal regions, especially those with a rough somatotopic mapping, represent the body-part-specific motor features of verb meanings, or what one might call the semantics of kinematics (for reviews, see Kemmerer, 2015a, 2015c, 2015d, 2015e; see also Figures 4.8 and 4.13, as well as Figure 2.6 in Chapter 2 and the section of that chapter on flexible processing). And yet Wurm and Lingnau (2015) ignore this literature. Moreover, a bit of reflection about the nature of verb meanings may help to explain why these researchers failed to find any significant involvement of the precentral motor cortices in capturing the intermediate and abstract levels of action generalization in their study. The English verbs *open*

---

[13] In contrast, as shown in Table 4.8, some Dogon languages, like Jamsay, have many transitive breaking verbs that do specify the kinds of actions that agents typically perform to detach or fragment objects in certain ways.

and *close* belong to the class of Change of State verbs, and as mentioned earlier, most of these verbs focus much more on the kinds of transformations that entities undergo than on the kinds of actions that sometimes bring them about. Hence, the verbs in this class tend to lack the sorts of fine-grained motor features that have been hypothesized to rely on the precentral motor cortices. This clearly applies to *open* and *close*, since both of these verbs embrace an extremely wide range of actions. What's ironic is that Wurm and Lingnau's (2015) own stimuli demonstrate these weak motor constraints quite nicely by showing that the broad concepts of opening and closing can accommodate movements as kinematically different as twisting and pulling/pushing. In short, it is not surprising that the precentral motor cortices did not distinguish between opening and closing events at intermediate and abstract levels of generalization, since the relevant action concepts don't have the sorts of motor features that could fulfill this function.

Interestingly, Wurm et al. (2016) conducted another fMRI study using a similar experimental paradigm, only this time the two kinds of actions were cutting and peeling, and the two kinds of objects were apples and potatoes. Notably, for both kinds of objects, the two kinds of actions involved the same tool (a small knife) as well as the same hand postures and movements, so they differed only in whether the objects were separated through the middle, in the case of cutting, or along the underside of the surface, in the case of peeling. When the researchers looked for brain regions that could discriminate between cutting and peeling at a concrete level of generalization that was restricted to just one kind of object, they found significant involvement of the LOTC, anterior SMG (extending superiorly into the intraparietal sulcus [IPS]), and vPMC. But when they looked for brain regions that could discriminate between the two types of actions at an abstract level of generalization that included both kinds of objects, they found significant involvement of just the LOTC and anterior SMG/IPS.

These results are obviously analogous to those from the previous study, and once again the researchers interpreted them as challenging theories that ascribe an important role of the precentral motor cortices to high-level action understanding. In this instance, the criticism does seem to have sharper teeth, but there are still some problems. For one thing, it may be unreasonable to expect arm/hand-related frontal regions to consistently distinguish between the two sets of action stimuli, since the kinematics were deliberately identical. If instead the kinematics had been different, these brain regions might have been recruited more reliably. As with the previous study, however, the key issue is whether the two action concepts that are putatively under investigation—namely, those encoded by the verbs *cut* and *peel*—have body-part-specific motor features that are defined narrowly and distinctively enough to plausibly be subserved by the appropriate body-part-specific motor cortices. For many other action concepts—e.g., those encoded by the verbs *wink, chomp, shrug, pinch, kneel,* and *tiptoe*—there do seem to be fairly well-circumscribed motor features. Whether the same applies to *cut* and *peel* is less certain, however, especially for the former verb, since it has a very general meaning.[14] Now, this issue could, in principle, be fruitfully

---

[14] In fact, the meaning of *cut* is so general that, as we have seen, Levin (1993) picked this verb to head the whole class of Cutting verbs, and many other linguists, including Majid and Bowerman (2007), have also used it this way.

investigated in a manner that brings together careful semantic analysis and sophisticated neuroimaging technology. But even though Wurm et al. (2016) took some initial steps in this direction, unfortunately they didn't get very far.

On the other hand, a major strength of Wurm et al.'s (2016) study has to do with an important finding that was not mentioned above. When the subjects performed a task that required them to attend to the objects rather than the actions in the stimuli, the fusiform gyrus was among the brain regions that could distinguish between cutting and peeling at an abstract level of generalization. This is a valuable result because, as noted in the earlier discussion of Kemmerer et al.'s (2008) study, verbs like *cut* and *peel* focus a great deal on the kinds of physical transformations that objects undergo. In fact, as already indicated, apart from the nature of the objects (which was irrelevant to the abstract level of generalization), the only difference between the videoclips of cutting and peeling was whether the separations were medial or superficial, so it makes sense that this factor turned out to influence the neural discrimination of the two types of actions, specifically in the form-sensitive ventral temporal cortex.

Having reviewed some of the neuroscientific literature on object-directed arm/hand actions, as well as the small set of fMRI studies that have concentrated on events of cutting, breaking, and opening, it is time to bring the typological literature back into the picture. To begin with, let's recall that Majid et al.'s (2007, 2008) statistical analyses of naming data from 28 languages revealed not only that cutting and breaking events tend to be treated as belonging to a composite semantic space that stands apart from opening events, but also that this semantic space seems to be structured in terms of three main parameters: (1) a continuous dimension that reflects the predictability of the locus of separation in the affected object, such that cutting events fall toward the high end of the spectrum, whereas breaking events fall toward the low end; (2) a dichotomous dimension that isolates tearing events from other kinds of cutting and breaking events; and (3) another dichotomous dimension that distinguishes between two subclasses of breaking events—smashing and snapping (see again Figure 4.10). We do not yet know exactly how these three semantic parameters are implemented in the brain, but because the typological data strongly suggest that they delineate a universal, language-independent framework that both guides and limits the language-specific conceptualization of cutting and breaking events, they should be given serious consideration in future neuroscientific research on these domains.

With regard to Dimension 1, it is undoubtedly the case that for events along the cutting/breaking continuum, a variety of factors influence whether the locus of separation is fairly predictable, thereby favoring categorization as a kind of cutting (e.g., slicing, dicing, carving, etc.), or fairly unpredictable, thereby favoring categorization as a kind of breaking (e.g., shattering, cracking, crumbling, etc.). Surely, though, two of the most critical factors are as follows. First, high predictability is associated much more with events in which an agent uses a sharp instrument, like a knife, to incise an object in a precise manner than with events in which an agent uses a blunt tool, like a hammer, to destroy an object in a haphazard manner. And second, high predictability is also associated much more with events in which the affected object is firm but yielding, like a carrot, than with events in which it is either very rigid, like a porcelain plate, or very soft, like an egg yolk.

These two factors help to flesh out Dimension 1, and some of the neuroscientific findings reviewed earlier provide valuable clues about their probable cortical underpinnings. Starting with the first, action-related factor, observed events in which people carefully use sharp instruments to linearly separate objects are not only likely to be nonverbally categorized as kinds of cutting, but are also likely to trigger distinctive patterns of brain activity in multiple nodes of the network for tool-mediated actions, including the pMTG, the SMG/AG/IPS, and the vPMC, as well as the medial fusiform cortex, which represents the shapes of tools (see Figure 4.14 together with Figure 3.2 in Chapter 3). In contrast, observed events that involve other kinds of agentively or non-agentively caused fragmentations of objects are not only likely to be nonverbally categorized as kinds of breaking, but are also likely to trigger other patterns of activity in the same regions, or in subsets of them. Turning to the second, object-related factor, we saw in Chapter 3 that the physical compositions of entities are represented primarily in the ventral temporal cortex, and it is possible that within this large territory the neuronal population codes for cuttable things tend to be segregated from those for breakable things. This proposal is admittedly quite speculative, but it is encouraging to note that an fMRI study by Hiramatsu et al. (2011) showed that objects made of different materials (e.g., wood, cloth, glass, etc.) do elicit significantly different activity patterns in this brain region (see the discussion of this study in the section of Chapter 3 on the constitution parameter of nominal classification systems).

With regard to Dimensions 2 and 3—i.e., the distinction between tearing events and other kinds of cutting/breaking events, and the distinction between smashing and snapping subtypes of breaking events—it is reasonable to suppose that in both cases the pertinent categorical contrasts correspond, for the most part, to different activity patterns in the motion-sensitive LOTC and the form/constitution-sensitive ventral temporal cortex. However, parietofrontal circuits for object-directed arm/hand actions may also come into play to some degree—e.g., snapping actions often involve the symmetrical application of bimanual force to the opposite ends of long, thin, brittle objects, like wooden sticks.

These hypotheses regarding the neural correlates of Dimensions 1, 2, and 3 could be tested in the future with fMRI studies that employ multivariate techniques. An important but difficult challenge, however, would be to ensure that the imaging results genuinely reflect the universal framework for nonverbally categorizing cutting and breaking events, as opposed to language-specific representations for verbally categorizing them. After all, it is essential to bear in mind that different languages use the framework in different ways, giving rise to a great deal of diversity in both the number of lexical-semantic distinctions that are made and the placement of their boundaries.

To recapitulate, here are some of the most striking manifestations of the sorts of variation that we encountered in our earlier overview of the typological investigation spearheaded by Majid and Bowerman (2007). At the two extremes of complexity, the 61 clips of multifarious separations were named with as few as three verbs in Yélî Dnye (Papuan, Rossel Island), but as many as 23 in Tzeltal (Mayan, Mexico). Although most languages distinguish between ideal instances of cutting and breaking events (as reflected by Dimension 1), they treat intermediate cases inconsistently, and in doing so they often make rather subtle distinctions—e.g., between cutting with a knife and cutting with scissors (Dutch, Indo-European, Netherlands), between cutting with a large knife and cutting with a small knife

(Tidore, West Papuan, Indonesia), or between cutting with a placed knife and cutting with a moving knife (Lao, Tai Kadai, Laos). It is common for languages to devote one or more verbs exclusively to tearing events (as reflected by Dimension 2), but many languages employ more general verbs instead—a semantic strategy exemplified by Otomi (Otomanguean, Mexico), which has a single verb that encompasses all sorts of separations of cloth, yarn, and rope by means of a knife, a chisel, a pair of scissors, or the agent's bare hands. Similarly, while there is a strong tendency for languages to lexically distinguish between smashing and snapping events (as reflected by Dimension 3), there are numerous exceptions—e.g., Hindi (Indo-European, India) and Tamil (Dravidian, India) both apply a relatively superordinate break-type verb to these kinds of situations. Another notable point is that even though most languages treat cutting and breaking events as forming a conceptual sphere apart from opening events, some languages have verbs that straddle this boundary—e.g., the verb *thuuth* in Kuuk Thaayorre (Pama-Nyungan, Australia) groups cutting/breaking events like plucking an eyebrow together with opening events like removing the lid from a teapot. Finally, the realm of opening events is itself a conceptual kaleidoscope, since a close look at it reveals complex patterns that shift from language to language, as illustrated by the radically cross-cutting categorization schemes in English and Korean (see again Figure 4.11).

These typological differences are not just curiosities. They demonstrate that different speech communities habitually operate with different—indeed, sometimes dramatically different—systems for categorizing the same experiential domains of cutting, breaking, and opening. These unique systems can be thought of as language-specific semantic maps across universal conceptual spaces, and their equally unique neural implementations may consist of idiosyncratic representational geometries in the brain regions that we have been discussing. Exploring this possibility would be a worthy goal for future research, since even a bit of progress could help to illuminate the cortical underpinnings of cultural variability in action concepts.

EVENTS OF PUTTING AND TAKING

Typology

Another domain of action that has been studied in semantic typology consists of events in which people put things in places and take them away. There are several reasons why such events have attracted the attention of typologists. For one thing, they are fundamental, ubiquitous aspects of human experience, and their prominence in daily life is echoed by the fact that *put* and *take* are among the most frequently used verbs in English. In addition, this realm of human activity is conceptually intriguing because it builds directly on the simpler domain of motion that we discussed earlier, specifically by encompassing situations in which a volitional agent causes a figure object to either enter into or exit from some kind of contiguous spatial relation (e.g., containment, support, attachment) to a ground object. Recent typological research has revealed many interesting cross-linguistic similarities and differences in the lexical and grammatical encoding of placement and removal events. Here, however, we will shine our spotlight on just two lexical-semantic issues: first, the level of specificity with

Table 4.9. List of 20 languages included in a typological study of events of putting and taking.

Language	Affiliation	Location
≠Ākhoe Hai‖om	Khoisan	Namibia
Basque	Isolate	Spain
German	Germanic	Germany
Hindi	Dravidian	India
Hungarian	Finno-Ugric	Hungary
Jahai	Mon-Khmer	Malaysia
Japanese	Unclear	Japan
Kalasha	Indo-Iranian	Pakistan
Kuuk Thaatorre	Pama Nyungan	Australia
Lowland Chontal	Tequistlatecan	Mexico
Mandarin Chinese	Sino-Tibetan	China
Moroccan Arabic	Semitic	Morocco
Polish	Slavic	Poland
Romansh	Romance	Switzerland
Spanish	Romance	Spain
Swedish	Germanic	Sweden
German	Germanic	Germany
Tamil	Dravidian	India
Tzeltal	Mayan	Mexico
Yélî Dnye	Papuan	Rossel Island

Based on Kopecka & Naramsimhan (2012).

which these kinds of events are categorized by verbs; and second, the extent to which they are treated symmetrically.[15]

Both of these issues were addressed in a detailed typological investigation directed, once again, by the Max Planck Institute for Psycholinguistics, the results of which are reported in a volume edited by Kopecka and Narasimhan (2012; for other studies, see Gullberg, 2011, and Slobin et al., 2011). Speakers of 20 genealogically and geographically diverse languages, listed in Table 4.9, were asked to describe 60 short videoclips, each 3–4 seconds long. In designing these clips, the researchers started with the core event schemas that underlie the prototypical meanings of *put* and *take*—in particular, "deliberately placing an object somewhere or removing it from somewhere under agentive control" (Narasimhan et al., 2012, p. 5). But they also made a concerted effort

---

[15] Some of the grammatical-semantic aspects of putting and taking verbs, such as their argument structure properties, have also been investigated from a typological perspective, but we will ignore them here. For details, see Kopecka and Narasimhan (2012), and for a few neuroscientific studies that have addressed this topic, see Kemmerer (2000a), Kemmerer and Gonzalez-Castillo (2010), and Christensen & Wallentin (2011).

to create a wide range of scenes that varied in ways which, according to previous typological work, were likely to reflect the semantic parameters that are most relevant to the cross-linguistic representation of placement and removal events. These parameters were as follows:

- the nature of the figure
- the nature of the ground
- the nature of the final/original spatial relation between figure and ground
- the manner in which the figure moves
- the agent's use of tools
- the agent's degree of intentionality and control.

Beginning with the issue of lexical-semantic specificity, an important question is whether it is common for languages to have highly general verbs like *put* and *take*, which encode concepts that are so schematic that they do not distinguish between different kinds of placement and removal events. According to Kopecka and Narasimhan's (2012) survey, the answer is no. Although a few of the languages in the sample—most notably, Hungarian (Finno-Ugric, Hungary), Kalasha (Indo-Iranian, Pakistan), Hindi (Dravidian, India), and Tamil (Dravidian, India)—did turn out to have basic verbs like *put* and *take* that speakers applied to a broad array of scenes, the vast majority of languages did not. Instead, speakers of the latter languages preferred to use variably sized sets of more specific verbs that subdivide the semantic space of placement and removal events into smaller categories delineated largely in terms of the parameters listed above.

To get an initial sense of how much diversity was discovered, here are the two ends of a continuum defined by the number of separate verbs that consultants in each language used to describe the 60 clips. At the low end, 10 speakers of Yélî Dnye (Papuan, Rossel Island) used only 27 verbs to name all of the events, and 73% of their responses involved just six core verbs, which are discussed further below (Levinson & Brown, 2012). At the high end, however, 12 speakers of Tzeltal (Mayan, Mexico) used a grand total of 88 distinct verbs to name the very same stimuli (Brown, 2012).[16]

Some of the cross-linguistic differences in this conceptual domain are nicely illustrated in Figure 4.15, which shows how six placement events—not derived from the 60 clips, but still related to them—are customarily referred to in English, German, and Tzeltal (Slobin et al., 2011). Although English has many specialized subclasses of putting verbs (Levin, 1993), all of them fall under the semantic rubric of the single, maximally austere verb that heads the whole category, namely *put*, and in fact this verb is the default choice for describing all six scenes, since each one shows an object either being placed unceremoniously on a horizontal surface or being inserted loosely in a container.

In contrast, German adopts a different strategy in which causative postural verbs, analogous to *sit, stand*, and *lie*, are regularly used to describe certain kinds of placement events (Serra Borneto, 1996; Slobin et al., 2011; Berthele, 2012; interestingly, many

---

[16] Interestingly, we noted in the previous section that the same two languages were also at the low and high ends of a comparable continuum involving events of cutting, breaking, and opening.

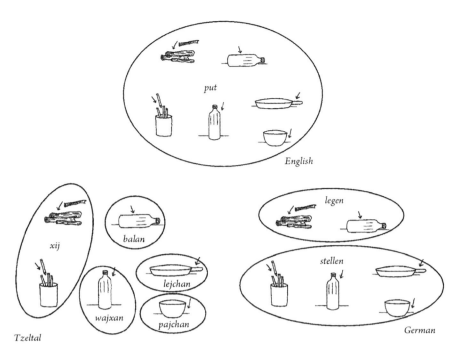

Figure 4.15. Cross-cutting classifications of the same six placement events in English, German, and Tzeltal.
Based on Slobin et al. (2011, pp. 153–154).

other languages adopt this strategy, too, as discussed by Newman, 2002; Lemmens, 2006; Viberg, 2006; Gullberg & Burenhult, 2012). The determination of which verb to use in a given situation depends primarily on a combination of geometric and functional factors, such as whether the figure's principal axis is oriented horizontally or vertically to the ground, and whether the figure has a base on which it typically rests. These sorts of factors dictate that *legen* "lie" is the most appropriate verb to describe two of the scenes in Figure 4.15, whereas *stellen* "stand" is the most appropriate verb to describe the other four.

Turning to Tzeltal, it employs yet another approach, one that takes into account even more fine-grained features of the figure and its induced spatial relation to the ground (Brown, 2012). As we first saw in Chapter 1, this language has over 250 elements that are known as dispositional predicates (for a cross-linguistic comparison of postural verbs and dispositional predicates, see Ameka & Levinson, 2007). They are derived from verb roots and provide rich information about the shapes, orientations, and configurations of objects, especially relative to each other. When Tzeltal speakers describe placement events, they typically use a construction that means "to cause relation X to come about," where the details of "relation X" are fleshed out by a particular dispositional predicate. Owing to the fact that many of these predicates encode a remarkable degree of spatial specificity, the six scenes in Figure 4.15 are described by no less than five separate predicates that make subtle distinctions not only between different kinds of objects (e.g., bowls, skillets, bottles, and stick-like things), but

Table 4.10. A sample of terms that speakers of Tzeltal (Mayan, Mexico) produced while describing 60 videoclips of placement and removal events.

Term	Gloss
lech/lejchan	'lie something down flat (nonflexible object)'
mejtzan	'put something lying on its side'
mojchan	'put something on its side, curved'
nujan	'set down inverted bowl-shaped thing'
pejchan	'put something 2D flat-lying'
suk	'insert stopper into tight fit, narrow opening'
tik'	'insert in container'
tujchan	'stand something long-thin vertically up'
t'uman	'put something (relatively small) into liquid so completely immersed'
mul koel	'immerse in water or granular objects'

From Brown (2012, p. 76).

also between different kinds of orientations (e.g., horizontal vs. vertical). Additional examples of Tzeltal placement concepts are provided in Table 4.10, which lists some of the responses that speakers gave to the standardized collection of 60 clips.

Kopecka and Narasimhan's (2012) survey uncovered a multitude of cross-linguistic similarities and differences in the meanings of putting and taking verbs, and these complex forms of patterned lexical-semantic variation involve all of the parameters listed earlier. In order to keep this review concise, however, we will just look briefly at a few more facets of the first three parameters—i.e., the nature of the figure, the nature of the ground, and the nature of the spatial relation between them. For instance, most of the languages in the sample have *pour*-type verbs which specify that the figure is a non-solid entity, but Polish takes this one step further by devoting distinct verbs to pouring liquids versus granular entities (Kopecka, 2012). It is also striking that Jahai (Mon-Khmer, Malaysia) has several highly specialized verbs for events in which the agent moves his/her own body parts to certain locations (Burenhult, 2012). Although the data are limited, it is clear that there are separate verbs for placing one's hand versus one's head somewhere; what's more, these verbs are sensitive to whether the given body part is inserted into the ground object or moved onto its horizontal surface.

Some other interesting results pertain to verbs for dressing. Many of the languages in the sample have such verbs, but they vary greatly in the specificity of the encoded concepts. For example, both Tzeltal (Mayan, Mexico) and Basque (isolate, Spain) have general dressing verbs that apply to all, or almost all, types of clothing (Brown, 2012; Ibarretxe-Antuñano, 2012). But Mandarin Chinese has separate verbs for dressing one's trunk versus one's extremities (Chen, 2012); ≠Ākhoe Hai‖om (Khoisan, Namibia) has separate verbs for putting on headgear, garments, and footwear (Rapold, 2012); and Jahai (Mon-Khmer, Malaysia) has an even more richly developed "donning" lexicon, with separate verbs for putting on a loincloth, girding a string around one's waist, putting a ring on one's finger, putting on a headband, adorning oneself with leaves, skewering an oblong object through one's hair, applying fat to one's face, and putting a porcupine's quill through one's septum (Burenhult,

Table 4.11. Symmetrical sets of postural putting and taking verbs in Yélî Dnye (Papuan, Rossel Island).

Putting Verbs	Taking Verbs
yé 'put sitting, put something down'	*ngî* 'take sitting, take something which sits'
kââ 'put standing, stand something up'	*y:oo* 'take standing, take something which stands'
t:oo 'put hanging, hang something up'	*ngee* 'take hanging, take something which hangs'

From Levinson & Brown (2012, p. 279).

2012). Not surprisingly, these verbs were not elicited by any of the clips, but were instead identified by Burenhult during his fieldwork with Jahai speakers. Additional cross-linguistic differences in verbs for dressing are described by Bowerman (2005).

Last but not least, we must address the question of whether languages tend to treat placement and removal events symmetrically. One of the most robust results of Kopecka and Narasimhan's (2012) typological investigation is that, even though these are converse behaviors, there is a strong propensity for languages to make more lexical-semantic distinctions between goal-oriented placement events than between source-oriented removal events. However, it turns out that this asymmetry is consistent with other data indicating that, compared to sources of movement, goals not only receive greater grammatical elaboration in languages worldwide (Ikegami, 1987), but also receive more attention from both adults and infants (Regier & Zheng, 2007; Lakusta et al., 2007).

At the same time, though, it is notable that Kopecka and Narasimhan's (2012) survey disclosed a major exception to this cross-linguistic bias toward asymmetry. As mentioned earlier, in Levinson and Brown's (2012) study of putting and taking verbs in Yélî Dnye (Papuan, Rossel Island), a whopping 73% of the 10 consultants' naming responses consisted of just six core verbs. These items are shown in Table 4.11, which indicates that they actually form two perfectly symmetrical triads of monomorphemic postural predicates. One triad specifies whether a placed object canonically "sits," "stands," or "hangs," and the other specifies whether a removed object canonically "sits," "stands," or "hangs."[17] In addition, analyses of the remaining 27% of the responses revealed that even though some of the clips were described with more precise goal-oriented putting verbs, most of these items had corresponding source-oriented taking verbs with equivalent semantic granularity. This kind of parity, with closely matching divisions of the placement subdomain and the removal subdomain, appears to be rather rare.

[17] Canonical object postures in Yélî Dnye are, for the most part, conventional and not always intuitive, as shown by the following examples: "a plate or bowl 'stands' on a table, people 'sit' but animals 'stand,' and a shoe 'hangs' on someone's leg, the sun 'sits' but the moon 'hangs'" (Levinson & Brown, 2012, p. 276). For novel objects, however, the choice of a postural verb depends, as in German and other languages, on geometric and functional factors.

Neurobiology

The cortical underpinnings of putting and taking verbs have not yet been carefully explored in any language—not even in English. Still, the typological findings described above do appear to have some interesting theoretical implications for neuroscientific research on action concepts, and these implications could potentially be tested in future studies. As we have seen, much of the cross-linguistic diversity in the lexical encoding of placement and removal events does not involve their dynamic aspects— i.e., the agentively instigated and controlled movements of figure objects to and from ground objects—but instead involves their static aspects—i.e., the inherent properties of the figure and ground objects themselves, and the nature of the final/original spatial relation between them. Hence, the brain regions that are most relevant to this cross-linguistic diversity are not those that have traditionally been associated with action concepts—i.e., the motion-related LOTC and certain motor-related parietofrontal circuits—but rather those that contribute to the semantic representation of objects and static spatial relations—i.e., the ventral temporal cortex (see Chapter 3) and the inferior parietal lobule (see Chapter 5). These points are developed below.

As just suggested, because much of the typological variation in the meanings of putting and taking verbs involves the inherent properties of figure and ground objects, it is reasonable to suppose that these cross-linguistic differences depend, for the most part, on the ventral temporal cortex, together with a few other object-related brain regions. To elaborate this proposal, let's return to the six placement events shown in Figure 4.15. Whereas English speakers tend to name all of them with the generic, object-neutral verb *put*, Tzeltal speakers usually refer to them in more nuanced ways by using several fine-grained, object-sensitive verbs that discriminate between figures with bottle-like, bowl-like, skillet-like, and stick-like shapes (see also Table 4.10). According to the hypothesis under consideration here, although both groups of speakers have category-specific representations for these kinds of objects in the functional topographies of their ventral temporal cortices, English speakers do not incorporate them directly into the meanings of putting verbs, but Tzeltal speakers do. Similarly, we observed that while some languages (e.g., English) lack specialized verbs for dressing, others (e.g., Mandarin Chinese, ≠Ākhoe Hai‖om, and Jahai) have dedicated "donning" lexicons that vary in complexity, with different sets of verbs specifying the placement of particular kinds of clothing, jewelry, and other ornaments on particular body parts. As before, the basic idea regarding the neural substrates of such concepts is as follows. Across all cultures, the shapes of the various kinds of things that people don are represented primarily in the ventral temporal cortex, and the shapes of the body parts that they are applied to are represented primarily in and around the EBA; however, in some languages but not others, certain pairs of these two types of cortical object representations are prescribed as filling the figure and ground slots of certain putting verbs. Yet another conjecture— one that complements those just offered—is that higher-level transmodal brain regions, including but not necessarily limited to the ATL, are essential for capturing the language-specific integrative patterns that determine which kinds of conceptual components are systematically conjoined to form the meanings of putting verbs.[18]

---

[18] This proposal is analogous to one formulated earlier in this chapter, near the end of the section on motion events.

We also noted earlier that a great deal of the typological variation in the meanings of putting and taking verbs has to do with the final/original spatial relation between figure and ground objects. For example, looking once again at Figure 4.15, it can be seen that in both Tzeltal and German, but not in English, speakers tend to use different verbs to describe events in which an agent places a bottle upright versus sideways on a horizontal surface. Moreover, in German and many other languages, the relevant verbs are causative postural predicates that mean, basically, "to put in a standing position" and "to put in a lying position." (As indicated earlier, these kinds of languages often have one or more additional terms meaning "to put in a sitting position" and/or "to put in a hanging position.") What is the neurobiological basis of this cross-linguistically common, but far from universal, process of anthropomorphically projecting canonical human body postures onto inanimate entities? More specifically, what sorts of cortical representations and computations underlie the selection of particular postural verbs in particular referential situations? With respect to the two events involving the bottle in Figure 4.15, in order for a German speaker to correctly choose *stellen* in one case and *legen* in the other, he or she must not only identify the principal axis of the bottle, but also determine its orientation relative to the supporting surface. A single-cell recording study in rhesus monkeys suggests that the intrinsic axes of objects are stored in the ventral temporal cortex together with other geometric features (Hung et al., 2012), and a number of neuropsychological studies and fMRI studies in humans suggest that the orientations of objects are computed in the posterior parietal cortex, especially in the right hemisphere (Turnbull et al., 1995, 1997; Karnath et al., 2000; Harris et al., 2001; Valyear et al., 2006; Martinaud et al., 2016). These findings provide a few hints about the neural substrates of postural verb use, but they are only indirectly related to this topic. For instance, the data on orientation judgments are limited by the fact that all of the studies just cited involve an egocentric, viewer-based frame of reference; in contrast, the kinds of orientation judgments that German speakers must make in order to select appropriate postural verbs usually involve an allocentric, object-based frame of reference, because what matters is the angle of the figure relative to the ground, not relative to the viewer. Perhaps, though, cognitive neuroscientists will soon begin to directly investigate the cortical underpinnings of postural verbs. After all, these terms are used quite frequently in German and other languages, like Swedish, whose speakers are readily available for research purposes.

SERIAL VERB CONSTRUCTIONS

Typology

In the three previous sections, we concentrated on the lexical encoding of particular domains of action concepts, addressing them from both typological and neurobiological perspectives. Now, in this section and the next, we turn our attention to two grammatically based strategies of event representation that, while not restricted to particular domains, are nonetheless relevant to cognitive neuroscience because they differ in several ways from the strategies that are typically used in English and in most of the other languages that have dominated research on the neural substrates of conceptual knowledge. Specifically, this section deals with serial verb constructions, and the next one deals with verbal classification systems.

Serial verb constructions (SVCs) are well-documented in languages across much of the globe, including Africa, Southeast and East Asia, Indonesia, Papua New Guinea, Australia, Oceania, and the Americas (Lefebvre, 1991; Durie, 1997; Crowley, 2002; Aikhenvald & Dixon, 2006; Senft, 2008; Bisang, 2009; Foley, 2010; Haspelmath, 2016; Aikhenvald, 2018a). Although SVCs are manifested in many diverse ways, they have the following properties in common (Haspelmath, 2016):

- two or more verbs, each of which can in principle occur independently, co-occur in a single clause without being connected by a formal linking element
- they share at least one argument, usually either an agent or a patient
- they have the same values for tense, aspect, mood, affirmative/negative polarity, and spatial/temporal modification, all of which are expressed by elements that either precede the first verb or follow the last verb
- they are pronounced with a single intonation contour, like single-verb clauses
- when they jointly encode a causal or sequential chain, they occur in a tense-iconic order, such that the verb expressing the cause or the earlier event precedes the verb expressing the effect or the later event

Like most other familiar European languages, English lacks fully productive SVCs, but it does allow a limited number of "quasi-SVCs" in imperatives and a few other environments, as illustrated by sentences like *Go get the milk* and *Come eat with me* (Pullum, 1990). Some examples of genuine SVCs in languages that regularly employ them are shown below (Haspelmath, 2016):

Nêlêmwa-Nixumwak (Austronesian, New Caledonia)

I	*fuk*	*ulep*	*daxi*	*ni*	*fwaa-mwa*
3SG	fly	cross.threshold	up.away	in	hole-house

"It flies into the house."

Tariana (North Arawak, Brazil)

nhuta	*nu-thaketa-ka*	*di-ka-pidana*
1SG.take	1SG-cross.CAUS-SUBORD	3SG-see-REM.PST

"He saw that I took it across."

White Hmong (Hmong-Mien, Southwestern China)

nws	*xuab*	*riam*	*txiav*	*nqiaj*	*qaib*
3SG	grasp	knife	cut	meat	chicken

"She cut some chicken meat with a knife." (Literally: "She took a knife she cut chicken meat.")

SVCs are quite interesting from a semantic perspective because they bear directly on the question of what constitutes a unitary conceptual event. In fact, much of the literature on SVCs has focused on this issue. Unlike concrete objects such as cats and dogs, most events in the world do not have clear-cut boundaries; instead, they must be mentally segmented and packaged by the creatures that perceive them. Needless to say, this has significant implications for how people talk about events. As Foley (2010,

p. 84) observes, "Just how the tangled unindividuated stream of events gets reported in inventories and sequences of linguistic expressions, prototypically verbs, is subject to a great deal of cross-linguistic variation. . . ." He goes on to elaborate this point by comparing the different ways in which several New Guinea languages express the concept encoded by the English verb *kill*, and his analysis is well worth summarizing here, since it clearly reveals how SVCs explicitly represent the sub-events of complex events in a compact fashion that treats them as parts of a larger whole.

Foley begins by showing that the concept encoded by *kill* can be decomposed as follows, using the approach proposed by Rappaport Hovav and Levin (1998):

$$[[x \, ACT_{<MANNER>} \, CAUSE \, [BECOME \, [y_{<DEAD>}]]]]$$

According to this formula, *kill* means that someone/something (x) performs an action in some manner, and this action causes someone/something (y) to become dead. Next, Foley notes that one New Guinea language, namely Yimas, also encodes the notion "kill" with a single monomorphemic verb root:

> Yimas (Lower Sepik, Papua New Guinea)
>
> *namot* *numpran* *na-mpu-tu-t*
>
> man.PL   pig.SG   3SG.OBJ-3.PL.SUBJ-kill-PERF
>
> "The men killed the pig."

But then he points out that another New Guinea language called Numbami expresses the same notion in an SVC that contains two separate but cohesively integrated verbs, with *lapa* "hit" encoding the causing event and *uni* "dead" encoding the resulting state:

> Numbami (Austronesian, Papua New Guinea)
>
> *kolapa* *i-lapa*   *bola* *uni*
>
> boy   3SG.REALIS-hit   pig   dead
>
> "The boy killed the pig."

Importantly, the meaning of *lapa* "hit" has been grammaticalized so that it denotes any act of killing, regardless of whether it involves clubbing, stabbing, shooting, or some other method. The reason this matters is because it implies that the sequence *lapa uni* "hit dead" "represents a lexicalization for 'kill,' albeit one in an SVC rather than a monomorphemic verb root as in Yimas, but still a unique lexical item" (Foley, 2010, p. 85).

Moving on to Watam, which is yet another New Guinea language, Foley demonstrates that it does not really have a single, monomorphemic or multimorphemic lexical item for "kill"; instead, it encodes this notion in numerous SVCs, each of which denotes a different type of killing, as shown in the following examples:

Watam (Lower Sepik, Papua New Guinea)

- *rug minik*—hit die
- *wak minik*—sever die

- *rutki minik*—slash die
- *rutki yak minik*—slash cut.open die
- *arig minik*—shoot die
- *arig turka minik*—shoot pierce die
- *mo minik*—do die

These SVCs are similar, at least in content, to English expressions like *They pummeled/hacked/knifed/shot him to death*. But as some of the examples indicate, when a speaker wants to convey even more information about the manner of killing, he or she can expand the SVC from two to three elements; and conversely, when a speaker wants to omit manner information entirely, he or she can use the default SVC *mo minik* "do die," which leaves the causing event unspecified but is still a two-element expression and hence no more basic than the others. As Foley (2010, p. 86) observes, in this language "there is no fixed sequence of lexemes covering the semantic range of 'kill,' but rather strings productively produced by syntactic rules." It is notable, however, that even though these SVCs are semantically and syntactically flexible in the ways just described, they always treat the designated complex events as unitary, since they are monoclausal, susceptible to full scopal coverage by various operators (e.g., tense, mood, negation), and consistently pronounced with a single intonation contour.

Other findings provide further evidence that, in general, SVCs unpack complex events while still representing them as conceptually coherent and tight-knit. For instance, this point is nicely illustrated by the difference between the two sentences from Taba (Austronesian, Indonesia) shown below:

Taba (Austronesian, Indonesia)

n=babas	*welik*	*n=mot*	*do*
3SG=bite	pig	3SG=die	REALIS

  "It bit the pig dead."

n=babas	*welik,*	*n=ha-mot*	*i*
3SG=bite	pig,	3SG=CAUS-die	3SG

  "It bit the pig and killed it."

The first sentence contains an SVC, and it entails that the pig's death is "a direct and immediate consequence of the pig's being bitten" (Bowden, 2001, p. 297). In contrast, the second one contains coordinated clauses separated by a pause, and it allows for the possibility that the pig's death occurred after "a considerable period of time" and was "a quite indirect consequence of having been bitten," such as having eventually resulted from blood loss (Bowden, 2001, p. 297; see also Croft, 2012, p. 348).

Likewise, the following sentences from Lao (Tai Kadai, Laos) could both refer to the same real-world scenario, but the first one uses an SVC and hence portrays the temporally sequenced activities as segments of an overarching unitary event, whereas the second one uses separate, overtly linked clauses and hence portrays the very same activities as being quite distinct from each other. According to Enfield (2015b, p. 112),

"The difference in description is one of conceptual closure. In [the first sentence] they are component events of a single conceptual event, while in [the second one] they are each separate events in themselves."

Lao (Tai Kadai, Laos; numbers signify tones)

- *laaw2*   *paj3*   *talaat5*   *sùù4*   *khùang1*   *maa2*
  3SG   go   market   buy   stuff   come
  "S/he has come (here) from going and buying stuff at the market."
  (Or: "S/he has been to the market and bought stuff.")

- *laaw2*   *paj3*   *talaat5*   *lèka*   *sùù4*   *khùang1*   *lèka*   *maa2*
  3SG   go   market   LINKER   buy   stuff   LINKER   come
  "S/he went to the market, and then bought stuff, and then came (here)."

Furthermore, by drawing on data involving co-speech manual gestures in Avetime (Kwa, Ghana), Defina (2016) obtained additional support for the view that SVCs encode unitary conceptual events. In particular, she found that SVCs tend to occur with single gestures that are closely aligned with the boundaries of those constructions, whereas other kinds of complex clauses tend to occur with multiple gestures that coincide with separate verbs.

There is, however, an intriguing constraint on SVCs, which is that in many languages they can only be applied to events that are publicly recognized as familiar, natural, or typical, and therefore part of the cultural common ground (Bruce, 1988; Durie, 1997; Enfield, 2015b). For example, in White Hmong (Hmong-Mien, Southwestern China) the SVC in the first sentence shown below is perfectly acceptable because "whenever the *qeej* 'bamboo pipe' is played, the performer's feet and body move and sway in time to the music. Playing and dancing are not two events but one" (Jarkey, 1991, p. 170; quoted by Durie, 1997, p. 329). In contrast, the SVC in the second sentence is regarded as ungrammatical because dancing and listening to music are conventionally construed as distinct events. Hence, they must be expressed by separate coordinated clauses, as in the third sentence.

White Hmong (Hmong-Mien, Southwestern China)

- *nws*   *dhia*   *tshov*   *qeej*
  3SG   dance   blow   bamboo.pipes
  "He dances playing the pipes."

- *nws   *dhia*   *mloog*   *nkauj*
  3SG   dance   listen   song
  "He dances listening to music."

- *nws*   *dhia*   *thiab*   *mloog*   *nkauj*
  3SG   dance   and   listen   song
  "He dances and listens to music."

Finally, this brief overview of SVCs would not be complete without mentioning that some of the most fascinating discoveries derive from an extraordinary language called Kalam (Trans-New Guinea, Papua New Guinea; Pawley, 1987, 1993, 2008, 2011). As noted in Chapter 1, this language only has about 130 verb roots, and they are routinely serialized to express complex events. Two different types of SVCs have been distinguished. First, "compact SVCs" capture complex events whose constituent sub-events tend to be temporally close and causally connected. Over 500 such constructions have been recorded, and they fall into a variety of classes according to their semantic and syntactic makeup. Table 4.12 provides some examples from the classes for transfer/connection events, transporting events, and resultative or change of state events. As can be seen, most compact SVCs contain just two verb roots, but some have three or more.

Second, "narrative SVCs" squeeze into a single clause a long series of verb roots—indeed, up to nine or ten—so as to reduce an entire plot to its minimal components. As Pawley (2011, p. 29) notes, "narrative SVCs tell a short story, or parts of a story, in highly compressed form." They, too, fall into many classes, one of the largest of which involves successful collecting episodes. Such episodes have five main stages: (1)

Table 4.12. Examples of three classes of compact serial verb constructions (SVCs) in Kalam (Trans-New Guinea, Papua New Guinea).

A. SVCs Denoting Transfer/Connection Events

ag ñ-	say transfer	'tell something to someone'
d jak ñ-	get stand connect	'stand something against a place'
d ñ-	get transfer	'give something to someone personally (e.g., by hand)'
g ñ-	do transfer	'fit something in position, connect to something'
ju ñ-	withdraw transfer	'return something to its owner, give back'

B. SVCs Denoting Transporting Events

d ap-	get come	'bring something'
d am-	get go	'take something'
d am yok-	get go move.away	'get rid of something, take something away'
d ap tan-	get come ascend	'bring something up, fill something'
d ap tan jak-	get come rise reach	'bring something to the top, fill something up'

C. SVCs Denoting Resultative or Change of State Events

pak cg-	strike adhere	'stick something on, cause something to adhere'
pak wk-	strike shattered	'knock something to bits, shatter something'
pak sug-	strike extinguished	'put out'
taw pag yok-	step.on broken displace	'break something off by stepping on it'
tb kluk yok-	cut gouge displace	'gouge something out'

From Pawley (2011, pp. 28–29).

movement to the scene of collecting; (2) collecting; (3) transport to the scene of processing; (4) processing; and (5) coda (e.g., sleeping or going home). Although some narrative SVCs only encode a few consecutive stages of a successful collecting episode, many encode all five. For instance, in the following sentence, the first verb (*am* "go") encodes stage 1; the second (*pu* "hit"), third (*wk* "smash"), and fourth (*d* "get") encode stage 2; the fifth (*ap* "come") encodes stage 3; the sixth (*agi* "ignite") encodes stage 4; and the seventh (*kn* "sleep") encodes stage 5:

Kalam (Trans-New Guinea, Papua New Guinea)

kik	*am*	*mon*	*pu*-*wk*	*d*	*ap*	*agi*	*kn*-ya-k
they	go	wood	hit-smash	get	come	ignite	sleep-3PL-PAST

It can be seen, however, that all of these verbs are very short, so the whole sequence can easily be uttered within a single intonation contour. A rough English translation of the sentence would necessarily be much longer and probably require several clauses, as in "They went and gathered firewood and brought it, made a fire, and slept" (Pawley, 2011, p. 16). Despite their remarkable semantic density, narrative SVCs represent complex events as unitary, just like compact SVCs and the other kinds of SVCs discussed earlier. In fact, Pawley (2011) points out that Kalam speakers use them when they do *not* want to individuate the discrete stages of episodes or elaborate on their details, but instead want to portray them as cohesive parts of a larger situation.

Neurobiology

As with events of putting and taking, there has not yet been any neuroscientific work that directly addresses SVCs. These sorts of complex predicates are still quite relevant, however, to research on how our brains perceive and conceptualize actions. The following discussion provides some support for this claim by focusing on two related issues: first, the segmentation of experiences into coherent events; and second, the binding of multifarious conceptual features into "chunked" representations.

Regarding the first issue, a small but growing literature has been documenting how people segment continuous streams of information into discrete events at multiple timescales and hierarchical levels (for reviews, see Kurby & Zacks, 2008; Radvansky & Zacks, 2014; Richmond & Zacks, 2017). For instance, an activity like brushing one's teeth can easily be viewed as a bounded event, but it can also be seen as consisting of several shorter and more fine-grained sub-events (e.g., putting toothpaste on the toothbrush, moving it to one's mouth, etc.); in addition, it can be construed as just one stage of a longer and more overarching macro-event (e.g., getting ready for work). A number of fMRI studies have investigated the neural substrates of event segmentation by first presenting participants with movies or narratives and then identifying the brain regions in which significant changes in signal strength correspond to subjectively recognized transitions between events (Zacks et al., 2001, 2010; Speer et al., 2007; Whitney et al., 2009; Baldassano et al., 2015; Zadbood et al., 2017; see also Hasson et al., 2015). Interestingly, these studies suggest that as events increase in temporal duration and hierarchical level, they are segmented by brain regions that lie further along the cortical continuum extending from peripheral sensory/motor systems up to the highest transmodal hubs, where the greatest effects have been found in certain lateral and medial parietal areas—in particular, the angular gyrus and the territory comprising the posterior cingulate gyrus, precuneus, and retrosplenial cortex.

How do SVCs fit into this picture? We argued earlier that they encode unitary conceptual events, and if this is really the case, their boundaries should elicit, in representationally appropriate brain regions, the types of shifts in neural dynamics that have been associated with event segmentation. For instance, SVCs for relatively small-scale events, like the fixed expression for "kill" in Numbami (i.e., *lapa uni* "hit dead") and the hundreds of compact SVCs in Kalam (see again Table 4.10), can be expected to trigger neural markers for event segmentation at low to mid points along the cortical continuum just mentioned, whereas SVCs for relatively large-scale events, like the Lao example given earlier (i.e., the one containing the integrated sub-events of going to the market, buying things, and returning) and the various kinds of narrative SVCs in Kalam, would be more likely to evoke such effects at mid to high points. Moreover, it seems reasonable to predict that when an SVC is contrasted with an expression that encodes similar content but in separate, coordinated clauses (as in the minimal pairs from Taba and Lao discussed earlier), the following results should be observed regarding neural markers for event segmentation. Although both constructions should elicit a marker at the end, the one for the SVC should be stronger and at a somewhat higher level of the cortical continuum than the one for the coordinate construction. Additionally, the coordinate construction should elicit a marker after each internal clause, and while the SVC might also elicit such markers for sub-events, they should be weaker than those in the coordinate construction. Now, these proposals are obviously quite speculative, but they have the virtue of being testable, and in any case their main purpose is simply to stimulate interest in examining more closely the relevance of SVCs to neuroscientific research on event segmentation. After all, the primary communicative function of these typologically unique linguistic devices is to allow speakers to portray events as being conceptually unitary, regardless of their duration or degree of internal complexity.

SVCs are also pertinent to the second issue referred to above—namely, the binding of disparate experiential attributes into holistic concepts. It appears that in many languages a large proportion of SVCs are not computed "on the fly," but are instead retrieved from long-term memory as precompiled items whose meanings are intricate yet more or less fixed. Even the knotty narrative SVCs in Kalam are based on deep-seated templates for multi-stage episodes. It therefore seems justifiable to assume that, in general, SVCs place heavy demands on the integrative mechanisms that form distilled or chunked conceptual representations—i.e., representations that glue together the multifarious semantic features that are often widely distributed across sensory, motor, and affective systems. We have already noted at several points in this book that these integrative mechanisms reside in transmodal hubs, with the ATL playing an especially important role. For instance, it is well-established that as the featural complexity of concepts increases, patients with semantic dementia, who suffer from ATL atrophy, perform progressively worse (Lambon Ralph & Patterson, 2008). These considerations suggest that the ATL may be critical for conjoining the conceptual components of SVCs and that, as a consequence, it may be recruited with increasing intensity as these components increase in number. Furthermore, depending on their content, some of the action concepts encoded by SVCs may also rely on certain sectors of the prefrontal cortex that have been implicated in "structured event complexes," which are long-term records of the types of characters, objects, settings, and social and emotional properties of various kinds of temporally sequenced, hierarchically organized activities, such as going out to dinner, shopping for groceries, and doing the laundry (for a review, see Grafman & Krueger, 2009). As before, these are testable hypotheses, but their main purpose here is simply to encourage other scholars to begin thinking about, and perhaps even investigating, the many ways in which SVCs can inform contemporary research on the neural substrates of action concepts.

VERBAL CLASSIFICATION SYSTEMS
Typology

Although nominal classification systems have been extensively studied (see Chapter 3), verbal classification systems, which are similar in some respects, have not been examined in nearly as much depth. Still, the literature on this topic has been growing, and a substantial amount has been learned about such systems in Northern Australian languages, where they are quite common (Capell, 1979; Wilson, 1999; McGregor, 2002, 2006, 2013; Schultze-Berndt, 2000, 2006, 2017; see also Baker & Harvey, 2010).

In these languages, the verb lexicon contains two separate classes of items. First, there is a relatively small set of so-called "generic" verbs (also known as "inflecting verbs") that encode very schematic types of events and are obligatorily tagged with pronominal affixes and tense/aspect/mood markers. Although this class is always closed, its size varies greatly across languages, ranging from just six in Malak-Malak to several hundred in some of the Worrorran and Nyulnyulan languages. On average, however, there are typically between 20 and 40 members, and even in those languages with much larger numbers of items, usually only about 10 or 20 participate in the kind of complex predicate formation described below. The second class consists of so-called coverbs (also known as "preverbs"). They are open-ended and express a wide variety of specific event-related meanings, but they cannot take any inflections.

In ordinary discourse, every finite clause must include a generic verb, which implies that speakers must constantly keep track of how events should be categorized according to the coarse-grained concepts encoded by the generic verbs in their language. Although these generic verbs are sometimes used on their own, they are often combined with one or more coverbs to form complex predicates that simultaneously represent events at two different levels of abstraction—one fairly austere, and the other more elaborate. For instance, in the following sentence, which is from Jaminjung (Mirndi, Australia), the generic verb (highlighted with a double underline) is *jga* "go," and the preceding coverbs (highlighted with a single underline) are *yugung* "run," which expresses a particular manner of motion, and *walig* "around," which expresses a particular path (Schultze-Berndt, 2006, p. 83):

jalig=malang	*yugung*	*walig*	*ga-jga-ny=nu*
child=GIVEN	run	around	3SG-go-PST=3SG.OBL

"the child ran around for him"

Importantly, the generic verb in this example can also combine with many other manner of motion coverbs (glossed roughly as "walk," "fly," "jump," "roll," "crawl," "stagger," "limp," "wade," "swim," "sneak," etc.) and many other path coverbs (glossed roughly as "go back and forth," "take a turnoff," "go past a point or through a volume," "keep going in the same direction," etc.) (Schultze-Berndt, 2006, pp. 92–93). What this shows is that generic verbs have a classificatory function not only with respect to the extra-linguistic world of events, but also with respect to the intra-linguistic world of coverbs.

In addition, it is notable that while there is, not surprisingly, some cross-linguistic variation in the content of the schematic event concepts encoded by generic verbs, there is also a great deal of consistency. This was demonstrated by McGregor (2002), who investigated 33 Northern Australian languages with verbal classification systems and found that most of them have inventories of generic verbs that include the following 14 items, indexed here by rough English glosses: "sit/be," "stand," "fall," "put," "become," "go," "carry," "catch/get," "hit," "poke," "throw," "say/do," "give," and "see." These glosses are definitely informative, but they should be taken with a grain of salt, since they only offer glimpses of the recurrent verb meanings that they aim to capture. In actuality, many of these meanings are more abstract than the glosses suggest, and many of them also exhibit different forms of polysemy in different languages.

To convey a better, but still limited, sense of the nature of generic verb meanings, Table 4.13 provides not only single-word English glosses, but also more detailed semantic characterizations, of the 26 items that comprise the major generic verbs in Jaminjung (Schultze-Berndt, 2000). Following the lead of the Natural Semantic Metalanguage research program (e.g., Goddard & Wierzbicka, 1994, 2002; Wierzbicka, 1996; Goddard, 2008), these semantic characterizations are formulated in very simple terms, and Schultze-Berndt (2000, p. 401) cautions that they should not be regarded as "psychologically real." On the other hand, in line with the sorts of grounded theories of semantic cognition reviewed in Chapter 2, she also emphasizes that, as in other languages with verbal classification systems, all of the generic verbs in Jaminjung cover events that correspond to basic human experiences. In fact, as shown in Table 4.13, they can be grouped into the following domains: location, existence, possession, and change of locative relation; translational motion; contact/force; burning/cooking; "say/do"; caused change of possession; and a few other conceptual fields exemplified by verbs for perception ("see"), consumption ("eat"), and creation ("make").

Neurobiology

Sadly, Jaminjung only has a few speakers left, and many other Northern Australian languages with verbal classification systems are also endangered. Nevertheless, it is still worthwhile for cognitive neuroscientists studying conceptual knowledge to be aware of such languages, because they show that the human brain is naturally capable of creating and using a unique strategy for describing events that involves the simultaneous deployment of both coarse-grained (i.e., relatively abstract) and fine-grained (i.e., relatively concrete) verb classes.

Since it would probably be premature to speculate about the specific networks of modal and transmodal cortical systems that underlie the meanings of generic verbs, we will briefly address a different issue instead, albeit one that may turn out to be

Table 4.13. Single-word glosses and more detailed semantic characterizations of the 26 generic verbs in Jaminjung (Mirndi, Australia), organized by domain.

Location, Existence, Possession, and Change of Locative Relation

yu	be	- 'x is located at y'
		- 'x is (involved) in a state/activity'
muwa	have	- 'x is located at y & y controls the location of x'
ardba	fall	- 'x comes to be in a locative relation with respect to y'
arra	put	- 'x causes y to be in a locative relation with respect to y'
		- 'x transforms itself (y) into z'
		- 'x causes y to change its configuration'
		- 'x (human) causes y to be accessible to z'
		- 'x (human) conventionally calls y by a word "z"'

Translational Motion

ijga	go	'x moves along a path'
		'x moves to a state'
		'x is (involved) in a state/activity for a long time'
ruma	come	'x moves along a path which is oriented toward the deictic center'
uga	take	'x moves along a path & y is located at x & x controls the location of y'
		'y is located at x for a long time & x controls the location of y'
		'x (animate) has y in mind'
		'x (animate) hears y'
		'x applies force on y by means of x's body weight'
anjama	bring	'x moves along a path which is oriented toward the deictic center & y is located at x & x controls y'
unga	leave	'x purposefully moves along a path which is oriented away from y'
arrga	approach	'x purposefully moves along a path which is oriented towards y'
warda-garra	follow	'x purposefully moves along a path which is oriented towards y and in the same direction in which y is moving'

Contact/Force

mili/angu	get/handle	'x is in contact with y with a movable (body) part or instrument & x affects y'
		'x (animate) is in contact with y through its lower senses'
		'x is in the same place as y & x affects y'
		'x attempts to make contact with y'
ma	hit	'x makes an impact on y & x affects y'

Table 4.13. Continued

Contact/Force		
		'x completely affects y'
		'x emerges'
ina(ngga)	chop	'x makes an impact on y with the edge of a body part or instrument & x affects y'
inama	kick/step	'x makes an impact on y with the foot & x affects y'
		'x makes an impact on y, moving on a downward trajectory, & x affects y'
ijja/yaluga	poke	'x makes an impact on y with the pointed end of a body part or instrument & x affects y'
wa	bite	'x makes forceful contact with y with the mouth part & x affects y'
		'x causes y to experience pain like from a bite & x affects y'
wardgiya	throw	'x causes y to move along a trajectory determined by gravity or the direction of force applied'

Burning/Cooking		
irna	burn	'x is affected by heat'
irriga	cook	'x affects y by means of heat'

The Polyfunctional 'Say/Do' Verb		
yu(nggu)	say/do	'x internally causes, and gives immediate evidence of, an event "e"'

Caused Change of Possession		
ngarna	give	'x (animate) causes y to be located at z (animate), such that x controls y'
		'x (animate) transmits y (information) to z (animate)'
		'x/z (animate) say "y" to one another'
		'x (animate) directs event "e" at z & x affects z'
yungga	take away	'x (animate) causes y to be removed from its location at z (animate), and from the control of z'

Other Major Verbs		
ngawu	see	'x (animate) directs one's eyes at y & x visually perceives y'
minda	eat	'x (animate) takes y into x's mouth'
(ma)linyma	make	'x brings y into existence (from something)'
		'x causes y to bring about an event "e"'

From Schultze-Berndt (2000, pp. 402–403).

indirectly relevant to the neural substrates of generic verb meanings. In particular, it is striking that the distinction between generic verbs and coverbs in seemingly exotic languages like Jaminjung has a loose parallel—certainly not a perfect one, but a loose one—in the distinction between "light" verbs and "heavy" verbs in more familiar languages like English (Butt, 2010). Light verbs are always small in number, and they have very schematic meanings that, interestingly enough, tend to correspond to some of the glosses of generic verbs in Table 4.13, with English examples including *have, go, come, get, do, give, take,* and *make.* Moreover, these verbs often have auxiliary-like syntactic properties (e.g., *We're going to eat*), and they frequently serve as verb-slot-fillers in idioms (e.g., *have a rest, go crazy, give a shout, take a bath, make love*). In contrast, heavy verbs usually number in the thousands; they have richly nuanced meanings (e.g., *embellish, titillate, grumble, dither, confirm*); and they never have auxiliary-like or idiomatic slot-filling functions. Importantly, pycholinguistic and electrophysiological studies have revealed significant processing differences between these two types of verbs (Wittenberg & Piñango, 2011; Wittenberg et al., 2014a, 2014b), and neuropsychological studies have shown that they sometimes dissociate from each other in brain-damaged patients, with agrammatic Broca's aphasics exhibiting worse production of light verbs than heavy verbs, and anomic aphasics exhibiting the opposite performance profile (Breedin et al., 1998; see also Gordon & Dell, 2003). Taken together, these considerations suggest that both of the verb class distinctions that we have been discussing—the one between generic verbs and coverbs, and the one between light verbs and heavy verbs—may derive, at least partly, from the same deep-seated aspects of the neural architecture of language. And if this is the case, it follows that as we learn more about how the meanings of light verbs are implemented in the brain, we may also gain some insight, albeit very indirectly and loosely, into the neural substrates of generic verb meanings.

CONCLUSION

This chapter has focused on the complex conceptual universe of actions, with the aim of surveying some recent findings from semantic typology and exploring their implications for cognitive neuroscience. The major highlights are briefly summarized below, beginning with cross-linguistic similarities that may reflect fundamental, pan-human ways in which actions are conceptualized, and then turning to cross-linguistic differences that reveal the remarkable range of cultural diversity in this realm of semantic cognition.

Regarding cross-linguistic similarities, we have seen that many genealogically and geographically diverse languages converge on some common strategies for categorizing certain domains of action. For instance, in the domain of motion events, there is a strong tendency for languages to have translation equivalents of the English verbs *walk* and *run*, presumably because they encode the two most biomechanically stable human gaits. Moreover, these verbs usually anchor variably sized clusters of other verbs for more specialized forms of walking and running. Although these typological trends may not seem very surprising, they have nontrivial neuroscientific consequences, since they predict that for speakers of different languages all over the world, the action concepts associated with walking and running will have fairly consistent, and clearly distinguished, representations in the relevant brain regions—most notably, the LOTC and precentral motor cortices.

Additional insights of a more sophisticated nature involve, at higher levels of semantic generalization, the comparable ways in which different languages carve up the closely related domains of cutting, breaking, and opening events. Statistical analyses of naming data suggest that most languages treat the first two domains as not only being more similar to each other than to the third, but as belonging to a single semantic framework that is structured in terms of one continuous dimension (the predictability of the locus of separation in the affected object) and two dichotomous dimensions (tearing events versus all others, and smashing events versus snapping events). These basic conceptual dimensions are valuable "targets" for neuroscientific investigation because they can account for a great deal of data involving the cross-linguistic encoding of cutting and breaking events, and hence may constitute universal, or at least widely shared, aspects of semantic cognition. We argued earlier that these dimensions probably depend, to varying degrees, on the tightly interconnected brain areas that subserve the observation and execution of object-directed actions, including the mirror system and the tool network, but a series of carefully designed fMRI studies would be necessary to begin elucidating the details of the underlying cortical architecture.

Yet another example of how cross-linguistic similarities in verb meanings can inform neuroscientific research on action concepts involves the striking correspondences that have been documented between, on the one hand, generic verbs in seemingly exotic languages with verbal classification systems, and on the other hand, light verbs in more familiar kinds of languages. The key finding is that both types of verbs tend to encode the same sorts of highly schematic events in such domains as location, motion, possession, contact, and existence. These cross-linguistic patterns are clearly relevant to cognitive neuroscience, since they provide precious clues about what may be the most fundamental representational spaces for action in the human brain.

Shifting to cross-linguistic differences, we have encountered numerous manifestations of substantial variation involving the inventories of verbs that subdivide particular domains of action into distinct categories. For instance, several studies have found that (despite the commonalities just noted) when speakers of different languages name standardized videoclips of actions in certain domains—specifically, motion events, events of cutting and breaking, and events of putting and taking—they produce profoundly different sets of verbs that group the very same stimuli into radically mismatching categories. Needless to say, such dramatic cross-linguistic differences in lexical-semantic specificity have significant repercussions for cognitive neuroscience, since they suggest that cultures vary greatly in the precise functional topographies of the cortical circuits supporting many domains of action concepts. In addition, at a more systemic level of semantic structure, considerable cross-linguistic diversity has been found in the combinations of conceptual components that are preferentially lexicalized by verbs—e.g., [motion + manner] versus [motion + path] versus [motion + figure]. These contrasting conflation patterns may be underpinned by the ATL and/or other transmodal hubs, but further research is needed to test this hypothesis.

Finally, we examined two kinds of grammatically based strategies of action representation that are quite different from those found in English and other familiar European languages. First, serial verb constructions (SVCs) consist of strings of verbs—usually just two or three, but as many as nine in Kalam (Trans-New Guinea, Papua New Guinea)—that encode the separate phases of complex events while still treating those events as unitary. SVCs are routinely used by speakers of hundreds of languages in many parts of the world, and they have interesting connections with neuroscientific research on event segmentation and conceptual feature binding. Second, verbal classification systems require speakers to habitually categorize events at both a coarse-grained level, with generic verbs, and a fine-grained level, with coverbs. These fascinating systems are prevalent in the languages of Northern Australia, and they bear on cognitive neuroscience because, as mentioned earlier, the austere meanings of generic verbs seem to reflect the most elementary ways in which people classify the events they experience.

5

SPATIAL RELATIONS

Languages use surprisingly different criteria to calculate similarities and differences among spatial configurations, and this means that their spatial categories cross-cut and intersect each other in complex ways.
—Melissa Bowerman (1996, p. 160)

INTRODUCTION

People worldwide talk on a daily basis about the locations of objects and actions in the three-dimensional world that surrounds them, and they usually refer to those locations by using a small, closed class of grammatical morphemes that tend to have fairly schematic spatial meanings, like the prepositions *on, in, around, in front of,* and *in back of,* and the demonstratives *here* and *there.* But even though native English speakers find these particular terms to be perfectly natural and employ them quite frequently, there is actually a vast range of coding possibilities in the complex conceptual realm of categorical spatial relations, and languages vary tremendously in which ones they adopt, while still conforming to some overarching patterns.

Ever since the mid-1980s, research on the linguistic representation of spatial relations has burgeoned, and there is now a large literature that addresses many empirical and theoretical aspects of this topic, not only with regard to English, but embracing a broad array of other languages too (Talmy, 1983; Herskovits, 1986; Landau & Jackendoff, 1993; Svorou, 1994; Bowerman & Choi, 2001; Levinson, 2003b; Tyler & Evans, 2003; van der Zee & Slack, 2003; Coventry & Garrod, 2004; Carlson & van der Zee, 2005; Levinson & Wilkins, 2006a; Aurnague et al., 2007; Feist, 2008; Evans & Chilton, 2010; Diessel, 2014; Johannes et al., 2015; Landau, 2016). Surprisingly, however, very little of this work has had any impact on cognitive neuroscience, and the vast majority of researchers who study the cortical underpinnings of concrete conceptual knowledge have ignored spatial relations completely, preferring to focus on objects and actions instead. Due to this rather stark asymmetry, this chapter has a somewhat different organization than the previous two. The first section focuses entirely on cross-linguistic similarities and differences in the grammatical-semantic representation of three main types of spatial relations: topological, projective, and deictic. Then the last section addresses a number of neuroscientific issues, including a review of what has been learned so far about the implementation of these kinds of concepts in the brain, and a discussion of how the typological literature can both inspire and guide future research in this important but relatively neglected area of inquiry.[1]

TYPOLOGY

Very few languages have a word for "space" in the general sense employed by philosophers and scientists such as Newton, Leibniz, Kant, and Einstein. However, current evidence suggests that all languages do have *Where* questions (Ulltan, 1978) that elicit answers in which the figure object—i.e., the thing to be located—is described as being within a search domain defined by some kind of categorical spatial relation to a ground object—i.e., a thing that serves as a point of reference (Talmy, 1983). As mentioned earlier, we will focus here on three main classes of spatial relations: topological, projective, and deictic. All of them are encoded to different degrees in different languages, and although they interact in complex ways, each one usually constitutes a fairly independent semantic field that is partitioned into distinct categories by a specialized set of grammatical morphemes.

Topological relations

According to the loose, non-mathematical sense of topology employed in much of the research on spatial semantics, topological relations involve not only certain types of allocentric contiguity between figure and ground objects, but also various force-dynamic and functional features, such as the notions of support and containment captured by the English prepositions *on* and *in*, respectively.[2] In an influential article, Landau and Jackendoff (1993) point out that the spatial concepts found in English prepositions are extremely schematic and coarse, since they place few geometric constraints on figure and ground objects. They also argue that these sorts of concepts are likely to be cross-linguistically universal. For example, based on the observation that English prepositions are insensitive to the specific shapes of figure and ground objects, they state that no language should have a locative element like the hypothetical *sprough*, which means "reaching from end to end of a cigar-shaped object," as in *The rug extended sprough the airplane.* Similarly, given that English prepositions do not discriminate between the subregions of containers, they propose that no language will manifest a locative element like the hypothetical *plin*, which means "contact with the inner surface of a container," as in *Bill sprayed paint plin the tank.*

This view has been challenged, however, by studies that have revealed considerable variation in the kinds of topological relations that are grammaticalized in different languages. Levinson (2003b, pp. 63, 72) notes, for instance, that the putative non-existence of an expression like *sprough* is directly contradicted by Karuk (Hokan, Northwestern United States), which has a suffix *-vara* meaning "in through a tubular

---

[1] Parts of this chapter are based on Kemmerer (2006b, 2010).

[2] Interestingly, one recent study focuses on a language, namely Palikur (North Arawak, Brazil), that has a closed class of frequently used spatial terms which appear to encode pure topological notions in the true mathematical sense—e.g., interior, boundary, extendedness, connectedness, symmetry, and so forth (Green & Green, 2017).

space." Similarly, expressions of the *plin* type, which specify subregions of containers, have been attested in Makah (Wakashan, Northwestern United States), which has suffixes encoding locations such as "at the rear of a house" and "at the head of a canoe" (Davidson, 1999). Equally if not more threatening to Landau and Jackendoff's (1993) theory is Tzeltal (Mayan, Mexico), which describes topological relations with a large but, importantly, closed class of dispositional predicates that specify detailed geometric distinctions involving figure and ground objects (Brown, 1994, 2006). When combined with the single, all-purpose relational marker *ta*, these words extensively cross-classify spatial arrays that would be described in English by using semantically more general prepositions like *on* and *in*. Thus, if asked "Where are the tortillas?" an English speaker might reply simply "On the table"—a statement that reduces the tortillas to a mere point or shapeless blob. However, a Tzeltal speaker would probably select one of several terms that encode information about the shape or arrangement of the tortillas, such as *pakal* if they are folded or *latzal* if they are stacked. A variety of other examples are shown in Figure 5.1 (see also Figure 4.15 and Table 4.10 in Chapter 4, together with the associated text.)

Some especially intriguing insights about both similarities and differences in the cross-linguistic representation of topological relations come from a pioneering study that was conducted by Bowerman and Pederson (1992) at the Max Planck Institute for Psycholinguistics. Although the original report was never published, it has been widely cited and discussed, and its main contents are clearly summarized by Bowerman and Choi (2001; see also Gentner & Bowerman, 2009). In short, speakers of 38 languages from 25 genealogical groups were asked to describe the locations of objects portrayed in a carefully designed set of 71 drawings (see Appendix 4 of Levinson & Wilkins, 2006a). The various scenes contrasted along a large number of partially overlapping spatial dimensions that the investigators believed to be relevant to the cross-linguistic encoding of topological relations. Some of the most critical features are described below and exemplified by the six stimuli at the top of Figure 5.2.

a. support from below (e.g., cup on table, pen on desk)
b. "clingy" attachment (i.e., adhesion or surface tension, e.g., bandaid on leg, rain drops on window)
c. hanging over/against (e.g., picture on wall, coat on bannister)
d. fixed attachment (e.g., handle on door, telephone on wall)
e. point-to-point attachment (e.g., apple on twig, balloon on string)
f. full inclusion (e.g., apple in bowl, rabbit in cage).

The investigators identified some fascinating forms of constrained cross-linguistic variation regarding which terms cover which situations. Five of the attested patterns are illustrated in Figure 5.2, and Bowerman and Choi's (2001, pp. 484–485) explications of them are as follows, quoted in full but with minor changes to fit the current context:

1. One term for situations (a)–(e) and another for (f). This is a common pattern, followed by languages as diverse as English, Hebrew, Hungarian, and Mopan Mayan. In English, (a)–(e) are covered by *(be) on* and (f) by *(be) in*.

Y-UTIL man, house
'at its-inside'

PACHAL apple, bowl
'in a bowl-shaped container
canonically sitting'

WAXAL water, bottle
'in a taller-than-wide rectangular
or cylindrical object vertically
standing'

T'MUL apple, water
'immersed in liquid in a
container'

TIK'IL bull, corral
'having been inserted into a
container with a narrow opening'

XIJIL pencils, cup
'of long-thin object, having been
inserted carefully into a bounded
object'

XOJOL coffeebag, pot
'having been inserted singly into
a closely fitting container'

TZ'APAL stick, ground
'having been inserted at end into
supporting medium'

Figure 5.1. Some dispositional predicates in Tzeltal (Mayan, Mexico) that, when combined with the general-purpose locative marker *ta*, encode topological relations in which the figure is positioned at least partly within a bounded region of the ground. Below each diagram, the appropriate Tzeltal term is provided first, followed by the English names of the depicted figure and ground objects, and finally the rough meaning of the Tzeltal term in single quotes.
Adapted from Brown (1994, p. 767).

2. One term for (a) and another for (f). Neither term is used for (b)–(e); these situations are covered instead by a general locative word or inflection—also applicable to (a) and (f)—that indicates only that there is *some* spatial relationship between the figure and the ground, normally understood as the most canonical one for the objects in question. This pattern, also common, is found for example in Japanese and Korean, in which the terms used to encode situations (a) and (f) are nominals: e.g., Japanese *ue* "upper region, top, above," and *naka* "interior region."

3. One term for (a)–(b), another for (c)–(e), and still another for (f). This pattern is rare in the languages Bowerman and Pederson looked at, occurring only in Dutch

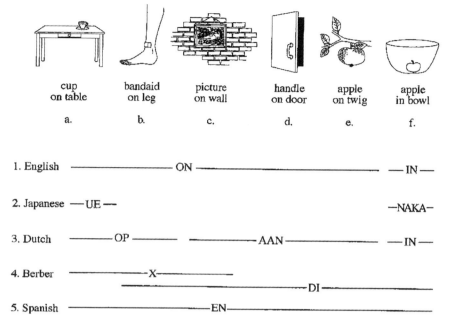

Figure 5.2. A cross-linguistically based similarity gradient of topological relations extending from surface support—(a) "cup on table"—to full containment—(f) "apple in bowl"—and illustrated by the referential patterns of spatial terms in several languages (1–5). Note that even though these patterns don't match perfectly, they all conform to the constraint that if a term covers more than one segment of the continuum, it covers the intervening segments too.
From Bowerman & Choi (2001, p. 485).

(German is similar but not identical).[3] The three Dutch terms, all prepositions, are *op* (for a–b), *aan* (c–e), and *in* (f). *Op* and *aan* are both usually translated as *on* in English. The difference between them for situations like those shown in Figure 5.2 has to do with the force dynamics of the situation (Bowerman, 1996). If the figure is conceptualized as acted on by a salient force, usually gravity, that must be counteracted if the figure is to stay in contact with the ground, *aan* is selected (e.g., picture on wall). But if the figure is seen as resting comfortably on the ground with no "pull" toward separation, *op* is chosen (e.g., cup on table, bandaid on leg).

4. One term for (a)–(c) and another for (b)–(f). A language of this type is Berber, with the prepositions *x* and *di* (roughly "on" and "in"); similar but not identical is Finnish, with the locative case endings *-lla* and *-ssa* (again, roughly "on" and "in"). What is new and surprising here is the extension of an "in"-type morpheme to many situations that English categorizes as "on" relations; note also that there is some overlap in the range of the "on"-"in" terms.

---

[3] A recent study found, however, that both Frisian (Germanic, Netherlands) and Schwyzerdütsch (Germanic, Switzerland) pattern like Dutch (Majid et al., 2015).

5. One term for the whole range from (a) to (f), e.g., the Spanish preposition *en*, normally translated in English as either *in* or *on*. (Spanish speakers can, if they desire, be more explicit, distinguishing (a) as *encima (de)* "on top (of)" and (f) as *dentro (de)* "inside (of).")

Despite such diversity, the 38 languages that Bowerman and Pederson (1992) examined do not vary arbitrarily, but instead conform to an implicit similarity gradient that orders topological relations along the lines shown at the top of Figure 5.2, with the left end anchored in a prototypical situation of support from below—(a) "cup on table"—and the right end anchored in a prototypical situation of containment—(f) "apple in bowl." The intermediate situations are arranged according to the degree to which they can be construed as similar to one of these two extremes, as revealed by the referential ranges of spatial terms. For instance, languages of the Dutch type (pattern 3) extend the term for situation (a) to situation (b); languages of the Berber type (pattern 4) extend it one step further to situation (c); and languages of the English type (pattern 1) extend it all the way to situation (e). Crucially, the researchers found that across all the languages in their sample, if a term covers more than one segment of the continuum, it covers all the intervening segments as well. Taken together, these results suggest that even though languages differ substantially in how they categorize topological relations, they seem to be constrained by an underlying similarity gradient that may reflect the inherent biases of the brain.

Additional evidence for this view comes from a number of more recent studies that used Bowerman and Pederson's (1992) stimuli to explore the topological coding systems of many other languages around the world (Levinson & Meira, 2003; Levinson & Wilkins, 2006a; Feist, 2008; Berthele et al., 2015; Majid et al., 2015; see also Khetarpal et al., 2009; Croft, 2010; Regier et al., 2013). Here, however, we will restrict our attention to Feist's (2008) investigation, which focused on the 24 languages listed in Table 5.1. Speakers of these languages were asked to describe the locations of objects in 29 drawings, all but two of which were taken from Bowerman and Pederson's (1992) battery. Some of the languages turned out to have extremely general spatial terms that speakers employed in virtually all of their descriptions, much like the Japanese terms discussed earlier in connection with pattern 2 in Figure 5.2. But Feist (2008) found that most of the languages have more semantically specific locative morphemes that speakers applied in more selective ways. To investigate the similarities among all of the pooled naming responses, she performed a multidimensional scaling analysis that yielded the graph shown in Figure 5.3. Along the y axis, the situations clearly vary with respect to the vertical placement of the figure relative to the ground. Of greater interest for present purposes, however, is the distribution of pictures along the x axis. It can be seen that the leftmost cluster includes the prototypical situation of support from below—i.e., "cup on table"—and the rightmost cluster includes the prototypical situation of containment—i.e., "apple in bowl." Strikingly, these two situations are identical to the two ends of the continuum in Figure 5.2. Moreover, several other aspects of that continuum are also manifested here. For instance, the cluster just to the right of the one anchored by the "cup on table" picture includes not only the labeled "laundry on clothesline" picture but also the "bandaid on leg" picture, which, as noted earlier, is likewise ordered just to the right of the "cup on table" picture along the similarity gradient in Figure 5.2. Now, Feist (2008) explicitly states that the

Table 5.1. List of 24 languages included in Feist's (2008) study of topological spatial relations.

Language	Affiliation	Location
Polish	Indo-European	Poland
Russian	Indo-European	Russia
Croatian	Indo-European	Croatia
German	Indo-European	Germany
Swedish	Indo-European	Sweden
Italian	Indo-European	Italy
French	Indo-European	France
Hindi	Indo-European	India
Hebrew	Afro-Asiatic	Israel
Hungarian	Uralic	Hungary
Cantonese	Sino-Tibetan	China
Telugu	Dravidian	India
Turkish	Altaic	Turkey
Tagalog	Austronesian	Philippines
Japanese	Isolate	Japan
Korean	Koreanic	Korea
Indonesian	Austronesian	Indonesia
Egyptian Arabic	Afro-Asiatic	Egypt
Bangla (Bengali)	Indo-European	Bangladesh
English (American)	Indo-European	United States
Thai	Tai-Kadai	Thailand
Mongolian	Altaic	Mongolia
Vietnamese	Austro-Asiatic	Vietnam
Mandarin	Sino-Tibetan	China

Based on Feist (2008, p. 1181).

arrangement of pictures along the x axis in Figure 5.3 closely matches, and hence statistically reinforces, the continuum discovered by Bowerman and Pederson (1992) and discussed by Bowerman and Choi (2001). But she characterizes it somewhat differently, since she emphasizes that the more a situation can be construed as involving either attachment or containment, the more it entails locational control of the figure by the ground. A virtue of this approach is that it dovetails nicely with other recent work on spatial semantics, like Coventry and Garrod's (2004) "functional geometry" theory, which is based on a wealth of data indicating that, as already mentioned, force-dynamic and functional features play a prominent role in many topological relations (see also Carlson & van der Zee, 2005; Landau, 2016).

It is quite remarkable that the ways in which genealogically and geographically disparate languages categorize topological relations appear to be shaped by the largely convergent similarity scales shown in Figures 5.2 and 5.3. Indeed, these findings raise the tantalizing possibility that the cross-linguistic construal of topological relations

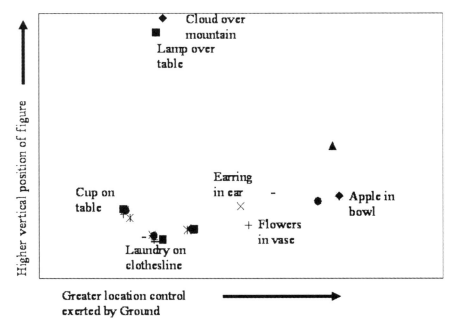

Figure 5.3. Results of a multivariate statistical analysis of pooled naming data for topological relations, derived from speakers of the 24 languages listed in Table 5.1. Each point represents one picture, and selected points have been labeled for ease of exposition. Within the plot, the closer two points are to each other, the more likely the corresponding pictures are to be named the same way. The x axis reflects the degree of locational control of the figure by the ground, with support-like situations involving weak locational control toward the left (e.g., "cup on table"), and containment-like situations involving strong locational control toward the right (e.g., "apple in bowl"). The y axis reflects the higher vertical position of the figure relative to the ground. From Feist (2008, p. 1186).

is strongly influenced by innate neurocognitive predispositions. Caution is definitely warranted, however, because exceptions to the observed tendencies have been documented. Kutscher (2011) argues, for instance, that Laz (Kartvelian, Turkey) conveys topological relations with so-called preverbs whose meanings do not depend on functional-geometric notions like surface support and containment, but rather on other kinds of semantic parameters that collectively contradict the ON-IN ordering system proposed by Levinson and Meira (2003)—a system which is quite comparable to the similarity scales presented above. As an illustration, the boldface font in Figure 5.4 highlights the fact that the preverb *ce-* covers discontinuous parts of the depicted gradient, applying to the situations "hat on head" and "apple in bowl," but not to the intervening situations "cork in bottle" and "box in bag," both of which are referred to with *dolo-* instead. These seemingly peculiar referential patterns are actually well-motivated, though, since *ce-* denotes topological relations that result from the figure moving downward along a vertically oriented path into contact with the ground, and *dolo-* denotes topological relations in which part of the figure occupies an opening at the top of a roughly cylindrically shaped object. It is also notable that the leftmost situation, "cup on table," can be described with either of two preverbs: *ce*, if the speaker

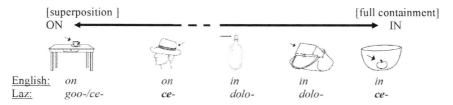

Figure 5.4. The referential distribution of the preverb *ce-* in Laz (Kartvelian, Turkey) violates the cross-linguistic tendency for spatial terms to cover continuous segments of the ON-IN similarity gradient that extends from situations involving superposition (i.e., surface support)—"cup on table"—to situations involving full containment—"apple in bowl." The particular gradient shown here is from Levinson and Meira (2003) and does not perfectly match either the one at the top of Figure 5.2 or the one along the *x* axis in Figure 5.3; however, all three gradients are closely related and based on substantial cross-linguistic data. See the main text for discussion of the meanings of *ce-*, *dolo-*, and *goo-*. From Kutscher (2011, p. 25).

wants to draw attention to the downward path that the cup presumably traversed to become located on the table; or *goo-*, if the speaker wants to emphasize that the table is a horizontal surface. This last aspect of Figure 5.4 is relatively trivial, however, because the key point is that the broader referential range of *ce-* clearly violates the common constraint that if a spatial term covers more than one segment of the continuum, it covers all the intervening segments as well. Thus, Laz underscores the importance of cultural conventions in the cross-linguistic treatment of topological relations.

Projective relations

Projective relations involve locating the figure within a search domain that radiates out some distance from the ground along a particular angle or line. This class of categorical spatial relations breaks down into several subclasses, each of which exhibits substantial, but not unlimited, cross-linguistic variation. The following survey draws heavily on the theoretical frameworks and empirical analyses provided by Levinson (2003b) and Levinson and Wilkins (2006a). According to Levinson (2003b, p. 76), languages use, to varying degrees, three frames of reference for encoding primarily horizontal projective relations: "the intrinsic system, which projects out a search domain from a named facet of a landmark [i.e., ground] object; the relative system, which imports the observer's bodily axes and maps them onto the ground object thus deriving named angles; and the absolute system, which uses a fixed set of bearings or a conceptual 'slope' to define a direction from a ground object." In the following subsections, we will first look closely at how these three frames of reference are manifested cross-linguistically, and then we will briefly discuss the encoding of projective relations along the vertical dimension.

The intrinsic frame of reference

The first locative strategy has two steps: the speaker identifies a salient part or facet of the ground—e.g., the "front"—and then extracts from the designated component an angle which extends outward a certain distance, thereby defining a search domain within which the figure can be found—e.g., *The man is in front of the house*. In English this system operates mainly by imposing on the ground a six-sided, box-like "armature"

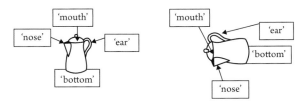

Figure 5.5. Application of the body-part-based intrinsic frame of reference in Tzeltal (Mayan, Mexico) to some of the facets of a teapot pot. Note that the assignment of terms is not affected by the pot's orientation relative to the observer, but is instead object-centered.
From Levinson (2003a, p. 78).

that yields a front, back, top, bottom, and two lateral (i.e., left and right)sides as the major intrinsic parts. Functional criteria are often used to identify, for instance, the "front" of an object based on factors like the typical direction of the perceptual apparatus (for animate entities), the typical direction of motion (for vehicles), or the typical direction of encounter (for houses, computers, etc.). Some objects resist this decompositional approach because they lack the relevant intrinsic asymmetries—e.g., English speakers usually do not construe trees and mountains as having fronts and backs. But judgments of this nature vary across languages—e.g., in Chamus (Nilo-Saharan, Kenya) the front of a tree is the side it leans toward, or, if it is vertical, the side with the biggest branch or the most branches, and in Kikuyu (Nilo-Saharan, Kenya) the front of a mountain is the side opposite its steepest side (Heine, 1997a, p. 13).

As mentioned near the end of Chapter 1, it is cross-linguistically common for locative terms employing the intrinsic frame of reference to derive historically from body part terms (Svorou, 1994; Heine, 1997a; Heine & Kuteva, 2002). This can be seen in the English example used earlier—*The man is in front of the house*—and in a number of fixed English expressions like *the face of a cliff, the mouth of a cave, the eye of a hurricane, the nose of an airplane, the head of a nail, the neck of a guitar, the arm/leg of a chair,* etc. In many languages, however, the body-part-based intrinsic system is much more complex and productive, requiring regular linguistically driven visual analysis of the axial geometry as well as the major and minor protrusions of inanimate objects so that the relative appropriateness of different body part terms can be computed instantly on the basis of these inherent properties, i.e., independent of the object's orientation or the speaker's viewpoint. Perhaps the best-studied language of this type is Tzeltal (Mayan, Mexico), in which even an object as seemingly nondescript as a stone may be assigned a "face," a "nose," an "ear," a "back," a "belly," or any of about 15 other quasi-metaphorical body parts in order to specify that a figure is located within a search domain projected from one of these facets (Levinson, 1994). For instance, in Tzeltal an *s-jol* (best translated as "head") is a protrusion that can be found at one end of an object's major axis and that has a gently curved, circular outline with only minor concavities on either side. To further illustrate how this system works, some of the body-part-based facets of a teapot are shown in Figure 5.5.[4]

---

[4] An important caveat, however, is that in Tzeltal the intrinsic frame of reference is only used to locate a figure in the region of space that is very close to the designated part of the ground. When a figure is separated from the ground by a larger distance, a different set of locative terms is applied—specifically, terms based on an absolute frame of reference, as indicated below.

The relative frame of reference

To describe spatial arrays in which the figure is at some remove from the ground, but the ground is classified as "unfeatured" by the intrinsic system of the given language, the front/back and left/right axes of the observer's body can sometimes be introduced to provide a frame of reference for structuring the scenario. This increases the complexity of the spatial relations from binary (figure and ground) to ternary (figure, ground, and observer). Thus, whereas *The man is in front of the house* specifies a binary relation in which the figure is located with respect to an intrinsic facet of the ground, *The man is in front of the tree* specifies a ternary relation in which the figure is located with respect to a non-intrinsic facet of the ground that can only be identified by taking into account the observer's perspective.

The type of relative system found in English involves imposing on the ground the mirror reflection of the observer's bodily axes, as shown in Figure 5.6a. A mirror flips the front/back axis but not the left/right axis of the object it reflects. Accordingly, to designate the figure as being *in front of* or *in back of* the ground, the observer's front/back axis is mapped onto the ground under 180° rotation, so that *The man is in front of the tree* means "From this viewpoint, the man is in a search domain projected from the side of the tree that faces me." And to designate the figure as being *left* or *right* of the ground, directions are projected laterally from the ground along angles that correspond to the observer's left/right axis.

Besides the English system, there are two other logical possibilities for organizing the relative frame of reference on the horizontal plane, and both are utilized by other languages (Levinson, 2003b, pp. 84–89). One strategy, exemplified by some dialects of Tamil (Dravidian, India), involves mapping the observer's bodily axes onto the ground under complete 180° rotation, generating not only front/back reversal but also left/right reversal. Thus, the Tamil expression for *The man is in front of the tree* has the same meaning as it does in English, but the expression for *The man is to the left of the tree* means that he is located in the region that English speakers would consider "to the right," as shown in Figure 5.6b. The other strategy, exemplified by Hausa (Chadic, Nigeria), involves translating the observer's bodily axes directly to the ground without any rotation whatsoever, so that the expression for *The man is in front of the tree* means that he is located in the region that English speakers would consider "in back of," but *The man is to the right of the tree* means the same thing as it does in English, as shown in Figure 5.6c.

The absolute frame of reference

The third type of angular specification on the horizontal plane involves an absolute frame of reference that provides a set of fixed bearings, like the compass points north, south, east, and west. These bearings define "an infinite sequence of parallel lines—a conceptual 'slope'—across the environment" (Levinson, 2003b, p. 90). To indicate the location of a figure with respect to a ground, one projects an angle from the latter to the former, determines the orientation of that angle in relation to the permanent grid, and selects the appropriate term—e.g., *The farm is south of the town*.

Absolute systems are fundamentally geocentric in nature, and languages typically base their terms on stable environmental features like celestial azimuths, mountain slopes, and river drainages. For instance, Warrwa (Nyulnyulan, North Australia) has

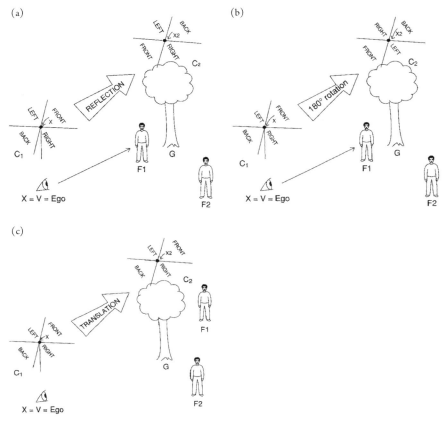

Figure 5.6. Three variants of the relative frame of reference. (a) Reflection, exemplified by English, in which the viewer's bodily axes are mapped onto the ground using a mirror-reversal strategy, so that F1 is in front of the tree and F2 is to the right of it. (b) 180º rotation, exemplified by Tamil (Dravidian, India), in which the viewer's bodily axes are mapped onto the ground by fully rotating them 180º, so that F1 is in front of the tree and F2 is to the left of it. (c) Translation, exemplified by Hausa (Chadic, Nigeria), in which the viewer's bodily axes are directly translated to the ground, so that F1 is in front of the tree and F2 is to the right of it.
Abbreviations: C = coordinate system; V = viewer; F = figure; G = ground.
From Levinson (2003a, pp. 86–88).

a system that is anchored in the cardinal directions (McGregor, 2006). As shown in Figure 5.7, the fundamental roots are *yardayi* (or *yawan*) "north," *yalmban* "south," *banu* "east," and *kularr* (or *wardiya*) "west," but there are also many words that are derived from these elements and that have complex meanings like *banuwu* "coming from the east," *banuwurdany* "going toward the east," and *banurarri* "the east-facing side of something." This is not unusual, since numerous North Australian languages have intricate lexicons that are built around the core terms for cardinal directions, as illustrated in Table 5.2, which provides a sample of compass-point derivatives in Kayardild (Tangic, North Australia) that are based on the root *ri* "east" (Evans, 2010). Returning once again to Tzeltal (Mayan, Mexico), it has a different kind of absolute

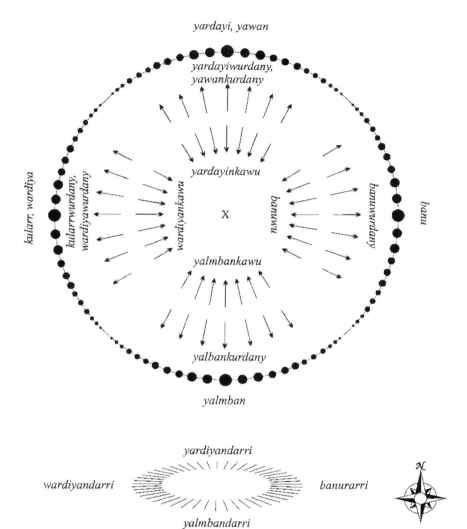

Figure 5.7. The absolute frame of reference in Warrwa (Nyulnyulan, North Australia) is anchored in the cardinal directions. The top panel shows the four directions in relation to a speaker whose location is marked by X. The terms outside the circle correspond roughly to the English words *north, south, east*, and *west*, and as the size of the dots increases along the line of the circle, so does the applicability of these terms to the directions that the dots represent. The terms inside the circle encode motion either toward or away from the speaker along the directions indicated by the arrows, with arrow length symbolizing appropriateness. The bottom panel shows the four terms for the northern, southern, eastern, and western sides or aspects of physical entities.
From McGregor (2006, p. 150).

Table 5.2. Some Kayardild (Tangic, North Australia) compass-point derivatives, based on the root *ri-*"east."

Form	Meaning
riya	east
rilungka	to the east, eastward
riyananganda	to the east of
rilumbanda	easterner
riinda	moving from the east
riliida	heading ever eastward
riliji	far to the east
rinlinda	at the eastern extremity of
ringurrnga	east across a geographical discontinuity
riinkirida	at the boundary you meet moving from the east toward the point of speech
rimali	hey you in the east!
riinmali	hey you coming from the east!
rilumali	hey you going eastward!
rilumirdamirda	in the dugong grounds to the east
rilunganda	easterly wind
riluayaanda	previous night's camp in the east
rilijatha	turn (self) around to the east
rilijulutha	move something to the east; sleep with one's head to the east
rimarutha	look to the east
riinmarutha	look from the east

From Evans (2010, p. 164).

system that, as shown in Figure 5.8, is anchored in the mountain incline of the local landscape, giving rise to three directional terms: *ajk'ol* "uphill" (roughly south), *alan* "downhill" (roughly north), and *jejch* "across" (either east or west) (Brown & Levinson, 1993; Brown, 2006). Finally, systems based on water flow are frequently used in several Australian and Austronesian languages (e.g., McGregor, 1990; Adelaar, 1997; McKenzie, 1997; Schultze-Berndt, 2006).

Remarkably enough, in some languages speakers routinely employ an absolute frame of reference, rather than a relative one, even when the figure is at a fairly short distance from the ground. This is demonstrated in a compelling manner by Levinson's (2003b, p. 114) account of Guugu Yimithirr (Pama-Nyungan, Australia):

> In GY, in order to describe someone as standing in front of the tree, one says something equivalent (as approximate) to "George is just north of the tree," or, to tell someone to take the next left turn, "go north," or, to ask someone to move over a bit, "move a bit east," or, to instruct a carpenter to make a door jamb vertical, "move it a little north," or, to tell someone where you left your tobacco, "I left it on the southern edge of the western table in your house," or, to ask someone to turn off the camping gas stove,

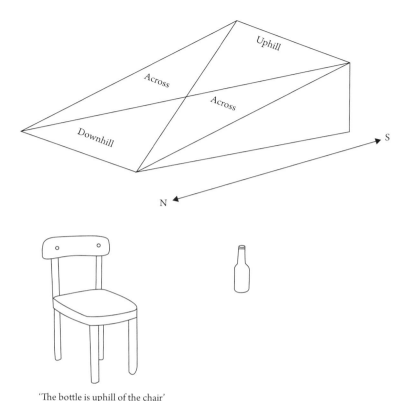

'The bottle is uphill of the chair'

Figure 5.8. The absolute frame of reference in Tzeltal (Mayan, Mexico) is anchored in the slope of the dominant hill where the language is chiefly spoken.
From Brown (2006, p. 265).

"turn the knob west," and so on. So thoroughgoing is the use of cardinal directions in GY that just as we think of apicture as containing virtual space, so that we describe an elephant as behind a tree in a children's book(based on apparent occlusion), so GY speakers think about it as an oriented virtual space: if I am looking atthe book facing north, then the elephant is north of the tree, and if I want you to skip ahead in the book Iwill ask you to go further east (because the pages would then be flipped from east to west).

In the same vein, Evans (2010, pp. 163–165) offers the following eye-opening anecdote about his experience of learning Kayardild (Australian, North Australia):

I suddenly had to add a whole new channel of ongoing attention to how I thought about space. I needed touse "dead reckoning," orienting to the points of the compass for every waking moment, if I was to followwhat was being said, and talk in a way that people would understand. . . . It is not that I never thought bycompass before learning Kayardild. Sometimes I had needed to do it, in occasional boy-scout mode, when orienteering, or navigating a city with a grid layout. And if someone had sprung the command to "pointnorth" upon me, I could eventually have answered after checking for the sun or shadows out the window. But the experience of speaking Kayardild was something quite different—an incessant need always to know the compass directions, and always to attend to them, or face an embarrassment equivalent to not knowing my wife's name, or not noticing whether you are male or female.

The vertical dimension

With regard to the linguistic encoding of projective relations along the vertical dimension, the three frames of reference just discussed—intrinsic, relative, and absolute—often coincide and yield the same answer to *Where* questions (Levinson, 2003b, p. 75). For example, consider a scene in which a fly hovers above an upright bottle. The figure is "above" the ground according to all three criteria: it is located within the search domain that radiates from the top of the bottle (intrinsic frame); it is higher than the bottle in the observer's visual field (relative frame); and it is higher than the bottle along the vertical axis defined by gravity (absolute frame). However, as a number of experiments have shown (e.g., Friederici & Levelt, 1990; Carlson-Radvansky & Irwin, 1993; Carlson, 1999), the three frames of reference can be manipulated independently of each other (e.g., by rotating either the ground or the observer, or, more radically, by shifting the entire array to a zero gravity environment) to create special situations in which they yield conflicting answers to *Where* questions. Also, although English clearly distinguishes *above/over* from *on* according to whether the figure contacts the ground, this may be the result of splitting into two subcategories the cross-linguistically more common (and perhaps conceptually more basic) category of superadjacency, which is neutral with respect to contact and is directly encoded in languages like Japanese and Arrernte (Pama-Nyungan, Australia; Levinson & Meira, 2003; Levinson & Wilkins, 2006b). This is one of several ways in which the vertical dimension interacts with topology. Another manifestation of this interaction is that *over* and *under* are not synonymous with *above* and *below*, respectively, because the former prepositions have a functional-geometric component that makes them more suitable than the latter for describing spatial arrays that involve an encompassment relation. For instance, it is more felicitous to say that a penny is *under* than *below* an inverted cup on a table (Coventry et al., 2001).

Deictic relations

Deixis involves the many ways in which the interpretation of utterances depends on aspects of the speech situation (Fillmore, 1997). In the present context, the most relevant deictic expressions are demonstrative adverbs and pronouns, like the English contrastive pairs *here/there* and *this/that*. These spatial terms are deictically anchored because the ground that serves as a point of reference for locating the figure is not some entity outside the speech situation, but rather the speech participants themselves—either the speaker, the addressee, or both. It is generally believed that all human languages have demonstratives; moreover, these terms tend to be historically quite old, they are among the first words that children acquire, and they are often (or, in some languages, always) accompanied by angle-specifying pointing gestures. The primary spatial parameter that demonstratives encode is radial distance from the deictic center; however, as described below, some languages encode other parameters as well (for reviews and perspectives, see Diessel, 1999, 2006, 2014; Dixon, 2003; Burenhult, 2008; for a recent collection of cross-linguistic studies, see Levinson et al., 2018; and for discussions of important social factors, see Enfield, 2003; Jungbluth, 2003; Hanks, 2005; Peeters &Özyürek, 2016).

In a sample of 234 languages from diverse families and geographical regions, Diessel (2005) found that the kind of demonstrative system manifested in English, with a binary proximal/distal distinction, is actually the most frequent, showing up in 127 (54%) of the languages. However, this is the minimal type of system, and other languages exhibit systems of greater complexity. For example, some languages include the addressee as a possible deictic center. Such person-oriented systems come in several varieties. One type, exemplified by Pangasinan (Western Austronesian, Philippines), has a three-way contrast between "near speaker,""near addressee," and "far from both speaker and addressee," while another type, exemplified by Quileute (Chimakuan, Northwestern United States), has a four-way contrast between "near speaker,""near addressee,""near both speaker and addressee," and "far from both speaker and addressee." These person-oriented systems resemble the English two-term system insofar as they specify just two zones—proximal and distal. The key difference is that person-oriented systems require the speaker to perform more elaborate spatial calculations which take into account not only his or her own egocentric frame of reference, but also that of the addressee. Perhaps for this reason, person-oriented systems are relatively rare. A more common way to increase the complexity of a demonstrative system is to partition the dimension of distance into more fine-grained zones. Eighty-eight (38%) of the languages in Diessel's (2005) sample follow this strategy by distinguishing between three zones—proximal, medial, and distal. Spanish and Yimas (Lower Sepik, Papua New Guinea) have systems like this. A very small proportion of languages (less than 4% in Diessel's sample) go one step further by distinguishing between four zones—proximal, medial, distal, and very distal. Tlingit (Na Dane, Yukon) is the most often cited example. There are even reports of languages with demonstrative systems that encode five distance contrasts (Anderson & Keenan, 1985), but Diessel (1999, 2005) supports Fillmore (1997), who maintains that systems with more than four terms invariably draw upon other spatial parameters.

These other parameters include elevation, visibility, geography, and movement. Elevation is a common component of demonstrative systems in several language areas, including a few pockets of the Americas, the territory in and around Tibet, the Caucasus, Indonesia, New Guinea, and Australia. For instance, Schapper (2014) analyzes seven languages belonging to the Alor-Pantar family in Indonesia and shows that all of them prominently feature elevation in their demonstrative systems, often together with some of the other spatial parameters just mentioned. As an illustration, Table 5.3 indicates that the system in Western Pantar makes not only a proximal/distal distinction but also a level/high/low distinction; and what's more, both of these distinctions cross-cut a visible/invisible distinction that breaks down further according to a specific/nonspecific distinction, yielding a grand total of 20 terms. It is also notable that, as exemplified by Dyirbal (Pama-Nyungan, Australia) in Table 5.4, some languages incorporate salient aspects of the local geography into their demonstrative systems, making contrasts like uphill/downhill, upriver/downriver,

Table 5.3. Demonstratives in Western Pantar (Alor-Pantar, Indonesia).

	Demonstratives			
	Visible		*Invisible*	
	Specific	*Nonspecific*	*Specific*	*Nonspecific*
Proximal	*saiga*	*aiga*	*sigamme*	*igamme*
Distal	*saina*	*aina*	*sinamme*	*inamme*
Level	*smaugu*	*maugu*	*smaume*	*maume*
High	*sraugu*	*daugu*	*sraume*	*daume*
Low	*spaugu*	*paugu*	*spaume*	*paume*

Adapted from Schapper (2014, p. 263).

inland/seawards, or upcoast/downcoast. Yet another spatial parameter, albeit one that has not been documented very frequently, involves movement of the figure relative to the deictic center. Diessel (1999, pp. 45–47) points out, for example, that both Nunggubuyu (Australian, North Australia) and Kiowa (Kiowa-Tanoan, Oklahoma) have demonstratives that specify whether the figure is moving toward the speaker, away from the speaker, or across the speaker's line of sight.

These sorts of conceptual contrasts are certainly intriguing, but some languages encode even more unusual ones. Central Yup'ik (Eskimo-Aleut, Alaska), for instance, is widely regarded as having an extremely elaborate demonstrative system that makes a fundamental, and highly idiosyncratic, three-way distinction which interacts with no less than 10 other semantic features, as shown in Table 5.5. Jacobson's (1984, p. 653) illuminating account of the three primary categories is worth quoting in full:

Table 5.4. Demonstratives in Dyirbal (Pama-Nyungan, Australia).

Form	Meaning
dayi	uphill + proximal
daya	uphill + medial
dayu	uphill + distal
baydi	downhill + proximal
bayda	downhill + medial
baydu	downhill + distal
dawala	upriver + medial
dawalu	upriver + distal
balbala	downriver + medial
balbulu	downriver + distal
guya	across the river

Adapted from Dixon (1972, p. 48).

Table 5.5. Demonstratives in Central Yup'ik (Eskimo-Aleut, Alaska). Only the "localis case" forms of the demonstrative adverbs are shown here; the complete paradigm includes six other sets of inflectional forms for each root (i.e., for each cell in the table). Moreover, demonstrative pronouns constitute a separate paradigm of even greater complexity.

Extended (moving, long, or of large extent)	Restricted (stationary, localized, visible)	Obscured (stationary and indistinct or out of sight)	
maani	wani	—	here, near speaker
tamaani	tuani	—	there, near listener
avani	yaani	amani	over there, yonder
agaani	ikani	akmani	across a prominent feature of topography
qavani	kiani	qamani	inside, inland, upriver
qagaani	keggani	qakmani	outside
un'gani	uani	cakmani	toward the exit (from inside), toward the coast, downriver
unani	kanani	camani	down below, toward the river
pavani	piani	pamani	back, away from the river
pagaami	pikani	pakmani	up above

From Jacobson (1984, pp. 661–662).

In the chart the first vertical column, labeled *extended*, consists of those demonstratives which are used to refer to an entity or area that is in sight and that is extended to some length, moving from one place to another, or of broad expanse. The extended demonstratives may be characterized as those which refer to an entity or area which requires more than a single glance to be seen. The second vertical column, labeled *restricted*, includes those demonstratives which refer to an entity or area that is in sight and that is restricted in size and is not in motion (or whose motion is confined to a restricted area). In other words, restricted demonstratives are those which refer to an entity or area which may be seen fully in a single glance. The third vertical column, labeled *obscured*, includes those demonstratives which refer to an entity or area that is not in sight, or not clearly perceptible.

Intersecting these peculiar categories are the following features that speakers must also habitually attend to in order to use the system effectively: "near speaker"; "near addressee"; "far from both speaker and addressee"; "across a barrier (e.g., a road or fence)"; "inside, inland, or upriver"; "outside"; "toward the exit (from inside), toward the coast, or downriver"; "down below, or toward the river"; "back, or away from the river"; and "up above." These features clearly involve some of the spatial parameters discussed earlier—in particular, distance, elevation, and geography—but they include other distinctions as well, like inside/outside. Moreover, almost all of the possible combinations of these features with the three cross-cutting conceptual components (i.e., extended/restricted/obscured) are realized by separate but largely parallel groups of demonstrative adverbs and demonstrative pronouns that are also inflected for numerous cases, giving rise to an enormous inventory of over 400 terms. For the sake of simplicity, only the "localis case" forms of the adverbs are shown in Table 5.5. Needless to say, though, we are dealing here with a system of extraordinary structural and functional intricacy.

Finally, it is instructive to consider the demonstrative system in Jahai (Mon-Khmer, Malaysia), since it makes a very interesting spatial distinction that has not yet been observed in any other language (Burenhult, 2008). This system treats the speech situation itself as a circular or oval bubble that forms between two individuals as soon as they enter into a speaker/addressee relationship. This bubble constitutes the deictic center, and its two intrinsic parts, namely the speaker and addressee, serve as ground objects for locating figure entities through the appropriate use of two exterior-directed demonstratives—one that is speaker-anchored and means essentially "that/there, outside my side of our speech perimeter," and another that is addressee-anchored and means essentially "that/there, outside your side of our speech perimeter."

The spatial concepts encoded by these terms were investigated by placing a cup at each of 32 positions—16 arranged circularly around a speaker, and 16 arranged circularly around an addressee—and repeatedly asking seven consultants, "If I place the cup here, can I say _____?" Figure 5.9a shows that when the two interlocutors are facing each other, the speaker-anchored exterior demonstrative applies to referents located within the sector of space that is projected out roughly to the sides of and behind the speaker, whereas the addressee-anchored exterior demonstrative applies to referents located within the corresponding, symmetrically opposite sector of space that is projected out from the addressee. Figure 5.9b shows that when the two interlocutors are oriented in a line, with one behind the other and both facing the same direction, if the speaker is in front, the speaker-anchored exterior term covers the semi-circular field anterior to that participant, and if the addressee is in front, the addressee-anchored exterior term likewise covers the semi-circular field anterior to that participant. Lastly, Figure 5.9c shows that when the two interlocutors are sitting side-by-side and facing the same direction, with the speaker to the left of the addressee, each term again demarcates an exterior search domain that is projected out 180° from each participant; however, these domains do not coincide perfectly with the regions to the left of the speaker and to the right of the addressee, but are instead skewed a bit posteriorly, which suggests that in this context the interactive bubble (i.e., the interior of the speech situation) is biased toward the front.

Two other aspects of the exterior demonstratives in Jahai are also worth noting. First, neither distance nor visibility are relevant. For instance, Burenhult (2008) reports a scene in which a man uses the speaker-anchored term to refer to a potential hunting site that is no less than three kilometers upstream from the speech situation, on his side. He is not sure about the name of the place, but his interlocutor supplies it, using the correct addressee-anchored term. The greatest distance for which exterior-oriented demonstrative reference has been documented is approximately 50 kilometers. Second, unlike most other spatial deictics, these demonstratives directly encode *angular* search domains and hence do not require co-speech pointing gestures to provide directional information. Burenhult (2008) speculates that this unique semantic property of the terms may be a cultural reflection of the high frequency of Jahai interactions in which manual pointing is either ineffective or inappropriate. Here are

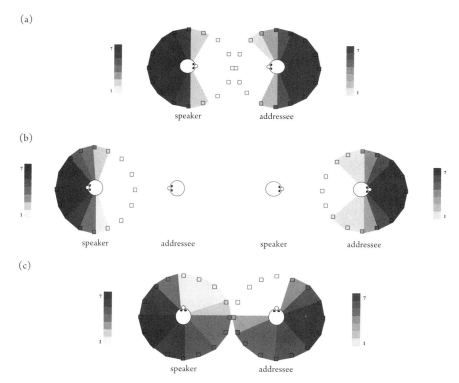

Figure 5.9. Results from an investigation of the demonstrative system in Jahai (Mon-Khmer, Malaysia). The squares indicate the different locations where a cup was placed—16 around the speaker, and 16 around the addressee—and the degree of shading indicates the number of consultants (1–7) who stated that for a given location it would appropriate to use either the speaker-anchored or the addressee-anchored exterior demonstrative. (a) Face-to-face conversational situation. (b) Aligned conversational situation with either the speaker in front of the addressee (left) or the addressee in front of the speaker (right). (c) Side-by-side conversational situation. From Burenhult (2008, pp. 127–129).

a few examples. Pointing is ineffective during group movement (a common activity in this nomadic, foraging society), because such movement typically involves walking in a single line along narrow trails through dense rain-forest with little eye contact. Furthermore, pointing is actually taboo in a variety of situations. For instance, it would be "unthinkable" to point to one's destination while traveling to a hunting, fishing, or gathering site, "for fear of revealing one's intentions to the potential game, catch, or harvest" (Burenhult, 2008, pp. 133–134). Thus, the angular search domains that are directly specified by exterior demonstratives clearly help to compensate for these kinds of pointing restrictions, among others.

NEUROBIOLOGY

Unfortunately, the neural substrates of linguistically encoded concepts for categorical spatial relations have not yet received much attention. Moreover, almost all of the studies that have explored this topic so far have been restricted to English, and almost none have tried to determine whether the different classes and subclasses of spatial relations described above have different cortical underpinnings. Nevertheless, a number of interesting discoveries have been made, and they should serve as a springboard for future investigations that will hopefully draw much more extensively on the well-developed and highly relevant literature in semantic typology.

The importance of the left inferior parietal lobule

As noted in previous chapters, when we look out at the world, incoming visual signals are rapidly propagated through multiple retinotopically mapped occipital areas and then passed on to the temporal and parietal lobes for higher-level processing (Wandell et al., 2007). One major stream extends into the ventral temporal cortex and is sometimes called the "what" pathway because it is devoted to recognizing objects on the basis of their shapes, colors, and apparent textures (see Figure 3.2 and the associated text in Chapter 3). Another major stream extends into the posterior parietal cortex and is sometimes called the "how" pathway because it implements the kinds of visuomotor transformations that are necessary to program object-directed actions—for example, converting the position of a hammer encoded in eye-centered coordinates into its position encoded in hand-centered coordinates so it can be grasped, and retrieving knowledge about how this particular type of tool should be manipulated to fulfill its function of hitting other things, such as nails (see Figures 3.2 and 4.14 and the associated text in Chapters 3 and 4). Importantly, the occipitoparietal stream has also been referred to as the "where" pathway because it contributes to the spatial localization of objects not only in relation to the viewer—or, more accurately, the viewer's body parts—but also in relation to each other (for a classic survey of a wide range of data, see Ungerleider & Mishkin, 1982). Furthermore, there is now substantial evidence that, as originally proposed by Kosslyn (1987), the following two types of spatial relations have hemispheric asymmetries: first, coordinate spatial relations, which involve precise metric specifications of distance and orientation, are computed predominantly (but not exclusively) in the right inferior parietal lobule (IPL); and second, categorical spatial relations, which involve groupings of locations that are treated as equivalence classes, are computed predominantly (but not exclusively) in the left IPL (for reviews, see Jager & Postma, 2003, and Laeng et al., 2003; see also the special issue of *Neuropsychologia, 44/9,2006*; for more recent developments, see Amorapanth et al., 2010).

In light of these considerations, it is reasonable to suppose that the left IPL plays a vital role in representing all of the different classes and subclasses of categorical spatial relations that we discussed earlier in the context of cross-linguistic data. Indeed, Landau and Jackendoff (1993) formulated just such a hypothesis in their influential paper, and Landau (2016) recently refined that proposal by pointing out that prepositions for topological relations, like *on* and *in*, may be especially dependent on the left IPL because their force-dynamic features are somewhat similar to the kinds of goal-directed causal interactions between objects (e.g., between hammers and nails) that this brain region captures. As indicated below, functional neuroimaging studies with healthy subjects, as well as neuropsychological studies with brain-damaged patients, suggest that the meanings of terms for both topological and projective relations do in fact rely on the left IPL—particularly the supramarginal gyrus (SMG), and to some degree also the angular gyrus (AG).

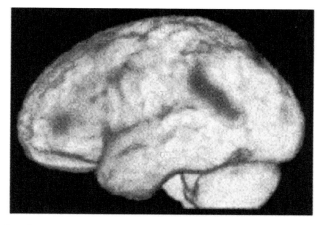

Figure 5.10. Significant activity in the left inferior parietal lobule (IPL), including the supramarginal gyrus (SMG) and angular gyrus (AG), during a task in which subjects produced English locative prepositions to name topological and projective spatial relations, compared to a task in which they produced English nouns to name objects. A color version is in the color plates section. From Emmorey et al. (2005, p. 837).

Let's focus first on functional neuroimaging data. Damasio et al. (2001) conducted a PET study in which English speakers viewed drawings of static spatial relations between objects (e.g., a spoon in a bowl) and performed two tasks: naming the figure with an appropriate noun, and naming the spatial relation between figure and ground with an appropriate preposition. When the condition of naming objects was subtracted from that of naming spatial relations, the largest and strongest area of activity was in the left SMG. It is also notable that these results were later replicated in another PET study by Emmorey et al. (2005), as shown in Figure 5.10. Although it is not clear exactly which prepositions were targeted for production in these studies, it appears that a mixture of topological and projective terms were included, which suggests that the left SMG may represent the meanings of both.

Several fMRI studies that have concentrated on prepositions for projective relations have likewise observed significant activity in the left IPL—usually in just the SMG, but sometimes in just the AG instead. For instance, in a study by Noordzij et al. (2005) the experimental condition involved judging whether phrases containing the spatial terms *left of* and *right of* (e.g., *triangle left of circle*)[5] matched subsequently presented pictures or phrases, and the baseline condition involved judging whether phrases containing the nonspatial term *and* (e.g., *triangle and circle*) matched subsequently presented pictures or phrases. When the researchers contrasted the experimental condition against the baseline condition, they found that only one brain area was engaged, namely the left SMG. What's more, this activity was present regardless of whether the second stimulus on each trial was a picture or a phrase, which suggests that the SMG may process prepositional meanings in a manner that is independent of such stimulus-specific factors. Further support for this notion comes from a follow-up study by Struiksma et al. (2011) which

---

[5] Note that these uses of the terms involved the relative frame of reference.

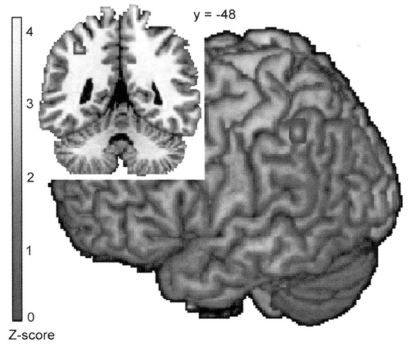

Figure 5.11. Significant activity for both sighted and congenitally blind subjects in the left supramarginal gyrus (SMG) during a task that required comprehension of the expressions *left of* and *right of*, compared to a task that required comprehension of the term *together*. A color version is in the color plates section.
From Struiksma et al. (2011, p. 8).

found that when both sighted and congenitally blind subjects performed purely linguistic versions of essentially the same tasks that Noordzij et al. (2005) employed, the spatial terms selectively triggered overlapping activity for both groups of subjects in, once again, the left SMG, as shown in Figure 5.11. It's also worth mentioning, however, that somewhat different results were obtained in an earlier study by Baciu et al. (1999) that had the following conditions: judging whether a dot was above or below a horizontal line (a categorical spatial relation), and judging whether a dot was within a certain distance of a horizontal line (a coordinate spatial relation). When these conditions were contrasted against each other, activations were found not in the SMG but rather in the AG, with left-hemisphere dominance for the categorical task and right-hemisphere dominance for the coordinate one. Still, much more work would obviously be needed to determine whether the two main gyri comprising the left IPL make different contributions to the two subclasses of projective prepositions that were investigated in these fMRI studies, with the SMG potentially being more specialized for terms like *left/right* than *above/ below*, and the AG potentially having the opposite profile.

Another approach to this whole topic was taken by Amorapanth et al. (2010), who conducted an fMRI study in which subjects performed a one-back matching task in two conditions that had identical stimuli. On each trial, they saw a photograph of two objects (e.g., a stapler and a coffee mug) in a particular configuration, with an arrow pointing to one of them (the figure). In the spatial condition, they indicated whether the figure-ground relation in the current picture matched the one in the previous picture, and although no prepositions were used in either the stimuli or the responses, the spatial relations were of the topological and projective types denoted by the terms *on, in, left of, right of, in front of, in back of, above*, and *below*.[6] In the object condition, the subjects indicated whether both objects in the current picture matched those in the previous picture. When the researchers contrasted the spatial condition against the object condition, they found greater activity in the left than the right IPL (and also equivalent activity in both superior parietal lobules; for related data, see Conder et al., 2017). It is not clear, though, whether the left IPL activity was fairly evenly distributed or concentrated more in either the SMG or the AG, since the researchers treated the entire IPL as a region of interest.

Turning now to neuropsychological data, the largest study to date was carried out by Tranel and Kemmerer (2004; see also Kemmerer & Tranel, 2000, 2003, and Kemmerer, 2005). Their aim was to identify the neural basis of impaired knowledge of the meanings of 12 prepositions—four encoding topological relations (*on, in, around*, and *through*), and eight encoding projective relations (*in front of, in back of, above, below, over, under, beside*, and *between*). The materials included both prototypical and non-prototypical uses of *on* and *in*, and both intrinsic and relative frames of reference for *in front of* and *in back of*. The following four tasks, each of which involved most if not all of the prepositions just mentioned, were administered to 78 brain-damaged patients with focal lesions distributed widely across the left and right hemispheres:

- Naming ($N = 80$ items): For each item, the participant is shown a spatial array of objects and is asked to orally name the location of one object relative to another.
- Matching ($N = 50$ items): For each item, the participant is shown three spatial arrays of objects together with a preposition and is asked to choose which array best represents the meaning of the preposition.
- Odd One Out ($N = 45$ items): For each item, the participant is shown three spatial arrays of objects and is asked to choose which one involves a type of relationship that is different from the other two. (Although this task does not require knowledge of the phonological or orthographic forms of English prepositions, it does require knowledge of their language-specific meanings, for reasons discussed by Kemmerer and Tranel, 2000.)
- Verification ($N = 44$ items): For each item, the participant is shown a spatial array of unrecognizable shapes together with a preposition and is asked to decide whether the preposition correctly describes the location of the white object relative to the black one(s).

Overall, the 78 patients displayed a complex pattern of associations and dissociations across the four tasks, such that some patients failed none of them, others failed just one, others two, others three, and others all four. Given this variability, the

---

[6] It appears that all of the projective relations involved the relative frame of reference, but the authors were not explicit about this.

researchers first formed two groups of patients in the following manner. They reasoned that the patients who failed all four tasks ($N = 6$) most likely had impaired knowledge of the meanings of spatial prepositions, whereas the patients who failed only one task ($N = 9$) most likely had unimpaired knowledge of those meanings (but perhaps had idiosyncratic disturbances involving certain processes uniquely required by certain tasks). Next, the researchers created separate lesion overlap maps for the two groups of patients. And finally, they contrasted the map for the impaired group against the one for the unimpaired group. This subtraction revealed that, as shown in Figure 5.12, defective knowledge of the meanings of spatial prepositions was associated with damage in just a few areas of the left hemisphere—specifically, parts of both the SMG and AG, the adjacent posterior sector of the superior temporal gyrus, the frontal operculum, and the white matter underlying all of these regions.

A limitation of this study is that the researchers did not analyze the data for topological and projective prepositions separately, but instead lumped both types of terms together. It is noteworthy, however, that for two of the six patients who failed all four tasks, detailed error analyses were reported in other papers, and they exposed pervasive deficits affecting all 12 prepositions (Kemmerer & Tranel, 2000, 2003). It is also interesting that, in other assessments, the six impaired patients not only displayed relatively preserved knowledge of object and action concepts, but also performed well on several standardized tasks that probed their working memory capacity and their

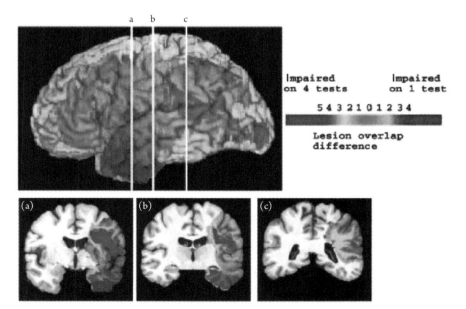

Figure 5.12. Results from Tranel and Kemmerer's (2004) neuropsychological study of English locative prepositions. The lesion overlap map of 6 patients who failed all 4 tasks was contrasted against the lesion overlap map of 9 patients who failed only 1 task. The color bar indicates the number of lesions in the subtraction image at each voxel, and the white lines indicate the planes of the coronal sections depicted below. A color version is in the color plates section.
From Tranel & Kemmerer (2004, p. 740).

non-linguistic visuospatial abilities. Thus, it is likely that their profound difficulties with spatial prepositions reflected genuine disturbances of the meanings of these terms, and were not byproducts of other cognitive or perceptual problems.

In a closely related line of work that used voxel-based lesion-symptom mapping, researchers in Anjan Chatterjee's lab at the University of Pennsylvania have published several papers providing further evidence that damage to the left IPL tends to impair knowledge of the types of categorical spatial relations that are encoded by English prepositions (Wu et al., 2007; Amorapanth et al., 2010, 2012). First of all, Wu et al. (2007) found that in a group of 14 patients with left-hemisphere lesions, those who had damage in many of the same areas identified by Tranel and Kemmerer (2004)— including, most importantly, parts of the SMG and AG, as shown in Figure 5.13— performed significantly worse, relative to patients without such damage, on a task that required them to match simple sentences containing spatial prepositions (e.g., *The circle is above the square*) with one of four pictures. The relevant prepositions were *on, in, through, above, below, next to,* and *far from.* Second, in a study involving 17 patients with left-hemisphere lesions and 17 patients with right-hemisphere lesions, Amorapanth et al. (2010) found that, once again, damage to the left SMG and AG (and also, but much more mildly, to the right SMG and AG) was linked with impaired processing of categorical spatial relations, specifically on a task that required the patients to match, on each trial, a spatial array of objects with one of four others. These arrays were comparable to those that the same researchers used in a "companion" fMRI study that was reported in the same paper and that we discussed earlier. Third, in another study with the same patients, Amorapanth et al. (2012) tried to elucidate the neural substrates of spatial semantics in greater detail by distinguishing between, as they put it, "those meanings associated with (1) phonological and orthographic representations, or *words,*(2) richly textured images, or *pictures,* and (3) simplified abstract images, or *schemas*" (p. 235). In short, they gave the patients four separate matching tasks that involved different combinations of these three kinds of stimuli, and obtained a complex set of results that not only provided additional, albeit modest, support for the link between spatial prepositions and the left SMG, but also suggested that, more generally, the left-hemisphere bias for categorical spatial relations is integrally tied to the linguistic labeling of such relations.

Having reviewed a number of functional neuroimaging studies and neuropsychological studies that implicate the left IPL in the spatial meanings of English prepositions,

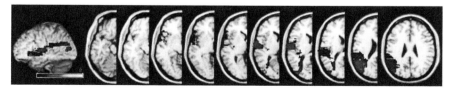

Figure 5.13. Results from Wu et al.'s (2007) neuropsychological study of English locative prepositions. Colored voxels, which include sectors of the left inferior parietal lobule (IPL), indicate areas where patients with lesions performed significantly worse than patients without lesions on a task that required them to match sentences containing prepositions (e.g., *The circle is above the square*) with one of four pictures. A color version is in the color plates section.
From Wu et al. (2007, p. 1549).

it is time to return to the broader cross-linguistic perspective that we started with and consider some of the questions that it raises—questions that could potentially be addressed in future work. First of all, the fundamental semantic distinction between topological and projective relations is reliably reflected by different classes of terms in languages worldwide, but whether these classes recruit different sectors of the left IPL is still unknown. Although the studies summarized above suggest that the spatial meanings of at least some terms of both types rely on this large brain region, they don't provide any insight into the more specific cortical organization of these two kinds of concepts. It seems likely, however, that some progress toward deciphering this organization could be made by tackling the problem head-on with a carefully designed fMRI protocol that is applied to several well-chosen languages.

Another issue that warrants serious attention involves the role of the left IPL in representing the similarity gradient that, as we saw earlier, orders topological relations along a conceptual continuum that extends from a prototypical *on*-like situation of support from below (e.g., "cup on table") to a prototypical *in*-like situation of full containment (e.g., "apple in bowl"). Although different versions of this gradient have been described by different researchers (see again Figures 5.2–5.4 and the associated text), they are all quite comparable, and, most importantly, they seem to capture an intricate set of neurocognitive biases that both guide and constrain the ways in which languages all over the globe categorize topological relations. Given the impressive cross-linguistic explanatory power that the ON-IN gradient appears to possess, determining whether—and, if so, exactly how—it is implemented in the left IPL would be a significant achievement. It would also be a very difficult undertaking, however, because the many types of topological relations that constitute the ordered segments of the continuum are not all distinguished by any one language; instead, different combinations of adjacent segments tend to be encoded by different grammatical morphemes in different languages, as shown in Figure 5.2. Hence, any attempt to use fMRI to disclose the representational geometry of the similarity gradient in the left IPL would not only need to present participants with multiple pictures instantiating each of the distinct types of topological relations, but would also need to ensure that the participants process those relations in an implicit manner, without labeling them in language-specific ways. To design and run such a study would be extremely challenging, but it would probably be worth the effort, since a positive outcome would begin to illuminate the neural substrates of some of the most intensively investigated and well-supported cross-linguistic tendencies in the field of semantic typology.

Of course, it would also be worthwhile to directly explore, from a neuroscientific perspective, the sorts of language-specific idiosyncrasies that allowed researchers to infer the underlying similarity gradient in the first place. Looking once again at Figure 5.2 and the associated text, what stands out most strongly is that languages like English, Japanese, Dutch, Berber, and Spanish (among many others) divide the very same continuum of spatial scenes into a complex matrix of cross-cutting categories. And yet, just as the meanings of *on* and *in* seem obvious and straightforward to native speakers of English, so the unique concepts encoded by each of the other languages undoubtedly seem perfectly natural to its native speakers. How are all these concepts—cut from the same cloth, but with very different boundaries—implemented in the fine-grained functional topography of the left IPL? Given the close relationship between this research problem and the one outlined in the previous paragraph (i.e., the one involving the neural basis of the similarity gradient), it might be fruitful to pursue both in parallel.

Separate studies would be needed, however, to examine the cortical foundations of other forms of language specificity in the encoding of topological relations. For instance, as illustrated in Figure 5.1 and discussed in the associated text, the dispositional predicates that speakers of Tzeltal (Mayan, Mexico) use to refer to these kinds of spatial relations are cross-linguistically unusual because many of them incorporate not only locational and force-dynamic/functional information about the contiguous relation between figure and ground entities, but also details about the shape, arrangement, and constitution of those entities. To take a couple of examples, *xijil* specifies that the figure is a long thin object, like a pencil, and *tik'il* specifies that the ground is a container with a narrow opening, like a corral. Thus, it seems likely that in the brains of Tzeltal speakers, the multifaceted meanings of these sorts of terms depend not only on the "where"/"how" pathway that extends into the left IPL, but also on the "what" pathway that extends into the ventral temporal cortex. Moreover, the different kinds of semantic features that these two streams represent may be integrated in a transmodal region such as the anterior temporal lobe (ATL).

Neural substrates of intrinsic, relative, and absolute frames of reference

Some of the functional neuroimaging studies and neuropsychological studies summarized above suggest that the left IPL contributes to the meanings of terms for projective relations, but none of them sought to determine whether different neural networks subserve the different frames of reference that these terms draw upon. One recent fMRI study, however, did address this issue and obtained intriguing results.

Janzen et al. (2012) scanned subjects while they performed a sentence-picture verification task that required them to judge, on each trial, whether a written sentence correctly described a subsequently presented line drawing. In the baseline trials, the sentences referred to nonspatial situations, like *The ball is green*, whereas in the critical trials, they expressed projective relations, like *The ball is in front of the man*, that were ambiguous because they could be interpreted according to either an intrinsic frame of reference or a relative frame of reference. In one block of trials, the subjects received feedback consistent with the intrinsic frame, and in another block that contained the very same stimuli, they received feedback consistent with the relative frame. In neither block, however, were they told in advance which frame was appropriate, so the feedback was essential for informing them about the proper frame on those trials when they mistakenly adopted the wrong one. Such incorrect judgments were few in number, however, and, not surprisingly, were concentrated near the beginning of each block, which suggests that the feedback was effective at inducing selection of the right frame.

The researchers carried out numerous analyses of the imaging data, some focusing on just the sentence phase or just the picture phase of the trials, and some contrasting the two frame-specific conditions against the baseline trials or against each other. Overall, the main findings were as follows. First, the intrinsic frame of reference was linked with significant activity in several brain regions that included, most notably, the left middle/inferior occipital cortex and the left parahippocampal gyrus. Given that the intrinsic frame involves the projection of search domains from salient parts of ground objects, these results make sense, since the lateral occipital cortex is a mid-level visual area that tracks the shape features of perceived objects (e.g., Cant & Goodale, 2007; Freud et al., 2013; Emberson et al., 2017), and the parahippocampal gyrus is a high-level visual area that contributes not only to the shape features of object concepts (e.g., Tyler et al., 2013; Liuzzi et al., 2015; Bonner et al., 2016), but also to the recognition of entire scenes that are characterized by both the identities of, and the spatial relations between, particular kinds of objects or navigational landmarks (e.g., Epstein & Kanwisher, 1998; Aguirre & D'Esposito, 1999; MacEvoy & Epstein, 2011). Second, use of the relative frame of reference engaged a left superior parietofrontal network. Although this network did not include the IPL (contrary to some of the studies reviewed earlier), its recruitment may reflect the fact that the relative frame is viewer-centered (i.e., egocentric) and therefore anchored in the observer's own bodily based sensorimotor axes, which are known to be represented primarily in dorsal areas, as discussed in Chapter 4 (see also Committeri et al., 2004).

These findings are certainly valuable, but they are also rather limited, since they only provide some initial hints about the cortical underpinnings of two frames of reference (intrinsic and relative) associated with two terms (*in front of* and *behind*) in one language (English). Needless to say, many other phenomena involving the cross-linguistic encoding of projective relations remain to be investigated from a neuroscientific perspective.

Regarding the intrinsic frame of reference, we noted earlier that it is often structured by expressions that derive historically from body part terms, and in some languages the regular use of such expressions requires complex visuospatial analyses of the axial and contour features of inanimate ground objects (Svorou, 1994; Heine, 1997a; Heine & Kuteva, 2002). For instance, to return briefly to Figure 5.5, if a speaker of Tzeltal (Mayan, Mexico) wanted to say that something was located near a particular part of a teapot, he or she would probably anchor the search domain by using the most appropriate body part term to designate the relevant part of the pot—e.g., calling the spout a nose, the handle an ear, or the top a mouth. This raises the question of how the meanings of such terms are implemented in the brains of Tzeltal speakers. One possibility that warrants further consideration is that they depend on populations of neurons in, or perhaps just anterior to, the left extrastriate body area (EBA)—a region that, as discussed in Chapter 3, not only represents the shapes of actual body parts (for reviews, see Peelen & Downing, 2007; Downing & Peelen, 2011, 2016; see also Figure 3.5 and the associated text), but also appears to be sensitive to the metaphorical applications of body part terms to inanimate entities (Kemmerer & Tranel, 2008; Lacey et al., 2017; see also Figure 3.6 and the associated text).

Regarding the relative frame of reference, we have seen that its use in connection with the English terms *left of* and *right of* has been linked with the left SMG (Noordzij et al., 2005; Struiksma et al., 2011), and its use in connection with the English terms *in front of* and *behind* has been linked with a left superior parietofrontal network (Janzen et al., 2012). It is worth recalling, however, that English employs a specific version of the relative frame of reference—namely, the "reflection" strategy—and two other versions have also been documented in other languages (see Figure 5.6 and the associated text). First, there is the "180° rotation" strategy, exemplified by Tamil (Dravidian, India), in which the viewer's bodily axes are mapped onto the ground by fully rotating them 180°, so that the front/back axis is the same as in the reflection strategy, but the left/right axis is flipped. And second, there is the "translation" strategy, exemplified by Hausa (Chadic, Nigeria), in which the viewer's bodily axes are directly translated to the ground, so that the left/right axis is the same as in the reflection strategy, but the front/back axis is flipped. These alternative versions of the relative frame of reference are undoubtedly self-evident to the speech communities that use them on a daily basis to refer to the locations of objects, but their neural substrates are completely unknown.

Finally, regarding the absolute frame of reference, the long passages from Levinson (2003b) and Evans (2010) that are quoted in the section on semantic typology clearly demonstrate that many languages make extensive use of geocentric coordinate systems that are based on natural phenomena like celestial azimuths and mountain slopes. To employ such systems accurately, habitually, effortlessly, and at multiple scales ranging from inches to miles, speakers must constantly monitor their own orientation, and the spatial relations between objects in their environment, with respect to a set of fixed bearings. How do they do this? Many nonhuman species have evolutionarily specialized sensory devices that enable them to use absolute coordinates for navigation (for a recent collection of articles on this topic, see the September 10, 2018, special issue of *Current Biology*). To take a few examples, some species of migratory birds have light-absorbing molecules in their retinae that are sensitive to the magnetic field of the earth and that may enable them to see this information as patterns of color or light intensity (Ritz et al., 2004); sea turtles have the biological equivalent of a magnetically based global positioning system that allows them to pinpoint their location relative to geographically large target areas (Luschi et al., 2007); and desert locusts perceive polarization patterns in the blue sky and use them as cues for spatial orientation (Homberg, 2015). But we humans obviously lack such amazing adaptations. Hence, the superb sense of direction displayed by people in "absolute" communities—a sense comparable in precision to that of homing pigeons (Levinson, 2003b, p. 232)—is most likely a knock-on effect of culture. Indeed, Levinson (2003b) elaborates this line of argumentation in detail, with the central claim being that the incessant use of a linguistically encoded absolute frame of reference greatly enhances the following cognitive capacities:

- the ability to mentally form and maintain an oriented survey map of a large terrain—i.e., a map that represents the distances and angles between places, is viewer-independent, and is oriented according to a grid of fixed bearings, like the compass points north, south, east, and west;
- the ability to instantly determine which cardinal direction one is facing by attending to cues like the path of the sun, the incline of the land, the direction of the wind, the alignment of sand dunes, the flight vectors of migratory birds, etc.;
- and the ability to dead reckon, which essentially involves monitoring how far one has traveled on each heading.

Recent research has begun to explore the neural substrates of several aspects of these cognitive capacities (for a review, see Chrastil, 2013; see also Epstein et al., 2017). For instance, data from diverse brain mapping techniques strongly suggest that dead reckoning (a.k.a. path integration) depends on a distributed network that includes the hippocampus, the retrosplenial cortex, and the medial prefrontal cortex, each of which may contribute to different components of the ability (e.g., Wolbers et al., 2007; Baumann & Mattingley, 2010; Sherrill et al., 2013; Marchette et al., 2014; Yamamoto et al., 2014; Chrastil et al., 2015, 2016). Although the subjects in these investigations were not nearly as good at dead reckoning as most people in "absolute" communities, it is notable that an anatomically focused study did find that as task performance increased, so did the amount of gray matter in the regions just mentioned (Chrastil et al., 2017). This discovery is especially pertinent here, since it predicts that these regions may have, on average, significantly greater volume in people who live in "absolute" communities than in people who live in "relative" ones. On the other hand, the cortical underpinnings of the other two abilities described above—namely, building oriented survey maps (as opposed to unoriented ones) and instantly determining cardinal directions—have not been carefully examined and therefore remain rather mysterious, even though such abilities are second nature to people in "absolute" communities. The upshot: a major challenge for future neuroscientific work will be to shed some light on the biological mechanisms that allow speakers of languages like Guugu Yimithirr (Pama Nyungan, Australia) to formulate and understand, without any difficulty whatsoever, statements like "I left my tobacco on the southern edge of the western table in your house" (Levinson, 2003b, p. 114).

Neural substrates of demonstratives

As yet very few studies have explored the cortical underpinnings of demonstratives. This topic is ripe for rigorous investigation, however, because some of the cross-linguistic properties of these terms may be related to recent neuroscientific findings about the representation of egocentrically anchored space. Although we experience the space around us as being unified and seamless, our brains actually carve it up into different sectors by means of multiple, anatomically and functionally segregated circuits. In particular, during the past 30 years, a great deal has been learned about two distinct parietofrontal circuits—one that represents near or peripersonal space, which extends roughly to the perimeter of arm's reach, and another that represents far or extrapersonal space, which extends outward from that fuzzy boundary (for reviews, see Berti & Rizzolatti, 2002; di Pellegrino & Làdavas, 2015; Cléry et al., 2015; see also Graziano, 2018). This fundamental division of labor is widely believed to reflect computational differences in the kinds of sensorimotor control that are most commonly required for each sector of space—specifically, interacting with objects in the near sector, and visually scanning them in the far sector. A few of the many interesting aspects of these cortical circuits are shown in Figures 5.14 and 5.15. For instance, some of the cells in the circuit for near space are associated with—indeed, representationally locked onto—certain body parts, like the face, arm, hand, or chest, and have bimodal responses, firing not only when an object is seen to enter a bubble of space surrounding the given body part, but also when that part is touched (Fogassi et al., 1996). In addition, the boundary between the two sectors of space is plastic and can be dynamically influenced by a variety of factors, including tool use (e.g., Berti & Frassinetti, 2000), the changing mobility of one's limbs (e.g., Lourenco & Longo, 2009), the relative desirability of objects (e.g., Valdés-Conroy et al., 2012), emotions like claustrophobic fear (e.g., Lourenco et al., 2011), and interactions with other individuals (e.g., Teneggi et al., 2013). Furthermore, the circuit for near space is immediately adjacent to, and

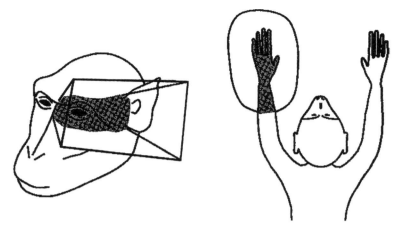

Figure 5.14. Typical bimodal responses of peripersonal neurons in the polysensory zone of the macaque frontal cortex. One neuron responded to a touch on the left side of the face around the eye (shaded area shows the region responsive to touch) and to the sight of objects near the left side of the face (boxed area shows the visually responsive region). Another neuron responded to a touch on the left arm and hand and to the sight of objects in the space near the hand. From Graziano (2018, p. 35).

even partly coextensive with, the mirror neuron system, so it is not surprising that it too has mirror-like properties, responding both when an observer sees an object that is close to his or her own hand, and when he or she sees an object that is close to someone else's hand but, from his or her own perspective, located in far space (Brozzoli et al., 2013; see also Ishida et al., 2010; Brozzoli et al., 2014).

Does the existence of separate circuits for near and far space provide the biological basis for Diessel's (2005) discovery that the majority of languages worldwide have demonstrative systems that encode a binary proximal/distal contrast? Perhaps, but the precise nature of the relationship between these perceptual and typological phenomena is not clear, and several competing factors need to be considered.

On the positive side, some studies do suggest that there are rough correspondences between proximal demonstratives and near space on the one hand, and distal demonstratives and far space on the other. In an experiment that was designed to elicit demonstratives without the participants realizing that their language was being tested, Coventry et al. (2008) found that when objects were within reach, English and Spanish speakers preferred to use proximal terms (*this* in English and *este* in Spanish), but when objects were beyond reach, they preferred to use non-proximal ones (*that* in English and either *ese* or *aquel* in Spanish) (see also Maes & de Rooij, 2007; Coventry et al., 2014). Similarly, in an experiment in which Dutch speakers were asked to produce demonstratives to describe scenes in which a person pointed to one of two objects at different distances, Peeters et al. (2015) found that they strongly favored proximal terms (*dit* or *deze*) for objects near the person, and distal terms (*dat* or *die*) for objects far from the person. Furthermore, in an experiment that focused on judgments of the (in)congruity between phrases and scenes, Stevens and Zhang (2013) found that English speakers tended to match proximal demonstratives (as in

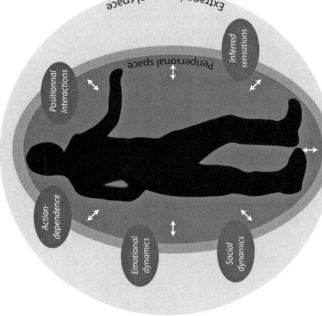

(b)

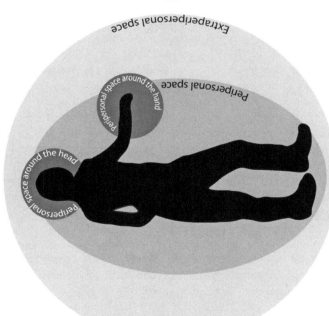

(a)

Figure 5.15. Some properties of the cortical representation of near or peripersonal space and far or extrapersonal space. (a) Head and arm/hand peripersonal spaces have a privileged representation compared to the rest of the body. (b) The boundary between near and far space representations is plastic and dynamic, under the influence of a variety of endogenous and exogenous factors.
From Cléry et al. (2015, p. 319).

this one) with objects in speaker-associated near space, and distal demonstratives (as in *that one*) with objects in either hearer-associated far space or non-associated far space (see also Coello & Bonnotte, 2013). In this connection, it is also notable that, according to a brief remark by Levinson (2012a, p. xiii), "in Yélî Dnye [Papuan, Rossel Island] the proximal deictic can only be used for objects in, or at least potentially in, one's grasp."

On the negative side, however, a number of other findings suggest that the cross-linguistically common conceptual distinction between proximal and distal demonstratives cannot be reduced in any straightforward way to the presumably universal perceptual distinction between near and far space. For one thing, setting aside rare languages like Yélî Dnye, it only takes a bit of reflection to realize that demonstratives are not restricted to more or less fixed sectors of space such as within vs. beyond arm's reach; instead, the distances they specify are variables that are assigned values on-the-fly by contextual semantic and pragmatic factors, thereby allowing speakers to expand or contract the referential range of demonstratives as needed (Kemmerer, 1999). For instance, Talmy (1988, pp. 168–169) used the sentences *This speck is smaller than that speck* and *This planet is smaller than that planet* to illustrate how the proximal/distal contrast is not rigid but flexible: "The scenes referred to by these sentences differ greatly, involving tiny objects millimeters apart to huge objects parsecs apart; therefore, the scenes' differences as to the magnitude of size or distance must arise from the lexical elements, they cannot be traced to the deictics. . . ." In a similar vein but from an experimental perspective, Bonfiglioli et al. (2009) found that even when the target objects for reach-to-grasp movements were all located at different positions *within peripersonal space*, Italian speakers still displayed significant sensitivity to the proximal/distal contrast in their language (e.g., *questo* vs. *quello*), since they not only reacted faster to objects that were very close (12 cm away) when those objects were named with proximal rather than distal terms, but also reacted faster to objects that were less close but still within arm's reach (30 cm away) when those objects were named with distal rather than proximal terms. In addition, social circumstances often modulate the use of spatial demonstratives, as shown by Peeters et al. (2015), who obtained electrophysiological evidence that in a situation like a face-to-face conversation involving two Dutch speakers, it is acceptable for one of them to use a proximal term to refer to an object located anywhere within the shared space between them, regardless of who it is closer to (see also Jungbluth, 2003; Peeters & Özyürek, 2016). Contrary to the authors' interpretation, however, this particular finding may not be completely at odds with the view that the proximal/distal distinction in demonstratives is somehow connected with the near/far distinction in perception, since it may fit with the recent discovery that, as mentioned earlier, the cortical circuit for near space is also strongly influenced by social circumstances (Brozzoli et al., 2013; Teneggi et al., 2013; see also Ishida et al., 2010; Brozzoli et al., 2014). Further research is needed to explore this topic in greater depth.

Now, given the many positive and negative factors that we have considered, it appears that any plausible account of the relationship between the cross-linguistic proximal/distal distinction and the perceptual near/far distinction must ultimately be quite subtle and nuanced. Extending some of Anderson's (2010) ideas about "neural reuse," one could speculate that when demonstrative systems develop, they often exploit, recycle, or redeploy the two parietofrontal circuits for near and far space in the following selective manner: they tend to retain the basic contrast between two egocentrically anchored sectors of space, but they no longer restrict it to the zones delimited by the peripersonal/extrapersonal boundary; instead, they allow speakers to apply it flexibly so as to accommodate a wide spectrum of semantic and pragmatic contexts. Still, despite whatever superficial appeal this line of thinking may have, it would need to be fleshed out much more fully in order to constitute a viable hypothesis, and it would also need to be linked, in one way or another, to the sorts of grounded theories of conceptual knowledge that we encountered in Chapter 2.

So far our discussion of the neural substrates of demonstratives has focused entirely on the most frequent kind of distance-based distinction, namely proximal/distal. Earlier, however, we reviewed many other kinds of demonstrative systems, and they too pose important challenges for future neuroscientific research on the conceptualization of spatial relations. For instance, continuing with the primary semantic parameter of radial distance from the deictic center, as many as 88 (38%) of the 234 languages in Diessel's (2005) global sample have three-term systems that distinguish between proximal, medial, and distal (e.g., Yimas, Lower Sepik, Papua New Guinea), so it is definitely worthwhile to ask how such systems are implemented in the brain, especially in light of the fact that they clearly deviate from the primitive perceptual platform provided by the two parietofrontal circuits for near and far space. We have also seen that a very small proportion of languages—just 4% of Diessel's (2005) sample—have four-term systems that add a category called "very distal" (e.g., Tlingit, Na Dane, Yukon), and their cortical underpinnings are likewise mysterious. On the other hand, we noted that some languages have person-oriented systems that include a term for "near addressee" (e.g., Pangasinan, Western Austronesian, Philippines), and it is exciting to imagine that the regular use of such a term may recruit the mirror-like function of the cortical circuit for near space (Brozzoli et al., 2013; see also Ishida et al., 2010; Brozzoli et al., 2014). Similarly, the recent discovery that this circuit can be modulated by social interaction may have some bearing on the unique type of demonstrative system in Jahai (Mon-Khmer, Malaysia), which distinguishes between the interior, the speaker-anchored exterior, and the addressee-anchored exterior of the roughly circular bubble of space formed by two individuals in a conversational dyad (see again Figure 5.9 and the associated text). Finally, any comprehensive neuroscientific account of demonstratives would have to address the numerous complexities found in systems that incorporate other semantic parameters, such as elevation, visibility, geography, and movement (see again Tables 5.3 and 5.4 and the associated text), with the most daunting gauntlet undoubtedly being thrown down by the extraordinarily intricate system in Central Yup'ik, which has over 400 terms (see again Table 5.5 and the associated text). The richly specified concepts encoded by these terms are most likely distributed across multiple modal and transmodal cortical areas, and mapping out that neurotopography, even in rough outline, would be a tremendous achievement, to say the least.

CONCLUSION

During the past few decades, a great deal of research in semantic typology has focused on the major classes and subclasses of categorical spatial relations that are encoded cross-linguistically. In our brief review of this large literature, we emphasized two important generalizations. First, a number of patterns have been identified that lend some coherence to each of the semantic fields comprising this complex conceptual realm. Here are a few salient examples that are worth reiterating: regarding topological relations, a similarity gradient that extends from a prototypical *on*-like situation of surface support (e.g., "cup on table") to a prototypical *in*-like situation of full containment (e.g., "apple in bowl") recurs across many languages; regarding projective relations, most languages have several sets of expressions that instantiate up to three frames of reference (intrinsic, relative, and absolute); and regarding deictic relations, over 50% of languages have demonstrative systems that specify a binary proximal/distal contrast. Second, despite these cross-linguistic tendencies, there is still a huge amount of variation involving the specific concepts that are grammaticalized, which suggests that every language has, to some degree, its own distinctive spatial ontology, with idiosyncratic notions ranging from Tzeltal's *waxal* ("the figure is in a taller-than-wide rectangular or cylindrical ground that is vertically standing"), to Laz's *ce-* ("the figure is in a static location that resulted from its downward movement into contact with the ground"), to Central Yup'ik's *camani* ("the figure is a stationary, obscured entity that can be found either down below the speaker or toward the river"). Together, these two generalizations provide valuable clues about both the natural predispositions and the cultural plasticity of the neurocognitive architecture that underlies the conceptualization of categorical spatial relations.

Somewhat surprisingly, however, only a few serious efforts have been made so far to elucidate this architecture. To be sure, there is mounting evidence that the left IPL is a key cortical region for representing the meanings of English locative prepositions, and one fMRI study has tried to disentangle the neural correlates of intrinsic and relative frames of reference. But when these investigations are considered in the context of the preceding typological survey of the kinds of categorical spatial relations that are encoded cross-linguistically, it immediately becomes clear that the research done so far is merely spadework, and that most of this rich neurocognitive terrain remains to be mined. Here are just a few of the many open questions that we highlighted as potential topics for future exploration. Do the meanings of topological and projective terms recruit largely overlapping or largely segregrated sectors of the left IPL? Within this region, what is the representational geometry of the cross-linguistically common ON-IN similarity gradient described earlier? In languages that use grammaticalized body part terms to structure the intrinsic frame of reference, are the meanings of those terms represented in, or perhaps just anterior to, the left EBA? What brain mechanisms underlie the amazing ability of some cultures to constantly keep track of, and talk about, the locations of objects according to an absolute frame of reference that is based on, say, the cardinal directions, or the incline of the local landscape? And finally, how do demonstrative systems that make a proximal/distal distinction relate to the two cortical circuits for near and far space?

PART III

Broader Questions

6

HOW DO LANGUAGE-SPECIFIC CONCEPTS
RELATE TO COGNITION?

The "linguistic relativity principle"... means, in informal terms, that users of markedly different grammars are pointed by their grammars toward different types of observations and different evaluations of externally similar acts of observation, and hence are not equivalent as observers but must arrive at somewhat different views of the world.
—Benjamin Lee Whorf (1956, p. 221)

INTRODUCTION

In the previous three chapters we surveyed a great deal of typological data showing that even though the roughly 6,500 languages of the world display some interesting similarities in their conceptual representation of objects, actions, and spatial relations, they exhibit far more differences. These pervasive cross-linguistic differences are manifested not only in the lexical partitioning and packaging of particular semantic domains, but also in the aspects of experience that speakers must regularly encode in grammatical constructions and hence habitually track. Since we have already discussed the implications of these findings for contemporary research on the neural substrates of conceptual knowledge, we will now step back from the details and ask a much broader question: How do language-specific concepts relate to cognition? The interaction between language and thought has fascinated scholars and laypeople alike for centuries, but during the past few decades this complex topic has gained significance from the discovery that, as just mentioned, the amount of cross-linguistic diversity in both lexical and grammatical semantics is much greater than often assumed.

The first two sections of this chapter draw upon psychological and neuroscientific studies to support two seemingly contradictory but actually complementary claims: many forms of cognition do not depend on language-specific concepts; nonetheless, such concepts do sometimes influence a variety of cognitive processes, in keeping with Whorf's (1956) linguistic relativity hypothesis (or at least with a weak version of it). The last section then addresses some interpretive issues regarding recent neuroscientific evidence that some verbal and nonverbal semantic tasks have partly shared cortical underpinnings.

MANY FORMS OF COGNITION DO NOT DEPEND ON LANGUAGE-SPECIFIC CONCEPTS

Sanity check

Let's begin by acknowledging that it's clearly possible for thought to occur without language. Here are five fairly straightforward and uncontroversial points that justify this assumption. First, impressive cognitive capacities have been documented in many nonhuman species that lack full-fledged language, including monkeys and apes (e.g., Tomasello & Call, 1997), dogs and wolves (e.g., Hare & Tomasello, 2005), dolphins and whales (e.g., Whitehead & Rendell, 2014), ravens and crows (e.g., Emery & Clayton, 2004), squid and octopuses (e.g., Godfrey-Smith, 2016), and even honeybees (e.g., Chittka, 2017). Second, preverbal infants evince fundamental forms of "core knowledge" about objects, substances, magnitudes, animals, and people (e.g., Spelke, 2016). Third, just because a particular language happens to lack a word or morpheme for a particular concept doesn't mean that the speakers of that language never employ that concept. In the domain of kinship, for example, the English term *uncle* doesn't distinguish between someone's mother's brother and someone's father's brother, but it seems safe to say that most English speakers can still understand and appreciate these contrasting matrilineal and patrilineal relations, especially at large family gatherings when failing to do so could be embarrassing. Fourth, Malt et al. (2010, p. 33) make the following incisive observation: "It must logically be true that any useful conceptual distinction that is directly reflected in language had to have been noticed by humans before the words labeling that distinction came about." And fifth, Pinker (1994, p. 57) draws attention to the fact that some thoughts are hard to express: "We have all had the experience of uttering or writing a sentence, then stopping and realizing that it wasn't exactly what we meant to say. To have that feeling, there has to be a 'what we meant to say' that is different from what we said."

Psychological support

Turning to specific studies, several psychological experiments have revealed situations in which people's thoughts are more tightly linked to the world than to words. As indicated below, such findings have emerged for all three of the conceptual realms that we concentrated on earlier: objects, actions, and spatial relations.

Regarding objects, in Chapter 3 we saw that many studies have reported substantial cross-linguistic variation in the naming of familiar household containers and drinking vessels such as boxes, bottles, jars, cups, mugs, glasses, and so forth (Kronenfeld et al., 1985; Malt et al., 1999, 2003; Ameel et al., 2008; Pavlenko & Malt, 2011; Majid et al., 2015; Whelpton et al., 2015). Crucially, we noted that in Malt et al.'s (1999) investigation, even though speakers of English, Argentinian Spanish, and Mandarin Chinese manifested strikingly different patterns of sorting these kinds of objects according to language-specific names, they manifested remarkably similar patterns of sorting the very same objects according to physical similarity, functional similarity, and overall similarity. These results imply that, at least in this rather small semantic sphere, people have two sets of concepts that only partially overlap: one that varies greatly across languages and is used largely for talking about the designated types of objects, and another that is more or less independent of language and is used largely for directly interacting with those objects.

Regarding actions, in Chapter 4 we saw that one of the most intensively studied manifestations of cross-linguistic variation involves the lexicalization of motion events. To briefly recapitulate a key distinction made by Talmy's (1985, 1991, 2000) typological framework, in satellite-framed languages (henceforth S-languages) like English, manner is preferentially encoded by the main verb and path by a so-called "satellite," such as a prepositional phrase (e.g., *The bottle floated into the cave*), whereas in verb-framed languages (henceforth V-languages) like Spanish, path is preferentially encoded by the main verb and manner by an optional, and often omitted, adverbial adjunct in a syntactically subordinate clause (e.g., *La botella entró a la cueva flotando* "The bottle entered the cave floating"). Due in part to these contrasting lexicalization patterns, S-languages tend to develop much richer inventories of manner verbs than V-languages, and moreover these finely distinguished manner verbs are not just static dictionary entries but are actively used in a wide range of settings, including spontaneous conversation, creative writing, newspaper reporting, describing pictures of motion events, and naming videoclips of motion events (Slobin, 2000, 2003). Several studies have shown, however, that even though speakers of S- and V-languages often represent motion events differently during online language processing, they tend to represent them in more or less the same ways during certain kinds of nonverbal tasks. For example, Gennari et al. (2002) found that after English and Spanish speakers passively viewed videoclips of motion events without any instruction to label them, they performed quite comparably on an old-new recognition memory task and also on a task that required them to judge which of two choice videoclips was more similar to a pivot videoclip—one that had the same manner but a different path, or one that had the same path but a different manner. Analogous results were obtained by Papafragou et al. (2002) in a study that involved speakers of English and Modern Greek, the latter being a V-language. And in a subsequent study by Papafragou et al. (2006), it was found that while English speakers express manner more frequently than Greek speakers when describing motion events, the rate at which Greek speakers do so increases significantly when manner cannot be inferred from the context—a result which suggests that these speakers do monitor information about manner for pragmatic purposes, despite the fact that the syntactic structure of their language doesn't compel them to encode it.

Finally, regarding spatial relations, in Chapter 5 we saw that although English distinguishes *on* from *above/over*, many other languages—perhaps even the majority (Levinson & Meira, 2003; Levinson & Wilkins, 2006b)—have morphemes that encode the general notion of superadjacency, which is neutral with respect to whether the figure contacts the ground. Korean is one such language, and to investigate whether this form of cross-linguistic variation influences nonverbal spatial memory, Munnich et al. (2001) asked speakers of English and Korean to perform two tasks with the same stimuli, which consisted of spatial arrays showing a ball in any of 72 locations superadjacent to a table. In the naming task subjects completed the sentence *The ball is ____ the table* (or the equivalent sentence in Korean). In the memory task they viewed an array for 500 msec, and then after a 500 msec delay they saw another array which they judged as being either the same as or different from the initial one. In the naming task the English speakers consistently employed the lexical contrast between *on* and *above/over*, whereas the Korean speakers rarely mentioned the contact/noncontact distinction. In the memory task, however, the two groups of subjects had almost identical patterns of accuracy for all 72 locations, including an advantage for locations aligned with the surface of the table. This study therefore suggests that nonverbal spatial memory is not significantly affected by whether the contact/noncontact distinction is linguistically encoded on a regular basis throughout one's life. In other words, even though Korean does not force speakers to fractionate the category of superadjacency according to the presence or absence of contact between figure and ground, this spatial distinction is nevertheless perceptually prominent enough to modulate the operation of recognition memory in Korean speakers.[1]

Taken together, these experimental findings indicate that some cognitive processes involving objects, actions, and spatial relations are not constrained by the meanings of particular words in particular languages, but instead reflect strategies of categorization, problem-solving, and decision-making that are common across different speech communities.

Neuroscientific support

A number of neuroscientific studies also suggest that thinking often transcends language-specific concepts. Let's begin with some relevant research involving brain-damaged patients. Many aphasic individuals are impaired on both verbal and non-verbal semantic tasks (for a review, see Gainotti, 2014), but many others, including some who display total or near-total language loss, can still conduct a host of sophisticated cognitive operations, such as adding, subtracting, multiplying, and dividing; solving problems that require causal or logical reasoning; inferring other people's mental states from their behavior; and successfully navigating complex environments (for a review, see Federenko & Varley, 2016).

An especially interesting case of the latter type of patient is Brother John, a 50-year-old epileptic man who worked as an editor of letters for his religious order (Lecours & Joanette, 1980). Although he suffered primarily from short seizures (1–5 minutes, up to 5 times a day), he sometimes experienced long "spells" (1–11 hours, about once a month). During the initial phase of a spell, all of his linguistic abilities, including inner speech, would temporarily shut down, but most of his non-linguistic abilities would remain intact. Thus, he could still recognize objects and events, use tools and utensils, find his way around familiar buildings and towns, adapt to unexpected situational changes, and carry out instructions that he was given previously. For instance, the researchers told him that at different intervals over the course of a spell he should record himself trying to speak correctly, and he was able to both recall and execute these instructions. Indeed, he still knew how to use a tape recorder by inserting a cassette, turning certain knobs, pushing certain buttons, etc., and according to Lecours and Joanette (1980, p. 20), "Brother John maintains . . . that he need not tell himself

---

[1] Notably, Holmes et al. (2017) recently found that, contra Munnich et al. (2001), whether one's native language obligatorily marks the contact/noncontact distinction *can* affect one's non-linguistic sensitivity to this distinction; however, such sensitivity is modulated by the immediate linguistic context.

the words 'tape recorder,' 'magnetic tape,' 'red button on the left,' 'turn,' 'push,' and so forth, nor any sequential arrangement of these words into appropriate phrases and sentences, in order to be capable of properly operating a tape recorder."

On one dramatic occasion, Brother John was traveling by train from Italy to a small village in Switzerland that he had never visited before, and immediately upon reaching his destination he suddenly found himself reduced to a state of global aphasia by the abrupt onset of a spell. Despite this affliction, however, he was still able to gather his suitcases, disembark from the train, present his transportation papers to the attending agent, look for and find a hotel, show the registration clerk his passport and medic-alert bracelet, mime his desire for a room, unlock the door with a key, go to the restaurant, and point to an item on the menu that he hoped would be good but that turned out, unfortunately, to be a dish he detested. After returning to his room and sleeping for several hours, he awoke with his linguistic functions restored, and then went back down to the desk clerk to apologize for his "foolish" behavior.

Now, because most of the findings that Lecours and Joanette (1980) report are from informal observations rather than carefully controlled experiments, there is not enough data to justify the inference that Brother John's spells rendered him completely incapable of accessing language-specific concepts. Nonetheless, the following points are both undeniable and significant: first, the spells did prevent him from producing and comprehending (even during covert self-talk) the words that encode those concepts; and second, despite this profound handicap, he could still think and act quite intelligently.

It is also noteworthy that a few studies of semantic dementia (SD) have revealed double dissociations between verbal and nonverbal semantic tasks. As discussed in Chapter 2, SD is a devastating disease in which conceptual knowledge gradually erodes due to progressive tissue loss and hypometabolism in the anterior temporal lobes (ATLs) bilaterally. Early on, however, some patients exhibit hemispheric asymmetries in their ATL dysfunction and, importantly, also manifest corresponding differences in their conceptual deficits. In particular, patients with predominantly left-sided ATL atrophy generally have more trouble with verbal than nonverbal semantic tasks, whereas those with predominantly right-sided ATL atrophy generally display the opposite performance profile (e.g., Gorno-Tempini et al., 2004; Snowden et al., 2004, 2012; Acres et al., 2009; Butler et al., 2009; Mion et al., 2010; Mesulam et al., 2013; for a review, see Gainotti, 2015).

Further evidence that some forms of cognition do not rely on language-specific concepts comes from fMRI studies involving healthy participants. For instance, a number of investigations have compared the activity patterns evoked by verbal and nonverbal semantic tasks and found differences not only in the ATLs (consistent with the data from SD), but also in several other cortical regions above and beyond those that only represent the contrasting kinds of stimuli (see the meta-analysis by Rice et al., 2015; see also Krieger-Redwood et al., 2015; Federenko & Varley, 2016; Amit et al., 2017; Hoffman & Lambon Ralph, 2018).

In addition, a remarkable study by Honey et al. (2012) revealed that when English and Russian speakers listened to translations of the same 11-minute-long story, their brains responded in strikingly similar ways, with nearly equal within-group and between-group correlations among time-locked neural signals in many higher-order temporal, parietal, and frontal areas, both laterally and medially and in both left and right hemispheres, as shown in Figure 6.1. Because the purpose of translation is, as

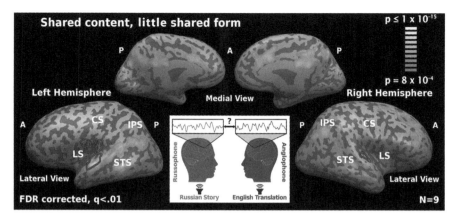

Figure 6.1. Results from Honey et al.'s (2012) fMRI study in which English speakers and Russian speakers listened to translations of the same story. The cortical areas highlighted in the orange-to-yellow spectrum had significantly correlated signal fluctuations in the two groups of subjects, suggesting shared narrative content. The areas outlined in red were commonly engaged when both groups of subjects heard the Russian version of the story, so they reflect responses restricted primarily to Russian phonetic forms. A color version is in the color plates section.
Abbreviations: A = anterior; P = posterior; LS = lateral sulcus; CS = central sulcus; STS = superior temporal sulcus; IPS = intraparietal sulcus.
From Honey et al. (2012, p. 15281).

Jackendoff (1997, p. 183) put it, "to preserve the thought behind the expression," it is reasonable to suppose that these shared cortical responses, most of which occurred in transmodal regions, reflect a level of narrative comprehension that transcends language-specific concepts. And this is, in fact, Honey et al.'s (2012, p. 15282) interpretation. What's more, they conclude that their findings pose "a serious challenge to the strong Whorfian view that linguistic peculiarities substantially determine what individuals perceive and think (Whorf, 1956)." On the other hand, it is important to bear in mind that, as noted in Chapter 1, translation is rarely if ever perfect, especially when it comes to whole stories. Hence, we should not dismiss the possibility that the activity patterns depicted in Figure 6.1 may not be limited to a language-independent level of understanding, but may also reflect the retrieval of some lexical-semantic and grammatical-semantic structures that differ between English and Russian.[2] In

---

[2] For just one example of lexical-semantic differences, recall the discussion in Chapter 3 of the contrasting categories of drinking vessels in English and Russian (see Table 3.4 and the associated text). And with regard to grammatical-semantic differences, many manifestations could easily be adduced. For instance, English makes abundant use of articles to encode distinctions involving definiteness and specificity, whereas Russian does not (following the trend of 90% of the world's languages; see Dixon, 2010a, p. 160, and Dixon, 2016, p. 82). Conversely, like all Slavic languages, Russian has rich inflectional paradigms for case, aspect, and many other features, whereas English does not (for some representative analyses from the perspective of cognitive linguistics, see Divjak & Kochańska, 2007; see also Laura Janda's extensive research on grammatical-semantic phenomena in Russian: http://ansatte.uit.no/laura.janda/).

principle, this hypothesis could be tested by combining comparative conceptual analyses of the two versions of the narrative with comparative multivariate pattern analyses of the two sets of neuroimaging data.

LANGUAGE-SPECIFIC CONCEPTS NONETHELESS DO INFLUENCE SOME FORMS OF COGNITION
The linguistic relativity hypothesis

As just mentioned, Honey et al. (2012, p. 15282) reject "the strong Whorfian view that linguistic peculiarities substantially determine what individuals perceive and think (Whorf, 1956)." Such an extreme view is really just a straw man, however, since no one familiar with modern psychology and neuroscience seriously endorses it. Moreover, even though Whorf himself did make some pretty bold statements, passages like the following suggest that he didn't hold a deeply deterministic view either: "the apprehension of space is given in substantially the same form by experience irrespective of language" (1956, p. 158), and "visual perception is basically the same for all normal persons past infancy, and conforms to definite laws" (1956, p. 163).

Rather, the main proposal for which Whorf is famous—or infamous, depending on one's perspective—is the linguistic relativity hypothesis. Here is the essence of the argument in the form of a short syllogism:

- *Premise 1*: Different languages provide their speakers with different conventionalized conceptual systems.
- *Premise 2*: The conceptual system of a given language sometimes influences how speakers think during nonverbal tasks.
- *Conclusion*: Therefore, speakers of different languages sometimes think differently during nonverbal tasks.

The truth of the first premise is indisputable. Indeed, from Whorf's early 20th century predecessors (especially Franz Boas and Edward Sapir) up to the present, research in semantic typology has disclosed a tremendous amount of diversity in how languages represent numerous domains of human experience. In Chapters 3, 4, and 5 we looked in detail at how this diversity is manifested in the large conceptual realms of objects, actions, and spatial relations, and in Chapter 1 we briefly noted that considerable variation has also been found in many other semantic spheres, such as colors, landscapes, odors, temperatures, emotions, numbers, kinship, time periods, and sources of knowledge (i.e., evidentiality). As a refresher, here are a few examples. Unlike English, Miraña (Witotoan, Peru/Columbia) has an inventory of 66 shape-based classifiers that speakers must selectively combine with nouns whenever they refer to concrete entities (Seifart, 2009; see Table 3.9 in Chapter 3 and the associated text). Unlike English, Kalam (Trans-New Guinea, Papua New Guinea) only has about 130 verb roots in its entire lexicon, and speakers must serialize them in chains of up to nine elements in order to describe complex events (Pawley, 1987, 1993, 2008, 2011; see Table 4.12 in Chapter 4 and the associated text). And unlike English, Central Yup'ik (Eskimo-Aleut, Alaska) has an enormous demonstrative system with over 400 multimorphemic terms, so that when speakers want to indicate deictic spatial relations, they must take into account not only a primary three-way distinction between "extended," "restricted," and "obscured," but also 10 other cross-cutting spatial features as well as a variety of inflectional cases (Jacobson, 1984; see Table 5.5 in Chapter 5 and the associated text).

The second premise, which is more subtle than the first, can be fleshed out as follows. As just stated, the unique conceptual system of a given language forces its speakers to make certain category distinctions rather than others. And because those speakers must repeatedly attend to those distinctions (especially the ones that are grammatically encoded) when they communicate with each other, they develop a special kind of expertise that is culturally shared and involves not only the efficient on-line processing of the pertinent language-specific concepts, but also the intuitive sense that those concepts are, for the most part, natural and obvious (for further discussion of this topic, see the beginning of Chapter 1). As a result, those concepts are sometimes activated during nonverbal tasks too, accentuating certain aspects of experience and thereby facilitating classification, reasoning, decision-making, and behavior. In an insightful paper about the linguistic relativity hypothesis, Reines and Prinz (2009, p. 1030) express this key notion as follows: "By labeling things, language draws our attention to features of the world, and noticing these features becomes habitual. Those habits bias which of the many discernable categories we recognize by default, and may even impose category boundaries we would not notice otherwise."

Now, if the second premise, like the first, is true, the conclusion, which is the heart of the linguistic relativity hypothesis, must be treated as plausible. What, then, is the empirical status of the second premise, and, by extension, of the linguistic relativity hypothesis? Because the claim is not that language *always determines* cognition (a radical view that we refuted in the previous section), but rather that it *sometimes influences* cognition, one should expect to find inconsistent effects that are modulated by many factors. And if one looks back over the last 50 years or so of research on this topic, that's pretty much what one sees. For instance, in the previous section we discussed several studies which found that speakers of different languages perform certain nonverbal tasks in similar ways that reflect language-independent representations and processes, rather than in different ways that reflect language-specific concepts; however, a number of other studies have obtained results of the latter kind instead, in line with the argument presented above (for a book-length survey, see Everett, 2013; for other reviews and perspectives, see Gumperz & Levinson, 1996; Gentner & Goldin-Meadow, 2003; Reines & Prinz, 2009; Wolff & Holmes, 2011; Lupyan, 2012a, 2012b; Pavlenko, 2014; Lupyan & Bergen, 2016; Casasanto, 2016, 2017; see also the special 2016 issue of *Language Learning* [volume 66, issue 3]). Given this long history of seemingly contradictory outcomes, Byland and Athanasopoulos (2014, p. 953) recently made the following trenchant remark: "In view of the available empirical evidence, it becomes clear that, instead of asking whether language influences thought or not, we should ask which cognitive processes are affected by which linguistic categories under which circumstances." This statement nicely captures the nuanced position that appears to be adopted by most of the leading figures currently working on the linguistic relativity hypothesis. But because a detailed review of this large literature would take us too far afield, we will only consider a few of the multifarious studies that have generated results in keeping with the claim that speakers of different languages do sometimes think differently during nonverbal tasks.

Psychological support

As before, it's worthwhile to concentrate on the three large conceptual realms that we covered in Chapters 3, 4, and 5—namely, objects, actions, and spatial relations.

Regarding objects, several studies have found that the way people perform certain kinds of nonverbal tasks depends, in part, on whether their language has a rich nominal classification system. English lacks such a system, and, like other languages of this type, most of its words for inanimate objects are count nouns whose meanings generally include information about the geometric properties of the designated entities. Conversely, as discussed in Chapters 1 and 3, in many languages that do have well-developed nominal classification systems, the vast majority of words for inanimate objects are mass nouns that denote unformed substances, and speakers must combine them with shape-related classifiers in order to individuate particular entities. For instance, in Yucatec (Mayan, Mexico) the classifier *tz'iit* is used for long thin things (i.e., those that are saliently one-dimensional), and, in cookie-cutter fashion, it imposes this configuration on whatever type of material is denoted by the noun it occurs with. Thus, when it occurs with *ha'as* ("banana stuff"), the whole phrase refers to a banana; when it occurs with *kib'* ("wax"), the whole phrase refers to a candle; and when it occurs with *che'* ("wood"), the whole phrase refers to a stick (see the right-hand column of Table 1.3 in Chapter 1).

In a series of experiments, Lucy and Gaskins (2001, 2003) sought to determine whether the different types of object representation exhibited by nouns in English and Yucatec have significant effects on nonverbal cognition, with the specific predictions being that, at least in some situations, English speakers would preferentially attend more to the shapes than the material compositions of objects, whereas Yucatec speakers would display the opposite tendency. To test these predictions, the researchers employed a similarity judgment task in which, on every trial, subjects were first shown three stimuli: a pivot object (e.g., a plastic comb with a handle), a choice object with the same shape as the pivot but a different material (e.g., a wooden comb with a handle), and a choice object with the same material as the pivot but a different shape (e.g., a plastic comb without a handle). The subjects then had to decide which choice object was more like the pivot. The results confirmed the predictions, since the English-speaking subjects grouped the objects according to shape most of the time (77%), whereas the Yucatec-speaking subjects grouped them according to material most of the time (61%).

Interestingly, subsequent studies have shown that these sorts of preferences can change as a function of learning a second language that has the other type of object representation. For instance, Japanese has a nominal classification system that is roughly analogous to the one in Yucatec, and while Japanese speakers who are monolingual gravitate toward material-based similarity judgments, those who have acquired English as a second language are more likely to make shape-based similarity judgments (Cook et al., 2006; Athanasopoulos, 2007; Athanasopoulos & Kasai, 2008).

At this juncture, it worth noting that when people perform the kinds of similarity judgment tasks that were employed in these investigations, their decisions may be influenced by inner speech, i.e., silent self-talk (a phenomenon that is discussed more fully in a separate subsection later in this chapter). Although some scholars take this to be a serious limitation, it does not imply that the tasks themselves are actually verbal rather than nonverbal, because it remains the case that neither the stimuli nor the responses involve words. If some subjects covertly name the stimuli while performing the task, this only serves to demonstrate that language invades their thinking, and as Byland and Athanasopoulos (2014, p. 963) point out, "the issue at stake is not really whether nonverbal tasks are impervious to linguistic influence, but empirically spelling out the extent to which and just precisely in which ways language intrudes into nonverbal behavior (i.e., the Whorfian problem)."

An especially compelling manifestation of such intrusion comes from Srinivasan (2010), who compared Mandarin Chinese, a language in which many nouns are assigned specific shape-related classifiers, with English and Russian, both of which are non-classifier languages. In the main experiment, speakers of all three languages performed a speeded numerical task that discouraged strategic planning. On each trial, they saw a visual array of objects and had to count, as quickly as possible, the number of items belonging to a target category while ignoring the intermixed items belonging to a different category. The key finding was that, compared to the English and Russian speakers, the Mandarin speakers took significantly longer to count target objects (e.g., spatulas) when they were presented together with distractors that had the same Mandarin classifier (e.g., brooms) than when they were presented together with distractors that had a different Mandarin classifier (e.g., pants). This interference effect is quite interesting because it suggests that even though the Mandarin speakers could have accomplished the task most efficiently by *not* retrieving classifiers, it appears that they still retrieved them in an impulsive manner that was driven by the mere sight of the objects they applied to, with the result that their responses were delayed.

Shifting to actions, let's consider once again the fact that although the path component of motion events is prominently encoded in both S- and V-languages, the manner component tends to be represented much more often, and much more precisely, in S- than V-languages (Slobin, 2000, 2003, 2004). Earlier we noted that despite this distinction, speakers of the two types of languages have been found to perform quite similarly on some kinds of nonverbal tasks (Gennari et al., 2002; Papafragou et al., 2002, 2006). Now, however, we will see that they have also been found to perform quite differently on other kinds of nonverbal tasks (Kersten et al., 2010; Filipović, 2011).

For instance, Kersten et al. (2010) conducted a very clever study in which monolingual speakers of English (an S-language) and monolingual speakers of Spanish (a V-language) were told that four different species of bug-like creatures had been discovered on Mars, each of which was referred to simply by a number. On every trial of the key experiment, the subjects were instructed to classify a creature moving around on a computer screen as belonging to one of the four species, and then they were given feedback regarding the correctness of their response. Based on this trial-by-trial feedback, they could, in principle, gradually infer which attributes, and which values of those attributes, were most relevant to categorizing the creatures. In the two main conditions, manner of motion and path of motion were the pertinent attributes, and both of them had four values. The critical findings were as follows. In the manner condition, the English speakers performed significantly better than the Spanish speakers; however, in the path condition, the two groups performed the same. These results support the linguistic relativity hypothesis because the English speakers, but not the Spanish speakers, already had a deeply entrenched habit of attending to manner for linguistic purposes, and this perceptual bias presumably helped them notice the relevance of manner in the novel category-learning situation; in contrast, the two groups were equally likely to consider the relevance of path, since that component of motion events is encoded with comparable frequency in both languages.

In another interesting study, Filipović (2011) obtained evidence that the differential treatment of manner information in S- and V-languages also influences speakers' nonverbal memory for motion events. In the first part of the experiment, she showed monolingual English and Spanish speakers a block of videoclips, each of which lasted roughly six seconds and portrayed a person either locomoting in three manners (e.g., limping out of a building, staggering down a sidewalk, and marching around a corner) or executing several non-locomotive activities (e.g., opening a book, leafing through it, and closing it). Half of the subjects in each group described what they saw, and the other half simply watched the videoclips. In the second part of the experiment, the subjects performed a two-minute distractor task that involved counting randomized letters in a 10 x 10 grid. And in the last part, they viewed another block of videoclips and indicated, for each one, whether they had seen an identical sequence of events in the first block. In actuality, all of the motion-related videoclips in the second block differed from those in the first block with respect to just one of the three manners, and while half of the non-motion-related videoclips in the second block likewise differed from those in the first block with respect to just one of the three sub-events, the other half did not differ at all. Analyses of the data revealed that the English speakers had significantly better memory than the Spanish speakers for the motion-related videoclips, but not for the non-motion-related videoclips. Moreover, neither group's memory was affected by whether or not they described the videoclips in the first block. These findings suggest that because English places greater weight than Spanish on the manner features of motion events, English speakers are more likely than Spanish speakers to not only notice these features in perceived situations, but also store them in long-term memory, in case that information needs to be recalled and potentially reported at some future time.

Lastly, we turn to the domain of categorical spatial relations. It has been investigated quite intensively from the perspective of the linguistic relativity hypothesis, and a number of studies have shown that the language one speaks can both decrease and increase one's perceptual sensitivity to certain kinds of spatial relations.

We saw in the previous section that even though Korean does not lexicalize the contact/noncontact distinction, speakers were still influenced by it when they performed a nonverbal memory task (Munnich et al., 2001). There is also evidence, however, that in some cases sensitivity to a particular categorical spatial distinction is present in infancy but then gradually diminishes during language acquisition because the distinction is not captured by the language being learned. This type of scenario is illustrated by a study that focused on the following contrast between English and Korean strategies for describing actions involving topological relations of containment (McDonough et al., 2003). The English expression *put in* specifies that a figure object ends up occupying the interior of a ground object, but it is neutral with respect to whether the former entity fits tightly or loosely within the latter. In Korean, on the other hand, the notion of containment is subdivided into two different categories: *kkita* designates the creation of a tight-fitting relation between figure and ground (e.g., putting a CD in its case), and *nehta* designates the creation of a loose-fitting relation between figure and ground (e.g., putting an apple in a bowl). Using a preferential looking paradigm as an indirect measure of perceptual categorization, McDonough et al. (2003) found that infants as young as nine months of age, from both English- and Korean-speaking environments, discriminated between tight and loose containment events (see also Hespos & Spelke, 2004). This kind of spatial sensitivity is clearly useful for infants growing up in Korean-speaking environments, but it is ultimately less valuable for infants growing up in English-speaking environments, and in fact when adult speakers of each language were given the same preferential looking task, the Korean speakers exhibited sensitivity to the tight/loose distinction, but the English speakers did not. In another experiment that evaluated the adult speakers' recognition of the distinction more explicitly, subjects observed the enactment of three tight containment events and one loose containment event, and then answered the question "Which is the odd one?" Significantly more Korean- than English-speaking adults based their choice on degree of fit (80% vs. 37%).

McDonough et al. (2003) interpreted their findings as evidence that when language-specific spatial categories are being learned, the perceptual judgments that are necessary to use them efficiently become increasingly automatic and habitual. Thus, Korean speakers implicitly monitor the tightness of fit of containment relations because the grammatical system of their language regularly forces them to encode distinctions along this parameter. However, spatial sensitivities that are not needed in order to use the local language may fade—e.g., English speakers can safely ignore the tight/loose contrast much of the time. As the researchers point out, the loss of sensitivity to the tight/loose contrast is remarkably similar to another dramatic instance of perceptual tuning that takes place during early language development—specifically, the loss of phonetic contrasts that are not phonemic in the target language (for a review, see Kuhl, 2004).

There are also reasons to believe that language can cause speakers to become more attuned to particularly subtle or non-obvious types of spatial relations. Bowerman and Choi (2003, p. 417) note that in cases like this, "an important stimulant to comparison can be hearing the same word. As the child encounters successive uses of the word, she 'tries' (although this process is presumably rarely if ever conscious) to align the referent situations and work out what they have in common. Sometimes . . . there is no existing concept that does the job, and the child has to construct a new one to account for the distribution of the word." An excellent example is a topological term in Tiriyó (Cariban, Brazil), namely *awee*, which refers to situations in which a figure object is suspended from part of a ground object and hangs down on either side of it, hence treating as equivalent such superficially diverse spatial arrays as a necklace around a person's neck, a tablecloth draped over a table, and a clothespin dangling from a line (Meira, 2006). It is not known whether infants are sensitive to this idiosyncratic spatial category, but it seems likely that they are not and that they must therefore gradually construct the concept through multiple exposures to *awee* when acquiring Tiriyó. Another good example is the Chamus (Nilo-Saharan, Kenya) strategy of treating the intrinsic front of a tree as either the side it leans toward or, in case it is perfectly vertical, the side with the biggest branch or the most branches (Heine, 1997a, p. 13). It seems safe to assume that these are features of trees that English speakers do not usually register, although Chamus speakers must attend to them in order to use the grammatical system of the language appropriately. In this manner, language can be said to provide "on-the-job training for attention" (Smith et al., 2002). And as Majid (2002) observes, it is useful to think of this form of linguistically driven perceptual tuning as similar to the novice-to-expert shift in categorization abilities that is known to engender more refined representations for the target domain (Palmeri et al., 2004).

So far, the most systematic investigation of language-specific influences on cognitive representations of space has been conducted by Stephen Levinson and his colleagues at the Max Planck Institute for Psycholinguistics (see especially Levinson, 2003b, and Majid et al., 2004; see also Haun et al., 2006, 2011; Haun & Rapold, 2009). This line of work has provoked a vigorous debate (see especially the exchange between Li & Gleitman, 2002, and Levinson et al., 2002; see also Li et al., 2011; Li & Abarbanell, 2018). But we will not address the many contentious issues here; instead, we will simply highlight some of the experiments which suggest that there are deep cognitive consequences of speaking a language that characterizes projective spatial relations either predominantly in terms of a relative frame of reference, like English, or predominantly in terms of an absolute frame of reference, like Warrwa (Nyulnyulan, North Australia).

The main method in these experiments involves a rotation paradigm that makes it possible to identify the frame of reference that subjects use to carry out various types of nonverbal cognitive tasks—for instance, memory tasks that require both recognition and recall, maze tasks that require tracking motion trajectories, reasoning tasks that require transitive inferences, and dance-learning tasks that require moving one's arms and hands in particular directions. To take a straightforward example, in one of the memory tasks subjects are first seated at a table on which three toy animals are lined up headed leftward, or north, and then they are rotated 180° and seated at a different table where they must arrange an identical set of toy animals so that they are just as before, with an emphasis on reconstructing the linear order. If subjects orient the animals in a leftward direction, they are invoking a relative frame of reference that takes into account their own egocentric coordinates, but if they orient the animals in a rightward (i.e., northerly) direction, they are invoking an absolute frame of reference that is anchored in environmental coordinates. When performing this type of task, as well as many others that use the rotation paradigm, subjects tend to follow the spatial coding pattern of their native language. Such results have been obtained with speakers of a variety of "relative" languages—e.g., English, Dutch, Japanese, Yucatec (Mayan, Mexico), and Kgalagadi (Khoisan, Namibia)—and a variety of "absolute" languages—e.g., Guugu Yimithirr (Pama-Nyungan, Australia) Tzeltal (Mayan, Mexico), Longgu (Austronesian, Solomon Islands), Belhare (Sino-Tibetan, Nepal), and Hai‖om (Khoisan, Namibia).

Levinson (2003b) argues that these effects are due to the fact that relative and absolute frames of reference are incommensurable. For instance, from the proposition *The knife is to the right of the fork* one cannot derive the proposition *The knife is to the south of the fork*, or vice versa. According to Levinson (2003b, pp. 290–291), this has serious implications:

Once a language has opted for one of these frames of reference and not the other, all the systems that support language, from memory, to reasoning, to gesture, have to provide information in the same frame of reference. If I remember an array as *The knife is to the right of the fork* but live in a community where no left/right terminology or computation is part of everyday life, I simply will not be able to describe it. For my memory will have failed to support the local description system, in, say, terms of north and south. The use of language thus forces other systems to come into line in such a way that semantic parameters in the public language are supported by internal systems keeping track of all experience coded in the same parameters.

Neuroscientific support

Consistent with the widespread neglect of semantic typology in cognitive neuroscience, as yet only a few studies have used modern brain mapping methods to test the linguistic relativity hypothesis. On the bright side, however, some striking discoveries have already been made (for a review, see Thierry, 2016).

For instance, in a seminal electrophysiological investigation, Thierry et al. (2009) took advantage of the fact that although both English and Greek have just one basic color term for green, they differ in their categorization of blue, such that English has, again, just one basic color term, but Greek has two—one for dark blue (*ble*) and another for light blue (*ghalazio*). In the main experiment, the researchers recorded the event-related potentials (ERPs) of both English speakers and Greek speakers while they performed an oddball detection task that required them to press a button every time they saw a square (probability 20%) within a stream of circles (probability 80%). Crucially, as shown in Figure 6.2a, each stimulus was one of four colors—dark green, light green, dark blue, or light blue—and within a given block of trials the most frequent stimuli were circles with either dark or light luminance (standard, probability 70%), and the least frequent stimuli were circles with the contrasting luminance, i.e., light if the standard was dark, and vice versa (deviant, probability 10%). The key finding was that, as shown in Figure 6.2b, the visual mismatch negativity (vMMN), which is a reliable index of the rapid, unconscious, and pre-attentive detection of rare visual stimuli, was similar for the two groups of speakers when they saw deviant shades of green, but was significantly greater for the Greek speakers than the English speakers when they saw deviant shades of blue. Importantly, when the subjects were debriefed, none of them gave any indication of knowing that the critical stimulus dimension was luminance, nor did any of them report subvocally naming the colors. Thus, these remarkable results demonstrate that even when the color of an object is irrelevant to a person's task, that person's brain still implicitly categorizes the color in a way that is influenced by his or her native language, and it does so in a fraction of a second, without the person even realizing what has happened (for a closely related study, see Athanasopoulos et al., 2010).

In another electrophysiological investigation that employed the same kind of oddball paradigm, Boutonnet et al. (2013) capitalized on the fact that while English has different labels for cups and mugs, Spanish has just one label (*taza*) for both. ERPs were recorded from English and Spanish speakers while they viewed a series of grayscale photographs of a cup, a mug, and a bowl, with the task being to press a button whenever they saw a bowl (probability 5%). In one block of trials the cup served as the standard (probability 80%) and the mug as the deviant (probability 15%), and in another block these roles were reversed. As expected, the English speakers, but not the Spanish speakers, exhibited deviant-related negativities very much like vMMNs in response to the infrequent cups and mugs, presumably reflecting the automatic

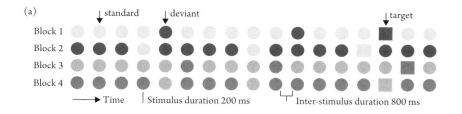

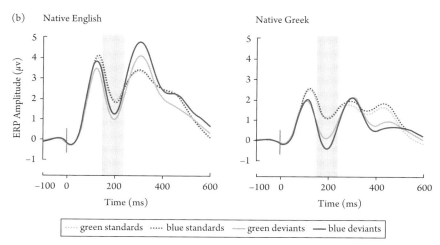

Figure 6.2. Design and results of Thierry et al.'s (2009) electrophysiological study of linguistic effects on color perception. (a) Sample stimulus sequences presented in four blocks. Subjects monitored for squares, which occurred rarely (probability 20%) in streams of circles, most of which had a "standard" color (e.g., light blue, probability 70%), but some of which had a "deviant" color (e.g., dark blue, probability 10%). (b) When English and Greek speakers saw green deviants (solid green waves), the visual mismatch negativity (vMMN), relative to green standards (dotted green waves), was similar in the two groups. However, when the two groups saw blue deviants (solid blue waves), the vMMN, relative to blue standards (dotted blue waves), was significantly greater (i.e., more negative) for the Greek speakers than the English speakers, suggesting that within 200 msec the former speakers automatically categorize the stimuli according to the distinction between two basic color terms—*ble* ("dark blue") and *ghalazio* ("light blue"). A color version is in the color plates section. From Thierry et al. (2009, pp. 4567–4568).

registration of this conceptual distinction by the former group, but not by the latter group. These findings provide further evidence that language-specific word meanings are often activated in an unconscious, pre-attentive manner when their referents are perceived.

The electrophysiological studies summarized above support the notion that one's visual system is, at least to some degree, shaped by the typologically unique lexical-semantic properties of one's language. It is essential to realize, however, that even though this notion may seem radical to some readers, it actually follows quite naturally from the combination of two well-established points that are both fundamental to this whole book: first, that concrete word meanings vary greatly across languages; and second, that they are anatomically grounded in high-level sensory, motor, and affective brain regions. Still, experimental work on what Thierry (2016) calls "neurolinguistic relativity" has only just begun, and much more research is needed to explore the idea that the cortical underpinnings of perception are sculpted, in part, by language-particular semantic structures. This proposal predicts, for example, that during ordinary instances of nonverbal perception, processing in modality-specific cortical regions often engages representations that constitute the modality-specific components of word meanings which are typologically unique to the given person's language. Furthermore, it also predicts that this engagement sometimes modulates subsequent processing in ways that are, *ipso facto*, linguistically biased (though not necessarily linguistically constrained). In the coming years, these predictions, among others, could potentially be tested by using the rapidly improving types of fMRI techniques that allow investigators to characterize and compare the representations carried by complex multivoxel patterns of cortical activity.[3]

Inner speech

In the last few subsections, we have considered several sources of support for the linguistic relativity hypothesis, which maintains that language sometimes influences other forms of cognition. It is worth emphasizing, however, that every human language constitutes, in and of itself, a unique form of cognition, since it provides its speakers with an idiosyncratic inventory of prepackaged, conventionalized concepts that have been honed over a long period of cultural history for the purpose of interpersonal communication (see the notion of "thinking for speaking" developed by Slobin, 1996; see also Tomasello, 1999, p. 150). Moreover, it is far from trivial that people actively employ these language-specific concepts not only when they overtly talk to each other, but also when they covertly talk to themselves.

In fact, recent research suggests that inner speech is one of the most salient aspects of most people's mental lives. Studies using a method called Descriptive Experience Sampling (DES)—in which, several times a day, volunteers report whatever they were aware of right before hearing a random beep—have revealed that, on average, people engage in silent self-talk 23% of the time, which is nearly a quarter of their waking moments (for reviews, see Hurlburt et al., 2013; Alderson-Day & Fernyhough, 2015). And as Fernyhough (2016, p. 66) points out, all of this inner speech is manifested in multiple ways:

---

[3] It is widely accepted that perception arises from a complex interplay between bottom-up sensory inputs and top-down cognitive expectations (for reviews, see Clark, 2013; Panichello et al., 2013; Summerfield & de Lange, 2014). In this connection, a recent study found that when people were shown ambiguous images, the prior presentation of lexical cues—in particular, English nouns—not only facilitated both recognition and discrimination, but also increased the power of posterior alpha-band (8–14 Hz) oscillations (which have been linked with top-down effects) right before each stimulus, thereby modulating the early stages of visual processing (Samaha et al., 2016). These findings provide electrophysiological evidence that word meanings can influence perception. However, I am not aware of any neuroscientific studies that have carefully compared two or more languages to determine whether lexically and/or grammatically encoded concepts can influence perception in clearly language-specific ways.

Internal self-talk can convey emotions as varied as curiosity, outrage, interest, and boredom. It can come with a range of bodily concomitants: some folk experience it as emerging from their torso or chest, while others feel it as emanating from the head, sometimes even from particular parts of the cranium (front, back, or side). Inner speech can be addressed to the self, to another individual or to no one in particular, and it can even happen in another person's voice. . . . People can talk to themselves at almost the same time as they are speaking out loud, and can sometimes be thinking things that are different from what their external voice is saying.

In addition, inner speech has been found to have several functions (again, see Alderson-Day & Fernyhough, 2015). It contributes to cognitive development during childhood; it facilitates executive operations such as task switching, planning, and reasoning; it improves motivation and self-regulation in a variety of situations that range from inhibiting impulses to competing in sports; and it enhances communal relations by allowing people to privately replay past dialogues and simulate future ones so as to determine the most prudent course of social behavior. Furthermore, some forms of psychopathology have been linked with disturbances of inner speech, as illustrated by the auditory hallucinations that afflict people with schizophrenia and the dark ruminations that plague people with depression. It is also notable that a major aim of mindfulness meditation is to detach oneself from the nearly constant stream of inner speech so as to treat it objectively and non-judgmentally as just another transient process that, like every experience, simply flows through the mind.

Over the course of recorded history, a number of famous philosophers and psychologists, including Plato, Immanuel Kant, Ludwig Wittgenstein, Max Müller, and John Watson, have maintained that thought is basically reducible to inner speech. This claim is surely too strong because, as we saw in the first section of this chapter, many forms of cognition do not necessarily rely on language. But on the other hand, it would also be wrong to regard inner speech as insignificant, given the discoveries mentioned earlier about the frequency and functionality of this well-known yet deeply personal phenomenon.

Against this background, I would like to suggest that inner speech becomes even more intriguing, and even more relevant to the complex relation between language and thought, when it is viewed from the perspective of semantic typology. After all, it is only from this perspective that one can fully appreciate the fact that the covert voices that jabber away inside our heads so much of the time always use words and constructions that reflect the unique conceptual inventories of specific languages. The ramifications of this important point can be clarified by briefly considering, once again, a few of the many cases of cross-linguistic semantic diversity that we encountered in previous chapters.

Here are three examples. First, in several languages of the Tucanoan family (Columbia/Brazil), whenever speakers make declarative past-tense statements, they must use one of five evidential markers to indicate whether the source of the information is visual, nonvisual, apparent, reported, or assumed (see Table 1.7 in Chapter 1 and the associated text). Second, in Dakota (Siouan, North and South Dakota), there is no single, all-purpose possession marker; instead, speakers must use different grammatical devices to represent the following kinds of possessed objects: body parts construed as being particularly subject to willpower (e.g., mouth, eye, hand); other body parts (e.g., nose, ribs, lungs); both consanguineal and affinal kin; and ownable things (see the subsection on split possession in Chapter 3). And third, in Arrernte (Pama-Nyungan, Australia), action verbs are often inflected for no less than 14 types of associated motion (e.g., "do coming," "do going back," "do upwards," "do downwards," "go and do," "do and go," "go back and do," "do and go back," etc.), which implies that speakers regularly construe human behaviors as taking place in the context of prior, concurrent, or subsequent motion events with particular trajectories (see Table 4.4 in Chapter 4 and the associated text).

These examples illustrate how, as Whorf (1956, p. 221) put it, "users of markedly different grammars are pointed by their grammars toward different types of observations...." The key point here, however, is that these cross-linguistic and, by extension, cross-cultural differences in conceptualization are strongly realized not only when speakers overtly produce and comprehend utterances, but also when they covertly talk to themselves. And so, if the finding that English speakers engage in self-talk nearly a quarter of the time generalizes to speakers of the thousands of other languages around the world (an issue that clearly warrants more research), it seems quite likely that a great deal of the thinking that people conduct on a daily basis is suffused with language-specific semantic structures (for further discussion, see Pavlenko, 2014, pp. 207-224).

PARTLY SHARED NEURAL SUBSTRATES FOR VERBAL AND NONVERBAL SEMANTIC TASKS: INSIGHTS AND UNCERTAINTIES

During the past few decades, many studies have employed both verbal and nonverbal semantic tasks to investigate the organization of conceptual knowledge in the brain. In the first section of this chapter, we noted that these two types of tasks often recruit partly distinct high-level cortical regions, in line with the view that the representations and processes used for understanding words are not entirely the same as those used for understanding pictures. In this last section, we will focus instead on evidence that the two types of tasks also tend to have partly shared neural substrates—e.g., similar activity patterns in healthy subjects, and similar deficit-lesion patterns in brain-damaged patients—suggesting that they frequently draw upon common cognitive resources. As we will see, in some cases it is likely that the similar results for verbal and nonverbal tasks reflect the retrieval of the very same conceptual properties, which may transcend cross-linguistic differences in meaning. In other cases, however, the correct interpretation is less clear, not only because the tasks have fewer constraints, but also because of complications introduced by cross-linguistic semantic variation. Once again, we will concentrate on studies that have dealt with objects, actions, and spatial relations.[4]

Regarding objects, numerous studies have reported partly shared neural substrates for verbal and nonverbal semantic tasks (for a review of neuropsychological studies,

---

[4] Interestingly, several studies have found that a bilateral network of mostly transmodal cortical areas is similarly engaged when people watch movies, describe those movies in spoken narratives, and listen to such narratives (e.g., Baldassano et al., 2015; Chen et al., 2017; Zadbood et al., 2017). These studies are not discussed here, however, because all of the movie conditions included conversations between characters and hence were not entirely nonverbal.

see Gainotti, 2014; for PET and fMRI studies see Vandenberghe et al., 1996; Chao et al., 1999; Chee et al., 2000; Boronat et al., 2005; Shinkareva et al., 2011; Visser et al., 2012; Devereux et al., 2013; Fairhall & Caramazza, 2013; Chen et al., 2018). To illustrate how these two types of tasks sometimes tap the same conceptual properties, here are three closely related studies that used both words and pictures to probe people's knowledge of the manipulation and function features of tools. First, Buxbaum and Saffran (2002) found that brain-damaged patients with limb apraxia due to left inferior parietal lesions were more impaired at judging whether certain tools are manipulated in similar ways than whether they are used for similar functions, and, crucially, this dissociation was manifested for both word and picture versions of the tasks. Second, in a subsequent fMRI study by the same team, Boronat et al. (2005) found that when healthy participants made manipulation-based and function-based similarity judgments for tools that were presented as both words and pictures, the manipulation condition engaged the left inferior parietal lobule significantly more than the function condition, and, once again, this contrast was manifested for both stimulus formats. Third, in another fMRI study, Chen et al. (2018) found that the activity patterns evoked by tools with similar manners of manipulation, but not those evoked by tools with similar functions, could be decoded from each other with a high degree of accuracy in the left inferior parietal lobule, regardless of whether the stimuli were words or pictures. Taken together, these results not only dovetail with a great deal of other evidence that the manipulation features of tool concepts depend on the left inferior parietal lobule (see Figure 4.14 and the associated text in Chapter 4), but also—and, in the current context, more importantly—suggest that these features are invariant to verbal and nonverbal forms of semantic access.

It is worth noting, however, that none of these studies took into account the fact that many tool concepts, such as those for familiar household containers and drinking vessels, differ substantially across languages, as shown by typological data indicating that naming patterns for the same arrays of objects criss-cross in complex ways that reflect variation in the relative weight of multiple features, including not just manipulation and function, but also shape, size, material, and cultural significance (see Tables 3.3–3.5 and the associated text in Chapter 3). As we saw in that chapter, and again in the first section of this chapter, Malt et al. (1999) found that despite such cross-linguistic diversity, speakers of English, Argentinian Spanish, and Mandarin Chinese performed more or less equally when asked to simply sort containers according to overall similarity. Thus, verbal and nonverbal object-related tasks yielded divergent results. On the other hand, in the second section of this chapter, we reviewed more recent research which showed that people sometimes perform nonverbal object-related tasks in ways that appear to be influenced by how they habitually conceptualize things for linguistic purposes. To briefly recapitulate the key points, using a triads paradigm that required participants to decide, on each trial, which of two choice objects was more like a pivot object, Lucy and Gaskins (2001, 2003) found that English speakers based their similarity judgments primarily on shape, in keeping with the shape bias of English count nouns, whereas Yucatec speakers based their similarity judgments primarily on material, in keeping with the material bias of Yucatec mass nouns (for analogous results comparing English and Japanese, see Cook et al., 2006; Athanasopoulos, 2007; Athanasopoulos & Kasai, 2008). Returning to the main thread, these findings are relevant to contemporary brain science because they raise the possibility that when studies reveal partly shared neural substrates for verbal and nonverbal semantic tasks, these cortical commonalities may not always reflect universal concepts; instead, they may sometimes reflect language-specific ones that people retrieve not just in response to verbal stimuli, but also in response to nonverbal stimuli, consistent with a weak Whorfian view.

This line of thinking is likewise pertinent to several studies that have focused on actions. For instance, as noted in Chapter 4, Kemmerer et al. (2012) reported an experiment in which 226 brain-damaged patients, most of whom suffered from strokes in various sectors of the left and right hemispheres, were given six standardized tasks that evaluated their conceptual knowledge of actions in both verbal and nonverbal ways. Poor performances on both types of tasks were significantly related to lesions in some of the same left frontal, temporal, and parietal regions (see Figure 4.13; see also Figure 4 in Kemmerer et al., 2012). In the current context, though, one of the nonverbal tasks—specifically, Picture Comparison—warrants special attention. On each trial of this task, participants must determine which of three photographs shows a different kind of action than the other two. Many of the trials are likely to be language-independent, and in fact a few patients passed this nonverbal task but failed most or even all of the verbal ones. However, as indicated in all of the neuropsychological studies that have employed this task (Kemmerer et al., 2001a, 2001b; Kemmerer & Tranel, 2003; Tranel et al., 2003; Kemmerer et al., 2012), some of the items appear to be biased by the idiosyncrasies of English verbs, since the correct picture—i.e., the "odd one out"—shows an action that is customarily named by a particular English verb, whereas both of the others show actions that are customarily named by another English verb. For example, on one trial the three pictures show what English speakers would describe as (i) a baby crawling, (ii) a person holding a baby, and (iii) two people holding hands. The right answer is (i), reflecting the distinction between crawling and holding, but this may not be so obvious to Spanish speakers, since they would probably use different verbs for all three pictures: (i) *un bebé gateando*, (ii) *una persona sosteniendo a un bebé*, and (iii) *dos personas tomados de la mano*. Moreover, when it comes to action concepts, many other languages around the world differ from English much more dramatically than Spanish (see Chapter 4), and it is unclear how their speakers would respond to the Picture Comparison task. Similar concerns can be raised about the nonverbal version of another standardized task—specifically, Kissing and Dancing—which also involves associative comparisons among pictures of actions and has been used in several neuropsychological studies (Bak & Hodges, 2003, 2004; Hillis et al., 2006).

In addition, such concerns apply to a recent fMRI study by Jouen et al. (2015) that had two conditions (see also Jouen et al., 2018). In the verbal condition, subjects read sentences describing certain kinds of actions (e.g., *The man climbs the ladder*); and in the nonverbal condition, they saw photographs of the corresponding kinds of actions. On 10% of the trials, they had to judge whether the given item had been previously presented, but otherwise their processing of the stimuli was unconstrained. As shown in Figure 6.3, a conjunction analysis of the imaging data revealed that both conditions jointly engaged the following modal and transmodal regions: in both hemispheres, several lateral temporal areas, the angular gyrus (BA39), and the retrosplenial cortex; and in just the left hemisphere, the temporoparietal junction, the temporal pole (BA38), the inferior frontal gyrus (BA45-46), the lateral (possibly hand-related) premotor cortex, and the parahippocampal gyrus. All of these regions have been linked either

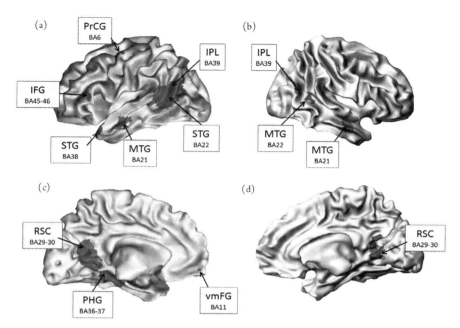

Figure 6.3. Results from Jouen et al.'s (2015) fMRI study in which participants read sentences describing certain kinds of actions (e.g., *The man climbs the ladder*) and saw photographs of the corresponding kinds of actions. The regions highlighted in red were commonly engaged in both conditions. (a) Left lateral view. (b) Right lateral view. (c) Left medial view. (d) Right medial view. A color version is in the color plates section.
Abbreviations: PrCG = precentral gyrus; IFG = inferior frontal gyrus; STG = superior temporal gyrus; MTG = middle temporal gyrus; IPL = inferior parietal lobule; RSC = retrosplenial cortex; PHG = parahippocampal gyrus; vmFG = ventromedial frontal gyrus.
From Jouen et al. (2015, p. 80).

with action concepts in particular or with semantic representations and computations in general, so the researchers were quite justified in concluding that their results disclose a complex neural architecture for action understanding that is "not limited to sensorimotor systems, but extends to the highest levels of cognition," and is accessed by both verbal and nonverbal stimuli (Jouen et al., 2015, p. 72). To their credit, they acknowledge that the subjects "might have explored the pictures . . . by a mentally evoked verbal description, which would thus activate the same neural structures as in the verbal task" (Jouen et al., 2015, p. 78). But they exclude this possibility on the grounds that, by itself, the picture condition did not engage many of the left perisylvian regions that are known to underlie phonological and syntactic processing. Indeed, it does seem likely that the common activity patterns triggered by the verbal and nonverbal stimuli reflect mental models of events that transcend language at least to some degree, and perhaps to a large degree, as in the behavioral studies of event cognition that we discussed in the first section of this chapter (Gennari et al., 2002; Papafragou et al., 2002, 2006). At the same time, though, it is also worth recalling that, as we saw in the previous section, people do sometimes respond to pictures and videos of actions in ways that are strongly influenced by language-specific strategies of conceptualization (Kersten et al., 2010; Filipović, 2011), and such Whorfian effects may involve semantic processing much more than phonological and syntactic processing. Thus, it remains possible that in Jouen et al.'s (2015) study the overlapping areas of activity for sentences and pictures reflect, to some extent, the retrieval of the cross-linguistically distinctive meanings of English action verbs and constructions not only in the verbal condition, but also in the nonverbal one.

Shifting, finally, to the domain of categorical spatial relations, analogous issues arise, but in this case the partly shared neural substrates for verbal and nonverbal semantic tasks can be interpreted more confidently in terms of language-specific concepts. As discussed in Chapter 5, several neuropsychological and functional neuroimaging studies have implicated the left inferior parietal lobule in the understanding of categorical spatial relations during both verbal and nonverbal semantic tasks (see especially Tranel & Kemmerer, 2004, and Amorapanth et al., 2012). However, because most of the nonverbal semantic tasks were based directly on the idiosyncratic meanings of English locative prepositions, all that can safely be inferred is that the left inferior parietal lobule underpins these particular concepts. It is worth emphasizing, though, that the focus here is on brain areas that are reliably recruited by both types of tasks. When differences are considered instead, it can be seen that some right-hemisphere parietal and frontal regions contribute more to the nonverbal than to the verbal representation and processing of both categorical and coordinate spatial relations, especially when the nonverbal tasks are independent of English prepositions (Kemmerer & Tranel, 2000; Amorapanth et al., 2010, 2012).

CONCLUSION

So, how do language-specific concepts relate to cognition? By now it should be clear that this question is fraught with complications, and that even though numerous advances have been made, the whole topic remains rather murky and mysterious. Many forms of cognition do not necessarily rely on language-specific concepts; however, such concepts nonetheless do sometimes influence how we think. A growing literature has been documenting weak Whorfian effects of this kind, but the precise circumstances under which they occur have yet to be elucidated. Moreover, the pace of progress in this line of inquiry has been much slower in cognitive neuroscience than in cognitive psychology, largely because, with some notable exceptions (Thierry, 2016), most researchers in the former field have not expressed much interest in the implications of cross-linguistic semantic diversity for mental representation and processing. On the other hand, many cognitive neuroscientists have shown that both verbal and nonverbal semantic tasks often have partly shared cortical underpinnings, as revealed by similar activity patterns in healthy subjects and similar deficit-lesion patterns in brain-damaged patients. Such findings are certainly interesting and valuable, but their interpretation is frequently difficult, since they could reflect language-independent concepts, language-specific ones, or a complex mixture of both. Hopefully, greater awareness of these issues in the future will lead to better experiments and hence deeper insights.

7

ARE WE EVER CONSCIOUS OF CONCEPTS?

... there really are no such things as conscious thoughts. ...
—Ray Jackendoff (2012, p. 84)

INTRODUCTION

Research on consciousness has made many advances during the past few decades (Boly et al., 2013; Block et al., 2014; Koch et al., 2016; Storm et al., 2017; see also the dual perspectives of Odegaard et al., 2017, and Boly et al., 2017).[1] However, apart from a few notable exceptions (Miller, 2007; Melloni & Singer, 2010; Aru et al., 2012b; de Graaf et al., 2012; Prinz, 2012; Pitts et al., 2014a), progress in elucidating the *neural* correlates of consciousness has been hampered by a lack of sufficient attention to the *cognitive* correlates of consciousness—that is, to the forms of mental representation that actually reach awareness. This is a critical issue, since the boundaries of what have been called "the admissible contents of experience" (Hawley & Macpherson, 2011) necessarily impose strict constraints on theories of how and why the human brain generates consciousness. Although this issue has not been adequately addressed in the neuroscientific literature, it has been the focus of intense debate in the philosophy of mind and related fields (e.g., see the collection of papers in Bayne & Montague, 2012a). The main controversy revolves around the following question: *Do the highest levels of mental representation—in particular, concepts and the thoughts they enter into—ever achieve consciousness when activated?* Two different positions have been disputed for centuries, with the liberal view giving this question a positive answer, and the conservative view giving it a negative one.

In this chapter I first describe both views in greater detail, and then I discuss how the long-standing conflict between them bears on several contemporary neuroscientific theories of consciousness. I do so, however, in a manner that is admittedly biased toward the conservative view, since I am among those who believe it is more consistent than the liberal view with a number of key findings. I focus first on the following two frameworks: Stanislas Dehaene's Global Neuronal Workspace Theory (Dehaene & Naccache, 2001; Dehaene & Changeux, 2011; Dehaene, 2014; Dehaene et al., 2014, 2017), and Giulio Tononi's Integrated Information Theory (Tononi,

---

[1] Most of this chapter is drawn from Kemmerer (2015b).

2004, 2008, 2012a, 2012b; Oizumi et al., 2014; Tononi & Koch, 2015; Tononi et al., 2016; Massimini & Tononi, 2018). I argue that because both of these approaches assume the liberal view, they are challenged in significant ways by data favoring the competing conservative view. I then turn to a third framework—namely, Jesse Prinz's Attended Intermediate-Level Representation Theory (Prinz, 2012), which is based partly on previous work by Jackendoff (1987; see also Jackendoff, 2012). I contend that because this approach explicitly endorses the conservative view, it has a unique advantage over the other two. I also point out, however, that it has independent shortcomings that prevent it from achieving optimal explanatory coherence. Finally, I conclude by emphasizing the need for researchers in the neuroscience of consciousness to realize that the question of whether concepts ever reach awareness is a significant one with major consequences for both theoretical frameworks and experimental investigations.[2]

COMPETING VIEWS

The liberal view

The central claim of the liberal view is that although concepts don't always reach awareness when activated, they frequently do, and in those situations they bring about a particular kind of experience that cannot be reduced to any form of verbal or nonverbal imagery but is instead distinctively cognitive in nature. This unique type of awareness is sometimes called "cognitive phenomenology" or "cognitive qualia," and it ostensibly cuts across the entire spectrum of mental activities that employ concepts, including thinking and reasoning, producing and comprehending language, and categorizing objects and events in the world.

As Bayne and Montague (2012b) point out, the liberal view has a long and illustrious history, having been endorsed by such luminaries as René Descartes, John Locke, George Berkeley, David Hume, Franz Brentano, Edmund Husserl, Immanuel Kant, William James, and G. E. Moore. In the early 20th century, the core members of the famous Würzburg school of psychology—namely, Oswald Külpe, Narziss Ach, and Karl Bühler—claimed to have discovered introspective evidence for a pure form of cognitive phenomenology that they called non-imagistic thought. And more recently, a number of philosophers have upheld the position that consciousness is not limited to the senses but encompasses high-level semantic knowledge, too. Here are a few representative examples, mostly drawn from Bayne and Montague (2012b):

> In addition to arguing that there is something it is like to think a conscious thought, I shall also argue that what it is like to think a conscious thought is distinct from what it is like to be in any other kind of conscious mental state, and that what it is like to think the conscious thought that p is distinct from what it is like to think any other conscious thought. . . . (Pitt, 2004, p. 2)

---

[2] A terminological note: Throughout this chapter, the words *consciousness*, *awareness*, and *experience* are used interchangeably.

Intentional states have a phenomenal character, and this phenomenal character is precisely the what-it-is-like of experiencing a specific propositional-attitude vis-à-vis a specific intentional content. Change either the attitude-type (believing, desiring, wondering, hoping, etc.) or the particular intentional content, and the phenomenal character thereby changes too. (Horgan & Tienson, 2002, p. 522)

. . . generally, as we think—whether we are speaking in complete sentences, or fragments, or speaking barely or not at all, silently or aloud—the phenomenal character of our noniconic thought is in continual modulation, which cannot be identified simply with changes in the phenomenal character of either vision or visualization, hearing or auralization, etc. (Siewert, 1998, p. 282, emphasis suppressed)

When I am now phenomenally aware of the telephone on my desk, I am aware of it *as a telephone* and as located at a particular place in my world. . . . Introspectively, all of this information is experienced as at least implicitly present as part of the phenomenal content of my perceptual state. (van Gulick, 1994, p. 34, emphasis added)

The liberal view is elaborated and defended more fully in the following additional references: Strawson (1994, 2012), Siegel (2005), Bayne (2009), Horgan (2012), Nes (2012), Pitt (2012), Shields (2012), Siewert (2012), Woodruff-Smith (2012), Jorba and Vicente (2014), Breyer and Gutland (2015), and Chudnoff (2015).

The conservative view

In sharp contrast to the liberal view, the conservative view maintains that we are never directly aware of concepts per se; instead, consciousness is always restricted to sensory, motor, and affective states. Proponents of this position typically argue that even though it sometimes seems as if our thoughts are conscious, this is just an illusion that stems from the tendency to mistakenly treat the verbal and nonverbal images that often accompany certain thoughts as being equivalent to the conceptual contents of those thoughts. Advocates of the conservative view also believe that while concepts can certainly influence perception, we only experience the sensory effects of such top-down processes, never the high-level causes.

Bayne and Montague (2012b) note that just as the liberal view has a rich historical background, so does the conservative view. Challenging the Würzburg psychologists mentioned earlier, both Wilhelm Wundt and Edward Titchener contended that introspection provides no convincing evidence that thought can be manifested in consciousness by itself—that is, independent of modality-specific imagery. Similarly, the notion that concepts have intrinsic qualia has been vigorously attacked by such famous philosophers as J. J. Smart, Gilbert Ryle, and Hilary Putnam. Moving closer to the present, during the past few decades many theorists have continued to challenge the notion of cognitive phenomenology, as illustrated by the following passages, mostly drawn from Bayne and Montague (2012b):

Should we include any mental states that are not feelings and experiences on the list of phenomenally conscious states? Consider my desire to eat ice cream. Is there not something it is like for me to have this desire? If so, is this state not phenomenally conscious? And what about the belief that I am a very fine fellow? Or the memory that September 2 is the date on which I first fell in love? . . . It seems to me not im-plausible to deal with these cases by arguing that insofar as there is any phenomenal or immediately experienced felt quality to the above states, this is due to their being accompanied by sensations or images or feelings that are the real bearers of the phe-nomenal character. (Tye, 1995, p. 4)

As best we can tell, believing that 17 is a prime number doesn't feel any different from believing that 19 is a prime number. Indeed, as best we can tell, neither of these states has any distinctive qualitative properties. Neither of them feels like much at all. (Nichols & Stich, 2003, p. 196)

Bodily sensations and perceptual experiences are prime examples of states for which there is something it is like to be in them. They have a phenomenal feel, a phenom-enology, or, in a term sometimes used in psychology, raw feels. Cognitive states are prime examples of states for which there is *not* something it is like to be in them, of states that lack a phenomenology. (Braddon-Mitchell & Jackson, 2007, p. 129, orig-inal emphasis)

I will argue . . . that the felt qualities of our thoughts can be completely accommodated by appeal to concomitant sensory imagery. (Prinz, 2012, p. 149)

The conservative view is elaborated and defended more fully in the following addi-tional references: Levine (1983), Jackendoff (1987, 2012), Clark (2000), Langsam (2000), Wilson (2003), Carruthers (2005), Robinson (2005, 2012), Damasio (2010), O'Callaghan (2011), Carruthers and Veillet (2012), Tye and Wright (2012), and Bayne and McClelland (2016).

Picking a side

As mentioned earlier, I strongly favor the conservative view over the liberal view. I will spell out the reasons for this preference in the next section, which focuses on how the conflict between these two opposing positions is relevant to some of the most promi-nent modern theories of consciousness.

Before proceeding, though, I would like to point out that the conservative view is entirely compatible with the sorts of grounded theories of conceptual knowledge that are elaborated in Chapter 2 and applied to specific semantic domains in Chapters 3, 4, and 5. One of the key claims shared by all of these theories is that the various sen-sory and motor components of concepts are stored in some of the same modality-specific cortical regions that underlie perceptual recognition and action planning. It is important to note, however, that, in keeping with the conservative view, the specific sectors of these regions that contribute to concepts appear to be segregated from those that contribute to consciousness. A compelling demonstration of this critical differ-ence comes from Willems et al. (2010b), who conducted an fMRI study in which the participants performed two tasks with printed verbs for hand actions, like *throw*. One task was lexical decision—a commonly used paradigm which involves determining whether each stimulus is a real word or a pseudoword, and which is known to trigger implicit semantic processing. The other task was to explicitly imagine executing the designated types of actions. Both tasks engaged the left premotor cortex, but, crucially, they engaged different sectors of it; moreover, the imagery task, but not the lexical decision task, also engaged a sector of the left primary motor cortex. These findings are consistent with many other studies which suggest that the motor features of verb meanings are represented in the left precentral motor cortices, with greater reliance on premotor than primary motor areas (for reviews, see Kemmerer, 2015a, 2015c, 2015d, 2015e; see also the treatments of this topic in Chapters 2 and 4). In the current context, however, what matters most is that the findings support the hypothesis that the modality-specific components of concepts depend on different neural mechanisms than the much richer conscious experiences that they apply to. For example, the motor component of the action concept encoded by the verb *throw* generalizes over an entire category of body movements, so it makes sense that this component is subserved in large part by the relatively high-level premotor cortex. In contrast, whenever one explicitly imagines throwing something, one must select specific settings for the parameters of grip type, force, and kinematics, so it makes sense that conscious motor simulations of throwing behaviors recruit not only the premotor cortex but also the lower-level primary motor cortex. This fits the conservative view that concepts are types, whereas experiences are tokens.

IMPLICATIONS FOR NEUROSCIENTIFIC THEORIES OF CONSCIOUSNESS

The Global Neuronal Workspace Theory (GNWT)

Summary of the GNWT

Building on a previous proposal by Baars (1988), the GNWT developed by Dehaene and colleagues holds that consciousness arises from a capacity-limited architecture that is adaptively designed to extract relevant information from a variety of mental systems and to make it broadly available for purposes such as linguistic encoding, memory storage, planning, and decision-making (Dehaene & Naccache, 2001; Dehaene & Changeux, 2011; Dehaene, 2014; Dehaene et al., 2014, 2017). During perception, a massive amount of information is processed unconsciously by specialized mechanisms that operate in parallel. Some of that information, however, is selected as being especially pertinent to the individual's present goals, and it then crosses the threshold of conscious access and enters the global workspace for flexible sharing. According to Dehaene (2014, p. 168), "this global availability of information is precisely what we subjectively experience as a conscious state."

Based on many experiments involving minimal contrasts between conscious and unconscious conditions, the GNWT maintains that conscious access has four neuronal signatures. First, starting roughly 300 msec after stimulus onset, there is a sudden ignition of activity that includes not only the regions that represent the specific content (e.g., color, shape, motion, etc.) of the given conscious state, but also the regions that comprise the backbone of the global workspace—namely, the dorsolateral prefrontal cortex, the anterior cingulate cortex, the inferior parietal cortex, and the precuneus, all of which form a so-called rich club network of tightly interconnected hubs (van den Heuvel & Sporns, 2011; van den Heuvel et al., 2012). Second, this widely distributed ignition is accompanied by a P300 event-related potential (ERP) component. Third, in conjunction with the P300 wave, there is a significant increase in high-frequency gamma-band (> 30 Hz) oscillations in the ignited regions. Finally, during the same time window, and with the help of thalamocortical loops, these regions become functionally integrated as a transiently stable coalition or "brain web" through synchronized reciprocal signals carried by long-distance excitatory axons.

Critique of the GNWT

Although the GNWT has many virtues, its putative signatures of consciousness are inconsistent with several empirical findings. For instance, although the dorsolateral prefrontal cortex is necessary for monitoring and maintaining perceptual information, it does not appear to be essential for consciously experiencing that information (Penfield & Evans, 1935; Mataró et al., 2001; Rounis et al., 2010; Frässle et al., 2014; see also Boly et al., 2017; Storm et al., 2017). In addition, there is evidence that the P300 wave and enhanced gamma oscillations reflect separate task-related post-perceptual processes, rather than the process of becoming aware of stimuli (Pitts et al., 2014a, 2014b).

Here, however, I focus on a different aspect of the GNWT—specifically, that it assumes, in line with the liberal view, that consciousness is not restricted to sensory, motor, and affective representations, but encompasses concepts as well. To be sure, Dehaene not only acknowledges, but also has played a major role in demonstrating, that concepts such as those denoted by numerals, words, and phrases can be processed outside of awareness (Dehaene et al., 1998, 2001; Naccache & Dehaene, 2001; Kouider & Dehaene, 2007; Van Gaal et al., 2014). But it is also quite clear from his book *Consciousness and the Brain* (Dehaene, 2014) that he believes that concepts, and the thoughts they enter into, are perfectly viable candidates for participating in the global workspace of experience, and that they actually serve important cognitive functions within that workspace. Indeed, the subtitle of his book is *Deciphering How the Brain Codes Our Thoughts,* and the expression "conscious thought" occurs at least half a dozen times throughout its pages (pp. 20, 53, 110, 146, 175, 251), including in the title of Chapter 4, "The Signatures of a Conscious Thought." In what follows, I consider five parts of the book where this notion of conscious thought is discussed, and in each case I argue that it is inconsistent with evidence which supports the opposite conservative view that thoughts are always hidden from awareness.

To begin, on pp. 145–148, Dehaene (2014) summarizes several intracranial recording studies that have revealed single neurons in the human anterior temporal lobes (ATLs) that respond fairly selectively to pictures of particular entities, including famous people like Bill Clinton and Jennifer Aniston, as well as famous locations like the Sydney Opera House and the World Trade Center (Kreiman et al., 2000, 2002; Quiroga et al., 2005, 2008a, 2008b). When a participant sees different pictures of the same person or place—e.g., assorted photographs, portraits, and line drawings of Bill Clinton—the firing rate of the relevant cell reliably tracks the invariant identity of that object, regardless of radical shifts in the fine-grained features of the images. Moreover, the cell's firing rate also follows the participant's reports of the visibility of the stimuli. In commenting on these findings, Dehaene states that what the discharge patterns index "is neither a global arousal signal nor myriad changing details, but the gist of the current picture—just the right sort of stable representation that we would expect to encode our conscious thoughts." In the same vein, he also states that when we observe such patterns, "we are witnessing the contents of consciousness."

These ATL cells do appear to contribute substantially to our conceptual knowledge of well-known people and places; indeed, that is why Quiroga (2012) calls them "concept cells." But the mere fact that their activation correlates with conscious experiences of these entities does not imply that their representational contents are an inherent part of such experiences (Aru et al., 2012b). On the contrary, two important points suggest that, in keeping with the conservative view, the concepts captured by these cells never reach awareness.

The first point involves the contrast between the striking specificity of experiences and the equally striking generality of concepts. Perhaps the most salient property of conscious states is their extraordinary degree of differentiation. Even if we restrict our attention to the visual domain, it is obvious that the number of potentially separate experiences is exceedingly large, limited only by one's imagination. The primary function of concepts, however, is to abstract away from all of this diversity so that certain aspects of experiences can be regarded as instances of more wide-ranging, similarity-based categories. In fact, according to the conservative view, it is precisely because concepts always transcend the experiences they apply to that they always remain unconscious. Both Prinz (2012) and Jackendoff (2012) underscore this point:

> When I look at a chair, try as I may, I only see a specific chair oriented in a particular way. . . . it's not clear what it would mean to say that one visually experiences chairness. What kind of experience would that be? A chair seen from no vantage point? A chair from multiple vantage points overlapping? A shape possessed by all chairs? Phenomenologically, these options seem extremely implausible. (Prinz, 2012, p. 74)

> Now the interesting thing is that everything you *perceive* is a particular individual (a token)—you can't perceive categories (types). And you can only *imagine* particular individuals—you can't *imagine* categories. If you try to imagine a type, say forks in general, your image is still a particular fork, a particular token. (Jackendoff, 2012, p. 130)

In the current context, what matters most is that this line of argumentation is not restricted to concepts for types of entities, like chairs and forks, but also applies to concepts for one-of-a-kind entities, like the well-known people and places that are represented by the sorts of ATL cells described above. Even though unique entities like these are significant enough to warrant dedicated concepts, they may still be consciously experienced in a vast if not infinite number of ways. For instance, nonliving things such as eminent landmarks can be seen under different lighting conditions, at different distances, from different angles, etc., and living things such as famous people can vary in their appearance even more, due to changes associated with facial expression, posture, hairstyle, age, etc. But while the specific ways that certain unique entities *look* to us may radically shift across different situations, the concepts that enable us to identify them remain relatively invariant. Moreover, and most critically, the activation of these concepts during the recognition process does not seem to add anything distinctively cognitive to the experience. For example, to reformulate Prinz's (2012, p. 74) statement, it's not clear what it would mean to experience "Bill Clinton-ness" or

"Jennifer Aniston-ness" in some sort of purely conceptual sense that goes beyond perceptual images. These observations support the hypothesis that, contrary to Dehaene's (2014, pp. 145–148) proposal, the concepts encoded by ATL cells never achieve consciousness; instead, they always perform their work beneath the surface of awareness.

The second point involves a set of neuropsychological studies that provide further evidence for this position. In particular, it has been repeatedly shown that dysfunction of the ATLs due to stroke, surgical resection, gradual deterioration, or congenital disease impairs the ability to recognize famous people like Bill Clinton and Jennifer Aniston, but does not impair the ability to consciously see their faces (A. R. Damasio et al., 1990; H. Damasio et al., 2004; Snowden et al., 2004; Avidan et al., 2014). This dissociation greatly strengthens the argument that whenever we see a familiar person, the relevant concept cells in the ATLs play an essential role in allowing us to identify them, but do not contribute directly to our conscious experience. Instead, the experience itself appears to be subserved by large assemblies of cells in the intermediate regions of the ventral face-processing network—i.e., the occipital face area and the fusiform face area—that represent the detailed visual features of faces (Tsao et al., 2008; Axelrod & Yovel, 2013; Von Der Heide et al., 2013; Rangarajan et al., 2014; Kanwisher, 2017; Landi & Freiwald, 2017).

Now, a critic, especially one who espouses the liberal view, might say that because perception is not driven entirely by bottom-up input, but is instead modulated by predictions and other kinds of prior representational states (Clark, 2013; Panichello et al., 2013; Summerfield & de Lange, 2014), it is certainly possible that in some situations one's concept of how a familiar person typically looks does in fact influence one's conscious experience of seeing them, if only in subtle ways. If that were the case, however, it would not imply that one is actually aware of the concept itself; rather, it would only imply that one is aware of the top-down effects of that concept (for relevant findings, see Hansen et al., 2006; Meteyard et al., 2007; Gendron et al., 2012; Lupyan & Ward, 2013).

Returning to Dehaene's (2014) book, on pp. 99–100 he elaborates the GNWT by comparing consciousness to the spokesperson of a large institution who voices the "common wisdom" extracted from different departments of a complex staff composed of thousands of specialist employees. While developing this analogy, he states that "like a presidential brief, the brain's conscious summary must contain an interpretation of the environment written in a 'language of thought' that is abstract enough to interface with the mechanisms of intention and decision making." How, though, could any level of representation that is abstract enough to bridge the gap between perception and behavior have any intrinsic qualia of its own, over and above the types of modality-specific qualia that are associated with the sensory and motor representations that must be connected with each other? Dehaene does not attempt to answer this question, nor does he acknowledge that it is a genuine issue. He simply adopts the liberal view that the concepts comprising the "language of thought" can reach awareness when activated, without either justifying that perspective or discussing the opposite conservative view that concepts always operate unconsciously.

Later in the same chapter, Dehaene (2014, p. 110) expands on the notion that consciousness is like a summary of relevant information by stating that it includes "a multisensory, viewer-invariant, and durable synthesis of the environment." But neither visual awareness nor any other form of experience contains viewer-invariant representations; on the contrary, possessing a first-person perspective—one that, for sighted people, is typically anchored behind the eyes—is often taken to be a fundamental requirement of bodily self-consciousness (Blanke & Metzinger, 2009). This is quite pertinent to our main topic because, according to the conservative view, one of the reasons why concepts cannot reach awareness is because they always generalize over particular perspectives. This key insight is nicely captured by Prinz (2012, p. 74) in the passage quoted earlier, where he makes what is essentially the following argument: the concept of a chair is viewer-invariant, which is to say that it covers all possible vantage points; however, it is impossible to see or imagine a chair from no vantage point or from multiple vantage points overlapping; therefore, it is impossible to directly experience the concept of a chair, i.e., "chairness" in the most general sense.

In another part of his book, Dehaene (2014, pp. 177–178) uses the example of Leonardo da Vinci's *Mona Lisa* to illustrate his idea that a conscious state is underpinned by millions of widely distributed neurons that represent different facets of the experience and that are functionally integrated through bidirectional, rapidly reverberating signals. Most importantly for present purposes, he claims that when we look at the classic painting, our global workspace of awareness includes not just its visual properties (e.g., the hands, eyes, and "Cheshire cat smile"), but also "fragments of meaning," "a connection to our memories of Leonardo's genius," and "a single coherent interpretation," which he characterizes as "a seductive Italian woman." This part of the book clearly reveals Dehaene's endorsement of the liberal view that concepts are among the kinds of information that can reach consciousness. The problem, however, is that he does not explicitly defend this position against the opposite conservative view, which denies that we can directly experience complex semantic structures like the one expressed by the phrase "a seductive Italian woman." The meaning of the word *seductive*, for instance, is highly abstract, since it applies not only to the nature of Mona Lisa's smile, but also to countless other visual and nonvisual stimuli that satisfy the conceptual criteria of, to quote from Webster's dictionary, "having tempting qualities." On the one hand, it is reasonable to suppose that there is something it is inimitably like, phenomenologically speaking, to perceive particular instances of seductive stimuli, such as Mona Lisa's smile. But on the other hand, it is extremely hard to imagine how anyone could directly experience seductiveness in some sort of general, all-encompassing sense. Hence the conservative view maintains that this concept, like all others, lacks intrinsic qualia.

Near the end of his book, Dehaene (2014, p. 251) proposes that "the human global neuronal workspace may be unique in its capacity to formulate conscious thoughts such as 'taller than Tom,' 'left of the red door,' or 'not given to John.'" Once again, though, advocates of the conservative view could argue that while the pronunciations of these phrases can certainly reach awareness, their compositional meanings are far too abstract to do so. For example, the expression *taller than Tom* encodes a comparative scalar relationship that could apply to an infinite number of entities whose extent along the dimension of height exceeds that of Tom but is otherwise unbounded (Bierwisch & Lang, 1989). One could generate a vast array of conscious mental images that depict this relationship in various ways, but none of them would be able to indicate, in a purely visual, nonsymbolic fashion, that the most important property is the relative height of the two objects. Turning to the expression *left of the red door*, it refers to a region of space that is determined in two steps: first, the left and right sides of the door are identified as the ones that correspond, in a mirror-reflecting manner, to the left and right sides of the viewer facing the door; and second, the target domain is specified by projecting out a moderate distance in the leftward direction defined by the horizontal left/right axis imposed on the door (Levinson, 2003; see Figure 5.6(a) and the associated text in Chapter 5 of this volume). As with the expression *taller than Tom*, it would be impossible for any particular image to indicate in a nonsymbolic fashion exactly how this spatial relationship is determined. It also bears mentioning that any conscious representation of the details of the situation described by the phrase *left of the red door* would need to portray the door as having a precise shape and a precise shade of red, thereby making the image in awareness much more specific than the actual content of the linguistically encoded concepts. Finally, the expression *not given to John* refers to an unrealized event, and for this reason it is quite difficult, to say the least, to understand how such a semantic structure could ever be directly experienced. What could it possibly be like to consciously represent the concept of negation in a way that fully complies with its extraordinary degree of abstractness (Horn, 1989)?

Before concluding this discussion of the GNWT, it is worthwhile to briefly invoke Block's (1995) distinction between phenomenal consciousness and access consciousness and to ask whether Dehaene (2014) might regard concepts, and the thoughts they enter into, as being available to awareness in the latter sense rather than the former. In the last chapter of his book, Dehaene (2014, p. 261) does mention some of Block's work, but unfortunately he does not address the distinction that Block proposed, so it is difficult to know where he stands on this issue. Nevertheless, some evidence that he might regard activated concepts as being potentially conscious in the access sense rather than the phenomenal sense comes from the fact that he frequently uses the expression "conscious access" not only in his book, but also in other presentations of his theory (Dehaene & Naccache, 2001; Dehaene & Changeux, 2011; Dehaene et al., 2014, 2017).

It is important to note, however, that Block's (1995) distinction is by no means uncontroversial, and some proponents of the conservative view reject it. Prinz (2012, p. 6) is one such scholar, as revealed by his remark that "information access seems conscious . . . when and only when it is accompanied by phenomenal experience." With respect to concepts, their retrieval is often accompanied by inner speech, visual images, and other forms of phenomenal experience, but the activated concepts themselves do not appear to have any uniquely cognitive qualia of their own, and this suggests that access consciousness may not exist as a special kind of awareness that is separate from phenomenal consciousness.

Consider, for example, the tip-of-the-tongue state, which occurs when you have accessed a particular concept—say, the one encoded by the word *pterodactyl*—but can't recall its name. While searching your memory for this elusive word, you might conjure up various kinds of verbal and nonverbal imagery, like saying to yourself, "It's a large flying dinosaur," and visualizing the appearance of the fearsome creature. But, as indicated earlier, these forms of modality-specific imagery do not actually constitute the concept, since the concept itself resides at a higher level of generalization. The key question, then, is this: Apart from such imagery, and from the frustrating sense of persistently groping for the desired word, what is left in your conscious awareness? According to the conservative view, nothing. Even though the meaning of the word continues to be activated, it does not have any inherent qualia of its own.

A similar situation involves the realization that what one has just said does not accurately express what one was trying to say. Besides showing that thought is independent of language, such events provide additional evidence for the conservative view, as Jackendoff (2012, pp. 90–91) explains:

> ... we can only be aware of the content of our thoughts if they're linked with pronunciation. So if we haven't yet turned a thought into words, we're only aware at best of *thinking going on*, not of exactly what the thought *is*. If we then utter a sentence, we can unconsciously compare the thought it expresses with the thought we intended to express, and we can get the feeling that the utterance is inadequate.

To summarize, the GNWT adopts the liberal view that activated concepts not only can, but often do reach awareness. Hence it is at odds with numerous empirical findings and theoretical arguments that favor the competing conservative view that concepts never reach awareness. This is arguably a significant limitation of the theory. Perhaps the most serious consequence is that the theory's characterization of the neuronal signatures of consciousness may turn out to be too broad. This is because over the course of their research on these signatures, Dehaene and his colleagues have not taken care to distinguish between, on the one hand, the sorts of sensory, motor, and affective representations that can occur in conscious experiences, and on the other hand, the sorts of high-level conceptual representations that—again, according to the conservative view—cannot.

Suppose, for example, that one suddenly saw a bicycle. According to the GNWT, the shapes, sizes, colors, and spatial arrangements of the object's parts would enter one's awareness after roughly 300 msec, and the resulting conscious state would be subserved by the synchronization of enhanced gamma oscillations in many populations of neurons distributed across not only certain visual areas of the brain, but also other areas involved in processes such as attention, short-term memory, and the widespread broadcasting of information. Now, assuming that one is familiar with bicycles, one's concept of a bicycle would also be activated—specifically, in a well-studied tool-related network consisting of certain temporal, parietal, and frontal areas (see Chapters 3 and 4)—and the activation of that concept would allow one to rapidly recognize the object and draw inferences about it (Grill-Spector & Kanwisher, 2005). This process of concept retrieval, however, would, according to the conservative view, take place unconsciously. So we are left with the following question: How exactly would the neural correlates of the *conscious perception* of the bicycle differ from the neural correlates of the *unconscious recognition* of the bicycle? This issue has yet to be rigorously investigated, but it must ultimately be resolved if genuine progress is to be made in the neuroscience of consciousness—once more, assuming the conservative view is actually correct.

The Integrated Information Theory (IIT)

Summary of the IIT

Originating from a previous proposal called the Dynamic Core Hypothesis (Tononi & Edelman, 1988; Edelman & Tononi, 2000), the IIT has been developed primarily by Tononi as a mathematical approach to measuring both the quantity and the quality of consciousness not only in biological organisms such as ourselves, but also, at least in principle, in artificial devices such as robots (Tononi, 2004, 2008, 2012a, 2012b; Oizumi et al., 2014; Tononi & Koch, 2015; Tononi et al., 2016; Massimini & Tononi, 2018). The IIT highlights the fact that a conscious state is simultaneously differentiated (i.e., every experience is unique insofar as it rules out a tremendous number of alternative possibilities) and integrated (i.e., every experience comprises a unified "scene" perceived from a particular perspective). It therefore predicts that variable degrees of awareness will be associated with variable degrees of differentiation and integration in the human thalamocortical system. Although this idea requires further refinement, it has been supported by studies involving not only healthy adults at different stages of the sleep-wake cycle (Massimini et al., 2005), but also brain-damaged patients in either vegetative or minimally conscious states (Casali et al., 2013). These studies employed complex analyses of neural activity that were indirectly based on the central construct of the IIT, namely a formula referred to as "phi" (φ), which is postulated to be a marker of consciousness, since it measures the amount of differentiated and integrated information in a system composed of multiple parts.

Concepts are major ingredients of the IIT, but they are defined in a technical manner as discrete mechanisms that are anatomically implemented by (sets of) neurons and that functionally specify irreducible cause-effect repertoires, where in each case the *cause* is the set of past inputs that give rise to the present on/off state of the mechanism, and the *effect* is the set of future consequences that follow from the present on/off state of the mechanism. Tononi maintains that such mechanisms are organized as nested hierarchies throughout the cerebral cortex, from the very lowest levels of representation to the very highest. In his scientific papers, most of the examples of this part of the framework are rather dense, but in his book, *Phi: A Voyage from the Brain to the Soul* (Tononi, 2012b), he presents a literary version of his theory, and in Chapter 19 he includes a fairly clear discussion of what he means by concepts. For instance, he writes that "we may discover a mechanism for detecting light in the center, another one for light on the left side, one for blue and one for red, one for oval and one for square shapes; one for noses, one for lips, and one for faces, and maybe even one for her, whoever she might be" (Tononi, 2012b, p. 201). All of these mechanisms are assumed to be separate concepts implemented by (sets of) neurons at different levels of the visual hierarchy, from V1 all the way up to the ATLs. Interestingly, Tononi argues that no single neuron, and hence no single concept, has any meaning independent of the various networks of mechanisms in which it is embedded, because the representational content of each one can only be identified by its relationship with, and especially its differentiation from, the others. He also argues, however, that whenever a multitude of concepts are co-activated in such a way that they collectively yield an irreducible cause-effect repertoire, the entire assembly constitutes a multifaceted "conceptual structure." And this in turn leads to what is, for present purposes, the most important aspect of the theory—specifically, its strong endorsement of the liberal view that concepts are conscious when activated.

This key assumption is explicitly formalized in the IIT as the "central identity" thesis, which asserts that "an experience is a maximally integrated conceptual (information) structure or quale—that is, a maximally irreducible constellation of points in qualia space" (Tononi, 2012a, p. 306). Indeed, according to the framework, at any given time whatever conceptual structure happens to be activated in an intricate information processing system such as a human brain "completely specifies 'what it is like to be' that particular mechanism in that particular state" (Tononi, 2012a, p. 306). Tononi and Koch (2015) elaborate this crucial claim by imagining a situation in which one watches a movie starring Jennifer Aniston (JA), and it is clear from their discussion that they believe one's experience would consist of a rapidly shifting series of fantastically complicated conceptual structures implemented by enormous neural networks distributed across the thalamocortical system. Some of the elements of these putative conceptual structures would change their on/off status quite frequently, like those subserved by the low-level cells in V1 that specify the orientations of edges in certain parts of the visual field. Other elements, however, would remain engaged for several seconds or even several minutes, like "the invariant concept 'JA's face,'" which is presumably subserved by high-level cells in the ATLs (Tononi & Koch, 2015, p. 9). In short, the IIT equates consciousness with concepts, regardless of their degree of complexity.

Critique of the IIT

Although this approach has many merits, it also has some serious weaknesses. In the current context, the most salient problem is that the IIT is incompatible with data supporting the conservative view that we are never aware of concepts. For instance, as argued earlier in connection with Dehaene's GNWT, even though one's concept of a famous person like Jennifer Aniston is activated whenever one sees, hears, or thinks about her, this does not entail that the concept itself is part of those experiences (Aru et al., 2012b). On the contrary, one's conscious perception of this particular actress in TV shows, movies, magazines, web sites, etc., would probably not be significantly different (apart from changes in the associated verbal and nonverbal imagery, and perhaps the lack of subtle top-down effects) if one didn't even recognize her due to having never learned her name and background or to having lost that knowledge as the result of ATL damage (A. R. Damasio et al., 1990; H. Damasio et al., 2004; Snowden et al., 2004; Avidan et al., 2014). This is because at any given moment one's awareness of Jennifer Aniston (or of anyone else, for that matter) is shaped not so much by one's degree of familiarity with that unique individual, but rather by such idiosyncratic and transient factors as whether one sees them from the front, the left, the right, half hidden behind a chair or table, sitting, standing, yawning, stretching, in candlelight, under a street lamp, through a fog, and so on (Millikan, 2014). According to the conservative view, the contents of consciousness consist of modality-specific details like these, not the high-level concepts that generalize over them.

A similar line of criticism also applies to Tononi's treatment of concepts of nonunique entities. For example, in Chapter 19 of *Phi*, one of the characters talks about how the machinery of conceptual representation could create "the idea of a triangle, wherever it may be, no matter how large or small, no matter where its corners are pointing, no matter whether equilateral, isosceles, or scalene" (Tononi, 2012b, p. 200). Even a concept as abstract as this would, according to the IIT, be conscious when activated. But how could the notion of a triangle possibly have any distinctive qualia? How could it ever be directly experienced? After all, no image could capture the conceptually vital fact that, as Tononi's character observes, a triangle must have three sides but need not have any particular size or shape. Similarly, Jackendoff (2012, p. 52) points out that nothing in a particular image of a triangle tells us that "having three sides is what's important for trianglehood." And he goes on to note that "once you state that as the critical feature, you've gone outside of what visual images can do."

In closing, the main message is that Tononi's IIT has the same significant limitation as Dehaene's GNWT. It assumes—incorrectly, according to the conservative view—that concepts can reach awareness when activated, and as a consequence its account of the neural underpinnings of consciousness appears to be too inclusive.

The Attended Intermediate-Level Representation Theory (AIRT)

Expanding on earlier work by Jackendoff (1987; see also Jackendoff, 2012), the AIRT developed by Prinz (2012) stands in sharp contrast to both the GNWT and the IIT because it adopts at the very outset the conservative view that we are never aware of concepts. In fact, based on the strength of the evidence for this view, Prinz (2012, p. 32) maintains that "an adequate theory should restrict consciousness to processes that lie outside of those systems that underwrite our highest cognitive capacities." Because the AIRT is among the few contemporary frameworks, if not the only one, that achieves this goal, its three major tenets are worth summarizing and evaluating here.

First, a central claim is that perceptual awareness arises at intermediate rather than low or high levels of sensory hierarchies. In the visual domain, for example, what we experience is a world of vividly colored objects with clear contours, located at different distances from us and framed by our own point of view. Such conscious states do not correspond to the "flat, disunified jumble" (Prinz, 2012, p. 51) that is encoded in V1, nor do they correspond to the abstract, viewer-invariant concepts that are encoded in high-level regions of the temporal, parietal, and frontal lobes. Rather, they correspond to the kinds of attribute-specific representations that are constructed by specialized cortical areas at more intermediate stages of the visual system. Exactly which areas are part of this privileged family is not yet clear, but Prinz suggests that likely candidates include V2, V3, V3A, V4, V5, V6, and V7, since they have been linked with the awareness of form, color, motion, depth, and perspective.

Second, the AIRT maintains that intermediate-level representations only become conscious when they are modulated by attention and thereby made available to working memory. Although the precise relationship between consciousness and attention has been, and continues to be, quite controversial, Prinz marshalls a substantial amount of psychological and neurobiological evidence to support his hypothesis. He also emphasizes that while conscious information must always be *accessible* to working memory, it need not always be *accessed* to working memory—as, for instance, when one only glimpses a tiny flash of light for a few milliseconds and does not subsequently reflect on that experience. This is an important point because it distinguishes the AIRT from the GNWT. As indicated earlier, the GNWT assumes that in order for information to reach awareness, it must be brought into the global workspace—that is, into the large-scale storage and broadcasting system that includes resources for working memory in the lateral prefrontal cortex. The AIRT rejects this requirement, however, and it is therefore more compatible than the GNWT with data suggesting that consciousness can occur without prefrontal involvement (e.g., see Kouider et al., 2007, and the comments on that study by Prinz, 2012, p. 31; see also Penfield & Evans, 1935; Mataró et al., 2001; Rounis et al., 2010; Frässle et al., 2014; Boly et al., 2017).

Third, the AIRT states that consciousness is neurophysiologically realized as what Prinz (2012) calls gamma vectorwaves. According to this conjecture, attending to an object causes the distributed intermediate-level neural populations that encode the various features of that object to become synchronized via enhanced and phased-locked oscillations in the gamma band—a phenomenon referred to as a gamma vectorwave. In addition, cells for qualitatively different features, such as shape and color, are proposed to have separate ultra-rapid spiking patterns that become coordinated at the coarser time scale of gamma. "By analogy," writes Prinz (2012, p. 141), "imagine playing two melodies on two different radios while raising and lowering their volume in sync. Each melody would remain intact, but they would now also be heard as parts of the same overarching sound pattern." This intriguing idea is bolstered by a large body of data, but like the GNWT and the IIT, it has several shortcomings. Most critically, during the conscious observation of recognizable objects, gamma responses are manifested in ways that violate the theory's predictions. For instance, in the mid-level areas that putatively subserve visual awareness, gamma responses do not reliably correlate with subjective reports (Aru et al., 2012a). Moreover, as noted earlier in the discussion of the GNWT, gamma responses increase greatly not only in mid-level areas, but also in many high-level areas, some of which contribute to conceptual knowledge and hence should *not* display any neurophysiological signatures of consciousness (Fisch et al., 2009; Gaillard et al., 2009). Thus, it remains mysterious how the brain regions that underlie our conscious perception of the visual world are operationally distinguished from those that underlie our unconscious understanding of that world.

In sum, because the AIRT adopts the conservative view that concepts never reach awareness, it may have a significant advantage over both the GNWT and the IIT. In addition, it synthesizes in a coherent manner a great deal of empirical and theoretical work in philosophy, psychology, and neuroscience. It is not without limitations, however. Most notably, although the gamma vectorwave proposal has several virtues, it—like all other attempts to pinpoint the neurophysiological signatures of consciousness—cannot explain all of the available data.

CONCLUSION

To elucidate the neural substrates of consciousness, it is first necessary to determine which mental representations in the flow of information processing do and do not reach awareness. The results of such an analysis can then be used to constrain the psychological phenomena for which unique neural correlates are sought.

According to the liberal view, the contents of experience include not only sensory, motor, and affective states, but also concepts and the thoughts they enter into. This view matches many people's intuitions. For instance, we spend much of our lives producing and comprehending language (both overtly and as inner speech), and it often seems as if these experiences are the equivalent of thinking. In addition, we are accustomed to recognizing objects and events quite rapidly and effortlessly, so it seems natural to suppose that we are directly aware of their meanings. But even though these considerations give some intuitive appeal to the liberal view, I have argued that a variety of other factors support the opposite conservative view, which maintains that concepts lack intrinsic qualia and always perform their functions beneath the surface of awareness. According to this alternative position, when we process spoken language, the only representations that reach awareness are the pronunciations of words, and they serve as conscious "handles" for the concepts that remain unconscious; likewise, when we recognize objects and events, the only representations that reach awareness are the superficial appearances of stimuli, and, again, they serve as conscious "handles" for the concepts that remain unconscious (Jackendoff, 2012).

If, as I suspect, the conservative view is correct, it will be necesssary for future research on the neuroscience of consciousness to distinguish between two levels of representation that are often engaged simultaneously in the brain: first, the kinds of sensory, motor, and affective representations that do reach awareness; and second, the kinds of conceptual representations that do not. I have shown that two of the most prominent and influential theories—namely, Dehaene's GNWT and Tononi's IIT—fail to draw this distinction because they assume the liberal view. And although a different framework—namely, Prinz's AIRT—does attempt to make the contrast, it unfortunately cannot account for all the available data.

As this field of inquiry moves forward, it will be essential for investigators to think more deeply about the critical question of whether we are ever aware of concepts. After all, even though I am admittedly biased toward the conservative view, I would be remiss if I did not acknowledge, once again in closing, that the debate between this view and the competing liberal view is by no means over. Indeed, the relevant literature contains far more issues and arguments than I have covered here. My hope is that more neuroscientists will begin to take a greater interest in this literature, and that their experimental and theoretical work will benefit from having done so.[3]

---

[3] One final remark: As indicated in the first footnote, most of the text of this chapter comes from a previously published paper (Kemmerer, 2015b). Shortly after it appeared, two philosophers published a lengthy commentary on it in the same journal (McClelland & Bayne, 2016). They challenged many of my arguments, and then we continued to wrestle with the issues in several rounds of animated email correspondence. I decided not to delve into this controversy here, but I would nevertheless like to make one point. Following several other scholars (e.g., Nelkin, 1989; Lormand, 1996), McClelland and Bayne support the plausibility of an intermediate position called "moderate conservatism," which maintains that activated concepts, and the thoughts they enter into, do figure in the contents of consciousness, but only in a non-phenomenal form, i.e., a form that lacks the sorts of qualia associated with sights, sounds, feelings, and so forth. As they observe, "... it seems *obvious* to us that there's a sense in which our thoughts are often conscious. How else can we express our thoughts if they are always unconscious?" (McClelland & Bayne, 2016, p. 3). The moderate view does indeed resolve this apparent paradox, which confronts the more extreme version of conservatism and makes it seem "strange and uncomfortable," to use Jackendoff's (2012, p. 5) terms. But even if one were to adopt the moderate view, it would still be prudent for neuroscientists to search for different neural signatures of phenomenal (i.e., sensory, motor, and affective) and nonphenomenal (i.e., conceptual) forms of consciousness, since these two forms would, by definition, be manifested quite differently in our minds.

FINAL REMARKS

Like any other language, English . . . has its own in-built culture-specific "forms of attention"—and native speakers of English are often blind to them because of their very familiarity. Often, this blindness to what is exceedingly familiar applies to Anglophone scholars
and leads to various forms of Anglocentrism in English-based human sciences, not only in
description but also in theory formation.
—Anna Wierzbicka (2014, p. 4)

Throughout our lives, from infancy onward, we interpret the world with concepts—
that is, with aggregated bits of distilled knowledge that allow us to understand diverse
domains of experience, such as people and places, objects and actions, properties and
relations, thoughts and feelings, and so forth. Over the course of development, as our
concepts increase in number and complexity, they come to form an intricately organized and adaptively deployed semantic system. Although this system always operates
beneath the surface of awareness, it is indispensable for the efficient flow of cognition
and behavior. Whenever we interact with our environment, our previously acquired
concepts support high-level perception by facilitating figure-ground segregation,
predicting likely entities and events, and controlling the spotlight of attention. During
the process of categorization, these concepts allow us to classify certain phenomena
as being particular tokens of more general types. And once we have recognized some
aspect of experience as belonging to a familiar category, we can use our long-term
knowledge about that category to draw multiple inferences, thereby going beyond the
information given. Concepts also serve as the basic building blocks of propositions and
play fundamental roles in reasoning, decision-making, and problem-solving. What's
more, they provide the necessary starting points for imagining an infinite variety of
counterfactual scenarios. And last but certainly not least, many concepts—indeed,
vast quantities of them—are symbolically encoded by the words and grammatical
constructions of specific languages; hence they constitute the most plentiful units of
publicly shared meaning for the speakers of those languages, establishing the semantic
bedrock of cultural common ground and enabling extremely rich forms of communication that are unparalleled in the animal kingdom.

   Because the native speakers of any given language learn the conceptual conventions
of that language at a very early age, it is not surprising that they often regard those socially standardized ways of carving up the world as being quite natural, perhaps even
inevitable. This sense of objectivity, however, is really just a powerful illusion, because
the fact of the matter is that, as research in semantic typology has incontrovertibly

shown, a huge proportion of the concepts encoded by specific languages are either unique to those languages or only found in a relatively small number of others. To be sure, the roughly 6,500 languages around the globe do have many lexical-semantic and grammatical-semantic similarities that are far from trivial. But they also vary greatly in several important ways, such as how they partition particular conceptual domains, how they map those domains onto syntactic categories, which distinctions they require speakers to habitually attend to, and how deeply they weave certain notions into the very fabric of their grammar. Copious examples of such cross-linguistic differences are scattered throughout the chapters in Part II of this book, and by this point it should be clear that they are not merely charming curiosities. On the contrary, they reveal the remarkable extent to which human cultures diverge in their representation of reality.

These insights from semantic typology have already had a major impact on several branches of psycholinguistics, but unfortunately they have not yet been taken seriously by the branch of cognitive neuroscience that focuses on how concepts are represented, organized, and processed in our brains. Now, it is undeniable that this field of investigation has made tremendous progress during the past few decades. For instance, as we have seen, there is mounting evidence that, at the level of widely distributed cortical networks, concrete concepts are not only anchored in modal systems for perception, action, and interoception, but also depend on transmodal systems for multidimensional integration. In addition, recent methodological breakthroughs have made it possible to determine, with increasing accuracy, which patterns of cortical activity are associated with which kinds of concepts, and how those patterns dynamically unfold on a millisecond time-scale, often under the influence of factors like task, context, and individual experience. Despite these impressive advances, however, the field as a whole has been significantly—and, it would appear, for the most part unwittingly—handicapped by the false assumption that the sorts of concepts that just happen to be encoded by the words and grammatical constructions of English and a few other familiar languages exemplify those that are found in languages worldwide. Because of this bias, which seems to be largely implicit, much of the work that has been done so far has been rather parochial. The central claim of this book is therefore as follows. As this field of research moves forward, it should, to the extent possible, expand its purview to embrace, on both empirical and theoretical fronts, the broad spectrum of cross-linguistic similarities and differences in the lexical and grammatical representation of meaning. Otherwise, it will never be able to achieve a truly comprehensive, pan-human account of the neural substrates of semantic knowledge.

To drive home this key point, here is one last illustration of cross-linguistic conceptual diversity and its implications for cognitive neuroscience. This particular example comes from one of the brightest luminaries in semantic typology, Stephen Levinson (2001, pp. 567–568), and it is especially instructive because it brings together all three of the domains that we concentrated on in Part II—namely, objects, actions, and spatial relations. The data involve the following English sentence and its translation into Tzeltal (Mayan, Mexico):

English: *Put the bowl behind the box*

Tzeltal:	*pach-an-a*	*bojch*	*ta*	*y-anil*	*te*	*karton-e*
	bowl.put-CAUSE-IMP	gourd.bowl	at	its-down	the	cardboard-DEIC

The Tzeltal sentence begins with the verb *pachana,* which is the imperative of the causative of the root *pach,* meaning "place a bowl-shaped vessel upright on a surface." As Levinson (2001, p. 567) observes, "This is one kind of semantic variation we may find across languages: familiar distinctions turning up in unfamiliar places, here bowl-shaped (or hemispherical) being a verbal rather than a nominal component." In the section of Chapter 4 called "Events of putting and taking," we saw that Tzeltal actually has a sizable number of placement verbs like this, all of which encode substantial geometric information about the shapes and orientations of the figure objects that are manipulated (see Figure 4.15[1] and the associated text). It is important to realize, however, that Tzeltal is not unique in this respect, since many other languages have the same kind of lexicalization pattern (Ameka & Levinson, 2007). In this context, it is also worth recalling that, as noted in Chapter 1, the Athabaskan languages of North America are famous for having several sets of so-called classificatory verbs for events of not only putting but also giving, taking, handling, etc., with each set consisting of multiple verbs that differ with regard to the type of object that is involved—e.g., small round things, large bulky things, flat flexible things, slender rigid things, etc. (see Table 1.5 and the associated text). For present purposes, the upshot is that these sorts of phenomena are quite relevant to cognitive neuroscience because they indicate that, compared to English, many other languages have far more action verbs that specify detailed object distinctions and that may therefore rely heavily on those brain regions that have traditionally been linked with nouns, such as the ventral temporal cortex.

Levinson (2001, p. 567) continues as follows: "Now consider *karton,* a Spanish loan, which in Tzeltal is semantically general across 'cardboard' rather than 'box'; this is a Mayan pattern whereby the basic nominal (other than names for humans, beasts and artifacts) denotes a substance rather than a thing (Lucy, 1992)." Of course, English has lots of mass nouns too, but Tzeltal pushes this approach to conceptualizing entities much farther, as Levinson shows: "Similarly *lo'bal* 'banana stuff' denotes the tree, the leaves, the roots as well as the fruit. . . . This is arguably somewhat different from a mere shuffling of semantic features, since we have no colloquial notion of 'banana essence' or 'stuff manufactured by banana genotype'. . . ." We touched on this topic in Chapters 1 and 3 (e.g., see Table 1.3 and the associated text), and it is worth returning to here because of its ramifications for cognitive neuroscience. In short, even though a great deal has been learned about the cortical underpinnings of object concepts, virtually nothing is known about the neural substrates of words like *lo'bal,* and part of the explanation for this gap may be that languages like Tzeltal have simply not been on most researchers' radar screens.

Finally, consider how the English preposition *behind* is rendered in Tzeltal as the phrase *ta yanil.* Levinson's (2001, pp. 567–568) account of the very weak correspondence between these two expressions is so shrewd that it deserves to be quoted in full:

> . . . although these terms may on an occasion of use have descriptive equivalence, they are actually not in the same intensional ballpark at all. English *behind* is ambiguous (between what I will call an intrinsic and a relative or "deictic" coordinate system), but is here used in the relative or "deictic" way, so that the utterance means that the box is between the speaker and the bowl. Tzeltal has no term equivalent to

---

[1] In that figure, the verb *pajchan* is the same one discussed here, but spelled with a "j."

either of these meanings of English *behind*. Tzeltal *ta yanil* 'at its down(hill)' (also ambiguous) here means something quite different, which may be specified in our concepts (not theirs) as lying in the quandrant bisected by the line North 010°—it is a cardinal direction term, which they think of in terms of a world essentially tilted North(-northeast)wards. These cardinal direction parameters (uphill, downhill, across) show up in a systematic range of vocabulary from motion verbs to words for edges. Clearly, we can't find any such semantic parameters built on the assumption of a tilted world showing up in English. This is [yet another] kind of semantic variation across languages. . . .

In Chapter 5 we discussed not only this particular instance of an absolute frame of reference, but also several others that have been documented in different languages around the globe (see Figures 5.7–5.8 and the associated text). As mentioned there, what is most amazing about these systems of spatial description is not the mere fact that they exist—after all, English has cardinal direction terms too—but rather the fact that speakers routinely and effortlessly use them to talk about the locations of objects at scales ranging from inches to miles. From our perspective, this appears to be a truly impressive cognitive feat, since it requires nearly constant attunement to the appropriate set of environmentally fixed bearings. But for the people who actually live in such "absolute" communities, always having immediate mental access to this frame of reference is not a big deal at all; it's just a kind of intuition that everyone shares and takes for granted—in other words, another form of cultural common ground. The following anecdote from Levinson (2003, p. 4) demonstrates this in a very compelling manner:

> Slus, a Mayan speaker of the language Tzeltal, says to her husband, facing an unfamiliar contraption, "Is the hot water in the uphill tap?" It is night, and we have just arrived at an alien hotel in a distant, unfamiliar city out of the hills. What does she mean? She means, it turns out, "Is the hot water in the tap that would lie in the uphill (southerly) direction if I were at home?"

As indicated in Chapter 5, much is now known about the neural basis of navigation, but the biological mechanisms that underlie the extraordinary spatial skills of people who live in "absolute" communities remain rather mysterious. Once again, this may be due in part to the widespread lack of familiarity with such communities.

It should now be apparent that even seemingly straightforward scenarios, like putting a bowl behind a box, are regularly construed in radically different ways by speakers of different languages—at least when they are preparing to describe such scenarios, and perhaps on many other occasions as well. Although we have restricted our attention to just two languages—English and Tzeltal—countless other conceptual contrasts, along with numerous overarching similarities, would undoubtedly emerge if we brought into the mix a large and carefully selected sample of the world's 6,500 languages. This is because, as Majid et al. (2008, pp. 247–248) point out, the primary insight of semantic typology is that "the precise makeup of categories varies across languages, with cross-cutting sets of elements falling together in some languages and apart in others in a kaleidoscope of recombinations." How are these complex patterns of meaning implemented in the human brain? Hopefully cognitive neuroscientists will not only begin to address this captivating question in the near future, but will also start producing informative answers to it.

REFERENCES

Abbi, A. (2011). Body divisions in Great Andamanese: Possessive classification, the semantics of inherency, and grammaticalization. *Studies in Language, 35,* 739–792.

Abbott, J. T., Griffiths, T. L., & Regier, T. (2016). Focal colors across languages are representative members of color categories. *Proceedings of the National Academy of Sciences, 113,* 11178–11183.

Acosta-Cabronero, J., Patterson, K., Fryer, T. D., Hodges, J. R., Pengas, G., Williams, G. B., & Nestor, P. J. (2011). Atrophy, hypometabolism, and white matter abnormalities in semantic dementia tell a coherent story. *Brain, 134,* 2025–2035.

Acres, K., Taylor, K. I., Moss, H. E., Stamatakis, E. A., & Tyler, L. K. (2009). Complementary hemispheric asymmetries in object naming and recognition: A voxel-based correlational study. *Neuropsychologia, 47,* 1836–1843.

Adelaar, K. A. (1997). An exploration of directional systems in West Indonesia and Madagascar. In G. Senft (ed.), *Referring to space: Studies in Austronesian and Papuan languages* (pp. 53–81). Oxford: Clarendon Press.

Adolphs, R., Tranel, D., & Damasio, A. R. (2003). Dissociable neural systems for recognizing emotions. *Brain and Cognition, 52,* 61–69.

Aggujaro, S., Crepaldi, D., Pistarini, C., Taricco, M., & Luzzatti, C. (2006). Neuroanatomical correlates of impaired retrieval of verbs and nouns: Interaction of grammatical class, imageability and actionality. *Journal of Neurolinguistics, 19,* 175–194.

Aglioti, S. M., Cesari, P., Romani, M., & Urgesi, C. (2008). Action anticipation and motor resonance in elite basketball players. *Nature Neuroscience, 11,* 1109–1116.

Aguirre, G. K., & D'Esposito, M. (1999). Topographical disorientation: A synthesis and taxonomy. *Brain, 122,* 1613–1628.

Aikhenvald, A. Y. (1994). Classifiers in Tariana. *Anthropological Linguistics, 36,* 407–465.

Aikhenvald, A. Y. (2000). *Classifiers: A typology of noun categorization devices.* New York: Oxford University Press.

Aikhenvald, A. Y. (2006). Classifiers and noun classes: Semantics. In K. Brown (ed.), *Encyclopedia of language and linguistics,* 2nd edition (pp. 463–470). Oxford: Elsevier.

Aikhenvald, A. Y. (2007). Classifiers in multiple environments: Baniwa of Içana/Kurripako—a North Arawak perspective. *International Journal of American Linguistics, 73,* 475–500.

Aikhenvald, A. Y. (2012). Round women and long men: Shape, size, and the meanings of gender in New Guinea and beyond. *Anthropological Linguistics, 54,* 33–86.

Aikhenvald, A. Y. (2017). A typology of noun categorization devices. In A. Y. Aikhenvald & R. M. W. Dixon (eds.), *The Cambridge handbook of linguistic typology* (pp. 361–404). Cambridge, UK: Cambridge University Press.

Aikhenvald, A. Y. (2018a). *Serial verbs.* New York: Oxford University Press.

Aikhenvald, A. Y. (ed.) (2018b). *The Oxford handbook of evidentiality*. New York: Oxford University Press.

Aikhenvald, A. Y., & Dixon, R. M. W. (eds.) (2006). *Serial verb constructions: A cross-linguistic typology*. New York: Oxford University Press.

Aikhenvald, A. Y., & Dixon, R. M. W. (eds.) (2013). *Possession and ownership: A cross-linguistic typology*. New York: Oxford University Press.

Aikhenvald, A. Y., & Dixon, R. M. W. (eds.) (2014). *The grammar of knowledge: A cross-linguistic typology*. New York: Oxford University Press.

Aikhenvald, A. Y., & Green, D. (1998). Palikur and the typology of classifiers. *Anthropological Linguistics, 40*, 429–480.

Alderson-Day, B., & Fernyhough, C. (2015). Inner speech: Development, cognitive functions, phenomenology, and neurobiology. *Psychological Bulletin, 141*, 931–965.

Allan, K. (1977). Classifiers. *Language, 53*, 284–310.

Allen, K., Pereira, F., & Botvinick, M., & Goldberg, A. E. (2012). Distinguishing grammatical constructions with fMRI pattern analysis. *Brain and Language, 123*, 174–182.

Almeida, J., Fintzi, A. R., & Mahon, B. Z. (2013). Tool manipulation knowledge is retrieved by way of the ventral visual object processing pathway. *Cortex, 49*, 2334–2344.

Ameel, E., Malt, B. C., & Storms, G. (2008). Object naming and later lexical development: From baby bottle to beer bottle. *Journal of Memory and Language, 58*, 262–285.

Ameka, F., & Essegbey, J. (2007). Cut and break verbs in Ewe and the causative alternation construction. *Cognitive Linguistics, 18*, 241–250.

Ameka, F., & Levinson, S. C. (2007). The typology and semantics of locative predicates: Posturals, positionals, and other beasts. *Linguistics, 45*, 847–872.

Amit, E., Hoeflin, C., Hamzah, N., & Federenko, E. (2017). An asymmetrical relationship between verbal and visual thinking: Converging evidence from behavior and fMRI. *NeuroImage, 152*, 619–627.

Amorapanth, P. X., Kranjec, A., Bromberger, B., Widick, P., Woods, A. J., Kimberg, D. Y., & Chatterjee, A. (2012). Language, perception, and the schematic representation of spatial relations. *Brain and Language, 120*, 226–236.

Amorapanth, P. X., Widick, P., & Chatterjee, A. (2010). The neural basis for spatial relations. *Journal of Cognitive Neuroscience, 22*, 1739–1753.

Andersen, E. (1975). Cups and glasses: Learning that boundaries are vague. *Journal of Child Language, 2*, 79–103.

Andersen, E. (1978). Lexical universals of body-part terminology. In J. H. Greenberg, C. A. Ferguson, & E. A. Moravcsik (eds.), *Universals of human language*, vol. 3 (pp. 335–368). Stanford: Stanford University Press.

Anderson, A. J., Binder, J. R., Fernandino, L., Humphries, C. J., Conant, L. L., Aguilar, M., Wang, X., Doko, D., & Raizada, R. D. S. (2017). Predicting neural activity patterns associated with sentences using a neurobiologically motivated model of semantic representation. *Cerebral Cortex, 27*, 4379–4395.

Anderson, L. B. (1982). The "perfect" as a universal and as a language-particular category. In P. J. Hopper (ed.), *Tense-aspect: Between semantics and pragmatics* (pp. 227–264). Amsterdam: John Benjamins.

Anderson, L. B. (1986). Evidentials, paths of change, and mental maps: Typologically regular asymmetries. In W. Chafe & J. Nichols (eds.), *Evidentiality: The linguistic encoding of epistemology* (pp. 273–312). Norwood: Ablex.

Anderson, M. L. (2010). Neural reuse: A fundamental organizational principle of the brain. *Behavioral and Brain Sciences, 33,* 245–266.

Anderson, S., & Keenan, E. (1985). Deixis. In T. Shopen (ed.), *Language typology and syntactic description,* vol. 3: *Grammatical categories and the lexicon* (pp. 259–307). Cambridge, UK: Cambridge University Press.

Andrews, M., Frank, S., & Vigliocco, G. (2014). Reconciling embodied and distributional accounts of meaning in language. *Topics in Cognitive Science, 6,* 359–370.

Aravena, P., Courson, M., Frak, V., Cheylus, A., Paulignan, Y., Deprez, V., & Nazir, T. (2014). Action *relevance* in linguistic context drives word-induced motor activity. *Frontiers in Human Neuroscience, 8,* 163.

Aravena, P., Delevoye-Turrell, Y., Deprez, V., Cheylus, A., Paulignan, Y., Frak, V., & Nazir, T. (2012). Grip force reveals the context sensitivity of language-induced motor activity during "action word" processing: Evidence from sentential negation. *PLoS ONE, 7,* e50287.

Arévalo, A., Baldo, J. V., & Dronkers, N. F. (2012). What do brain lesions tell us about theories of embodied semantics and the human mirror neuron system? *Cortex, 48,* 242–254.

Aristotle. (1961). *De anima, Books II and III,* trans. D. W. Hamlyn. Oxford: Oxford University Press. (Original work published in the 4th century B.C.)

Aru, J., Axmacher, N., Do Lam, A. T. A., Fell, J., Elger, C. E., Singer, W., & Melloni, L. (2012a). Local category-specific gamma band responses in the visual cortex do not reflect conscious perception. *Journal of Neuroscience, 32,* 14909–14914.

Aru, J., Bachmann, T., Singer, W., & Melloni, L. (2012b). Distilling the neural correlates of consciousness. *Neuroscience and Biobehavioral Reviews, 36,* 737–746.

Aske, J. (1989). Path predicates in English and Spanish: A closer look. *Proceedings of the 15th Annual Meeting of the Berkeley Linguistics Society* (pp. 1–14). Berkeley, CA: Berkeley Linguistics Society.

Athanasopoulos, P. (2007). Interaction between grammatical categories and cognition in bilinguals: The role of proficiency, cultural immersion, and language of instruction. *Language and Cognitive Processes, 22,* 689–699.

Athanasopoulos, P., Dering, B., Wigget, A., Kuipers, J. R., & Thierry, G. (2010). Perceptual shift in bilingualism: Brain potentials reveal plasticity in pre-attentive colour perception. *Cognition, 116,* 437–443.

Athanasopoulos, P., & Kasai, C. (2008). Language and thought in bilinguals: The case of grammatical number and nonverbal classification preferences. *Applied Psycholinguistics, 29,* 105–123.

Atkinson, J., Marshall, J., Woll, B., & Thacker, A. (2005). Testing comprehension abilities in users of British Sign Language following CVA. *Brain and Language, 94,* 233–248.

Atran, S. (1990). *Cognitive foundations of natural history.* Cambridge, UK: Cambridge University Press.

Atran, S., & Medin, D. (2008). *The native mind and the cultural construction of nature.* Cambridge, MA: MIT Press.

Augustinova, M., & Ferrand, L. (2014). Automaticity of word reading: Evidence from the semantic Stroop paradigm. *Current Directions in Psychological Science, 23,* 343–348.

Aurnague, M., Hickmann, M., & Vieu, L. (eds.). (2007). *Categorization of spatial entities in language and cognition.* Amsterdam: John Benjamins.

Avenanti, A., Candidi, M., & Urgesi, C. (2013). Vicarious motor activation during action perception: Beyond correlational evidence. *Frontiers in Human Neuroscience, 7,* 185.

Avidan, G., Tanzer, M., Hadj-Bouziane, F., Liu, N., Ungerleider, L. G., & Behrmann, M. (2014). Selective dissociation between core and extended regions of the face processing network in congenital prosopagnosia. *Cerebral Cortex, 24*, 1565–1578.

Axelrod, V., & Yovel, G. (2013). The challenge of localizing the anterior temporal face area: A possible solution. *NeuroImage, 81*, 371–380.

Aziz-Zadeh, L., Wilson, S. M., Rizzolatti, G., & Iacoboni, M. (2006). Congruent embodied representations for visually presented actions and linguistic phrases describing actions. *Current Biology, 16*, 1818–1823.

Baars, B. (1988). *A cognitive theory of consciousness.* Cambridge, UK: Cambridge University Press.

Baciu, M., Koenig, O., Vernier, M.-P., Bedoin, N., Rubin, C., & Segebarth, C. (1999). Categorical and coordinate spatial relations: fMRI evidence for hemispheric specialization. *NeuroReport, 10*, 1373–1378.

Bak, T. H., & Hodges, J. R. (2003). Kissing and dancing—A test to distinguish the lexical and conceptual contributions to noun/verb and action/object dissociation: Preliminary results in patients with frontotemporal dementia. *Journal of Neurolinguistics, 16*, 169–181.

Bak, T. H., & Hodges, J. R. (2004). The effects of motor neurone disease on language: Further evidence. *Brain and Language, 89*, 354–361.

Baker, B., & Harvey, M. (2010). Complex predicate formation. In M. Amberber, B. Baker, & M. Harvey (eds.), *Complex predicates: Cross-linguistic perspectives on event structure* (pp. 13–47). Cambridge, UK: Cambridge University Press.

Baldassi, C., Alemi-Neissi, A., Pagan, M., DiCarlo, J. J., Zecchina, R., & Zoccolan, D. (2013). Shape similarity, better than semantic membership, accounts for the structure of visual object representations in a population of monkey inferotemporal neurons. *PLOS Computational Biology, 9*, e1003167.

Baldassano, C., Chen, J., Zadbood, A., Pillow, J. W., Hasson, U., & Norman, K. A. (2016). Discovering event structure in continuous narrative perception and memory. *bioRxiv.*

Baroni, M., & Lenci, A. (2010). Distributional memory: A general framework for corpus-based semantics. *Computational Linguistics, 36*, 673–721.

Barrós-Loscertales, A., González, J., Pulvermüller, F., Ventura-Campos, N., Bustamante, J. C., Costumero, V., Parcet, A., & Ávila, C. (2012). Reading *salt* activates gustatory brain regions: fMRI evidence for semantic grounding in a novel sensory modality. *Cerebral Cortex, 22*, 2554–2563.

Barsalou, L. W. (2008). Grounded cognition. *Annual Review of Psychology, 59*, 617–645.

Barsalou, L. W. (2016). On staying grounded and avoiding Quixotic dead ends. *Psychonomic Bulletin & Review, 23*, 1122–1142.

Barsalou, L. W. (2017). Classification systems offer a microcosm of issues in conceptual processing: A commentary on Kemmerer (2016). *Language, Cognition, and Neuroscience, 32*, 438–443.

Barsalou, L. W., Santos, A., Simmons, W. K., & Wilson, C. D. (2008). Language and simulation in conceptual processing. In M. DeVega, A. M. Glenberg, & A. C. Graesser (eds.), *Symbols and embodiment* (pp. 245–283). New York: Oxford University Press.

Baumann, O., & Mattingley, J. B. (2010). Medial parietal cortex encodes perceived heading direction in humans. *Journal of Neuroscience, 30*, 12897–12901.

Bayne, T. (2009). Perception and the reach of phenomenal content. *The Philosophical Quarterly, 59*, 385–404.

Bayne, T., & McClelland, T. (2016). "Finding the feel": The matching content challenge to cognitive phenomenology. *Phenomenology and Mind, 10*, 26–43.

Bayne, T., & Montague, M. (eds.). (2012a). *Cognitive phenomenology.* New York: Oxford University Press.

Bayne, T., & Montague, M. (2012b). Cognitive phenomenology: An introduction. In T. Bayne & M. Montague (eds.), *Cognitive phenomenology* (pp. 1–34). New York: Oxford University Press.

Beauchamp, M. S., Lee, K. E., Argall, B. D., & Martin, A. (2004). Integration of auditory and visual information about objects in superior temporal sulcus. *Neuron, 41,* 809–823.

Beauchamp, M. S., & Martin, A. (2007). Grounding object concepts in perception and action. *Cortex, 43,* 461–468.

Bedny, M., Caramazza, A., Grossman, E., Pascual-Leone, A., & Saxe, R. (2008). Concepts are more than percepts: The case of action verbs. *Journal of Neuroscience, 28,* 11347–11353.

Bedny, M., Caramazza, A., Pascual-Leone, A., & Saxe, R. (2012). Typical neural representations of action concepts develop without vision. *Cerebral Cortex, 22,* 286–293.

Beavers, J., Levin, B., & Tham, S. W. (2010). The typology of motion expressions revisited. *Journal of Linguistics, 46,* 331–377.

Becker, A. J. (1975). A linguistic image of nature: The Burmese numerative classifier system. *Linguistics, 165,* 109–121.

Beilock, S. L., Lyons, I. M., Mattarella-Micke, A., Nusbaum, H. C., & Small, S. L. (2008). Sports experience changes the neural processing of action language. *Proceedings of the National Academy of Sciences, 105,* 13269–13273.

Berlin, B. (1978). Ethnobiological classification. In E. Rosch & B. B. Lloyd (eds.), *Cognition and categorization* (pp. 9–26). Hillsdale, NJ: Erlbaum.

Berlin, B. (1992). *Ethnobiological classification.* Princeton, NJ: Princeton University Press.

Berlin, B., Breedlove, D. E., & Raven, P. H. (1973). General principles of classification and nomenclature in folk biology. *American Anthropologist, 75,* 214–242.

Berlin, B., Breedlove, D. E., & Raven, P. H. (1974). *Principles of plant classification: An introduction to the botanical ethnography of a Mayan-speaking community in highland Chiapas.* New York: Academic Press.

Berlin, B., & Kay, P. (1969). *Basic color terms: Their universality and evolution.* Berkeley: University of California Press.

Berman, R. A., & Slobin, D. I. (1994). *Relating events in narrative: a crosslinguistic developmental study.* Mahwah, NJ: Erlbaum.

Berthele, R. (2012). On the use of PUT verbs by multilingual speakers of Romansch. In A. Kopecka & B. Narasimhan (eds.), *Events of putting and taking: A crosslinguistic perspective* (pp. 167–182). Amsterdam: John Benjamins.

Berthele, R., Whelpton, M., Næss, Å., & Duijff, P. (2015). Static spatial descriptions in five Germanic languages. *Language Sciences, 49,* 82–101.

Berti, A., & Frassinetti, F. (2000). When far becomes near: Remapping of space by tool use. *Journal of Cognitive Neuroscience, 12,* 415–420.

Berti, A., & Rizzolatti, G. (2002). Coding near and far space. In H.-O. Karnath, D. Milner, & G. Vallar (eds.), *The cognitive and neural bases of spatial neglect* (pp. 119–130). Oxford: Oxford University Press.

Besner, D., Stolz, J. A., & Boutilier, C. (1997). The Stroop effect and the myth of automaticity. *Psychonomic Bulletin & Review, 4,* 221–225.

Bi, Y. (2017). Nominal classification is not positive evidence for language relativity: A commentary on Kemmerer (2016). *Language, Cognition, and Neuroscience, 32,* 428–432.

Bi, Y., Han, Z., Zhong, S., Ma, Y., Gong, G., Huang, R., Song, L., Fang, Y., He, Y., & Caramazza, A. (2015). The white matter structural network underlying human tool use and tool understanding. *Journal of Neuroscience, 35,* 6822–6835.

Bickel, B. (2014). Linguistic diversity and universals. In N. J. Enfield, P. Kockelman, & J. Sidnell (eds.), *The Cambridge handbook of linguistic anthropology* (pp. 101–124). Cambridge, UK: Cambridge University Press.

Biederman, I. (1987). Recognition-by-components: A theory of human image understanding. *Psychological Review, 94,* 115–147.

Biederman, I. (1995). Visual object recognition. In S. M. Kosslyn & D. N. Osherson (eds.), *An invitation to cognitive science: Visual cognition,* vol. 2, 2nd edition (pp. 121–165). Cambridge, MA: MIT Press.

Biederman, I. (2013). Psychophysical and neural correlates of the phenomenology of shape. In L. Albertazzi (ed.), *Handbook of experimental phenomenology: Visual perception of shape, space, and appearance* (pp. 417–436). Malden, MA: Wiley-Blackwell.

Bierwisch, M., & Lang, E. (eds.) (1989). *Dimensional adjectives: Grammatical structure and conceptual interpretation.* New York: Springer.

Binder, E., Dovern, A., Hesse, M. D., Ebke, M., Karbe, H., Saliger, J., Fink, G. R., & Weiss, P. H. (2017). Lesion evidence for a human mirror neuron system. *Cortex, 90,* 125–137.

Binder, J. R. (2016). In defense of abstract conceptual representations. *Psychonomic Bulletin & Review, 23,* 1096–1108.

Binder, J. R., Conant, L. L., Humphries, C. J., Fernandino, L., Simons, S. B., Aguilar, M., & Desai, R. H. (2016). Toward a brain-based componential semantic representation. *Cognitive Neuropsychology, 33,* 130–174.

Binder, J. R., & Desai, R. H. (2011). The neurobiology of semantic memory. *Trends in Cognitive Sciences, 15,* 527–536.

Binder, J. R., & Fernandino, L. (2015). Semantic processing. In A. W. Toga (ed.), *Brain mapping: An encyclopedic reference* (pp. 445–454). New York: Elsevier.

Binder, J. R., McKiernan, K. A., Parsons, M. E., Westbury, C. F., Possing, E. T., Kaufman, J. N., & Buchanan, L. (2003). Neural correlates of lexical access during visual word recognition. *Journal of Cognitive Neuroscience, 15,* 372–393.

Binkofski, F., & Buxbaum, L. J. (2013). Two action systems in the human brain. *Brain and Language, 127,* 222–229.

Binney, R. J., Embleton, K. V., Jeffries, E., Parker, G. J. M., & Lambon Ralph, M. A. (2010). The ventral and inferolateral aspects of the anterior temporal temporal lobe are crucial in semantic memory: Evidence from a novel direct comparison of distortion-corrected fMRI, rTMS, and semantic dementia. *Cerebral Cortex, 20,* 2728–2738.

Binney, R. J., Hoffman, P., & Lambon Ralph, M. A. (2016). Mapping the multiple graded contributions of the anterior temporal lobe representational hub to abstract and social concepts: Evidence from distortion-corrected fMRI. *Cerebral Cortex, 26,* 4227–4241.

Bisang, W. (2009). Serial verb constructions. *Language and Linguistics Compass, 3,* 792–814.

Bisiacchi, P., Mondini, S., Angrilli, A., Marinelli, K., & Semenza, C. (2005). Mass and count nouns show distinct EEG cortical processes during an explicit semantic task. *Brain and Language, 95,* 98–99.

Blakemore, S. J., Bristow, D., Bird, G., Frith, C., & Ward, J. (2005). Somatosensory activations during the observation of touch and a case of vision-touch synaesthesia. *Brain, 128,* 1571–1583.

Blanke, O., & Metzinger, T. (2009). Full body illusions and minimal phenomenal selfhood. *Trends in Cognitive Sciences, 13,* 7–13.

Block, N. (1995). On a confusion about the function of consciousness. *Behavioral and Brain Sciences, 18,* 227–287.

Block, N., Carmel, D., Fleming, S. M., Kentridge, R. W., Koch, C., Lamme, V. A. F., Lau, H., & Rosenthal, D. (2014). Consciousness science: Real progress and lingering misconceptions. *Trends in Cognitive Sciences, 18,* 556–557.

Bloom, P. (2002). *How children learn the meanings of words.* Cambridge, MA: MIT Press.

Blouw, P., Solodkin, E., Thagard, P., & Eliasmith, C. (2016). Concepts as semantic pointers: A framework and computational model. *Cognitive Science, 40,* 1128–1162.

Boas, F. (1911). Introduction to *Handbook of American Indian languages.* Bulletin 40, Part I, pp. 1–83, Bureau of American Ethnology. Washington, DC: Government Printing Office. (Reprinted in 1966: F. Boas, *Introduction to Handbook of American Indian languages* & J. W. Powell, *Indian linguistic families of America North of Mexico.* Lincoln: University of Nebraska Press.)

Bohnemeyer, J. (2007). Morpholexical transparency and the argument structure of verbs of cutting and breaking. *Cognitive Linguistics, 18,* 153–178.

Bohnemeyer, J. (2019). *Ten lectures on field semantics and semantic typology.* Leiden: Brill.

Bohnemeyer, J., & Brown, P. (2007). Standing divided: Dispositional verbs and locative predications in two Mayan languages. *Linguistics, 45,* 1105–1151.

Boly, M., Massimini, M., Tsuchiya, N., Postle, B. R., Koch, C., & Tononi, G. (2017). Are the neural correlates of consciousness in the front or in the back of the cerebral cortex? Clinical and neuroimaging evidence. *Journal of Neuroscience, 37,* 9603–9613.

Boly, M., Seth, A. K., Wilke, M., Ingmundson, P., Baars, B., Laureys, S., Edelman, D. B., & Tsuchiya, N. (2013). Consciousness in humans and non-human animals: Recent advances and future directions. *Frontiers in Psychology, 4,* Article 625.

Bonfiglioli, C., Finocciaro, C., Gesierich, B., Rositani, F., & Vescovi, M. (2009). A kinematic approach to the conceptual representations of *this* and *that. Cognition, 111,* 270–274.

Bonner, M. F., & Grossman, M. (2012). Gray matter density of auditory association cortex relates to knowledge of sound concepts in primary progressive aphasia. *Journal of Neuroscience, 32,* 7986–7991.

Bonner, M. F., Peelle, J. E., Cook, P. A., & Grossman, M. (2013). Heteromodal conceptual processing in the angular gyrus. *NeuroImage, 71,* 175–186.

Bonner, M. F., Price, A. R., Peelle, J. E., & Grossman, M. (2016). Semantics of the visual environment encoded in parahippocampal cortex. *Journal of Cognitive Neuroscience, 28,* 361–378.

Bonner, M. F., Vesely, L., Price, C., Anderson, C., Richmond, L., Farag, C., Avants, B., & Grossman, M. (2009). Reversal of the concreteness effect in semantic dementia. *Cognitive Neuropsychology, 26,* 568–579.

Bonnici, H. M., Richter, F. R., Yazar, Y., & Simons, J. S. (2016). Multimodal feature integration in the angular gyrus during episodic and semantic retrieval. *Journal of Neuroscience, 36,* 5462–5471.

Borghesani, V., Pedregosa, F., Buiatti, M., Amadon, A., Eger, E., & Piazza, M. (2016). Word meaning in the ventral visual path: A perceptual to conceptual gradient of semantic coding. *NeuroImage, 143,* 128–140.

Borgo, F., & Shallice, T. (2003). Category specificity and feature knowledge: Evidence from new sensory-quality categories. *Cognitive Neuropsychology, 20,* 327–354.

Boronat, C. B., Buxbaum, L. J., Coslett, H. B., Tang, K., Saffran, E. M., Kimberg, D. Y., & Detre, J. A. (2005). Distinctions between manipulation and function knowledge of objects: Evidence from functional magnetic resonance imaging. *Cognitive Brain Research, 23*, 361–373.

Boulenger, V., Hauk, O., & Pulvermüller, F. (2009). Grasping ideas with the motor system: Semantic somatotopy in idiom comprehension. *Cerebral Cortex, 19*, 1905–1914.

Boutonnet, B., Dering, B., Viñas-Guasch, N., & Thierry, G. (2013). Seeing objects through the language glass. *Journal of Cognitive Neuroscience, 25*, 1702–1710.

Bowden, J. (2001). *Taba: Description of a South Halmahera language.* (Pacific Linguistics, 521.) Canberra: Research School of Pacific and Asian Studies, Australian National University.

Bowerman, M. (1996). The origins of children's spatial semantic categories: Cognitive versus linguistic determinants. In J. J. Gumperz & S. C. Levinson (eds.), *Rethinking linguistic relativity* (pp. 145–176). Cambridge, UK: Cambridge University Press.

Bowerman, M. (2005). Why can't you "open" a nut or "break" a cooked noodle? Learning covert object categories in action word meanings. In L. Gershkoff-Stowe & D. Rakison (eds.), *Building object categories in developmental time* (pp. 33–62). Mahwah, NJ: Erlbaum.

Bowerman, M., & Choi, S. (2001). Shaping meanings for language: Universal and language-specific in the acquisition of spatial semantic categories. In M. Bowerman & S. C. Levinson (eds.), *Language acquisition and conceptual development* (pp. 475–511). Cambridge, UK: Cambridge University Press.

Bowerman, M., & Choi, S. (2003). Space under construction: language-specific spatial categorization in first language acquisition. In D. Gentner & S. Goldin-Meadow (eds.), *Language in mind: Advances in the study of language and thought* (387–428). Cambridge, MA: MIT Press.

Bowerman, M., & Levinson, S. C. (eds.). (2001). *Language acquisition and conceptual development.* Cambridge, UK: Cambridge University Press.

Bowerman, M., & Pederson, E. (1992). Cross-linguistic perspectives on topological spatial relationships. Paper presented at the annual meeting of the American Anthropological Association, San Francisco, CA.

Boyd, R. (2018). *A different kind of animal: How culture transformed our species.* Princeton, NJ: Princeton University Press.

Boye, K. (2010). Semantic maps and the identification of cross-linguistic generic categories: Evidentiality and its relation to epistemic modality. *Linguistic Discovery, 8*. doi: 10.1349/PS1.1537-0852.A.361

Bracci, S., Caramazza, A., & Peelen, M. V. (2015). Representational similarity of body parts in human occipitotemporal cortex. *Journal of Neuroscience, 35*, 12977–12985.

Bracci, S., Cavina-Pratesi, C., Connolly, J. D., & Ietswaart, M. (2016). Representational content of occipitotemporal and parietal tool areas. *Neuropsychologia, 84*, 81–88.

Bracci, S., & Op de Beeck, H. (2016). Dissociations and associations between shape and category representations in the two visual pathways. *Journal of Neuroscience, 36*, 432–444.

Bracci, S., Ritchie, B., & Op de Beeck, H. (2017). On the partnership between neural representations of object categories and visual features in the ventral visual pathway. *Neuropsychologia, 105*, 153–164.

Braddon-Mitchell, D., & Jackson, F. (2007). *Philosophy of mind and cognition*, 2nd edition. Oxford: Blackwell.

Breedin, S. D., Saffran, E. M., & Schwartz, M. F. (1998). Semantic factors in verb retrieval: An effect of complexity. *Brain and Language, 63*, 1–31.

Breyer, T., & Gutland, C. (eds.). (2015). *Phenomenology of thinking: Philosophical investigations into the character of cognitive experiences.* New York: Routledge.

Bright, P., Moss, H. E., Stamatakis, E. A., & Tyler, L. K. (2008). Longitudinal studies of semantic dementia: The relationship between structural and functional changes over time. *Neuropsychologia, 46,* 2177–2188.

Brown, C. H. (1976). General principles of human anatomical partonomy and speculations on the growth of partonomic nomenclature. *American Ethnologist, 3,* 400–424.

Brown, C. H. (1984). *Language and living things: Uniformities in folk classification and naming.* New Brunswick, NJ: Rutgers University Press.

Brown, C. H. (2005a). Hand and arm. In M. Haspelmath, M. S. Dryer, D. Gil, & B. Comrie (eds.), *The world atlas of language structures* (pp. 522–525). Oxford: Oxford University Press.

Brown, C. H. (2005b). Finger and hand. In M. Haspelmath, M. S. Dryer, D. Gil, & B. Comrie (eds.), *The world atlas of language structures* (pp. 526–529). Oxford: Oxford University Press.

Brown, P. (1994). The INs and ONs of Tzeltal locative expressions: The semantics of static descriptions of location. *Linguistics, 32,* 743–790.

Brown, P. (2006). A sketch of the grammar of space in Tzeltal. In S. C. Levinson & D. Wilkins (eds.), *Grammars of space: Explorations in cognitive diversity* (pp. 230–272). Cambridge, UK: Cambridge University Press.

Brown, P. (2007). "She had just cut/broken off her head": Cutting and breaking verbs in Tzeltal. *Cognitive Linguistics, 18,* 319–330.

Brown, P. (2012). To "put" or to "take"? Verb semantics in Tzeltal placement and removal expressions. In A. Kopecka & B. Narasimhan (eds.), *Events of putting and taking: A crosslinguistic perspective* (pp. 55–78). Amsterdam: John Benjamins.

Brown, P., & Levinson, S. C. (1993). "Uphill" and "downhill" in Tzeltal. *Journal of Linguistic Anthropology, 3,* 46–74.

Brozzoli, C., Ehrsson, H. H., & Farnè, A. (2014). Multisensory representation of the space near the hand: From perception to action and interindividual interactions. *Neuroscientist, 20,* 122–135.

Brozzoli, C., Gentile, G., Bergouignan, L., & Ehrsson, H. H. (2013). A shared representation of the space near oneself and others in the human premotor cortex. *Current Biology, 23,* 1764–1768.

Bruce, L. (1988). Serialization: From syntax to lexicon. *Studies in Language, 12,* 19–49.

Bruffaerts, R., Dupont, P., Peeters, R., De Deyne, S., Storms, G., & Vandenberghe, R. (2013). Similarity of fMRI activity patterns in left perirhinal cortex reflects semantic similarity between words. *Journal of Neuroscience, 33,* 18597–18607.

Burenhult, N. (2006). Body part terms in Jahai. *Language Sciences, 28,* 162–180.

Burenhult, N. (2008). Spatial coordinate systems in demonstrative meaning. *Linguistic Typology, 12,* 99–142.

Burenhult, N. (2012). The linguistic encoding of placement and removal events in Jahai. In A. Kopecka & B. Narasimhan (eds.), *Events of putting and taking: A crosslinguistic perspective* (pp. 21–36). Amsterdam: John Benjamins.

Burenhult, N., & Levinson, S. C. (2008). Language and landscape: A cross-linguistic perspective. *Language Sciences, 30,* 135–150.

Butler, C. R., Brambati, S. M., Miller, B. L., & Gorno-Tempini, M. L. (2009). The neural correlates of verbal and nonverbal semantic processing deficits in neurodegenerative disease. *Cognitive and Behavioral Neurology, 22,* 73–80.

Butt, M. (2010). The light verb jungle: Still hacking away. In M. Amberber, B. Baker, & M. Harvey (eds.), *Complex predicates: Cross-linguistic perspectives on event structure* (pp. 48–78). Cambridge, UK: Cambridge University Press.

Buxbaum, L. J., & Saffran, E. M. (2002). Knowledge of object manipulation and object function: Dissociations in apraxic and nonapraxic subjects. *Brain and Language, 82,* 179–199.

Bybee, J. (2003). Cognitive processes in grammaticalization. In M. Tomasello (ed.), *The new psychology of language, volume 2* (pp. 145–167). New York: Erlbaum.

Byland, E., & Athanasopoulos, P. (2014). Linguistic relativity in SLA: Towards a new research programme. *Language Learning, 64,* 952–985.

Calder, A. J., Keane, J., Manes, F., Antoun, N., & Young, A. W. (2000). Impaired recognition and experience of disgust following brain injury. *Nature Neuroscience, 3,* 1077–1078.

Calvo-Merino, B., Grezes, J., Glaser, D. E., Passingham, R. E., & Haggard, P. (2006). Seeing or doing? Influence of visual and motor familiarity in action observation. *Current Biology, 16,* 1905–1910.

Campanella, F., D'Agostini, S., Skrap, M., & Shallice, T. (2010). Naming manipulable objects: Anatomy of a category-specific effect in left temporal tumours. *Neuropsychologia, 48,* 1583–1597.

Candidi, M., Sacheli, L. M., Mega, I., & Aglioti, S. M. (2014). Somatotopic mapping of piano fingering errors in sensorimotor experts: TMS studies in pianists and visually trained naives. *Cerebral Cortex, 24,* 435–443.

Canessa, N., Borgo, F., Cappa, S. F., Perani, D., Falini, A., Buccino, G., Tettamanti, M., & Shallice, T. (2008). The different neural correlates of action and functional knowledge in semantic memory: An fMRI study. *Cerebral Cortex, 18,* 740–751.

Cant, J. S., Arnott, S. R., & Goodale, M. A. (2009). fMR-adaptation reveals separate processing regions for the perception of form and texture in the human ventral stream. *Experimental Brain Research, 192,* 391–405.

Cant, J. S., & Goodale, M. A. (2007). Attention to form or surface properties modulates different regions of human occipitotemporal cortex. *Cerebral Cortex, 17,* 713–731.

Cant, J. S., & Goodale, M. A. (2011). Scratching beneath the surface: New insights into the functional properties of the lateral occipital area and parahippocampal place area. *Journal of Neuroscience, 31,* 8248–8258.

Capell, A. (1979). Classification of verbs in Australian languages. In S. A. Wurm (ed.), *Australian linguistic studies* (pp. 229–322). Canberra: Pacific Linguistics C-54.

Capitani, E., Laiacona, M., Mahon, B., & Caramazza, A. (2003). What are the facts of semantic category-specific deficits? A critical review of the clinical evidence. *Cognitive Neuropsychology, 20,* 213–262.

Caramazza, A., & Mahon, B. Z. (2003). The organization of conceptual knowledge: The evidence from category-specific semantic deficits. *Trends in Cognitive Sciences, 7,* 354–361.

Caramazza, A., & Shelton, J. R. (1998). Domain-specific knowledge systems in the brain: The animate-inanimate distinction. *Journal of Cognitive Neuroscience, 10,* 1–34.

Carlson, L. (1999). Selecting a reference frame. *Spatial Cognition and Computation, 1,* 365–379.

Carlson, L., & van der Zee, E. (2005), *Functional features in language and space: Insights from perception, categorization, and development.* New York: Oxford University Press.

Carlson, R., & Payne, D. (1989). Genitive classifiers. *Proceedings of the Fourth Annual Pacific Linguistics Conference* (pp. 89–119). Eugene: University of Oregon.

Carlson, T. A., Simmons, R. A., Kriegeskorte, N., & Slevc, I. R. (2014). The emergence of semantic meaning in the ventral temporal pathway. *Journal of Cognitive Neuroscience, 26,* 120–131.

Carlson-Radvansky, L. A., & Irwin, D. A. (1993). Frames of reference in vision and language: Where is above? *Cognition, 46,* 223–244.

Carota, F., Moseley, R., & Pulvermüller, F. (2012). Body-part-specific representations of semantic noun categories. *Journal of Cognitive Neuroscience, 24,* 1492–1509.

Carruthers, P. (2005). *Consciousness: Essays from a higher-order perspective.* New York: Oxford University Press.

Carruthers, P., & Veillet, B. (2012). The case against cognitive phenomenology. In T. Bayne & M. Montague (eds.), *Cognitive phenomenology* (pp. 35–56). New York: Oxford University Press.

Carter, R. (1976). Chipewyan classificatory verbs. *International Journal of American Linguistics, 42,* 24–30.

Casali, A. G., Gosseries, O., Rosanova, M., Boly, M., Sarasso, S., Casali, K. R., Casarotto, S., Bruno, M. A., Laureys, S., Tononi, G., & Massamini, M. (2013). A theoretically based index of consciousness independent of sensory processing and behavior. *Science Translational Medicine, 5,* 198ra105.

Casasanto, D. (2016). Linguistic relativity. In N. Riemer (ed.), *Routledge handbook of semantics* (pp. 158–174). New York: Routledge.

Casasanto, D. (2017). Relationships between language and cognition. In B. Dancygier (ed.), *Cambridge handbook of cognitive linguistics* (pp. 19–37). Cambridge, UK: Cambridge University Press.

Caspers, S., Zilles, K., Laird, A. R., & Eickhoff, S. B. (2010). ALE meta-analysis of action observation and imitation in the human brain. *NeuroImage, 50,* 1148–1167.

Cavina-Pratesi, Kentridge, R. W., Heywood, C. A., & Milner, A. D. (2010a). Separate processing of texture and form in the ventral stream: Evidence from fMRI and visual agnosia. *Cerebral Cortex, 20,* 433–446.

Cavina-Pratesi, Kentridge, R. W., Heywood, C. A., & Milner, A. D. (2010b). Separate channels for processing form, texture, and color: Evidence from fMRI adaptation and visual object agnosia. *Cerebral Cortex, 20,* 2319–2332.

Chan, A. M., Baker, J. M., Eskandar, E., Schomar, D., Ulbert, I., Marinkovic, K., Cash, S. S., & Halgren, E. (2011). First-pass selectivity for semantic categories in human anteroventral temporal lobe. *Journal of Neuroscience, 31,* 18119–18129.

Chao, L. L., Haxby, J. V., & Martin, A. (1999). Attribute-based neural substrates in temporal cortex for perceiving and knowing about objects. *Nature Neuroscience, 2,* 913–919.

Chao, L. L., & Martin, A. (1999). Cortical representation of perception, naming, and knowing about color. *Journal of Cognitive Neuroscience, 11,* 25–35.

Chappell, H., & McGregor, W. (eds.) (1995). *The grammar of inalienability: A typological perspective on body part terms and the part-whole relation.* Berlin: Mouton de Gruyter.

Charest, I., & Kriegeskorte, N. (2015). The brain of the beholder: Honouring individual representational idiosyncracies. *Language, Cognition, and Neuroscience, 30,* 367–379.

Chatterjee, A. (2008). The neural organization of spatial thought and language. *Seminars in Speech and Language, 29,* 226–238.

Chee, M. W. L., Weekes, B., Lee, K. M., Soon, C. S., Schreiber, A., Hoon, J. J., & Chee, M. (2000). Overlap and dissociation of semantic processing of Chinese characters, English words, and pictures: Evidence from fMRI. *NeuroImage, 12,* 392–403.

Chen, J. (2012). "She from the bookshelf take-descend-come the box": Encoding and categorizing placement events in Mandarin. In A. Kopecka & B. Narasimhan (eds.), *Events of putting and taking: A crosslinguistic perspective* (pp. 37–54). Amsterdam: John Benjamins.

Chen, L., & Rogers, T. T. (2014). Revisiting domain-general accounts of category specificity in mind and brain. *WIREs Cognitive Science, 5,* 327–344.

Chen, L., & Rogers, T. T. (2015). A model of emergent category-specific activation in the posterior fusiform gyrus of sighted and congenitally blind populations. *Journal of Cognitive Neuroscience, 27,* 1981–1999.

Chen, Q., Garcea, F. E., Jacobs, R. A., & Mahon, B. Z. (2018). Abstract representations of object-directed action in the left inferior parietal lobule. *Cerebral Cortex, 28,* 2162–2174.

Chen, Q., Garcea, F. E., & Mahon, B. Z. (2016a). The representation of object-directed action and function knowledge in the human brain. *Cerebral Cortex, 26,* 1609–1618.

Chen, Y., Shimotake, A., Matsumoto, R., Kunieda, T., Kikuchi, T., Miyamoto, S., Fukuyama, H., Takahashi, R., Ikeda, A., & Lambon Ralph, M. A. (2016b). The "when" and "where" of semantic coding in the anterior temporal lobe: Temporal representational similarity analysis of electrocortigram data. *Cortex, 79,* 1–13.

Chiou, R., & Lambon Ralph, M. A. (2016). Task-related dynamic division of labor between anterior temporal and lateral occipital cortices in representing object size. *Journal of Neuroscience, 36,* 4662–4668.

Chittka, L. (2017). Bee cognition. *Current Biology, 27,* R1049–R1053.

Chou, C. J., Huang, H. W., Lee, C. L., & Lee, C. Y. (2014). Effects of semantic constraint and cloze probability on Chinese classifier-noun agreement. *Journal of Neurolinguistics, 31,* 42–54.

Chou, T. L., Lee, S. H., Hung, S. M., & Chen, H. C. (2012). The role of inferior frontal gyrus in processing Chinese classifiers. *Neuropsychologia, 50,* 1408–1415.

Chouinard, P. A., & Goodale, M. A. (2010). Category-specific neural processing for naming pictures of animals and naming pictures of tools: An ALE meta-analysis. *Neuropsychologia, 48,* 409–418.

Chrastil, E. R. (2013). Neural evidence supports a novel framework for spatial navigation. *Psychonomic Bulletin & Review, 20,* 208–227.

Chrastil, E. R., Sherrill, K. R., Aselciogly, I., Hasselmo, M. E., & Stern, C. E. (2017). Individual differences in human path integration abilities correlate with gray matter volume in retrosplenial cortex, hippocampus, and medial prefrontal cortex. *eNeuro, 4,* e0346.

Chrastil, E. R., Sherrill, K. R., Hasselmo, M. E., & Stern, C. E. (2015). There and back again: Hippocampus and retrosplenial cortex track homing distance during human path integration. *Journal of Neuroscience, 35,* 15442–15452.

Chrastil, E. R., Sherrill, K. R., Hasselmo, M. E., & Stern, C. E. (2016). Which way and how far? Tracking of translation and rotation information for human path integration. *Human Brain Mapping, 37,* 3636–3655.

Christiansen, M. H., & Chater, N. (2008). Language as shaped by the brain. *Behavioral and Brain Sciences, 31,* 489–509; discussion, 509–558.

Christiansen, M. H., & Chater, N. (2016). *Creating language: Integrating evolution, acquisition, and processing.* Cambridge, MA: MIT Press.

Christensen, K. R., & Wallentin, M. (2011). The locative alternation: Distinguishing linguistic processing from error signals in Broca's region. *NeuroImage, 56,* 1622–1631.

Chudnoff, E. (2015). *Cognitive phenomenology.* New York: Routledge.

Chumbley, J. L., & Balota, D. A. (1984). A word's meaning affects the decision in lexical decision. *Memory and Cognition, 12,* 590–606.

Clark, A. (2000). *A theory of sentience.* New York: Oxford University Press.

Clark, A. (2013). Whatever next? Predictive brains, situated agents, and the future of cognitive science. *Behavioral and Brain Sciences, 36,* 181–204; discussion, 204–253.

Clark, E. V. (2004). How language acquisition builds on cognitive development. *Trends in Cognitive Sciences, 8,* 472–478.

Clarke, A. (2015). Dynamic information processing states revealed through neurocognitive models of object semantics. *Language, Cognition, and Neuroscience, 30,* 409–419.

Clarke, A., & Tyler, L. K. (2014). Object-specific semantic coding in human perirhinal cortex. *Journal of Neuroscience, 34,* 4766–4775.

Clarke, A., & Tyler, L. K. (2015). Understanding what we see: How we derive meaning from vision. *Trends in Cognitive Sciences, 19,* 677–687.

Cléry, J., Guipponi, O., Wardak, C., & Hamed, S. B. (2015). Neuronal bases of peripersonal and extrapersonal spaces, their plasticity and their dynamics: Knowns and unknowns. *Neuropsychologia, 70,* 313–326.

Coello, Y., & Bonnotte, I. (2013). The mutual roles of action representations and spatial deictics in French language. *Quarterly Journal of Experimental Psychology, 66,* 2187–2203.

Coello, Y., & Fischer, M. H. (eds.). (2015). *Perceptual and emotional embodiment: Foundations of embodied cognition,* vol. 1. New York: Psychology Press.

Cohen Kadosh, R., Henik, A., Rubinsten, O., Mohr, H., Dori, H., van de Ven, V., Zorzi, M., Hendler, T., Goebel, R., & Linden, D. E. J. (2005). Are numbers special? The comparison systems of the human brain investigated by fMRI. *Neuropsychologia, 43,* 1238–1248.

Collins, J. A., Montal, V., Hochberg, D., Quimby, M., Mandelli, M. L., Makris, N., Seeley, W. W., Gorno-Tempini, M. L., & Dickerson, B. C. (2017). Focal temporal pole atrophy and network degeneration in semantic variant primary progressive aphasia. *Brain, 140,* 457–471.

Committeri, G., Galati, G., Paradis, A. L., Pizzamiglio, L., Berthoz, A., & LeBihan, D. (2004). Reference frames for spatial cognition: Different brain areas are involved in viewer-, object-, and landmark-centered judgments about object location. *Journal of Cognitive Neuroscience, 16,* 1517–1535.

Comrie, B. (1989). *Language universals and linguistic typology,* 2nd edition. Chicago: University of Chicago Press.

Comrie, B. (2005). Numeral bases. In M. Haspelmath, M. S. Dryer, D. Gil, & B. Comrie (eds.), *The world atlas of language structures* (pp. 530–533). New York: Oxford University Press.

Conder, J., Fridriksson, J., Baylis, G. C., Smith, C. M., Boiteau, T. W., & Almor, A. (2017). Bilateral parietal contributions to spatial language. *Brain and Language, 164,* 16–24.

Connell, L., & Lynott, D. (2014). Principles of representation: Why you can't represent the same concept twice. *Topics in Cognitive Science, 6,* 390–406.

Connolly, A. C., Guntupalli, J. S., Gors, J., Hanke, M., Halchenko, Y. O., Wu, Y. C., Abdi, H., & Haxby, J. V. (2012). The representation of biological classes in the human brain. *Journal of Neuroscience, 32,* 2608–2618.

Contini, E. W., Wardle, S. G., & Carlson, T. A. (2017). Decoding the time-course of object recognition in the human brain: From visual features to categorical decisions. *Neuropsychologia, 105,* 165–176.

Contini-Morava, E., & Kilarski, M. (2013). Functions of nominal classification. *Language Sciences, 40,* 263–299.

Cook, V., Bassetti, B., Kasai, C., Sasaki, M., & Takahashi, J. (2006). Do bilinguals have different concepts? The case of shape and material in Japanese L2 users of English. *International Journal of Bilingualism, 10,* 137–152.

Cotelli, M., Borroni, B., Manenti, R., Alberici, A., Calabria, M., Agosti, C., Arévalo, A., Ginex, V., Ortelli, P., Binetti, G., Zanetti, O., Padovani, A., & Cappa, S. F. (2006). Action and object naming in frontotemporal dementia, progressive supranuclear palsy, and corticobasal degeneration. *Neuropsychology, 20,* 558–565.

Coutanche, M. N., & Thompson-Schill, S. L. (2015). Creating concepts from converging features in human cortex. *Cerebral Cortex, 25*, 2584–2593.

Coventry, K. R., & Garrod, S. C. (2004). *Saying, seeing, and acting: The psychological semantics of spatial prepositions.* New York: Psychology Press.

Coventry, K. R., Griffiths, D., & Hamilton, C. J. (2014). Spatial demonstratives and perceptual space: Describing and remembering object location. *Cognitive Psychology, 69*, 46–70.

Coventry, K. R., Prat-Sala, M., & Richards, L. (2001). The interplay between geometry and function in the comprehension of *over, under, above,* and *below. Journal of Memory and Language, 44*, 376–398.

Coventry, K. R., Valdés, B., Castillo, A., & Guijarro-Fuentes, P. (2008). Language within your reach: Near-far perceptual space and spatial demonstratives. *Cognition, 108*, 889–898.

Craig, C. (ed.) (1986). *Noun classes and categorization.* Amsterdam: John Benjamins.

Croft, W. (1991). *Syntactic categories and grammatical relations: The cognitive organization of information.* Chicago: University of Chicago Press.

Croft, W. (2001). *Radical construction grammar: Syntactic theory in typological perspective.* New York: Oxford University Press.

Croft, W. (2010). Relativity, linguistic variation, and language universals. *Cognitextes, 4.*

Croft, W. (2012). *Verbs: Aspect and causal structure.* New York: Oxford University Press.

Croft, W. (2017). Classifier constructions and their evolution: A commentary on Kemmerer (2016). *Language, Cognition, and Neuroscience, 32*, 425–427.

Croft, W., Barddal, J., Hollmann, W. Sotirova, V., & Taoka, C. (2010). Revising Talmy's typological classification of complex events. In H. C. Boas (ed.), *Contrastive construction grammar* (pp. 201–235). Amsterdam: John Benjamins.

Croft, W. & Poole, K. T. (2008). Inferring universals from grammatical variation: Multidimensional scaling for typological analysis. *Theoretical linguistics, 34*, 1–38.

Cross, E. S., Kraemer, D. J. M., De, A. F., Hamilton, A., Kelley, W. M., & Grafton, S. T. (2009). Sensitivity of the action observation network to physical and observational learning. *Cerebral Cortex, 19*, 315–326.

Crowley, T. (2002). *Serial verbs in Oceanic: A descriptive typology.* New York: Oxford University Press.

Crutch, S. J., & Warrington, E. K. (2007). The semantic organization of mass nouns: Evidence from semantic refractory access dysphasia. *Cortex, 43*, 1031–1124.

Crystal, D. (2000). *Language death.* Cambridge, UK: Cambridge University Press.

Cysouw, M. (2007). Building semantic maps: The case of person marking. In B. Wälchli & M. Miestamo (eds.), *New challenges in typology* (pp. 225–248). Berlin: Mouton.

Cysouw, M. (2010). Semantic maps as metrics on meanings. *Linguistic Discovery, 8.* doi: 10.1349/PS1.1537-0852.A.365

Dahl,Ö., & Velupillai, V. (2005). Tense and aspect. In M. Haspelmath, M. S. Dryer, D. Gil, & B. Comrie (eds.), *The world atlas of language structures* (pp. 266–281). New York: Oxford University Press.

Dalla Volta, R., Avanzini, P., De Marco, D., Gentilucci, M., & Fabbri-Destro, M. (2018). From meaning to categorization: The hierarchical recruitment of brain circuits selective for action verbs. *Cortex, 100*, 95–110.

Damasio, A. R. (1989a). Concepts in the brain. *Mind and Language, 4*, 24–28.

Damasio, A. R. (1989b). Time-locked multiregional retroactivation: A systems level proposal for the neural substrates of recall and recognition. *Cognition, 33*, 25–62.

Damasio, A. R. (2010). *Self comes to mind: Constructing the conscious brain*. New York: Pantheon.

Damasio, H., Grabowski, T. J., Tranel, D., Ponto, L. L. B., Hichwa, R. D., & Damasio, A. R. (2001). Neural correlates of naming actions and of naming spatial relations. *NeuroImage, 13*, 1053–1064.

Damasio, A. R., Tranel, D., & Damasio, H. (1990). Face agnosia and the neural substrates of memory. *Annual Review of Neuroscience, 13*, 89–109.

Damasio, H., Tranel, D., Grabowski, T. J., Adolphs, R., & Damasio, A. R. (2004). Neural systems behind word and concept retrieval. *Cognition, 92*, 179–229.

Davidson, M. (1999). Southern Wakashan locative suffixes: A challenge to proposed universals of closed-class spatial meaning. Paper presented at the Annual Meeting of the International Cognitive Linguistics Association, Stockholm, Sweden.

Davidson, W., Elford, L. W., & Hoijer, H. (1963). Athapaskan classificatory verbs. In H. Hoijer et al. (eds.), *Studies in the Athapaskan languages* (pp. 30–41). Berkeley: University of California Press.

Deen, B., & McCarthy, G. (2010). Reading about the actions of others: Biological motion imagery and action congruency influence brain activity. *Neuropsychologia, 48*, 1607–1615.

Defina, R. (2016). Do serial verb constructions describe single events? A study of co-speech gestures in Avetime. *Language, 92*, 890–910.

de Graaf, T. A., Hsieh, P. J., & Sack, A. T. (2012). The "correlates" in neural correlates of consciousness. *Neuroscience and Biobehavioral Reviews, 36*, 191–197.

De Grauwe, S., Willems, R. M., Rueschemeyer, S. A., Lemhöfer, K., & Schriefers, H. (2014). Embodied language in first- and second-language speakers: Neural correlates of processing motor verbs. *Neuropsychologia, 56*, 334–349.

Dehaene, S. (2014). *Consciousness and the brain: Deciphering how the brain codes our thoughts*. New York: Viking.

Dehaene, S., & Changeux, J. P. (2011). Experimental and theoretical approaches to conscious processing. *Neuron, 70*, 200–227.

Dehaene, S., Charles, L., King, J. R., & Marti, S. (2014). Toward a computational theory of conscious processing. *Current Opinion in Neurobiology, 25*, 76–84.

Dehaene, S., Lau, H., & Kouider, S. (2017). What is consciousness, and could machines have it? *Science, 358*, 486–492.

Dehaene, S., & Naccache, L. (2001). Towards a cognitive neuroscience of consciousness: Basic evidence and a workspace framework. *Cognition, 79*, 1–37.

Dehaene, S., Naccache, L., Le Clec'H, G., Koechlin, E., Mueller, M., Dehaene-Lambertz, G., van de Moortele, P. F., & Le Bihan D. (1998). Imaging unconscious semantic priming. *Nature, 395*, 597–600.

Dehaene, S., Naccache, L., Cohen, L., Le Bihan, D., Mangin, J. F., Poline, J. B., & Riviere, D. (2001). Cerebral mechanisms of word masking and unconscious repetition priming. *Nature Neuroscience, 4*, 752–758.

DeLancey, S. (1989). Klamath stem structure in genetic and areal perspective. *Papers from the 1988 Hokan-Penutian languages workshop* (pp. 31–39). Eugene, OR: University of Oregon.

DeLancey, S. (1996). *Argument structure of Klamath bipartite stems*. SSILA Conference, San Diego, CA.

Desai, R., Conant, L. L., Binder, J. R., Park, H., & Seidenberg, M. S. (2013). A piece of the action: Modulation of sensory-motor regions by action idioms and metaphors. *NeuroImage, 83*, 862–869.

Desai, R. H., Herter, T., Riccardi, N., Rorden, C., & Fridriksson, J. (2015). Concepts within reach: Action performance predicts action language processing in stroke. *Neuropsychologia, 71*, 217–224.

Devereux, B. J., Clarke, A., Marouchos, A., & Tyler, L. K. (2013). Representational similarity analysis reveals commonalities and differences in the semantic processing of words and objects. *Journal of Neuroscience, 33*, 18906–18916.

de Vignemont, F., Majid, A., Jolla, C., & Haggard, P. (2009). Segmenting the body into parts: Evidence from biases in tactile perception. *Quarterly Journal of Experimental Psychology, 62*, 500–512.

Diessel, H. (1999). *Demonstratives.* Amsterdam: John Benjamins.

Diessel, H. (2005). Distance contrasts in demonstratives. In M. Haspelmath, M. S. Dryer, D. Gil, & B. Comrie (eds.), *The world atlas of language structures* (pp. 170–173). New York: Oxford University Press.

Diessel, H. (2006). Demonstratives, joint attention, and the emergence of grammar. *Cognitive Linguistics, 17*, 463–490.

Diessel, H. (2014). Demonstratives, frames of reference, and semantic universals of space. *Language and Linguistics Compass, 8*, 116–132.

di Pellegrino, G., & Làdavas, E. (2015). Peripersonal space in the brain. *Neuropsychologia, 66*, 126–133.

Divjak, D., & Kochańska, A. (eds.). (2007). *Cognitive paths into the Slavic domain.* Berlin: Mouton de Gruyter.

Dixon, R. M. W. (1982). *Where have all the adjectives gone?* Berlin: Mouton.

Dixon, R. M. W. (1997). *The rise and fall of languages.* Cambridge, UK: Cambridge University Press.

Dixon, R. M. W. (2000). A typology of causatives: Form, syntax and meaning. In R. M. W. Dixon & A. Y. Aikhenvald (eds.), *Changing valency: Case studies in transitivity.* Cambridge, UK: Cambridge University Press.

Dixon, R. M. W. (2003). Demonstratives: A cross-linguistic typology. *Studies in Language, 27*, 62–112.

Dixon, R. M. W. (2010a). *Basic linguistic theory*, Vol. 1: *Methodology.* New York: Oxford University Press.

Dixon, R. M. W. (2010b). *Basic linguistic theory*, Vol. 2: *Grammatical topics.* New York: Oxford University Press.

Dixon, R. M. W. (2012). *Basic linguistic theory*, Vol. 3: *Further grammatical topics.* New York: Oxford University Press.

Dixon, R. M. W. (2016). *Are some languages better than others?* New York: Oxford University Press.

Domoto-Reilly, K., Sapolsky, D., Brickhouse, M., & Dickerson, B. C. (2012). Naming impairment in Alzheimer's disease is associated with left anterior temporal lobe atrophy. *NeuroImage, 63*, 348–355.

Dougherty, J. (1981). Salience and relativity in classification. In R. Casson (ed.), *Language, culture, and cognition* (pp. 163–180). New York: Macmillan.

Dove, G. (2011). On the need for embodied and disembodied cognition. *Frontiers in Psychology, 1*, 242.

Downing, P. E., & Peelen, M. V. (2011). The role of occipitotemporal body-selective regions in person perception. *Cognitive Neuroscience, 2*, 186–203.

Downing, P. E., & Peelen, M. V. (2016). Body selectivity in occipitotemporal cortex: Causal evidence. *Neuropsychologia, 83*, 138–148.

Dreyer, F. R., Frey, D., Arana, S., von Saldern, S., Picht, T., Vajkoczy, P., & Pulvermüller, F. (2015). Is the motor system necessary for processing action and abstract emotion words? Evidence from focal brain lesions. *Frontiers in Psychology, 6,* Article 1661.

Durie, M. (1997). Grammatical structures in verb serialization. In A. Alsina, J. Bresnan, & P. Sells (eds.), *Complex predicates* (pp. 289–354). Stanford: CSLI Publications.

Ebisch, S. J. H., Babiloni, C., Del Gratta, C., Ferretti, A., Perrucci, M. G., Caulo, M., Sitskoorn, M. M., & Romani, G. L. (2007). Human neural systems for conceptual knowledge of proper object use: A functional magnetic resonance imaging study. *Cerebral Cortex, 17,* 2744–2751.

Edelman, G. M., & Tononi, G. (2000). *A universe of consciousness: How matter becomes imagination.* New York: Basic Books.

Eliasmith, C. (2013). *How to build a brain: An architecture for neurobiological cognition.* New York: Oxford University Press.

Eliasmith, C., Stewart, T., Choo, X., Bekolay, T., DeWolf, T., Tang, Y., & Rasmussen, D. (2012). A large-scale model of the functioning brain. *Science, 338,* 1202–1205.

Emberson, L. L., Crosswhite, S. L., Richards, J. E., & Aslin, R. N. (2017). The lateral occipital cortex is selective for object shape, not texture/color, at six months. *Journal of Neuroscience, 37,* 3698–3703.

Emery, N. J., & Clayton, N. S. (2004). The mentality of crows: Convergent evolution of intelligence in corvids and apes. *Science, 306,* 1903–1907.

Emmorey, K., Damasio, H., McCullough, S., Grabowski, T. J., Ponto, L. L. B., Hichwa, R., & Bellugi, U. (2002). Neural systems underlying spatial language in American Sign Language. *NeuroImage, 17,* 812–824.

Emmorey, K., Grabowski, T. J., McCullough, S., Ponto, L. L. B., Hichwa, R., & Damasio, H. (2005). The neural correlates of spatial language in English and American Sign Language: A PET study with hearing bilinguals. *NeuroImage, 24,* 832–840.

Emmorey, K., McCullough, S., Mehta, S., Ponto, L. L. B., & Grabowski, T. J. (2013). The biology of linguistic expression impacts neural correlates for spatial language. *Journal of Cognitive Neuroscience, 25,* 517–533.

Enfield, N. (2003). Demonstratives in space and interaction: Data from Lao speakers and implications for semantic analysis. *Language, 79,* 82–117.

Enfield, N. (2007a). *A grammar of Lao.* Berlin: Mouton de Gruyter.

Enfield, N. (2007b). Lao separation verbs and the logic of event categorization. *Cognitive Linguistics, 18,* 287–296.

Enfield, N. (2015a). Linguistic relativity from reference to agency. *Annual Review of Anthropology, 44,* 207–224.

Enfield, N. (2015b). *The utility of meaning: What words mean and why.* New York: Oxford University Press.

Enfield, N., Majid, A., & van Staden, M. (2006). Cross-linguistic categorisation of the body. *Language Sciences, 28,* 137–147.

Epicurus. (1994). *The Epicurus reader: Selected writings and testimonia,* trans. B. Inwood & L. P. Gerson. (Original work published in the 4th century B.C.)

Epstein, R. A., & Kanwisher, N. (1998). A cortical representation of the local visual environment. *Nature, 392,* 598–601.

Epstein, R. A., Patai, E. Z., Julian, J. B., & Speiers, H. J. (2017). The cognitive map in humans: Spatial navigation and beyond. *Nature Neuroscience, 20,* 1504–1513.

Erdogan, G., Chen, Q., Garcea, F. E., Mahon, B. Z., & Jacobs, R. (2016). Multisensory part-based representations of objects in human lateral occipital complex. *Journal of Cognitive Neuroscience, 28,* 869–881.

Erk, K. (2012). Vector space models of word meaning and phrase meaning: A survey. *Language and Linguistics Compass, 6*, 635–653.

Essegbey, J. (2007). Cut and break verbs in Sranan. *Cognitive Linguistics, 18*, 231–240.

Evans, N. (1994). Kayardild. In C. Goddard & A. Wierzbicka (eds.), *Semantic and lexical universals: Theory and empirical findings* (pp. 203–228). Amsterdam: John Benjamins.

Evans, N. (2003). Context, culture, and structuration in the languages of Australia. *Annual Review of Anthropology, 32*, 13–40.

Evans, N. (2007). Standing up in your mind: Remembering in Dalabon. In M. Amberber (ed.), *The language of memory in a crosslinguistic perspective* (pp. 67–95). Amsterdam: John Benjamins.

Evans, N. (2010). *Dying words: Endangered languages and what they have to tell us.* West Sussex: Wiley-Blackwell.

Evans, N. (2011). Semantic typology. In J. J. Song (ed.), *The Oxford handbook of linguistic typology* (pp. 504–533). New York: Oxford University Press.

Evans, N., Gaby, A., Levinson, S., & Majid, A. (eds.) (2011). *Reciprocals and semantic typology.* Amsterdam: John Benjamins.

Evans, N., & Levinson, S. C. (2009). The myth of language universals: Language diversity and its implications for cognitive science. *Behavioral and Brain Sciences, 32*, 429–448; discussion, 448–492.

Evans, V., & Chilton, P. (eds.). (2010). *Language, cognition, and space: The state of the art and new directions.* London: Equinox.

Everett, C. (2013). *Linguistic relativity: Evidence across languages and cognitive domains.* Berlin: Mouton de Gruyter.

Fairhall, S. L., & Caramazza, A. (2013). Brain regions that represent amodal conceptual knowledge. *Journal of Neuroscience, 33*, 10552–10558.

Fedden, S., & Corbett, G. G. (2017). Gender and classifiers in concurrent systems: Refining the typology of nominal classification. *Glossa, 2*, Article 34.

Federenko, E., & Varley, R. (2016). Language and thought are not the same thing: Evidence from neuroimaging and neurological patients. *Annals of the New York Academy of Sciences, 1369*, 132–153.

Feist, M. I. (2008). Space between languages. *Cognitive Science, 32*, 1177–1199.

Fellbaum, C. (1998). *WordNet: An electronic lexical database.* Cambridge, MA: MIT Press.

Fernandino, L., Binder, J. R., Desai, R. H., Pendl, S. L., Humphries, C. J., Gross, W. L., Conant, L. L., & Seidenberg, M. S. (2016). Concept representation reflects multimodal abstraction: A framework for embodied semantics. *Cerebral Cortex, 26*, 2018–2034.

Fernandino, L., Humphries, C. J., Seidenberg, M. S., Gross, W. L., Conant, L. L., & Binder, J. R. (2015). Predicting brain activation patterns associated with individual lexical concepts based on five sensory-motor attributes. *Neuropsychologia, 76*, 17–26.

Fernandino, L., & Iacoboni, M. (2010). Are cortical maps based on body parts or coordinated actions? Implications for embodied semantics. *Brain and Language, 112*, 44–53.

Fernyhough, C. (2016). *The voices within: The history and science of how we talk to ourselves.* London: Wellcome Collection.

Fieder, N., Nickels, L., Biedermann, B., & Best, W. (2014). From "some butter" to "a butter": An investigation of mass and count representation and processing. *Cognitive Neuropsychology, 31*, 313–349.

Fieder, N., Nickels, L., Biedermann, B., & Best, W. (2015). How "some garlic" becomes "a garlic" or "some onion": Mass and count processing in aphasia. *Neuropsychologia, 75*, 626–645.

Filimon, F., Nelson, J. D., Hagler, D. J., & Sereno, M. I. (2007). Human cortical representations for reaching: Mirror neurons for execution, observation, and imagery. *NeuroImage*, *37*, 1315–1328.

Filimon, F., Rieth, C. A., Sereno, M. I., & Cottrell, G. W. (2014). Observed, executed, and imagined action representations can be decoded from ventral and dorsal areas. *Cerebral Cortex*, *25*, 3144–3158.

Filipović, L. (2007a). Language as a witness: Insights from cognitive linguistics. *Speech, Language, and the Law*, *14*, 245–267.

Filipović, L. (2007b). *Talking about motion: A crosslinguistic investigation of lexicalization patterns*. Amsterdam: John Benjamins.

Filipović, L. (2009). Motion events in eyewitness interviews, translation, and memory: Typological and psycholinguistic perspectives. *Language and Linguistics Compass*, *3*, 300–313.

Filipović, L. (2011). Speaking and remembering in one or two languages: Bilingual vs. monolingual lexicalization and memory for motion events. *International Journal of Bilingualism*, *15*, 466–485.

Fillmore, C. F. (1997). *Lectures on deixis*. Stanford: CSLI Publications.

Firth, J. R. (1957). *Papers in linguistics 1934–1951*. London: Oxford University Press.

Fisch, L., Privman, E., Ramot, M., Harel, M., Nir, Y., Kipervasser, S., Andelman, F., Neufeld, M. Y., Kramer, U., Fried, I., & Malach, R. (2009). Neural "ignition": Enhanced activation linked to perceptual awareness in human ventral stream visual cortex. *Neuron*, *64*, 562–574.

Fischer, M. H., & Coello, Y. (eds.) (2015). *Conceptual and interactive embodiment: Foundations of embodied cognition*, vol. 2. New York: Psychology Press.

Fogassi, L., Gallese, V., Fadiga, L., Luppino, G., Matelli, M., & Rizzolatti, G. (1996). Coding of peripersonal space in inferior premotor cortex (area F4). *Journal of Neurophysiology*, *76*, 141–157.

Foley, W. A. (2010). Events and serial verb constructions. In M. Amberber, B. Baker, & M. Harvey (eds.), *Complex predicates: Cross-linguistic perspectives on event structure* (pp. 79–109). Cambridge, UK: Cambridge University Press.

Frässle, S., Sommer, J., Jannsen, A., Naber, M., & Einhäuser, W. (2014). Binocular rivalry: Frontal activity relates to introspection and action but not to perception. *Journal of Neuroscience*, *34*, 1738–1747.

Frawley, W. (1992). *Linguistic semantics*. Hillsdale, NJ: Erlbaum.

Freud, E., Ganel, T., & Avidan, G. (2013). Representation of possible and impossible objects in the human visual cortex: Evidence from fMRI adaptation. *NeuroImage*, *64*, 685–692.

Freud, S. (1891/1953). *On aphasia* (E. Stengel, Trans.). New York: International University Press.

Friederici, A., & Levelt, W. J. M. (1990). Spatial reference in weightlessness: perceptual factors and mental representations. *Perception and Psychophysics*, *47*, 253–266.

Fuji, Y. (1999). The story of "break": Cognitive categories of objects and the system of verbs. In M. Hiraga, C. Sinha, & S. Wilcox (eds.), *Cultural, psychological, and typological issues in cognitive linguistics* (pp. 313–332). Amsterdam: John Benjamins.

Gaby, A. (2007). Describing cutting and breaking in Kuuk Thaayorre. *Cognitive Linguistics*, *18*, 263–272.

Gage, N., & Hickok, G. (2005). Multiregional cell assemblies, temporal binding, and the representation of conceptual knowledge in cortex: A modern theory by a "classical" neurologist, Carl Wernicke. *Cortex*, *41*, 823–832.

Gaillard, R., Dehaene, S., Adam, C., Clemenceau, S., Hasboun, D., Baulac, M., Cohen, L., & Naccache, L. (2009). Converging intracranial markers of conscious access. *PLOS Biology, 7,* e61.

Gainotti, G. (2006). Anatomical, functional, and cognitive determinants of semantic memory disorders. *Neuroscience and Biobehavioral Reviews, 30,* 577–594.

Gainotti, G. (2013). Controversies over the mechanisms underlying the crucial role of the left fronto-parietal areas in the representation of tools. *Frontiers in Psychology, 4,* Article 727.

Gainotti, G. (2014). Old and recent approaches to the problem of non-verbal conceptual disorders in aphasic patients. *Cortex, 53,* 78–89.

Gainotti, G. (2015). Is the difference between right and left ATLs due to the distinction between general and social cognition or between verbal and non-verbal representations? *Neuroscience and Biobehavioral Reviews, 51,* 296–312.

Gainotti, G., Ciaraffa, F., Silveri, M. C., & Marra, C. (2009). Mental representation of normal subjects about the sources of knowledge in different semantic categories and unique entities. *Neuropsychology, 23,* 803–812.

Gainotti, G., Spinelli, P., Scaricamazza, E., & Marra, C. (2013). The evaluation of sources of knowledge underlying different conceptual categories. *Frontiers in Human Neuroscience, 7,* Article 40.

Gallivan, J. P., McLean, D. A., Valyear, K. F., & Culham, J. C. (2013). Decoding the neural mechanisms of human tool use. *Elife, 2,* e00425.

Galton, C. J., Patterson, K., Graham, K., Lambon Ralph, M. A., Williams, G., Antoun, N., Sahakian, B. J., & Hodges, J. R. (2001). Differing patterns of temporal atrophy in Alzheimer's disease and semantic dementia. *Neurology, 57,* 216–225.

Gao, M. Y., & Malt, B. C. (2009). Mental representation and cognitive consequences of Chinese individual classifiers. *Language and Cognitive Processes, 24,* 1124–1179.

Garagnani, M., & Pulvermüller, F. (2016). Conceptual grounding of language in action and perception: A neurocomputational model of the emergence of category specificity and semantic hubs. *European Journal of Neuroscience, 43,* 721–737.

Garcea, F. E., & Mahon, B. Z. (2014). Parcellation of left parietal tool representations by functional connectivity. *Neuropsychologia, 60,* 131–143.

Garrard, P., Carroll, E., Vinson, D. P., & Vigliocco, G. (2004). Dissociating lexico-semantics and lexico-syntax in semantic dementia. *Neurocase, 10,* 353–362.

Gelman, S. A. (2003). *The essential child: Origins of essentialism in everyday thought.* New York: Oxford University Press.

Gelman, S. A., & Roberts, S. O. (2017). How language shapes the cultural inheritance of categories. *Proceedings of the National Academy of Sciences, 114,* 7900–7907.

Gendron, M., Barsalou, L., Lindquist, K. A., & Barrett, L. F. (2012). Emotion words shape emotion percepts. *Emotion, 12,* 314–325.

Gennari, S. P. (2012). Representing motion in language comprehension: Lessons from neuroimaging. *Language and Linguistics Compass, 6,* 67–84.

Gennari, S. P., Sloman, S. A., Malt, B. C., & Fitch, W. T. (2002). Motion events in language and cognition. *Cognition, 83,* 49–79.

Gentner, D., & Boroditsky, L. (2001). Individuation, relativity, and early word learning. In M. Bowerman & S. C. Levinson (eds.), *Language acquisition and conceptual development* (pp. 215–256). Cambridge, UK: Cambridge University Press.

Gentner, D., & Bowerman, M. (2009). Why some spatial semantic categories are harder to learn than others: The typological prevalence hypothesis. In J. Guo, E. Lieven, N. Budwig, S. Ervin-Tripp, K. Nakamura, & S. Ozcaliskan (eds.), *Crosslinguistic approaches to the psychology of language: Research in the tradition of Dan Isaac Slobin* (pp. 465–480). New York: Psychology Press.

Gentner, D., & Goldin-Meadow, S. (eds.). (2003). *Language in mind: Advances in the study of language and thought.* Cambridge, MA: MIT Press.

Gerfo, E. L., Oliveri, M., Torriero, S., Salerno, S., Koch, G., & Caltagirone, C. (2008). The influence of rTMS over prefrontal and motor areas in a morphological task: Grammatical vs. semantic effects. *Neuropsychologia, 46,* 764–770.

Gergely, G., & Csibra, G. (2003). Teleological reasoning in infancy: The naïve theory of rational action. *Trends in Cognitive Sciences, 7,* 287–292.

Giese, M. A. (2015). Biological and body motion perception. In J. Wagemans (ed.), *The Oxford handbook of perceptual organization* (pp. 575–600). New York: Oxford University Press.

Gil, D. (1995). Numeral classifiers. In M. Haspelmath, M. S. Dryer, D. Gil, & B. Comrie (eds.), *The world atlas of language structures* (pp. 226–229). Oxford: Oxford University Press.

Goddard, C. (ed.) (2008). *Cross-linguistic semantics.* Amsterdam: John Benjamins.

Goddard, C., & Wierzbicka, A. (1994). *Semantic and lexical universals: Theory and empirical findings.* Amsterdam: John Benjamins.

Goddard, C., & Wierzbicka, A. (eds.). (2002). *Meaning and universal grammar: Theory and empirical findings,* 2 volumes. Amsterdam: John Benjamins.

Goddard, C., & Wierzbicka, A. (2008). Contrastive semantics of physical activity verbs: "Cutting" and "chopping" in English, Polish, and Japanese. *Language Sciences, 31,* 60–96.

Godfrey-Smith, P. (2016). *Other minds: The octopus, the sea, and the deep origins of consciousness.* New York: Farrar, Straus & Giroux.

Goldberg, A. E. (1995). *Constructions: A Construction Grammar approach to argument structure.* Chicago: University of Chicago Press.

Goldberg, R. F., Perfetti, C. A., & Schneider, W. (2006a). Distinct and common cortical activations for multimodal semantic categories. *Cognitive, Affective, and Behavioral Neuroscience, 6,* 214–222.

Goldberg, R. F., Perfetti, C. A., & Schneider, W. (2006b). Perceptual knowledge retrieval activates sensory brain areas. *Journal of Neuroscience, 26,* 4917–4921.

Goldenberg, G., & Spatt, J. (2009). The neural basis of tool use. *Brain, 132,* 1645–1655.

Goldfarb, L., Aisenberg, D., & Henik, A. (2011). Think the thought, walk the walk: Social priming reduces the Stroop effect. *Cognition, 118,* 193–200.

González, J., Barros-Loscertales, A., Pulvermüller, F., Meseguer, V., Sanjuán, A., Belloch, V., & Ávila, C. (2006). Reading *cinnamon* activates olfactory brain regions. *NeuroImage, 32,* 906–912.

Gordon, J. K., & Dell, G. S. (2003). Learning to divide the labor: An account of deficits in light and heavy verb production. *Cognitive Science, 27,* 1–40.

Gorno-Tempini, M. L., Cipolotti, L., & Price, C. (2000). Category differences in brain activation studies: Where do they come from? *Proceedings of the Royal Society of London B, 267,* 1253–1258.

Gorno-Tempini, M. L., Rankin, K. P., Woolley, J. D., Rosen, H. J., Phengrasamy, L., & Miller, B. L. (2004). Cognitive and behavioral profile in a case of right anterior temporal lobe degeneration. *Cortex, 40,* 631–644.

Goschler, J., & Stefanowitsch, A. (eds.). (2013). *Variation and change in the encoding of motion events.* Amsterdam: John Benjamins.

Grafman, J., & Krueger, F. (2009). The prefrontal cortex stores structured event complexes that are the representational basis for cognitively derived actions. In E. Morsella, J. A. Bargh, & P.

M. Gollwitzer (eds.), *The Oxford handbook of human action* (pp. 197–213). New York: Oxford University Press.

Graziano, M. S. A. (2009). *The intelligent movement machine: An ethological perspective on the primate motor system*. Oxford: Oxford University Press.

Graziano, M. S. A. (2016). Ethological action maps: A paradigm shift for the motor cortex. *Trends in Cognitive Sciences, 20*, 121–132.

Graziano, M. S. A. (2018). *The spaces between us: A story of neuroscience, evolution, and human nature*. New York: Oxford University Press.

Graziano, M. S. A., & Aflalo, T. N. (2007). Mapping behavioural repertoire onto the cortex. *Neuron, 56*, 239–251.

Green, D. R., & Green, D. M. (2017). Thinking outside the box in the Palikur language: How properties of boundary and interior affect object and spatial concepts. Unpublished manuscript.

Greenwald, A. G. (2017). An AI stereotype catcher. *Science, 356*, 133–134.

Grewe, T., Bornkessel-Schlesewsky, I., Zysset, S., Wiese, R., von Cramon, D. Y., & Schlesewsky, M. (2007). The role of the posterior superior temporal sulcus in the processing of unmarked transitivity. *NeuroImage, 35*, 343–352.

Grèzes, J., Frith, C. D., & Passingham, R. E. (2004). Inferring false beliefs from the actions of oneself and others: An fMRI study. *NeuroImage, 21*, 744–750.

Grill-Spector, K., & Kanwisher, N. (2005). Visual recognition: As soon as you know it is there, you know what it is. *Psychological Science, 16*, 152–160.

Grill-Spector, K., & Weiner, K. S. (2014). The functional architecture of the ventral temporal cortex and its role in categorization. *Nature Reviews Neuroscience, 15*, 536–548.

Grinevald, C. (2000). A morphosyntactic typology of classifiers. In G. Senft (ed.), *Systems of nominal classification* (pp. 50–92). Cambridge: Cambridge University Press.

Grinevald, C. (2007). The linguistic categorization of spatial entities: Classifiers and other nominal classification systems. In M. Aurnague, M. Hickmann, & L. Vieu (eds.), *Categorization of spatial entities in language and cognition* (pp. 93–121). Amsterdam: John Benjamins.

Grisoni, L., Dreyer, F. R., & Pulvermüller, F. (2016). Somatotopic semantic priming and prediction in the motor system. *Cerebral Cortex, 26*, 2353–2366.

Grosbras, M. H., Beaton, S., & Eickhoff, S. B. (2012). Brain regions involved in human movement perception: A quantitative voxel-based meta-analysis. *Human Brain Mapping, 33*, 431–454.

Grossman, E. D. (2008). Neurophysiology of action recognition. In T. F. Shipley & J. M. Zacks (eds.), *Understanding events* (pp. 335–362). New York: Oxford University Press.

Grossman, M., Anderson, C., Khan, A., Avants, B., Elman, L., & McCluskey, L. (2008). Impaired action knowledge in amyotrophic lateral sclerosis. *Neurology, 71*, 1396–1401.

Guerssel, M., Hale, K., Laughren, M., Levin, B., & White Eagle, J. (1985). A crosslinguistic study of transitivity alternations. In W. H. Eilfort, P. D. Kroeber, & K. L. Peterson (eds.), *Papers from the parasession on causatives and agentivity at the 21st regional* meeting (pp. 48–63). Chicago: Chicago Linguistic Society.

Guillaume, A. (2016). Associated motion in South America: Typological and areal perspectives. *Linguistic Typology, 20*, 81–177.

Gullberg, M. (2011). Language-specific encoding of placement events in gestures. In J. Bohnemeyer & E. Pederson (eds.), *Event representation in language and cognition* (pp. 166–188). Cambridge, UK: Cambridge University Press.

Gullberg, M., & Burenhult, N. (2012). Probing the linguistic encoding of placement and re-moval events in Swedish. In A. Kopecka & B. Narasimhan (eds.), *Events of putting and taking: A crosslinguistic perspective* (pp. 1–20). Amsterdam: John Benjamins.

Gumperz, J. J., & Levinson, S. C. (eds.). (1996). *Rethinking linguistic relativity*. Cambridge, UK: Cambridge University Press.

Guo, C. C., Gorno-Tempini, M. L., Gesierich, B., Henry, M., Trujillo, A., Shany-Ur, T., Jovicich, J., Robinson, S. D., Kramer, J. H., Rankin, K. P., Miller, B. L., & Seeley, W. W. (2013). Anterior temporal lobe degeneration produces widespread network-driven dysfunction. *Brain, 136,* 2979–2991.

Guo, J., Lieven, E., Budwig, N., Ervin-Tripp, S., Nakamura, K., & Ozcaliksan, S. (eds.). (2008). *Crosslinguistic approaches to the study of language: Research in the tradition of Dan Isaac Slobin.* Philadelphia: Psychology Press.

Hammarström, H. (2016). Linguistic diversity and language evolution. *Journal of Language Evolution, 1,* 19–29.

Hanks, W. F. (2005). Explorations in the deictic field. *Current Anthropology, 46,* 191–220.

Hansen, T., Olkkonen, M., Walter, S., & Gegenfurtner, K. R. (2006). Memory modulates color appearance. *Nature Neuroscience, 9,* 1367–1368.

Hare, B., & Tomasello, M. (2005). Human-like social skills in dogs? *Trends in Cognitive Sciences, 9,* 439–444.

Harnad, S. (1990). The symbol grounding problem. *Physica D, 42,* 335–346.

Harris, I. M., Harris, J. A., & Caine, D. (2001). Object orientation agnosia: A failure to find the axis? *Journal of Cognitive Neuroscience, 13,* 800–812.

Harrison, K. D. (2007). *When languages die: The extinction of the world's languages and the erosion of human knowledge.* New York: Oxford University Press.

Haspelmath, M. (1997a). *Indefinite pronouns.* Oxford: Clarendon.

Haspelmath, M. (1997b). *From space to time: Temporal adverbials in the world's languages.* München: Lincom.

Haspelmath, M. (2003). The geometry of grammatical meaning: Semantic maps and cross-linguistic comparison. In M. Tomasello (ed.), *The new psychology of language,* 2nd edition (pp. 211–243). New York: Erlbaum.

Haspelmath, M. (2016). The serial verb construction: Comparative concept and cross-linguistic generalizations. *Language and Linguistics, 17,* 291–319.

Hasson, U., Chen, J., & Honey, C. J. (2015). Hierarchical process memory: Memory as an inte-gral component of information processing. *Trends in Cognitive Sciences, 19,* 304–313.

Hasson, U., Ghazanfar, A. A., Galantucci, B., Garrod, S., & Keysers, C. (2012). Brain-to-brain coupling: A mechanism for creating and sharing a social world. *Trends in Cognitive Sciences, 16,* 114–121.

Hasson, U., Nir, Y., Levy, I., Fuhrmann, G. & Malach, R. (2004). Intersubject synchronization of cortical activity during natural vision. *Science, 303,* 1634–1640.

Hauk, O. (2016). What does it mean? A review of the neuroscientific evidence for embodied lexical semantics. In G. Hickok & S. Small (eds.), *Neurobiology of language* (pp. 777–788). New York: Elsevier.

Hauk, O., Johnsrude, I., & Pulvermüller, F. (2004). Somatotopic representation of action words in human motor and premotor cortex. *Neuron, 41,* 301–307.

Hauk, O., & Pulvermüller, F. (2011). The lateralization of motor cortex activation to action words. *Frontiers in Human Neuroscience, 5,* Article 149.

Hauk, O., & Tschentscher, N. (2013). The body of evidence: What can neuroscience tell us about embodied semantics? *Frontiers in Psychology, 4*, Article 50.

Haun, D. B. M., & Rapold, C. (2009). Variation in memory for body movements across cultures. *Current Biology, 19*, R1068–R1069.

Haun, D. B. M., Rapold, C., Call, J., Janzen, G., & Levinson, S. C. (2006). Cognitive cladistics and cultural override in Hominid spatial cognition. *Proceedings of the National Academy of Sciences, 103*, 17568–17573.

Haun, D. B. M., Rapold, C., Janzen, G., & Levinson, S. C. (2011). Plasticity of human spatial memory: Spatial language and cognition covary across cultures. *Cognition, 119*, 70–80.

Hawley, K., & MacPherson, F. (eds.). (2011). *The admissible contents of experience.* New York: Wiley-Blackwell.

Haxby, J. V., Connolly, A. C., & Guntupalli, J. S. (2014). Decoding representational spaces using multivariate pattern analysis. *Annual Review of Neuroscience, 37*, 435–456.

Haynes, J. D. (2015). A primer on pattern-based approaches to fMRI: Principles, pitfalls, and perspectives. *Neuron, 87*, 257–270.

Haynie, H. J., & Bowern, C. (2016). Phylogenetic approach to the evolution of color term systems. *Proceedings of the National Academy of Sciences, 113*, 13666–13671.

Hays, T. E. (1983). Ndumba folk biology and general principles of ethnobiological classification and nomenclature. *American Anthropologist, 85*, 592–611.

Hayworth, K. J., & Biederman, I. (2006). Neural evidence for intermediate representations in object recognition. *Vision Research, 46*, 4024–4031.

Heath, J., & McPherson, L. (2009). Cognitive set and lexicalization strategy in Dogon action verbs. *Anthropological Linguistics, 51*, 38–63.

Heine, B. (1997a). *Cognitive foundations of grammar.* New York: Oxford University Press.

Heine, B. (1997b). *Possession: Cognitive sources, forces, and grammaticalization.* Cambridge, UK: Cambridge University Press.

Heine, B., Claudi, U., & Hünnemeyer, F. (1991). *Grammaticalization: A conceptual framework.* Chicago: University of Chicago Press.

Heine, B., & Kuteva, T. (2002). *World lexicon of grammaticalization.* Cambridge, UK: Cambridge University Press.

Heine, B., & Kuteva, T. (2007). *The genesis of grammar: A reconstruction.* New York: Oxford University Press.

Henrich, J. (2016). *The secret of our success: How culture is driving human evolution, domesticating our species, and making us smarter.* Princeton, NJ: Princeton University Press.

Henrich, J., Heine, S. J., & Norenzayan, A. (2010). The weirdest people in the world? *Behavioral and Brain Sciences, 33*, 1–23; discussion, 24–75.

Herbert, R., & Best, W. (2010). The role of noun syntax in spoken word production: Evidence from aphasia. *Cortex, 46*, 329–342.

Herskovits, A. (1986). *Language and spatial cognition: An interdisciplinary study of the spatial prepositions of English.* Cambridge, UK: Cambridge University Press.

Hespos, S. J., & Spelke, E. S. (2004). Conceptual precursors to language. *Nature, 430*, 453–456.

Heyes, C. (2018). *Cognitive gadgets: The cultural evolution of thinking.* Cambridge, MA: Belknap Press.

Hickok, G. (2014). *The myth of mirror neurons: The real neuroscience of communication and cognition.* New York: Norton.

Hickok, G., Pickell, H., Klima, E. S., & Bellugi, U. (2009). Neural dissociation in the production of lexical versus classifier signs in ASL: Distinct patterns of hemispheric asymmetry. *Neuropsychologia, 47*, 382–387.

Hillis, A. E., & Caramazza, A. (1991). Category-specific naming and comprehension impairment: A double dissociation. *Brain, 114*, 2081–2094.

Hillis, A. E., Heidler-Gary, J., Newhart, M., Chang, S., Ken, L., & Bak, T. H. (2006). Naming and comprehension in primary progressive aphasia: The influence of grammatical word class. *Aphasiology, 20*, 246–256.

Hiramatsu, C., Goda, N., & Komatsu, H. (2011). Transformation from image-based to perceptual representation of materials along the human ventral visual pathway. *NeuroImage, 57*, 482–494.

Hodges, J. R., Graham, N., & Patterson, K. (1995). Charting the progression in semantic dementia: Implications for the organization of semantic memory. *Memory, 3*, 463–495.

Hodges, J. R., & Patterson, K. (2007). Semantic dementia: A unique clinicopathological syndrome. *Lancet Neurology, 6*, 1004–1014.

Hoenig, K., Müller, C., Herrnberger, B., Sim, E. J., Spitzer, M., Ehret, G., & Kiefer, M. (2011). Neuroplasticity of semantic representations for musical instruments in professional musicians. *NeuroImage, 56*, 1714–1725.

Hoenig, K., Sim, E. J., Bochev, V., Herrnberger, B., & Kiefer, M. (2008). Conceptual flexibility in the human brain: Dynamic recruitment of semantic maps from visual, motion and motor-related areas. *Journal of Cognitive Neuroscience, 20*, 1799–1814.

Hoffman, P., Binney, R. J., & Lambon Ralph, M. A. (2015). Differing contributions of inferior prefrontal and anterior temporal cortex to concrete and abstract conceptual knowledge. *Cortex, 63*, 250–266.

Hoffman, P., & Lambon Ralph, M. A. (2013). Shapes, scents and sounds: Quantifying the full multi-sensory basis of conceptual knowledge. *Neuropsychologia, 51*, 14–25.

Hoffman, P., & Lambon Ralph, M. A. (2018). From percept to concept in the ventral temporal lobes: Graded hemispheric specialization based on stimulus and task. *Cortex, 101*, 107–118.

Hoffman, T., & Trousdale, G. (eds.) (2013). *The Oxford handbook of Construction Grammar.* New York: Oxford University Press.

Holmes, K. J., Moty, K., & Regier, T. (2017). Revisiting the role of language in spatial cognition: Categorical perception of spatial relations in English and Korean speakers. *Psychonomic Bulletin & Review, 24*, 2031–2036.

Homberg, U. (2015). Sky compass orientation in desert locusts: Evidence from field and laboratory studies. *Frontiers in Behavioral Neuroscience, 9*, Article 346.

Honey, C. J., Thompson, C. R., Lerner, Y., & Hasson, U. (2012). Not lost in translation: Neural responses shared across languages. *Journal of Neuroscience, 32*, 15277–15283.

Hopkins, N. A. (2012). The noun classifiers of Cuchumatán Mayan languages: A case of diffusion from Otomanguean. *International Journal of American Linguistics, 78*, 411–427.

Horgan, T. (2012). From agentive phenomenology to cognitive phenomenology. In T. Bayne & M. Montague (eds.), *Cognitive phenomenology* (pp. 57–78). New York: Oxford University Press.

Horgan, T., & Tienson, J. (2002). The intentionality of phenomenology and the phenomenology of intentionality. In D. Chalmers (ed.), *Philosophy of mind: Classical and contemporary readings* (pp. 520–533). New York: Oxford University Press.

Horn, L. R. (1989). *A natural history of negation.* Chicago: University of Chicago Press.

Hume, D. (1739/1978). *A treatise on human nature*, 2nd edition. Oxford: Oxford University Press.

Hummel, J. E., & Biederman, I. (1992). Dynamic binding in a neural network for shape recognition. *Psychological Review, 99*, 480–517.

Humphreys, G. F., Newling, K., Jennings, C., & Gennari, S. P. (2013). Motion and actions in language: Semantic representations in occipito-temporal cortex. *Brain and Language, 125*, 94–105.

Hunn, E. (1977). *Tzeltal folk zoology: The classification of discontinuities in nature*. New York: Academic Press.

Hung, C. C., Carlson, E. T., & Connor, C. E. (2012). Medial axial shape coding in macaque inferotemporal cortex. *Neuron, 74*, 1099–1113.

Huntenburg, J. M., Bazin, P. L., & Margulies, D. S. (2018). Large-scale gradients in human cortical organization. *Trends in Cognitive Sciences, 22*, 21–31.

Hurlburt, R. T., Heavey, C. L., & Kelsey, J. M. (2013). Toward a phenomenology of inner speaking. *Consciousness and Cognition, 22*, 1477–1494.

Huth, A. G., Nishimoto, S., Vu, A. T., & Gallant, J. L. (2012). A continuous semantic space describes the representation of thousands of object and action categories across the human brain. *Neuron, 76*, 1210–1224.

Huth, A. G., de Heer, W. A., Griffiths, T. L., Theunissen, F. E., & Gallant, J. L. (2016). Natural speech reveals the semantic maps that tile the human cerebral cortex. *Nature, 532*, 453–460.

Hwang, K., Palmer, E. D., Basho, S., Zadra, J. R., & Müller, R.-A. (2009). Category-specific activations during word generation reflect experiential sensorimotor modalities. *NeuroImage, 48*, 717–725.

Ibarretxe-Antuñano, I. (2012). Placement and removal events in Basque and Spanish. In A. Kopecka & B. Narasimhan (eds.), *Events of putting and taking: A crosslinguistic perspective* (pp. 123–144). Amsterdam: John Benjamins.

Ikegami, Y. (1987). "Source" and "Goal": A case of linguistic disymmetry. In R. Dirven & G. Radden (eds.), *Concepts of case* (pp. 122–146). Tübingen: Gunter Narr.

Imbert, C. (2012). Path: Ways typology has walked through it. *Language and Linguistics Compass, 6*, 236–258.

Ishibashi, R., Lambon Ralph, M. A., Saito, S., & Pobric, G. (2011). Different roles of lateral anterior temporal lobe and inferior parietal lobule in coding function and manipulation tool knowledge: Evidence from an rTMS study. *Neuropsychologia, 49*, 1128–1135.

Ishibashi, R., Pobric, G., Saito, S., & Lambon Ralph, M. A. (2016). The neural network for tool-related cognition: An activation likelihood estimation meta-analysis of 70 neuroimaging contrasts. *Cognitive Neuropsychology, 33*, 241–256.

Ishida, H., Nakajima, K., Inase, M., & Murata, A. (2010). Shared mapping of own and others' bodies in visuotactile bimodal area of monkey parietal cortex. *Journal of Cognitive Neuroscience, 22*, 83–96.

Jackendoff, R. (1987). *Consciousness and the computational mind*. Cambridge, MA: MIT Press.

Jackendoff, R. (1997). *The architecture of the language faculty*. Cambridge, MA: MIT Press.

Jackendoff, R. (2012). *A user's guide to thought and meaning*. New York: Oxford University Press.

Jacobs, R. H. A. H., Baumgartner, E., & Gegenfurtner, K. R. (2014). The representation of material categories in the brain. *Frontiers in Psychology, 5*, Article 146.

Jacobson, S. A. (1984). *Yup'ik Eskimo dictionary*. University of Alaska: Alaska Native Language Center.

Jacoby, L. L., Lindsay, D. S., & Hessels, S. (2003). Item-specific control of automatic processes: Stroop process dissociations. *Psychonomic Bulletin & Review, 10*, 638–644.

Jager, G., & Postma, A. (2003). On the hemispheric specialization for categorical and coordinate spatial relations: A review of the current evidence. *Neuropsychologia, 41*, 504–515.

Jakobson, R. (1959). Boas' view of grammatical meaning. *American Anthropologist, 61*, 139–145.

Janda, L. (2007). Aspectual clusters of Russian verbs. *Studies in Language, 31*, 607–648.

Janzen, G., Haun, D. B. M., & Levinson, S. C. (2012). Tracking down abstract linguistic meaning: Neural correlates of spatial frame of reference ambiguitiess in language. *PLoS ONE, 7*, e30657.

Jarkey, N. (1991). *Serial verbs in White Hmong: A functional approach*. Doctoral dissertation, University of Sydney.

Jastorff, J., & Orban, G. A. (2009). Human functional magnetic resonance imaging reveals separation and integration of shape and motion cues in biological motion processing. *Journal of Neuroscience, 29*, 7315–7329.

Jefferies, E. (2013). The neural basis of semantic cognition: Converging evidence from neuropsychology, neuroimaging, and TMS. *Cortex, 49*, 611–625.

Johannes, K., Wang, J., Papafragou, A., & Landau, B. (2015). Similarity and variation in the distribution of spatial expressions across three languages. *Proceedings of the 37th Annual Meeting of the Cognitive Science Society* (pp. 997–1002).

Johnson-Frey, S. H. (2004). The neural bases of complex tool use in humans. *Trends in Cognitive Sciences, 8*, 71–78.

Jorba, M., & Vicente, A. (2014). Cognitive phenomenology, access to contents, and inner speech. *Journal of Consciousness Studies, 21*, 74–99.

Jouen, A. L., Ellmore, T. M., Madden, C. J., Pallier, C., Dominey, P. F., & Ventre-Dominey, J. (2015). Beyond the word and image: Characteristics of a common meaning system for language and vision revealed by functional and structural imaging. *NeuroImage, 106*, 72–85.

Jouen, A. L., Ellmore, T. M., Madden-Lombardi, C. J., Pallier, C., Dominey, P. F., & Ventre-Dominey, J. (2018). Beyond the word and image: II- Structural and functional connectivity of a common semantic system. *NeuroImage, 166*, 185–197.

Jozwik, K. M., Kriegeskorte, N., & Mur, M. (2016). Visual features as stepping stones toward semantics: Explaining object similarity in IT and perception with non-negative least squares. *Neuropsychologia, 83*, 201–226.

Jungbluth, K. (2003). Deictics in the conversational dyad: Findings in Spanish and some crosslinguistic outlines. In F. Lenz (ed.), *Deictic conceptualisation of space, time and person* (pp. 13–40). Amsterdam: John Benjamins.

Kaiser, D., Azzalini, D. C., & Peelen, M. V. (2016). Shape-independent object category responses revealed by MEG and fMRI decoding. *Journal of Neurophysiology, 115*, 2246–2250.

Kalénine, S., Buxbaum, L. J., & Coslett, H. B. (2010). Critical brain regions for action recognition: Lesion symptom mapping in left hemisphere stroke. *Brain, 133*, 3269–3280.

Kan, I. P., Kable, J. W., Van Scoyoc, A., Chatterjee, A., & Thompson-Schill, S. L. (2006). Fractionating the left frontal response to tools: Dissociable effects of motor experience and lexical competition. *Journal of Cognitive Neuroscience, 18*, 267–277.

Kanwisher, N. (2017). The quest for the FFA and where it led. *Journal of Neuroscience, 37*, 1056–1061.

Karnath, H. O., Ferber, S., & Bulthoff, H. H. (2000). Neuronal representation of object orientation. *Neuropsychologia, 38*, 1235–1241.

Kay, P., Berlin, B., Maffi, L., Merrifield, W. R., & Cook, R. (2009). *The world color survey*. Stanford: CSLI.

Kay, P., & Maffi, L. (2005). Colour terms. In M. Haspelmath, M. S. Dryer, D. Gil, & B. Comrie (eds.), *The world atlas of language structures* (pp. 534–545). New York: Oxford University Press.

Kay, P., & Regier, T. (2003). Resolving the question of color naming universals. *Proceedings of the National Academy of Sciences, 100,* 9085–9089.

Kayaert, G., Biederman, I., Op de Beeck, H. P., & Vogels, R. (2005a). Tuning for shape dimensions in macaque inferior temporal cortex. *European Journal of Neuroscience, 22,* 212–224.

Kayaert, G., Biederman, I., & Vogels, R. (2005b). Representation of regular and irregular shapes in macaque inferotemporal cortex. *Cerebral Cortex, 15,* 1308–1321.

Keil, F. (1989). *Concepts, kinds, and cognitive development.* Cambridge, MA: MIT Press.

Kellenbach, M. L., Brett, M., & Patterson, K. (2001). Large, colorful or noisy? Attribute- and modality-specific activations during retrieval of perceptual attribute knowledge. *Cognitive, Affective, & Behavioral Neuroscience, 1,* 207–221.

Kemmer, S. (1993). *The middle voice.* Amsterdam: John Benjamins.

Kemmerer, D. (1999). "Near" and "far" in language and perception. *Cognition, 73,* 35–63.

Kemmerer, D. (2000a). Grammatically relevant and grammatically irrelevant features of verb meaning can be independently impaired. *Aphasiology, 14,* 997–1020.

Kemmerer, D. (2000b). Selective impairment of knowledge underlying prenominal adjective order: Evidence for the autonomy of grammatical semantics. *Journal of Neurolinguistics, 13,* 57–82.

Kemmerer, D. (2003). Why can you hit someone on the arm but not break someone on the arm? A neuropsychological investigation of the English body-part possessor ascension construction. *Journal of Neurolinguistics, 16,* 13–36.

Kemmerer, D. (2005). The spatial and temporal meanings of English prepositions can be independently impaired. *Neuropsychologia, 43,* 797–806.

Kemmerer, D. (2006a). Action verbs, argument structure constructions, and the mirror neuron system. In M. Arbib (ed.), *Action to language via the mirror neuron system* (pp. 347–373). Cambridge, UK: Cambridge University Press.

Kemmerer, D. (2006b). The semantics of space: Integrating linguistic typology and cognitive neuroscience. *Neuropsychologia, 44,* 1607–1621.

Kemmerer, D. (2010). A neuroscientific perspective on the linguistic encoding of categorical spatial relations. In V. Evans & P. Chilton (eds.), *Language, cognition, and space: The state of the art and new directions* (pp. 139–168). London: Equinox.

Kemmerer, D. (2014a). Body ownership and beyond: Some connections between cognitive neuroscience and linguistic typology. *Consciousness and Cognition, 26,* 189–196.

Kemmerer, D. (2014b). Word classes in the brain: Implications of linguistic typology for cognitive neuroscience. *Cortex, 58,* 27–51.

Kemmerer, D. (2015a). Are the motor features of verb meanings represented in the precentral motor cortices? Yes, but within the context of a flexible, multilevel architecture for conceptual knowledge. *Psychonomic Bulletin and Review, 22,* 1068–1075.

Kemmerer, D. (2015b). Are we ever aware of concepts? A critical question for the Global Neuronal Workspace, Integrated Information, and Attended Intermediate-Level Representation theories of consciousness. *Neuroscience of Consciousness, 1,* 1–10.

Kemmerer, D. (2015c). *Cognitive neuroscience of language: An introduction.* New York: Psychology Press.

Kemmerer, D. (2015d). Does the motor system contribute to the perception and understanding of actions? Reflections on Gregory Hickok's *The myth of mirror neurons: The real neuroscience of communication and cognition. Language and Cognition, 7,* 450–475.

Kemmerer, D. (2015e). Visual and motor features of action verbs: A cognitive neuroscience perspective. In R. G. de Almeida & C. Manouilidou (eds.), *Cognitive science perspectives on verb representation and processing* (pp. 189–212). New York: Springer.

Kemmerer, D. (2017a). Categories of object concepts across languages and brains: The relevance of nominal classification systems to cognitive neuroscience. *Language, Cognition, and Neuroscience, 32,* 401–424. (Target article for peer commentary.)

Kemmerer, D. (2017b). Some issues involving the relevance of nominal classification systems to cognitive neuroscience: Response to commentators. *Language, Cognition, and Neuroscience, 32,* 447–456.

Kemmerer, D., & Gonzalez-Castillo, J. (2010). The Two-Level Theory of verb meaning: An approach to integrating the semantics of action with the mirror neuron system. *Brain and Language, 112,* 54–76.

Kemmerer, D., Gonzalez-Castillo, J., Talavage, T., Patterson, S., & Wiley, C. (2008). Neuroanatomical distribution of five semantic components of verbs: Evidence from fMRI. *Brain and Language, 107,* 16–43.

Kemmerer, D., Miller, L., MacPherson, M. K., Huber, J., & Tranel, D. (2013). An investigation of semantic similarity judgments about action and non-action verbs in Parkinson's disease: Implications for the Embodied Cognition Framework. *Frontiers in Human Neuroscience, 7,* 146.

Kemmerer, D., Rudrauf, D., Manzel, K., & Tranel, D. (2012). Behavioral patterns and lesion sites associated with impaired processing of lexical and conceptual knowledge of actions. *Cortex, 48,* 826–848.

Kemmerer, D., & Tranel, D. (2000). A double dissociation between linguistic and perceptual representations of spatial relationships. *Cognitive Neuropsychology, 17,* 393–414.

Kemmerer, D., & Tranel, D. (2003). A double dissociation between the meanings of action verbs and locative prepositions. *NeuroCase, 9,* 421–435.

Kemmerer, D., & Tranel, D. (2008). Searching for the elusive neural substrates of body part terms: A neuropsychological study. *Cognitive Neuropsychology, 25,* 601–625.

Kemmerer, D., Tranel, D., & Barrash, J. (2001a). Patterns of dissociation in the processing of verb meanings in brain-damaged subjects. *Language and Cognitive Processes, 16,* 1–34.

Kemmerer, D., Tranel, D., & Barrash, J. (2001b). Addendum to "Patterns of dissociation in the processing of verb meanings in brain-damaged subjects." *Language and Cognitive Processes, 16,* 461–463.

Kemmerer, D., Tranel, D., & Zdanczyk, C. (2009). Knowledge of the semantic constraints on adjective order can be selectively impaired. *Journal of Neurolinguistics, 22,* 91–108.

Kemmerer, D., & Wright, S. K. (2002). Selective impairment of knowledge underlying reversative *un-* prefixation: Further evidence for the autonomy of grammatical semantics. *Journal of Neurolinguistics, 15,* 403–432.

Kemp, C., & Regier, T. (2012). Kinship categories across languages reflect general communicative principles. *Science, 336,* 1049–1054.

Kemp, C., Xu, Y., & Regier, T. (2018). Semantic typology and efficient communication. *Annual Review of Linguistics, 4,* 109–128.

Kersten, A. W., Meissner, C. A., Lechuga, J., Schwartz, B. L., Albrechtsen, J. S., & Iglesias, A. (2010). English speakers attend more strongly than Spanish speakers to manner or motion when classifying novel objects and events. *Journal of Experimental Psychology: General, 139,* 638–653.

Keysers, C., & Gazzola, V. (2006). Towards a unifying neural theory of social cognition. *Progress in Brain Research, 156,* 383–406.

Keysers, C., Wicker, B., Gazzola, V., Anotn, J. L., Fogassi, L., & Gallese, V. (2005). A touching sight: SII/PV activation during the observation and experience of touch. *Neuron, 42,* 335–346.

Khetarpal, N., Majid, A., & Regier, T. (2009). Spatial terms reflect near-optimal spatial categories. In N. Taatgen & H. Van Rijn (eds.), *Proceedings of the 37th Annual Conference of the Cognitive Science Society* (pp. 2396–2401).

Kiefer, M., & Pulvermüller, F. (2012). Conceptual representations in mind and brain: Theoretical developments, current evidence, and future directions. *Cortex, 48,* 805–825.

Kiefer, M., Sim, E.-J., Herrnberger, B., & Hoenig, K. (2008). The sound of concepts: Four markers for a link between auditory and conceptual brain systems. *Journal of Neuroscience, 28,* 12224–12230.

Kiefer, M., Sim, E.-J., Liebich, S., Hauk, O. & Tanaka, J. (2007). Experience-dependent plasticity of conceptual representations in human sensory-motor areas. *Journal of Cognitive Neuroscience, 19,* 525–542.

Kiefer, M., Trumpp, N., Herrnberger, B., Sim, E. J., Hoenig, K., & Pulvermüller, F. (2012). Dissociating the representation of action- and sound-related concepts. *Brain and Language, 122,* 120–125.

Kim, J. G., & Biederman, I. (2012). Greater sensitivity to nonaccidental than metric changes in the relations between simple shapes in the lateral occipital cortex. *NeuroImage, 63,* 1818–1826.

Klepp, A., Weissler, H., Niccolai, V., Terhalle, A., Geisler, H., Schnitzler, A., & Biermann- Ruben, K. (2014). Neuromagnetic hand and foot motor sources recruited during action verb processing. *Brain and Language, 128,* 41–52.

Koch, C., Massimini, M., Boly, M., & Tononi, G. (2016). Neural correlates of consciousness: Progress and problems. *Nature Reviews Neuroscience, 17,* 307–321.

Koenig, J. P., Mauner, G., Bienvenue, B., & Conklin, K. (2008). What with? The anatomy of a (proto)-role. *Journal of Semantics, 25,* 175–220.

Konkle, T., & Caramazza, A. (2013). Tripartite organization of the ventral stream by animacy and object size. *Journal of Neuroscience, 33,* 10235–10242.

Konkle, T., & Olivia, A. (2012). A real-world size organization of object responses in occipitotemporal cortex. *Neuron, 74,* 1114–1124.

Konner, M. (2002). *The tangled wing: Biological constraints on the human spirit,* 2nd edition. New York: Henry Holt.

Kopecka, A. (2012). Semantic granularity of placement and removal expressions in Polish. In A. Kopecka & B. Narasimhan (eds.), *Events of putting and taking: A crosslinguistic perspective* (pp. 327–348.). Amsterdam: John Benjamins.

Kopecka, A., & Narasimhan, B. (eds.). (2012). *Events of putting and taking: A crosslinguistic perspective.* Amsterdam: John Benjamins.

Koptjevskaja-Tamm, M. (ed.) (2015). *The linguistics of temperature.* Amsterdam: John Benjamins.

Koptjevskaja-Tamm, M., Vanhove, M., & Koch, P. (2007). Typological approaches to lexical semantics. *Linguistic Typology, 11,* 159–185.

Kouider, S., & Dehaene, S. (2007). Levels of processing during non-conscious perception: A critical review of visual masking. *Transactions of the Royal Society B: Biological Sciences, 362,* 857–875.

Kouider, S., Dehaene, S., Jobert, A., & Le Bihan, D. (2007). Cerebral bases of subliminal and supraliminal priming during reading. *Cerebral Cortex, 17,* 2019–2029.

Kosslyn, S. (1987). Seeing and imagining in the cerebral hemispheres: a computational approach. *Psychological Review, 94*, 148–175.

Kravitz, D. J., Saleem, K. S., Baker, C. I., Ungerleider, L. G., & Mishkin, M. (2013). The ventral visual pathway: An expanded neural framework for the processing of object quality. *Trends in Cognitive Sciences, 17*, 26–49.

Kreiman, G., Fried, I., & Koch, C. (2002). Single-neuron correlates of subjective vision in the human medial temporal lobe. *Proceedings of the National Academy of Sciences, 99*, 8378–8383.

Kreiman, G., Koch, C., & Fried, I. (2000). Category-specific visual responses of single neurons in the human medial temporal lobe. *Nature Neuroscience, 3*, 946–953.

Krieger-Redwood, K., Teige, C., Davey, J., Hymers, M., & Jefferies, E. (2015). Conceptual control across modalities: Graded specialization for pictures and words in inferior frontal and posterior temporal cortex. *Neuropsychologia, 76*, 92–107.

Kriegeskorte, N., & Kievit, R. A. (2013). Representational geometry: Integrating cognition, computation, and the brain. *Trends in Cognitive Sciences, 17*, 401–412.

Kriegeskorte, N., Mur, M., Ruff, D. A., Kiani, R., Bodurka, J., Esteky, H., Tanaka, K., & Bandettini, P. (2008a). Matching categorical object representations in inferior temporal cortex of man and monkey. *Neuron, 60*, 1126–1141.

Kriegeskorte, N., Mur, M., & Bandettini, P. (2008b). Representational similarity analysis: Connecting the branches of systems neuroscience. *Frontiers in Systems Neuroscience, 2*, Article 4.

Kronenfeld, D., Armstrong, J., & Wilmoth, S. (1985). Exploring the internal structure of linguistic categories: An extensionist semantic view. In J. Dougherty (ed.), *Directions in cognitive anthropology* (pp. 99–110). Champaign: University of Illinois Press.

Kuhl, P. K. (2004). Early language acquisition: Cracking the speech code. *Nature Reviews Neuroscience, 5*, 831–843.

Kuipers, J. R., van Koningsbruggen, M., & Thierry, G. (2013). Semantic priming in the motor cortex: Evidence from combined repetitive transcranial magnetic stimulation and event-related potentials. *Neuroreport, 24*, 646–651.

Kuno, S., & Takami, K. (2004). *Functional constraints in grammar: On the unergative-unaccusative distinction.* Amsterdam: John Benjamins.

Kurby, C. A., & Zacks, J. M. (2008). Segmentation in the perception and memory of events. *Trends in Cognitive Sciences, 12*, 72–79.

Kutscher, S. (2011). On the expression of spatial relations in Ardesen-Laz. *Linguistic Discovery, 9*.

Kwok, V., Niu, Z., Kay, P., Zhou, K., Mo, L., Jin, Z., So, K. F., & Tan, L. H. (2011). Learning new color names produces rapid increase in gray matter in the intact adult human cortex. *Proceedings of the National Academy of Sciences, 108*, 6686–6688.

Lacey, S., Stilla, R., Deshpande, G., Zhao, S., Stephens, C., McCormick, K., Kemmerer, D., & Sathian, K. (2017). Engagement of the left extrastriate body area during body-part metaphor comprehension. *Brain and Language, 166*, 1–18.

Laeng, B., Chabris, C. F., & Kosslyn, S. M. (2003). Asymmetries in encoding spatial relations. In K. Hugdahl & R. J. Davidson (eds.), *The asymmetrical brain* (pp. 303–339). Cambridge, MA: MIT Press.

Laiacona, M., Allamano, N., Lorenzi, L., & Capitani, E. (2006). A case of impaired naming and knowledge of body parts: Are limbs a separate subcategory? *Neurocase, 12*, 307–316.

Lakusta, L., Wagner, L., O'Hearn, K., & Landau, B. (2007). Conceptual foundations of spatial language: Evidence for a goal bias in infants. *Language Learning and Development, 3*, 179–197.

Laland, K. N. (2017). *Darwin's unfinished symphony: How culture made the human mind.* Princeton, NJ: Princeton University Press.

Lam, K., Bastiaansen, M. C. M., Dijkstra, T., & Rueschemeyer, S. A. (2017). Making sense: Motor activation and action plausibility during sentence processing. *Language, Cognition, and Neuroscience, 32,* 590–600.

Lambon Ralph, M. A. (2014). Neurocognitive insights on conceptual knowledge and its break-down. *Philosophical Transactions of the Royal Society, B, Biological Sciences, 369,* 20120392.

Lambon Ralph, M. A., Jefferies, E., Patterson, K., & Rogers, T. T. (2017). The neural and computational bases of semantic cognition. *Nature Reviews Neuroscience, 18,* 42–55.

Lambon Ralph, M. A., & Patterson, K. (2008). Generalization and differentiation in semantic memory. *Annals of the New York Academy of Sciences, 1124,* 61–76.

Lambon Ralph, M. A., Pobric, G., & Jefferies, E. (2009). Conceptual knowledge is underpinned by the temporal pole bilaterally: Convergent evidence from rTMS. *Cerebral Cortex, 19,* 832–838.

Lambon Ralph, M. A., Sage, K., Jones, R. W., & Mayberry, E. J. (2010). Coherent concepts are computed in the anterior temporal lobes. *Proceedings of the National Academy of Sciences, 107,* 2717–2722.

Landau, B. (2016). Update on "what" and "where" in spatial language: A new division of labor for spatial terms. *Cognitive Science, 41,* 321–350.

Landau, B., & Jackendoff, R. (1993). "What" and "where" in spatial language and spatial cognition. *Behavioral and Brain Sciences, 16,* 217–238.

Landauer, T., McNamara, D. S., Dennis, S., & Kintsch, W. (2013). *Handbook of latent semantic analysis.* East Sussex: Psychology Press.

Landauer, T., & Dumais, S. (1997). A solution to Plato's problem: The Latent Semantic Analysis theory of acquisition, induction and representation of knowledge. *Psychological Review, 104,* 211–240.

Landi, S. M., & Freiwald, W. A. (2017). Two areas for familiar face recognition in the primate brain. *Science, 357,* 591–595.

Langacker, R. W. (1987). Nouns and verbs. *Language, 63,* 53–94.

Langacker, R. W. (2011). Grammaticalization and Cognitive Grammar. In H. Narrog & B. Heine (ed.), *The Oxford handbook of grammaticalization* (pp. 79–91). New York: Oxford University Press.

Langsam, H. (2000). Experiences, thoughts, and qualia. *Philosophical Studies, 99,* 269–295.

Lebois, L. A. M., Wilson-Mendenhall, C. D., & Barsalou, L. W. (2015). Are automatic conceptual cores the gold standard of semantic processing? The context-dependence of spatial meaning in grounded congruency effects. *Cognitive Science, 39,* 1764–1801.

Lecours, A. R., & Joanette, Y. (1980). Linguistic and other psychological aspects of paroxysmal aphasia. *Brain and Language, 10,* 1–23.

Lefebvre, C. (ed.) (1991). *Serial verbs: Grammatical, comparative, and cognitive approaches.* Amsterdam: John Benjamins.

Lemmens, M. (2006). Caused posture: Experiential patterns emerging from corpus research. In A. Stefanowitsch & S. Gries (eds.), *Corpora in cognitive linguistics* (pp. 263–298). Berlin: Mouton de Gruyter.

Lescroart, M. D., Biederman, I., Yue, X., & Davidoff, J. (2010). A cross-cultural study of the representation of shape: Sensitivity to generalized cone dimensions. *Visual Cognition, 18,* 50–66.

Levin, B. (1993). *English verb classes and alternations.* Chicago: University of Chicago Press.

Levin, B., & Rappaport Hovav, M. (1995). *Unaccusativity: At the syntax-lexical semantics interface*. Cambridge, MA: MIT Press.

Levin, B., & Rappaport Hovav, M. (in press). Lexicalization patterns. In R. Truswell (ed.), *Oxford handbook of event structure*. New York: Oxford University Press.

Levine, J. (1983). Materialism and qualia. *Pacific Philosophical Quarterly, 64*, 354–361.

Levinson, S. C. (1994). Vision, shape, and linguistic description: Tzeltal body-part terminology and object description. *Linguistics, 32*, 791–856.

Levinson, S. C. (1996). Relativity in spatial conception and description. In J. J. Gumperz & S. C. Levinson (eds.), *Rethinking linguistic relativity* (pp. 177–202). Cambridge, UK: Cambridge University Press.

Levinson, S. C. (2003a). Language and mind: Let's get the issues straight! In D. Gentner & S. Goldin-Meadow (eds.), *Language in mind: Advances in the study of language and thought* (pp. 25–46). Cambridge, MA: MIT Press.

Levinson, S. C. (2003b). *Space in language and cognition: Explorations in cognitive diversity*. Cambridge, UK: Cambridge University Press.

Levinson, S. C. (2006). Parts of the body in Yélî Dnye, the Papuan language of Rossel Island. *Language Sciences, 28*, 221–240.

Levinson, S. C. (2007). Cut and break verbs in Yélî Dnye, the Papuan language of Rossel Island. *Cognitive Linguistics, 18*, 207–219.

Levinson, S. C. (2012a). Preface. In A. Kopecka & B. Narasimhan (eds.), *Events of putting and taking: A crosslinguistic perspective* (pp. xi–xv). Amsterdam: John Benjamins

Levinson, S. C. (2012b). The original sin of cognitive science. *Topics in Cognitive Science, 4*, 396–403.

Levinson, S. C., & Brown, P. (2012). Put and take in Yélî Dnye, the Papuan language of Rossel Island. In A. Kopecka & B. Narasimhan (eds.), *Events of putting and taking: A crosslinguistic perspective* (pp. 273–296). Amsterdam: John Benjamins.

Levinson, S. C., & Burenhult, N. (2009). Semplates: A new concept in lexical semantics? *Language, 85*, 153–174.

Levinson, S. C., Cutfield, S., Dunn, M., Enfield, N., Meira, S., & Wilkins, D. (eds.) (2018). *Demonstratives in cross-linguistic perspective*. Cambridge, UK: Cambridge University Press.

Levinson, S. C., Kita, S., Haun, D. B. M., & Rasch, B. H. (2002). Returning the tables: Language affects spatial reasoning. *Cognition, 84*, 155–188.

Levinson, S. C., & Meira, S. (2003). "Natural concepts" in the spatial topological domains—Adpositional meanings in crosslinguistic perspective: An exercise in semantic typology. *Language, 79*, 485–516.

Levinson, S. C., & Wilkins, D. P. (eds.) (2006a). *Grammars of space: Explorations in cognitive diversity*. Cambridge, UK: Cambridge University Press.

Levinson, S. C., & Wilkins, D. P. (2006b). Patterns in the data: Towards a semantic typology of spatial description. In S. C. Levinson & D. P. Wilkins (eds.), *Grammars of space: Explorations in cognitive diversity* (pp. 512–552). Cambridge, UK: Cambridge University Press.

Lewis, J. W. (2006). Cortical networks related to human use of tools. *The Neuroscientist, 12*, 211–231.

Li, P., & Abarbanell, L. (2018). Competing frames of reference in language and thought. *Cognition, 170*, 9–24.

Li, P., Abarbanell, L., Gleitman, L., & Papafragou, A. (2011). Spatial reasoning in Tenejapan Mayans. *Cognition, 120*, 33–53.

Li, P., & Gleitman, L. (2002). Turning the tables: Language and spatial reasoning. *Cognition, 83*, 265–294.

Lifshitz, M., Aubert-Bonn, N. A., Fischer, A., Kashem, I. F., & Raz, A. (2013). Using suggestion to modulate automatic processes: From Stroop to McGurk and beyond. *Cortex, 49*, 463–473.

Lin, L., Chen, G., Kuang, H., Wang, D., & Tsien, J. Z. (2007). Neural encoding of the concept of nest in the mouse brain. *Proceedings of the National Academy of Sciences, 104*, 6066–6071.

Lin, N., Bi, Y., Zhao, Y., Luo, C., & Li, X. (2015). The theory-of-mind network in support of action verb comprehension: Evidence from an fMRI study. *Brain and Language, 141*, 1–10.

Lin, N., Lu, X., Fang, F., Han, Z., & Bi, Y. (2011). Is the semantic category effect in the lateral temporal cortex due to motion property differences? *NeuroImage, 55*, 1853–1864.

Lin, N., Wang, X., Xu, Y., Wang, X., Hua, H., Zhao, Y., & Li, X. (2018). Fine subdivisions of the semantic network supporting social and sensory-motor semantic processing. *Cerebral Cortex, 28*, 2699–2710.

Lindsey, D. T., & Brown, A. G. (2006). Universality of color names. *Proceedings of the National Academy of Sciences, 103*, 16609–16613.

Lindsey, D. T., & Brown, A. G. (2009). World Color Survey color naming reveals universal motifs and their within-category diversity. *Proceedings of the National Academy of Sciences, 106*, 19785–19790.

Lingnau, A., & Downing, P. E. (2015). The lateral occipitotemporal cortex in action. *Trends in Cognitive Sciences, 19*, 268–277.

Liuzzi, A. G., Bruffaerts, R., Dupont, P., Adamczuk, K., Peeters, R., De Deyne, S., Storms, G., & Vandenberghe, R. (2015). Left perirhinal cortex codes for similarity in meaning between written words: Comparison with auditory word input. *Neuropsychologia, 76*, 4–16.

Locke, J. (1690/1959). *An essay concerning human understanding: In two volumes.* New York: Dover.

Looser, C. E., Guntupalli, J. S., & Wheatley, T. (2013). Multivoxel patterns in face-sensitive temporal regions reveal an encoding schema based on detecting life in a face. *Social, Cognitive, and Affective Neuroscience, 8*, 799–805.

López, A., Atran, S., Coley, J., Medin, D., & Smith, E. (1997). The tree of life: Universals of folk-biological taxonomies and inductions. *Cognitive Psychology, 32*, 251–295.

Lormand, E. (1996). Nonphenomenal consciousness. *Noûs, 30*, 242–261.

Lourenco, S. F., & Longo, M. R. (2009). The plasticity of near space: Evidence for contraction. *Cognition, 112*, 451–456.

Lourenco, S. F., Longo, M. R., & Pathman, T. (2011). Near space and its relation to claustro-phobic fear. *Cognition, 119*, 448–453.

Louv, R. (2008). *Last child in the woods: Saving our children from nature-deficit disorder.* Chapel Hill: Algonquin Books.

Louwerse, M. M. (2011). Symbol interdependency in symbolic and embodied cognition. *Topics in Cognitive Science, 3*, 273–302.

Lucy, J. (1992). *Grammatical categories and cognition: A case study of the linguistic relativity hypothesis.* Cambridge, UK: Cambridge University Press.

Lucy, J., & Gaskins, S. (2001). Grammatical categories and the development of classification preferences: A comparative approach. In S. Levinson & M. Bowerman (eds.), *Language acquisition and conceptual development* (pp. 257–283). Cambridge, UK: Cambridge University Press.

Lucy, J., & Gaskins, S. (2003). Interaction of language type and referent type in the development of nonverbal classification preferences. In D. Gentner & S. Goldin-Meadow (eds.),

Language in mind: Advances in the study of language and thought (pp. 465–492). Cambridge, MA: MIT Press.

Lüpke, F. (2007). "Smash it again, Sam": Verbs of cutting and breaking in Jalonke. *Cognitive Linguistics, 18*, 251–262.

Lupyan, G. (2012a). Linguistically modulated perception and cognition: The label-feedback hypothesis. *Frontiers in Psychology, 3*, Article 54.

Lupyan, G. (2012b). What do words do? Toward a theory of language-augmented thought. In B. H. Ross (ed.), *The psychology of learning and motivation*, vol. 57 (pp. 255–297). New York: Elsevier.

Lupyan, G. (2016). The centrality of language in human cognition. *Language Learning, 66*, 516–553.

Lupyan, G., & Bergen, B. (2016). How language programs the mind. *Topics in Cognitive Science, 8*, 408–424.

Lupyan, G., & Lewis, M. (in press). From words-as-mappings to words-as-cues: The role of language in semantic knowledge. *Language, Cognition, and Neuroscience.*

Lupyan, G., & Ward, E. J. (2013). Language can boost otherwise unseen objects into visual awareness. *Proceedings of the National Academy of Sciences, 110*, 1419–1424.

Luschi, P., Benhamoou, S., Girard, C., Ciccione, S., Roos, D., Sudre, J., & Benvenuti, S. (2007). Marine turtles use geomagnetic cues during open-sea homing. *Current Biology, 17*, 126–133.

Lynott, D., & Connell, L. (2010). Embodied conceptual combination. *Frontiers in Psychology, 1*, Article 212.

Lyons, I. M., Mattarella-Micke, A., Cieslak, M., Nusbaum, H. C., & Small, S. L. (2010). The role of personal experience in the neural processing of action-related language. *Brain and Language, 112*, 214–222.

MacEvoy, S. P., & Epstein, R. A. (2011). Constructing scenes from objects in human occipitotemporal cortex. *Nature Neuroscience, 14*, 1323–1329.

MacSweeney, M., Woll, B., Campbell, R., Calvert, G. A., McGuire, P. K., David, A. S., Simmons, A., & Brammer, M. J. (2002). Neural correlates of British Sign Language comprehension: Spatial correlates of topographic language. *Journal of Cognitive Neuroscience, 14*, 1064–1075.

Maes, A., & De Rooij, C. (2007). How do demonstratives code distance? In A. Branco, T. McEnery, R. Mitkov, & F. Silva (eds.), *Proceedings of the 6th Discourse Anaphora and Anaphor Resolution Colloquium* (pp. 83–89). Lagos, Pt: Centro Linguistica da Universidade do Porto.

Mahon, B. Z. (2015a). The burden of embodied cognition. *Canadian Journal of Experimental Psychology, 69*, 172–178.

Mahon, B. Z. (2015b). What is embodied about cognition? *Language, Cognition, and Neuroscience, 30*, 420–429.

Mahon, B. Z., Anzellotti, S., Schwarzbach, J., Zampini, M., & Caramazza, A. (2009). Category-specific organization in the human brain does not require visual experience. *Neuron, 63*, 397–405.

Mahon, B. Z., & Caramazza, A. (2008). A critical look at the embodied cognition hypothesis and a new proposal for grounding conceptual content. *Journal of Physiology—Paris, 102*, 59–70.

Mahon, B. Z., & Caramazza, A. (2009). Concepts and categories: A cognitive neuropsychological perspective. *Annual Review of Psychology, 60*, 27–51.

Mahon, B. Z., & Caramazza, A. (2011). What drives the organization of object knowledge in the brain? *Trends in Cognitive Sciences, 15*, 97–103.

Mahon, B. Z., Kumar, N., & Almeida, J. (2013). Spatial frequency tuning reveals interactions between the dorsal and ventral visual systems. *Journal of Cognitive Neuroscience, 25*, 862–871.

Mahon, B. Z., Milleville, S., Negri, G. A. L., Rumiati, R. I., Caramazza, A, & Martin, A. (2007). Action-related properties of objects shape object representations in the ventral stream. *Neuron, 55*, 507–520.

Maieron, M., Fabbro, F. & Skrap, M. (2013). Seeking a bridge between language and motor cortices: A PPI study. *Frontiers in Human Neuroscience, 7*, 249.

Majid, A. (2002). Frames of reference and language concepts. *Trends in Cognitive Sciences, 6*, 503–504.

Majid, A. (2008). Conceptual maps using multivariate statistics: Building bridges between typological linguistics and psychology. *Theoretical Linguistics, 34*, 59–66).

Majid, A. (2010). Words for parts of the body. In B. C. Malt & P. Wolff (eds.), *Words in the mind: How words capture human experience* (pp. 58–71). New York: Oxford University Press.

Majid, A. (2015). Comparing lexicons cross-linguistically. In J. R. Taylor (ed.), *The Oxford handbook of the word* (pp. 364–379). New York: Oxford University Press.

Majid, A., Boster, J. S., & Bowerman, M. (2008). The cross-linguistic categorization of everyday events: A study of cutting and breaking. *Cognition, 109*, 235–250.

Majid, A., & Bowerman, M. (eds). (2007). "Cutting and breaking" events: A crosslinguistic perspective. *Cognitive Linguistics, 18*(2) *[Special issue]*.

Majid, A., Bowerman, M., Kita, S., Haun, D. B. M., & Levinson, S. C. (2004). Can language restructure cognition? The case for space. *Trends in Cognitive Sciences, 8*, 108–114.

Majid, A., Bowerman, M., van Staden, M., & Boster, J. S. (2007). The semantic categories of cutting and breaking events: A crosslinguistic perspective. *Cognitive Linguistics, 18*, 133–152.

Majid, A., & Burenhult, N. (2014). Odors are expressible in language, as long as you speak the right language. *Cognition, 130*, 266–270.

Majid, A., Jordan, F., & Dunn, M. (2015). Semantic systems in closely related languages. *Language Sciences, 49*, 1–18.

Majid, A., & van Staden, M. (2015). Can nomenclature for the body be explained by embodiment theories? *Topics in Cognitive Science, 7*, 570–594.

Makris, S., & Urgesi, C. (2015). Neural underpinnings of superior action prediction abilities in soccer players. *Social, Cognitive, and Affective Neuroscience, 10*, 342–351.

Malchukov, A., & Comrie, B. (eds.). (2015). *Valency classes in the world's languages.* Berlin: Mouton de Gruyter.

Malikovic, A., Amunts, K., Schleicher, A., Mohlberg, H., Eickhoff, S. B., Wilms, M., Palomero-Gallagher, N., Armstrong, E., & Zilles, K. (2007). Cytoarchitectonic analysis of the human extrastriate cortex in the region of V5/MT+: A probabilistic, stereotaxic map of area hOc5. *Cerebral Cortex, 17*, 562–574.

Malone, P. S., Glezer, L. S., Kim, J., Jiang, X., & Riesenhuber, M. (2016). Multivariate pattern analysis reveals category-related organization of semantic representations in anterior temporal cortex. *Journal of Neuroscience, 36*, 10089–10096.

Malt, B. C. (1995). Category coherence in cross-cultural perspective. *Cognitive Psychology, 29*, 85–148.

Malt, B. C., Ameel, E., Imai, M., Gennari, S., Saji, S., & Majid, A. (2014). Human locomotion in languages: Constraints on moving and meaning. *Journal of Memory and Language, 74*, 107–123.

Malt, B. C., Gennari, S., & Imai, M. (2010). Lexicalization patterns and the world-to-words mapping. In B. C. Malt & P. Wolff (eds.), *Words and the mind: How words capture human experience* (pp. 29–57). New York: Oxford University Press.

Malt, B. C., Gennari, S., Imai, M., Ameel, E., Tsuda, N., & Majid, A. (2008). Talking about walking: Biomechanics and the language of locomotion. *Psychological Science, 19*, 232–240.

Malt, B. C., & Majid, A. (2013). How thought is mapped into words. *WIREs Cognitive Science*, *4*, 583–597.

Malt, B. C., Sloman, S. A., & Gennari, S. (2003). Universality and language specificity in object naming. *Journal of Memory and Language, 49*, 20–42.

Malt, B. C., Sloman, S. A., Gennari, S., Shi, M., & Wang, Y. (1999). Knowing vs. naming: Similarity and the linguistic categorization of artifacts. *Journal of Memory and Language, 40*, 230–262.

Malt, B. C., & Wolff, P. (eds.) (2010). *Words and the mind: How words capture human experience.* New York: Oxford University Press.

Man, K., Kaplan, J., Damasio, H., & Damasio, A. (2013). Neural convergence and divergence in the mammalian cerebral cortex: From experimental neuroanatomy to functional neuroimaging. *Journal of Comparative Neurology, 521*, 4097–4111.

Marchette, S. A., Vass, L. K., Ryan, J., & Epstein, R. A. (2014). Anchoring the neural compass: Coding of local spatial reference frames in human medial parietal lobe. *Nature Neuroscience, 17*, 1598–1606.

Margulies, D. S., Ghosh, S. S., Goulas, A., Falkiewicz, M., Huntenburg, J. M., Langs, G., Bezgin, G., Eickhoff, S. B., Castellanos, F. X., Petrides, M., Jefferies, E., & Smallwood, J. (2015). Situating the default-mode network along a principal gradient of macroscale cortical organization. *Proceedings of the National Academy of Sciences, 113*, 12574–12579.

Marinkovic, K., Dhond, R. P., Dale, A. M., Glessner, M., Carr, V., & Halgren E. (2003). Staiotemporal dynamics of modality-specific and supramodal word processing. *Neuron, 38*, 487–497.

Marques, J. F. (2007). The general/specific breakdown of semantic memory and the nature of superordinate knowledge: Insights from superordinate and basic-level feature norms. *Cognitive Neuropsychology, 24*, 879–903.

Martin, A. (2007). The representation of object concepts in the brain. *Annual Review of Psychology, 58*, 25–45.

Martin, A. (2009). Circuits in mind: The neural foundations for object concepts. In M. Gazzaniga (ed.), *The cognitive neurosciences*, 4th edition (pp. 1031–1046). Cambridge, MA: MIT Press.

Martin, A. (2016). GRAPES—Grounding representations in action, perception, and emotion systems: How object properties and categories are represented in the human brain. *Psychonomic Bulletin & Review, 23*, 979–990.

Martin, A., Simmons, W. K., Beauchamp, M. S., & Gotts, S. J. (2014). Is a single "hub," with lots of spokes, an accurate description of the neural architecture of action semantics? Comment on "Action semantics: A unifying framework for the selective use of multimodal and modality-specific object knowledge" by va Elk, van Shie, and Bekkering. *Physics of Life Reviews, 11*, 261–262.

Martin, A., & Weisberg, J. (2003). Neural foundations for understanding social and mechanical concepts. *Cognitive Neuropsychology, 20*, 575–587.

Martin, M., Beume, L., Kümmerer, D., Schmidt, C. S. M., Bormann, T., Dressing, A., Ludwig, V. M., Umarova, R. M., Mader, I., Rijntjes, M., Kaller, C. P., & Weiller, C. (2016). Differential roles of ventral and dorsal streams for conceptual and production-related components of tool use in acute stroke patients. *Cerebral Cortex, 26*, 3754–3771.

Martinaud, O., Mirlink, N., Bioux, S., Bliaux, E., Champmartin, C., Pouliquen, D., Cruypeninck, Y., Hannequin, D., & Gérardin, E. (2016). Mirrored and rotated stimuli are not th same: A neuropsychological and lesion mapping study. *Cortex, 78*, 100–114.

Massimini, M., Ferrarelli, F., Huber, R., Esser, S. K., Singh, H., & Tononi, G. (2005). Breakdown of cortical effective connectivity during sleep. *Science, 309*, 2228–2232.

Massimini, M., & Tononi, G. (2018). *Sizing up consciousness: Towards an objective measure of the capacity for experience*. New York: Oxford University Press.

Mataró, M., Juarado, A., Garcia-Sánchez, C., Barraquer, L., Costa-Jussa, F. R., & Junqué, C. (2001). Long-term effects of bilateral frontal brain injury: 60 years after injury with an iron bar. *Archives of Neurology, 58*, 1139–1142.

Matheson, H. E., & Barsalou, L. W. (2018). Embodiment and grounding in cognitive neuroscience. In J. Wixted, E. Phelps, L. Davachi, J. Serences, S. Ghetti, S. Thompson-Schill, & E. J. Wagenmakers (eds.), *The Stevens' handbook of experimental psychology and cognitive neuroscience*, 4th edition. Hoboken, NJ: Wiley.

Matsumoto, Y. (1993). Japanese numeral classifiers: A study on semantic categories and lexical organization. *Linguistics, 31*, 667–713.

Matsumoto, Y. (2003). Typologies of lexicalization patterns and event integration: Clarifications and reformulations. In S. Chiba et al. (eds.), *Empirical and theoretical investigations into language: A Festschrift for Masaru Kajita* (pp. 403–418). Tokyo: Kaitakusha.

Mayberry, E. J., Sage, K., & Lambon Ralph, M. A. (2011). At the edge of semantic space: The breakdown of coherent concepts in semantic dementia is constrained by typicality and severity but not modality. *Journal of Cognitive Neuroscience, 23*, 2240–2251.

Mayer, M. (1969). *Frog, where are you?* New York: Dial Press.

Mayka, M. A., Corcos, D. M., Leurgans, S. E., & Vaillancourt, D. E. (2006). Three-dimensional locations and boundaries of motor and premotor cortices as defined by functional brain imaging: A meta-analysis. *NeuroImage, 31*, 1453–1474.

McCarthy, R. A., & Warrington, E. K. (2016). Past, present, and prospects: Reflections 40 years on from the selective impairment of semantic memory (Warrington, 1975). *Quarterly Journal of Experimental Psychology, 69*, 1941–1968.

McClelland, T., & Bayne, T. (2016). Concepts, contents, and consciousness. *Neuroscience of Consciousness, 1*, 1–9.

McDonough, L., Choi, S., & Mandler, J. M. (2003). Understanding spatial relations: Flexible infants, lexical adults. *Cognitive Psychology, 46*, 229–259.

McGregor, W. B. (1990). *A functional grammar of Gooniyandi*. Amsterdam: John Benjamins.

McGregor, W. B. (2002). *Verb classification in Australian languages*. Berlin: Mouton de Gruyter.

McGregor, W. B. (2006). Prolegomenon to a Warrwa grammar of space. In S. C. Levinson & D. Wilkins (eds.), *Grammars of space: Explorations in cognitive diversity* (pp. 115–156). Cambridge, UK: Cambridge University Press.

McGregor, W. B. (2013). Comparing linguistic systems of categorisation. In L. Borin & A. Saxena (eds.), *Approaches to measuring linguistic differences* (pp. 387–427). Berlin: Mouton de Gruyter.

McKenzie, R. (1997). Downstream to here: Geographically determined spatial deictics in Aralle-Tabulahan (Sulawesi). In G. Senft (ed.), *Referring to space: Studies in Austronesian and Papuan languages* (pp. 221–249). Oxford: Clarendon Press.

Medin, D., & Atran, S. (eds.) (1999). *Folkbiology*. Cambridge, MA: MIT Press.

Meira, S. (2006). Approaching space in Tiriyó grammar. In S. C. Levinson and D. Wilkins (eds.), *Grammars of space: Explorations in cognitive diversity* (pp. 311–358). Cambridge, UK: Cambridge University Press.

Mellem, M. S., Jasmin, K. M., Peng, C., & Martin, A. (2016). Sentence processing in anterior superior temporal cortex shows a social-emotional bias. *Neuropsychologia, 89*, 217–224.

Melloni, L., & Singer, W. (2010). Distinct characteristics of conscious experience are met by large-scale neuronal synchronization. In E. K. Perry, D. Collerton, F. E. N. LeBeau, & H. Ashton (eds.), *New horizons in the neuroscience of consciousness* (pp. 17–28). Amsterdam: John Benjamins.

Mesulam, M. M., Wieneke, C., Hurley, R., Rademaker, A., Thompson, C. K., Weintraub, S., & Rogalski, E. J. (2013). Words and objects at the tip of the left temporal lobe in primary progressive aphasia. *Brain, 136*, 601–618.

Meteyard, L., Bahrami, B., & Vigliocco, G. (2007). Motion detection and motion words: Language affects low-level visual perception. *Psychological Science, 18*, 1007–1013.

Meteyard, L., Cuadrado, S. R., Bahrami, B., & Vigliocco, G. (2012). Coming of age: A review of embodiment and the neuroscience of semantics. *Cortex, 48*, 788–804.

Meyer, K., & Damasio, A. R. (2009). Convergence and divergence in a neural architecture for recognition and memory. *Trends in Neurosciences, 32*, 376–382.

Miller, S. M. (2007). On the correlation/constitution distinction problem (and other hard problems) in the scientific study of consciousness. *Acta Neuropsychiatrica, 19*, 159–176.

Millikan, R. G. (2014). An epistemology for phenomenology? In R. Brown (ed.), *Consciousness inside and out: Phenomenology, neuroscience, and the nature of experience* (pp. 13–26). New York: Springer.

Mion, M., Patterson, K., Acosta-Cabronero, J., Pengas, G., Izquierdo-Garcia, D., Hong, Y. T., Fryer, T. D., Williams, G. B., Hodges, J. R., & Nestor, P. J. (2010). What the left and right anterior fusiform gyri tell us about semantic memory. *Brain, 133*, 3256–3268.

Mitchell, T. M., Shinkareva, S. V., Carlson, A., Chang, K. M., Malave, V. L., Mason, R. A., & Just, M. A. (2008). Predicting human brain activity associated with the meanings of nouns. *Science, 320*, 1191–1195.

Mithun, M. (1999). *The languages of native North America*. Cambridge, UK: Cambridge University Press.

Mithun, M. (2004). The value of linguistic diversity: Viewing other worlds through North American Indian languages. In A. Duranti (ed.), *A companion to linguistic anthropology* (pp. 121–140). New York: Blackwell.

Mo, L., Xu, G., Kay, P., & Tan, L. H. (2011). Electrophysiological evidence for the left-lateralized effect of language on preattentive categorical perception of color. *Proceedings of the National Academy of Sciences, 108*, 14026–14030.

Molenberghs, P., Cunnington, R., & Mattingley, J. B. (2012). Brain regions with mirror properties: A meta-analysis of 125 human fMRI studies. *Neuroscience and Biobehavioral Reviews, 36*, 341–349.

Moody, C. L., & Gennari, S. P. (2010). Effects of implied physical effort in sensory-motor and prefrontal cortex during language comprehension. *NeuroImage, 49*, 782–793.

Moore, R., Donelson, K., Eggleston, A., & Bohnemeyer, J. (2015). Semantic typology: New approaches to crosslinguistic variation in language and cognition. *Linguistics Vanguard, 1*, 189–200.

Munnich, E., Landau, B., & Dosher, B. A. (2001). Spatial language and spatial representation: A cross-linguistic comparison. *Cognition, 81*, 171–208.

Munuera, J., Rigotti, M., & Salzman, C. D. (2018). Shared neural coding for social hierarchy and reward value in primate amygdala. *Nature Neuroscience, 21*, 415–423.

Mur, M., Meys, M., Bodurka, J., Goebel, R., Bandettini, P., & Kriegeskorte, N. (2013). Human object-similarity judgments reflect and transcend the primate-IT object representation. *Frontiers in Psychology, 4*, Article 128.

Murphy, C., Jefferies, E., Rueschemeyer, S. A., Sormaz, M., Wang, H., Margulies, D. S., & Smallwood, J. (2017). Isolated from input: Evidence of default mode network support for perceptually decoupled and conceptually guided cognition. *bioRxiv*.

Naccache, L., & Dehaene, S. (2001). The priming method: Imaging unconscious repetition priming reveals an abstract representation of number in the parietal lobes. *Cerebral Cortex, 11*, 966–974.

Narasimhan, B. (2007). Cutting, breaking, and tearing verbs in Hindi and Tamil. *Cognitive Linguistics, 18*, 195–206.

Narasimhan, B., Kopecka, A., Bowerman, M., Gullberg, M., & Majid, A. (2012). Putting and taking events: A crosslinguistic perspective. In A. Kopecka & B. Narasimhan (eds.), *Events of putting and taking: A crosslinguistic perspective* (pp. 1–20). Amsterdam: John Benjamins.

Narrog, H., & Heine, B. (eds.). (2011). *The Oxford handbook of grammaticalization*. New York: Oxford University Press.

Narrog, H., & Ito, S. (2007). Re-constructing semantic maps: The comitative-instrumental area. *Sprachtypologie und Universalienforschung, 60*, 273–292.

Nassi, J. J., & Callaway, E. M. (2006). Multiple circuits relaying primate parallel visual pathways to the middle temporal area. *Journal of Neuroscience, 26*, 12789–12798.

Nes, A. (2012). Thematic unity in the phenomenology of thinking. *The Philosophical Quarterly, 62*, 84–105.

Newman, J. (ed.) (1998). *The linguistics of giving*. Amsterdam: John Benjamins.

Newman, J. (ed.) (2002). *The linguistics of sitting, standing, and lying*. Amsterdam: John Benjamins.

Newman, J. (ed.) (2009). *The linguistics of eating and drinking*. Amsterdam: John Benjamins.

Nichols, J. (1988). On alienable and inalienable possession. In W. Shipley (ed.), *In honor of Mary Haas* (pp. 557–609). Berlin: Mouton de Gruyter.

Nichols, S., & Stich, S. (2003). How to read your own mind: A cognitive theory of self-consciousness. In Q. Smith & A. Jokic (eds.), *Consciousness: New philosophical essays* (pp. 157–200). New York: Oxford University Press.

Noordzij, M. L., Neggers, S. F. W., Ramsey, N. F., & Postma, A. (2005). Neural correlates of locative prepositions. *Neuropsychologia, 46*, 1576–1580.

Noppeney, U., & Price, C. J. (2002). Retrieval of visual, auditory, and abstract semantics. *NeuroImage, 15*, 917–926.

O'Callaghan, C. (2011). Against hearing meanings. *The Philosophical Quarterly, 61*, 783–807.

O'Connor, L. (2007). "Chop, shred, snap apart": Verbs of cutting and breaking in Lowland Chontal. *Cognitive Linguistics, 18*, 219–230.

Odegaard, B., Knight, R., & Lau, H. (2017). Should a few null findings falsify prefrontal theories of conscious perception? *Journal of Neuroscience, 37*, 9593–9602.

Oizumi, M., Albantakis, L., & Tononi, G. (2014). From the phenomenology to the mechanisms of consciousness: Integrated Information Theory 3.0. *PLoS Computational Biology, 10*, e1003588.

Oliver, R. T., Geiger, E. J., Lewandowski, B. C., & Thompson-Schill, S. L. (2009). Remembrance of things touched: How sensorimotor experience affects the neural instantiation of object form. *Neuropsychologia, 47*, 239–247.

Olson, I. R., McCoy, D., Klobusicky, E., & Ross, L. A. (2013). Social cognition and the anterior temporal lobes: A review and theoretical framework. *Social, Cognitive, and Affective Neuroscience, 8*, 123–133.

Orban, G. A., & Caruana, F. (2014). The neural basis of human tool use. *Fronties in Psychology*, 5, Article 310.

Orlov, T., Makin, T. R., & Zohary, E. (2010). Topographic representation of the human body in the occipitotemporal cortex. *Neuron, 68*, 586–600.

Osaka, N. (2009). Walk-related mimic word activates the extrastriate visual cortex in the human brain: An fMRI study. *Behavioural Brain Research, 198*, 186–189.

Osaka, N., Ikeda, T., & Osaka, M. (2012). Effect of intentional bias on agency attribution of animated motion: An event-related fMRI study. *PLoS ONE, 7*, e49053.

Pagel, M. (2012). *Wired for culture: Origins of the human social mind.* New York: Norton.

Palancar, E. L. (2007). Cutting and breaking verbs in Otomi: An example of lexical specification. *Cognitive Linguistics, 18*, 307–318.

Palmer, C. E., Bunday, K. L., Davare, M., & Kilner, J. M. (2016). A causal role for primary motor cortex in perception of observed actions. *Journal of Cognitive Neuroscience, 28*, 2021–2029.

Palmeri, T. J., Wong, A. C. N., & Gauthier, I. (2004). Computational approaches to the development of perceptual expertise. *Trends in Cognitive Sciences, 8*, 378–386.

Panichello, M. F., Cheung, O. S., & Bar, M. (2013). Predictive feedback and conscious visual experience. *Frontiers in Psychology, 3*, Article 620.

Panasiti, M. S., Porciello, G., & Aglioti, S. M. (2017). The bright and the dark sides of motor simulation. *Neuropsychologia, 105*, 92–100.

Papafragou, A., Massey, C., & Gleitman, L. (2002). Shake, rattle, 'n' roll: The representation of motion in language and cognition. *Cognition, 84*, 189–219.

Papafragou, A., Massey, C., & Gleitman, L. (2006). When English proposes what Greek presupposes: The cross-linguistic encoding of motion events. *Cognition, 98*, B75–B87.

Papeo, L., Negri, G. A. L., Zadini, A., & Rumiati, R. I. (2010). Action performance and action-word understanding: Evidence of double dissociations in left-damaged patients. *Cognitive Neuropsychology, 27*, 428–461.

Papeo, L., Rumiati, R. I., Cecchetto, C., & Tomasino, B. (2012). On-line changing of thinking about words: The effect of cognitive context on neural responses to verb reading. *Journal of Cognitive Neuroscience, 24*, 2348–2362.

Papeo, L., Vallesi, A., Isaja, A., & Rumiati, R. I. (2009). Effects of TMS on different stages of motor and non-motor verb processing in the primary motor cortex. *PLoS ONE, 4*, e4508.

Patterson, K., & Lambon Ralph, M. (2016). The hub-and-spoke hypothesis of semantic memory. In G. Hickok & S. Small (eds.), *Neurobiology of language* (pp. 765–775). New York: Elsevier.

Patterson, K., Nestor, P. J., & Rogers, T. T. (2007). Where do you know what you know? The representation of semantic knowledge in the brain. *Nature Reviews: Neuroscience, 8*, 976–987.

Pavlenko, A., & Malt, B. C. (2011). Kitchen Russian: Cross-linguistic differences and first-language object naming by Russian-English bilinguals. *Bilingualism: Language and Cognition, 14*, 19–45.

Pavlenko, A. (2014). *The bilingual mind and what it tells us about language and thought.* Cambridge, UK: Cambridge University Press.

Pawley, A. (1987). Encoding events in Kalam and English: Different logics for reporting experience. In R. S. Tomlin (ed.), *Coherence and grounding in discourse* (pp. 329–360). Amsterdam: John Benjamins.

Pawley, A. (1993). A language which defies description by ordinary means. In W. Foley (ed.), *The role of theory in language description* (pp. 87–129). Berlin: Mouton de Gruyter.

Pawley, A. (2006). On the size of the lexicon in preliterate language communities: Comparing dictionaries of Australian, Austronesia, and Papuan languages. In J. Genzon & M. Buckova (eds.), *Favete Linguis: Studies in honour of Viktor Krupa* (pp. 171–191). Bratislava: Institute of Oriental Studies.

Pawley, A. (2008). Compact versus narrative serial verb constructions in Kalam. In G. Senft (ed.), *Serial verb constructions in Austronesian and Papuan languages* (pp. 171–202). Canberra: Pacific Linguistics.

Pawley, A. (2011). Event representation in serial verb constructions. In J. Bohnemeyer & E. Pederson (eds.), *Event representation in language and cognition* (pp. 13–42). Cambridge, UK: Cambridge University Press.

Pecher, D., & Zwaan, R. A. (2017). Flexible concepts: A commentary on Kemmerer (2016). *Language, Cognition, and Neuroscience, 32,* 444–446.

Peelen, M. V., & Caramazza, A. (2012). Conceptual object representations in human anterior temporal cortex. *Journal of Neuroscience, 32,* 15728–15736.

Peelen, M. V., & Downing, P. E. (2007). The neural basis of visual body perception. *Nature Reviews Neuroscience, 8,* 636–648.

Peelen, M. V., Romagno, D., & Caramazza, A. (2012). Is verb selectivity in left posterior temporal cortex related to conceptual action knowledge? *Journal of Cognitive Neuroscience, 24,* 2096–2107.

Peeters, D., Hagoort, P., & Özyürek, A. (2015). Electrophysiological evidence for the role of shared space in online comprehension of spatial demonstratives. *Cognition, 136,* 64–84.

Peeters, D., & Özyürek, A. (2016). *This* and *that* revisited: A social and multimodal approach to spatial demonstratives. *Frontiers in Psychology, 7,* Article 222.

Pelgrims, B., Olivier, E., & Andres, M. (2011). Dissociation between manipulation and conceptual knowledge of object use in supramarginalis gyrus. *Human Brain Mapping, 32,* 1802–1810.

Pelphrey, K. A., Morris, J. P., & McCarthy, G. (2004). Grasping the intentions of others: The perceived intentionality of an action influences activity in the superior temporal sulcus during social perception. *Journal of Cognitive Neuroscience, 16,* 1706–1716.

Penfield, W., & Evans, J. (1935). The frontal lobe in man: A clinical study of maximal removals. *Brain, 58,* 115–133.

Penfield, W., & Rasmussen, T. (1950). *The cerebral cortex of man: A clinical study of localization of function.* New York: Macmillan.

Pereira, F., Gershman, S., Ritter, S., & Botvinick, M. (2016). A comparative evaluation of off-the-shelf distributed semantic representations for modelling behavioral data. *Cognitive Neuropsychology, 33,* 175–190.

Perniss, P., Vinson, D., Seifart, F., & Vigliocco, G. (2012). Speaking of shape: The effects of language-specific encoding on semantic representations. *Language and Cognition, 4,* 223–242.

Pinker, S. (1989). *Learnability and cognition: The acquisition of argument structure.* Cambridge, MA: MIT Press.

Pinker, S. (1994). *The language instinct: How the mind creates language.* New York: Morrow.

Pitt, D. (2004). The phenomenology of cognition, or, what is it like to think that P? *Philosophy and Phenomenological Research, 69,* 1–36.

Pitt, D. (2012). Introspection, phenomenality, and the availability of intentional content. In T. Bayne & M. Montague (eds.), *Cognitive phenomenology* (pp. 141–173). New York: Oxford University Press.

Pitts, M. A., Metzler, S., & Hillyard, S. A. (2014a). Isolating neural correlates of conscious perception from neural correlates of reporting one's perception. *Frontiers in Psychology, 5,* Article 1078.

Pitts, M. A., Padwal, J., Fennelly, D., Martinez, A., & Hillyard, S. A. (2014b). Gamma band activity and the P3 reflect post-perceptual processes, not visual awareness. *NeuroImage, 101,* 337–350.

Pobric, G., Jefferies, E., & Lambon Ralph, M. A. (2007). Anterior temporal lobes mediate semantic representation: Mimicking semantic dementia by using rTMS in normal participants. *Proceedings of the National Academy of Sciences, 104,* 20137–20141.

Pobric, G., Jefferies, E., & Lambon Ralph, M. A. (2009). The role of the anterior temporal lobes in the comprehension of concrete and abstract words: rTMS evidence. *Cortex, 45,* 1104–1110.

Pobric, G., Jefferies, E., & Lambon Ralph, M. A. (2010). Category-specific versus category-general semantic impairment induced by transcranial magnetic stimulation. *Current Biology, 20,* 964–968.

Porter, C. (2017). Reviving a lost language of Canada through film. *The New York Times,* June 11.

Posey, D. (1990). *Kayapó ethnoecology and culture.* London: Routledge.

Price, C. J., Noppeney, U., Phillips, J., & Devlin, J. T. (2003). How is the fusiform gyrus related to category-specificity? *Cognitive Neuropsychology, 20,* 561–574.

Primativo, S., Reilly, J., & Crutch, S. J. (2017). Abstract conceptual feature ratings predict gaze within written word arrays: Evidence from a visual wor(l)d paradigm. *Cognitive Science, 41,* 659–685.

Prinz, J. (2012). *The conscious brain: How attention engenders experience.* New York: Oxford University Press.

Proklova, D., Kaiser, D., & Peelen, M. V. (2016). Disentangling representations of object shape and object category in human visual cortex: The animate-inanimate distinction. *Journal of Cognitive Neuroscience, 28,* 680–692.

Pullum, G. K. (1990). Constraints on intransitive quasi-serial verb constructions in Modern Colloquial English. *Ohio State University Working Papers in Linguistics, 39,* 218–239.

Pulvermüller, F. (2005). Brain mechanisms linking language and action. *Nature Reviews Neuroscience, 6,* 576–582.

Pulvermüller, F. (2013a). How neurons make meaning: Brain mechanisms for embodied and abstract-symbolic semantics. *Trends in Cognitive Sciences, 17,* 458–470.

Pulvermüller, F. (2013b). Semantic embodiment, disembodiment, or misembodiment? In search of meaning in modules and neural circuits. *Brain and Language, 127,* 86–103.

Pulvermüller, F., Cooper-Pye, E., Dine, C., Hauk, O., Nestor, P. J., & Patterson, K. (2009). The word processing deficit in semantic dementia: All categories are equal, but some categories are more equal than others. *Journal of Cognitive Neuroscience, 22,* 2027–2041.

Pulvermüller, F., & Hauk, O. (2006). Category-specific conceptual processing of color and form in left fronto-temporal cortex. *Cerebral Cortex, 16,* 1193–1201.

Pulvermüller, F., Hauk, O., Nikulin, V., & Ilmoniemi, R. (2005). Functional links between motor and language systems. *European Journal of Neuroscience, 21,* 793–797.

Pye, C. (1996). K'iche' Maya verbs of breaking and cutting. In M Goodell & D. Ik Choi (eds.), *Kansas working papers in linguistics 21* (pp. 87–98). Lawrence: University of Kansas.

Pye, C., Loeb, D. F., & Pao, Y. Y. (1995). The acquisition of breaking and cutting. Paper presented at the 27th annual Child Language Research Forum.

Quandt, L. C., Cardillo, E. R., Kranjec, A., & Chatterjee, A. (2015). Fronto-temporal regions encode manner of motion in spatial language. *Neuroscience Letters, 609,* 171–175.

Quandt, L. C., & Chatterjee, A. (2015). Rethinking actions: Implementation and association. *WIREs Cognitive Science, 6,* 483–490.

Quiroga, R. Q. (2012). Concept cells: The building blocks of declarative memory functions. *Nature Reviews Neuroscience, 13*, 587–597.

Quiroga, R. Q., Kreiman, G., Koch, C., & Fried, I. (2008a). Sparse but not "grandmother-cell" coding in the medial temporal lobe. *Trends in Cognitive Neurosciences, 12*, 87–91.

Quiroga, R. Q., Mukamel, R., Isham, E. A., Malach, R., & Fried, I. (2008b). Human single-neuron responses at the threshold of conscious recognition. *Proceedings of the National Academy of Sciences, 105*, 3599–3604.

Quiroga, R. Q., Reddy, L., Kreiman, G., Koch, C., & Fried, I. (2005). Invariant visual representation by single neurons in the human brain. *Nature, 435*, 1102–1107.

Radvansky, G. A., & Zacks, J. M. (2014). *Event cognition*. New York: Oxford University Press.

Ramanan, S., Piguet, O., & Irish, M. (2018). Rethinking the role of the angular gyrus in remembering the past and imagining the future: The Contextual Integration Model. *The Neuroscientist, 24*, 342–352.

Ramayya, A. G., Glasser, M. F., & Rilling, J. K. (2010). A DTI investigation of neural substrates supporting tool use. *Cerebral Cortex, 20*, 507–516.

Rangarajan, V., Hermes, D., Foster, B. L., Weiner, K. S., Jacques, C., Grill-Spector, K., & Parvizi, J. (2014). Electrical stimulation of the left and right human fusiform gyrus causes different effects in conscious face perception. *Journal of Neuroscience, 34*, 12828–12836.

Rapold, C. J. (2012). The encoding of placement and removal events in ≠Ākhoe Hai||om. In A. Kopecka & B. Narasimhan (eds.), *Events of putting and taking: A crosslinguistic perspective* (pp. 73–98). Amsterdam: John Benjamins.

Raposo, A., Moss, H. E., Stamatakis, E. A., & Tyler, L. K. (2009). Modulation of motor, premotor cortices by actions, action words, and action sentences. *Neuropsychologia, 47*, 388–396.

Rappaport Hovav, M., & Levin, B. (1998). Building verb meanings. In M. Butt & W. Geuder (eds.), *The projection of arguments: Lexical and syntactic constraints* (pp. 97–134). Stanford: CSLI Publications.

Regier, T., Kay, P., & Cook, R. (2005). Focal colors are universal after all. *Proceedings of the National Academy of Sciences, 102*, 8386–8391.

Regier, T., Kay, P., & Khetarpal, N. (2007). Color naming reflects optimal partitions of color space. *Proceedings of the National Academy of Sciences, 104*, 1436–1441.

Regier, T., Khetarpal, N., & Majid, A. (2013). Inferring semantic maps. *Linguistic Typology, 17*, 89–105.

Regier, T., & Zheng, M. (2007). Attention to endpoints: A cross-linguistic constraint on spatial meaning. *Cognitive Science, 31*, 705–719.

Reich, D. (2018). *Who we are and how we got here: Ancient DNA and the new science of the human past*. New York: Pantheon.

Reilly, J., Rodriguez, A. D., Peelle, J. E., & Grossman, M. (2011). Frontal lobe damage impairs process and content in semantic memory: Evidence from category-specific effects in progressive nonfluent aphasia. *Cortex, 47*, 645–658.

Reines, M. F., & Prinz, J. (2009). Reviving Whorf: The return of linguistic relativity. *Philosophy Compass, 4*, 1022–1032.

Repetto, C., Colombo, B., Cipresso, P., & Riva, G. (2013). The effects of rTMS over the primary motor cortex: The link between action and language. *Neuropsychologia, 51*, 8–13.

Reynaud, E., Lesourd, M., Navarro, J., & Osiurak, F. (2016). On the neurocognitive origins of human tool use: A critical review of neuroimaging data. *Neuroscience and Biobehavioral Reviews, 64*, 421–437.

Rice, G. E., Lambon Ralph, M. A., & Hoffman, P. (2015). The roles of left versus right anterior temporal lobes in conceptual knowledge: An ALE meta-analysis of 97 functional neuroimaging studies. *Cerebral Cortex, 25*, 4374–4391.

Rice, S. (1998). Giving and taking in Chipewyan: The semantics of THING-marking classificatory verbs. In J. Newman (ed.), *The linguistics of giving* (pp. 97–134). Amsterdam: John Benjamins.

Rice, S., & Kabata, K. (2007). Crosslinguistic grammaticalization patterns of the ALLATIVE. *Linguistic Typology, 11*, 451–514.

Richerson, P., & Boyd, R. (2006). *Not by genes alone: How culture transformed human evolution.* Chicago: University of Chicago Press.

Richerson, P., & Christiansen, M. H. (eds.). (2013). *Cultural evolution: Society, technology, language, and religion.* Cambridge, MA: MIT Press.

Richmond, L. L., & Zacks, J. M. (2017). Constructing experience: Event models from perception to action. *Trends in Cognitive Sciences, 21*, 962–980.

Ritz, T., Thalu, P., Phillips, J. B., Wiltschko, R., & Wiltschko, W. (2004). Resonance effects indicate a radical-pair mechanism for avian magnetic compass. *Nature, 429*, 177–180.

Rizzolatti, G., Cattaneo, L., Fabbri-Destro, M., & Rozzi, S. (2014). Cortical mechanisms underlying the organization of goal-directed actions and mirror neuron-based action understanding. *Physiological Review, 94*, 655–706.

Roberson, D., & Hanley, J. R. (2010). Relatively speaking: An account of the relationship between language and thought in the color domain. In B. C. Malt & P. Wolff (eds.), *Words and the mind: How words capture human experience* (pp. 183–198). New York: Oxford University Press.

Robinson, W. S. (2005). Thoughts without distinctive non-imagistic phenomenology. *Philosophy and Phenomenological Research, 70*, 534–561.

Robinson, W. S. (2012). A frugal view of cognitive phenomenology. In T. Bayne & M. Montague (eds.), *Cognitive phenomenology* (pp. 197–214). New York: Oxford University Press.

Rogers, T. T., Graham, K. S., & Patterson, K. (2015). Semantic impairment disrupts perception, memory, and naming of secondary but not primary colours. *Neuropsychologia, 70*, 296–308.

Rogers, T. T., Hocking, J., Noppeney, U., Mechelli, A., Gorno-Tempini, M., Patterson, K., & Price, C. (2006). The anterior temporal cortex and semantic memory: Reconciling findings from neuropsychology and functional imaging. *Cognitive, Affective and Behavioral Neuroscience, 6*, 201–213.

Rogers, T. T., Lambon Ralph, M. A., Garrard, P., Bozeat, S., McClelland, J. L., Hodges, J. R., & Patterson, K. (2004). The structure and deterioration of semantic memory: A neuropsychological and computational investigation. *Psychological Review, 111*, 205–235.

Rohde, D. L. T., Gonnerman, L. M., & Plaut, D. C. (2005). An improved model of semantic similarity based on lexical co-occurrence. Unpublished manuscript.

Rosch, E., & Mervis, C. (1975). Family resemblances: Studies in the internal structure of categories. *Cognitive Psychology, 7*, 573–605.

Rounis, E., Maniscalco, B., Rothwell, J. C., Passingham, R. E., & Lau, H. (2010). Theta-burst transcranial magnetic stimulation to the prefrontal cortex impairs metacognitive visual awareness. *Cognitive Neuroscience, 1*, 165–175.

Sahlgren, M. (2008). The distributional hypothesis. *Italian Journal of Linguistics, 20*, 33–54.

Samaha, J., Boutonnet, B., & Lupyan, G. (2016). How prior knowledge prepares perception: Prestimulus oscillations carry perceptual expectations and influence early visual responses. *bioRxiv.*

Sapir, E. (1921). *Language: An introduction to the study of speech.* New York: Harcourt, Brace.

Saygin, A. P. (2012). Sensory and motor brain areas supporting biological motion perception: Neuropsychological and neuroimaging studies. In K. Johnson & M. Shiffrar (eds.), *People watching: Social, perceptual, and neurophysiological studies of body perception* (pp. 371–389). Oxford: Oxford University Press.

Saygin, A. P., McCullough, S., Alac, M., & Emmorey, K. (2010). Modulation of the BOLD response in motion sensitive lateral temporal cortex by real and fictive motion sentences. *Journal of Cognitive Neuroscience, 22,* 2480–2490.

Saygin, A. P., Wilson, S. M., Dronkers, N. F., & Bates, E. (2004). Action comprehension in aphasia: Linguistic and non-linguistic deficits and their lesion correlates. *Neuropsychologia, 42,* 1788–1804.

Schapiro, A. C., McClelland, J. L., Welbourne, S. R., Rogers, T. T., & Lambon Ralph, M. A. (2013). Why bilateral damage is worse than unilateral damage to the brain. *Journal of Cognitive Neuroscience, 25,* 2107–2123.

Schapper, A. (2014). Elevation in the spatial deictic systems of Alor-Pantar languages. In M. Klamer (ed.), *The Alor-Pantar languages: History and typology* (pp. 247–284). Berlin: Language Science Press.

Schuil, K. D. I., Smits, M., & Zwaan, R. A. (2013). Sentential context modulates the involvement of the motor cortex in action language processing: An fMRI study. *Frontiers in human neuroscience, 7,* 100.

Schultz, J., Imamizu, H., Kawato, M., & Frith, C. D. (2004). Activation of the human superior temporal gyrus during observation of goal attribution by intentional objects. *Journal of Cognitive Neuroscience, 16,* 1695–1705.

Schultze-Berndt, E. (2000). *Simple and complex verbs in Jaminjung.* MPI Series in Psycholinguistics 14. PhD dissertation, University of Nijmegen.

Schultze-Berndt, E. (2006). Sketch of a Jaminjung grammar of space. In S. C. Levinson & D. Wilkins (eds.), *Grammars of space: Explorations in cognitive diversity* (pp. 63–114). Cambridge, UK: Cambridge University Press.

Schultze-Berndt, E. (2017). Two classes of verbs in Northern Australian languages: implications for the typology of polycategoriality. In V. Vapnarsky & E. Veneziano (eds.), *Lexial polycategoriality* (pp. 243–272). Amsterdam: John Benjamins.

Schurz, M., Radua, J., Aichhorn, M., Richlan, F., & Perner, J. (2014). Fractionating theory of mind: A meta-analysis of functional brain imaging studies. *Neuroscience and Biobehavioral Reviews, 42,* 9–34.

Schwoebel, J., & Coslett, H. B. (2005). Evidence for multiple, distinct representations of the human body. *Journal of Cognitive Neuroscience, 17,* 543–553.

Searle, J. R. (1980). Minds, brains, and programs. *Behavioral and Brain Sciences, 3,* 417–424.

Seghier, M. L. (2013). The angular gyrus: Multiple functions and multiple subdivisions. *The Neuroscientist, 19,* 43–61.

Seifart, F. (2005). *The structure and use of shape-based noun classes in Miraña (North West Amazon).* MPI Series in Psycholinguistics 32. PhD dissertation, Radboud University.

Seifart, F. (2009). Multidimensional typology and Miraña class markers. In P. Epps & A. Arkhipov (eds.), *New challenges in typology: Transcending the borders and refining the distinctions* (pp. 365–385). Berlin: Mouton de Gruyter.

Seifart, F. (2010). Nominal classification. *Language and Linguistics Compass, 4,* 719–736.

Semaw, S., Rogers, M. J., Quade, J., Renne, P. R., Butler, R. F., Dominguez-Rodrigo, M., Stout, D., Hart, W. S., Pickering, T., & Simpson, S. W. (2003). 2.6-million-year-old stone tools and associated bones from OGS-6 and OGS-7, Gona, Afar, Ethiopia. *Journal of Human Evolution, 45*, 169–177.

Semenza, C., Mondini, S., & Cappelletti, M. (1997). The grammatical properties of mass nouns: An aphasia case study. *Neuropsychologia, 35*, 669–675.

Semin, G. R., & Smith, E. R. (eds.) (2008). *Embodied grounding: Social, cognitive, affective, and neuroscientific approaches.* Cambridge, UK: Cambridge University Press.

Senft, G. (ed.) (2000). *Systems of nominal classification.* Cambridge: Cambridge University Press.

Senft, G. (ed.) (2008). *Serial verb constructions in Austronesian and Papuan languages.* Canberra: Pacific Linguistics.

Sepulcre, J., Sabuncu, M. R., Yeo, T. B., Liu, H., & Johnson, K. A. (2012). Step-wise connectivity of the medial cortex reveals the multimodal organization of the human brain. *Journal of Neuroscience, 32*, 10649–10661.

Serra Borneto, C. (1996). *Liegen* and *stehen* in German: A study in horizontality and verticality. In E. Casad (ed.), *Cognitive linguistics in the redwoods* (pp. 459–505). Berlin: Mouton de Gruyter.

Sha, L., Haxby, J. V., Abdi, H., Guntupalli, S., Oosterhof, N. N., Halchenko, Y. O., & Connolly, A. C. (2015). The animacy continuum in the human ventral vision pathway. *Journal of Cognitive Neuroscience, 27*, 665–678.

Shapiro, L. (ed.) (2014). *The Routledge handbook of embodied cognition.* Routledge: New York.

Sharp, D. J., Scott, S. K., & Wise, R. J. S. (2004). Retrieving meaning after temporal lobe infarction: The role of the basal language area. *Annals of Neurology, 56*, 836–846.

Shay, E. A., Grimm, S., & Raizada, R. D. S. (2017). Commentary on Kemmerer: The challenges and rewards of trying to combine linguistics and cognitive neuroscience. *Language, Cognition, and Neuroscience, 32*, 433–437.

Shepard, R. N. (1992). The perceptual organization of colours. In J. Barkow, L. Cosmides, & J. Tooby (eds.), *The adapted mind: Evolutionary psychology and the generation of culture* (pp. 495–532). New York: Oxford University Press.

Sherrill, K. R., Erdem, U. M., Ross, R. S., Brown, T. I., Hasselmo, M. E., & Stern, C. E. (2013). Hippocampus and retrosplenial cortex combine path integration signals for successful navigation. Journal of Neuroscience, 33, 19304–19313.

Shetreet, E., Palti, D., Friedmann, N., & Hadar, U. (2007). Cortical representation of verb processing in sentence comprehension: Number of complements, subcategorization, and thematic frames. *Cerebral Cortex, 17*, 1958–1969.

Shibatani, M. (2006). On the conceptual framework for voice phenomena. *Linguistics, 44*, 217–269.

Shields, C. (2012). On behalf of cognitive qualia. In T. Bayne & M. Montague (eds.), *Cognitive phenomenology* (pp. 215–235). New York: Oxford University Press.

Shimotake, A., Matsumoto, R., Ueno, T., Kunieda, T., Saito, S., Hoffman, P., Kikuchi, T., Fukuyama, H., Miyamoto, S., Takahashi, R., Ikeda, A., & Lambon Ralph, M. A. (2014). Direct exploration of the role of the ventral anterior temporal lobe in semantic memory: cortical stimulation and local field potential evidence from subdural grid electrodes. *Cerebral Cortex, 25*, 3802–3817.

Shinkareva, S. V., Malave, V. L., Mason, R. A., Mitchell, T. M., & Just, M. A. (2011). Commonality of neural representations of words and pictures. *NeuroImage, 54*, 2418–2425.

Shtyrov, Y., Butorina, A., Nikolaeva, A., & Stroganova, T. (2014). Automatic ultrarapid activation and inhibition of cortical motor systems in spoken word comprehension. *Proceedings of the National Academy of Sciences*, E1918–E1923.

Shultz, S., & McCarthy, G. (2014). Perceived animacy influences the processing of human-like surface features in the fusiform gyrus. *Neuropsychologia, 60,* 115–120.

Sidnell, J., & Barnes, R. (2013). Alternative, subsequent descriptions. In M. Hayashi, G. Raymond, & J. Sidnell (eds.), *Conversational repair and human understanding* (pp. 322–342). Cambridge, UK: Cambridge University Press.

Siegel, S. (2005). Which properties are represented in perception? In T. S. Gendler & J. Hawthorne (eds.), *Perceptual experience* (pp. 481–503). New York: Oxford University Press.

Siewert, C. (1998). *The significance of consciousness.* Princeton, NJ: Princeton University Press.

Siewert, C. (2012). Phenomenal thought. In T. Bayne & M. Montague (eds.), *Cognitive phenomenology* (pp. 236–267). New York: Oxford University Press.

Simmons, W. K., & Barsalou, L. W. (2003). The similarity-in-topography principle: Reconciling theories of conceptual deficits. *Cognitive Neuropsychology, 20,* 451–486.

Simmons, W. K., Hamann, S. B., Harenski, C. N., Hu, X. P., & Barsalou, L. W. (2008). fMRI evidence for word association and situated simulation in conceptual processing. *Journal of Physiology, Paris, 102,* 106–119.

Simmons, W. K., Ramjee, V., Beauchamp, M. S., McRae, K., Martin, A., & Barsalou, L. W. (2007). A common neural substrate for perceiving and knowing about color. *Neuropsychologia, 45,* 2802–2810.

Siok, W. T., Kay, P., Wang, W. S. Y., Chan, A. H. D., Chen, L., & Luke, K. K. (2009). Language regions of brain are operative in color perception. *Proceedings of the National Academy of Sciences, 106,* 8140–8145.

Sirigu, A., Duhamel, J. R., & Poncet, M. (1991). The role of sensorimotor experience in object recognition. *Brain, 114,* 2555–2573.

Skelton, A. E., Catchpole, G., Abbott, J. T., Bosten, J. M., & Franklin, A. (2017). Biological origins of color categorization. *Proceedings of the National Academy of Sciences, 114,* 5545–5550.

Slobin, D. I. (1996). From "thought and language" to "thinking for speaking." In J. J. Gumperz & S. C. Levinson (eds.), *Rethinking linguistic relativity* (pp. 70–96). Cambridge, UK: Cambridge University Press.

Slobin, D. I. (2000). Verbalized events: A dynamic approach to linguistic relativity and determinism. In S. Niemeier & R. Dirven (eds.), *Evidence for linguistic relativity* (pp. 107–38). Amsterdam: Benjamins.

Slobin, D. I. (2001). Form-function relations: How do children find out what they are? In M. Bowerman & S. C. Levinson (eds.), *Language acquisition and conceptual development* (pp. 406–449). Cambridge, UK: Cambridge University Press.

Slobin, D. I. (2003). Language and thought online: cognitive consequences of linguistic relativity. In D. Gentner & S. Goldin-Meadow (eds.), *Language in mind: advances in the study of language and thought* (pp. 157–192). Cambridge, MA: MIT Press.

Slobin, D. I. (2004). The many ways to search for a frog: Linguistic typology and the expression of motion events. In S. Strömqvist & L. Verhoeven (eds.), *Relating events in narrative: Typological and contextual perspectives* (pp. 219–258). Mahwah, NJ: Erlbaum.

Slobin, D. I. (2006). What makes manner of motion salient? Explorations in linguistic typology, discourse, and cognition. In M. Hickmann & S. Robert (eds.), *Space in languages: Linguistic systems and cognitive categories* (pp. 59–81). Amsterdam: John Benjamins.

Slobin, D. I., Bowerman, M., Brown, P., Eisenbeiß, S., & Narasimhan, B. (2011). Putting things in places: Developmental consequences of linguistic typology. In J. Bohnemeyer & E. Pederson (eds.), *Event representation in language and cognition* (pp. 134–165). Cambridge, UK: Cambridge University Press.

Slobin, D. I., & Hoiting, N. (1994). Reference to movement in spoken and signed languages: Typological considerations. *Proceedings of the 20th Annual Meeting of the Berkeley Linguistics Society* (pp. 487–505). Berkeley: Berkeley Linguistics Society.

Slobin, D. I., Ibarretxe-Antuñano, I., Kopecka, A., & Majid, A. (2014). Manners of human gait: A crosslinguistic event-naming study. *Cognitive Linguistics, 25*, 701–741.

Sloman, S., & Malt, B. C. (2003). Artifacts are not ascribed essences, nor are they treated as belonging to kinds. *Language and Cognitive Processes, 18*, 563–582.

Smith, E., Shoben, E., & Rips, L. (1974). Structure and process in semantic memory. *Psychological Review, 81*, 214–241.

Smith, K. (2013). Reading minds. *Nature, 502*, 428–430.

Smith, L. B., Jones, S. S., Landau, B., Gershkoff-Stowe, L., & Samuelson, L. (2002). Object name learning provides on-the-job training for attention. *Psychological Science, 13*, 13–19.

Snell-Hornby, M. (1983). *Verb descriptivity in German and English: A contrastive study in semantic fields*. Heidelberg: Carl Winter.

Snowden, J. S., Thompson, J. C., & Neary, D. (2004). Knowledge of famous faces and names in semantic dementia. *Brain, 127*, 860–872.

Snowden, J. S., Thompson, J. C., & Neary, D. (2012). Famous people knowledge and the right and left temporal lobes. *Behavioral Neurology, 25*, 35–44.

Soroli, E. (2012). Variation in spatial language and cognition: Exploring visuo-spatial thinking and speaking cross-linguistically. *Cognitive Processing, 13*, 333–337.

Speer, N. K., Zacks, J. M., & Reynolds, J. R. (2007). Human brain activity time-locked to narrative event boundaries. *Psychological Science, 18*, 449–455.

Spelke, E. S. (2016). Cognitive abilities of infants. In R. J. Sternberg, S. T. Fiske, & D. J. Foss (eds.), *Scientists making a difference* (pp. 228–232). Cambridge, UK: Cambridge University Press.

Spunt, R. P., Kemmerer, D., & Adolphs, R. (2016). The neural basis of conceptualizing the same action at different levels of abstraction. *Social, Cognitive, and Affective Neuroscience, 11*, 1141–1151.

Srinivasan, M. (2010). Do classifiers predict differences in cognitive processing? A study of nominal classification in Mandarin Chinese. *Language and Cognition, 2*, 177–190.

Stassen, L. (1997). *Intransitive predication*. New York: Oxford University Press.

Stassen, L. (2009). *Predicative possession*. New York: Oxford University Press.

Steels, L., & Belpaeme, T. (2005). Coordinating perceptually grounded categories through language: A case study for colour. *Behavioral and Brain Sciences, 28*, 469–489; discussion, 489–529.

Sterelny, K. (2012). *The evolved apprentice: How evolution made humans unique*. Cambridge, MA: MIT Press.

Stevens, W. D., Tessler, M. H., Peng, C. S., & Martin, A. (2015). Functional connectivity constrains the category-related organization of human ventral occipitotemporal cortex. *Human Brain Mapping, 36*, 2187–2206.

Stevens, J., & Zhang, Y. (2013). Relative distance and gaze in the use of entity-referring spatial demonstratives: An event-related potential study. *Journal of Neurolinguistics, 26*, 31–45.

Stilla, R., & Sathian, K. (2008). Selective visuo-haptic processing of shape and texture. *Human Brain Mapping, 29*, 1123–1138.

Stolz, T., Kettler, S., Stroh, C., & Urdze, A. (eds.). (2008). *Split possession*. Amsterdam: John Benjamins.

Storm, J. F., Boly, M., Casali, A. G., Massimini, M., Olcese, U., Pennartz, C. M. A., & Wilke, M. (2017). Consciousness regained: Disentangling mechanisms, brain systems, and behavioral responses. *Journal of Neuroscience, 37*, 10882–10893.

Strawson, G. (1994). *Mental reality*. Cambridge, MA: MIT Press.

Strawson, G. (2012). Cognitive phenomenology: Real life. In T. Bayne & M. Montague (eds.), *Cognitive phenomenology* (pp. 285–325). New York: Oxford University Press.

Striem-Amit, E., Vannuscorps, G., & Caramazza, A. (2017). Sensorimotor-independent development of hands and tools selectivity in the visual cortex. *Proceedings of the National Academy of Sciences, 114*, 4787–4792.

Strömqvist, S., & Verhoeven, L. (eds.). (2004). *Relating events in narrative: typological and contextual perspectives*. Mahwah, NJ: Erlbaum.

Stout, D., & Hecht, E. E. (2015). Neuroarchaeology. In E. Bruner (ed.), *Human paleoneurology* (pp. 145–175). New York: Springer.

Struiksma, M. E., Noordzij, M. L., Neggers, S. F. W., Bosker, W. M., & Postma, A. (2011). Spatial language processing in the blind: Evidence for a supramodal representation and cortical reorganization. *PLoS ONE, 6*, e24253.

Summerfield, C., & de Lange, F. P. (2014). Expectation in perceptual decision making: Neural and computational mechanisms. *Nature Reviews Neuroscience, 15*, 745–56

Svorou, S. (1994). *The grammar of space*. Amsterdam: John Benjamins.

Taler, V., Jarema, G., & Saumier, D. (2005). Semantic and syntactic aspects of the mass/count distinction: A case study of semantic dementia. *Brain and Cognition, 57*, 222–225.

Talmy, L. (1983). How language structures space. In H. Pick & L. Acredolo (eds.), *Spatial orientation: Theory, research, and application* (pp. 225–282). New York: Plenum Press.

Talmy, L. (1985). Lexicalization patterns: Semantic structure in lexical forms. In T. Shopen (ed.), *Linguistic typology and syntactic description*, vol. 3: *Grammatical categories and the lexicon* (pp. 57–149). Cambridge, UK: Cambridge University Press.

Talmy, L. (1988). The relation of grammar to cognition. In B. Rudska-Ostyn (ed.), *Topics in cognitive linguistics* (pp. 166–205). Amsterdam: John Benjamins.

Talmy, L. (1991). Path to realization: A typology of event conflation. *Proceedings of the 17th Annual Meeting of the Berkeley Linguistics Society* (pp. 480–519). Berkeley: Berkeley Linguistics Society.

Talmy, L. (2000). *Toward a cognitive semantics II: Typology and process in concept structuring*. Cambridge, MA: MIT Press.

Talmy, L. (2009). Main verb properties and equipollent-framing. In J. Guo, E. Lieven, N. Budwig, S. Ervin-Tripp, K. Nakamura, & S. Özçalikan (eds.), *Crosslinguistic approaches to the psychology of language: Research in the tradition of Dan Isaac Slobin* (pp. 389–403). New York: Psychology Press.

Talmy, L. (2016). Properties of main verbs. *Cognitive Semantics, 2*, 133–163.

Tan, L. H., Chan, A. H. D., Kay, P., Khong, P. L., Yip, L. K. C., & Luke, K. K. (2008). Language affects patterns of brain activation associated with perceptual decision. *Proceedings of the National Academy of Sciences, 105*, 4004–4009.

Tanaka, K. (2003). Columns for complex visual object features in the inferotemporal cortex: Clustering of cells with similar but slightly different stimulus selectivities. *Cerebral Cortex, 13*, 90–99.

Tanaka, S., & Fujita, I. (2015). Computation of object size in visual cortical area V4 as a neural basis for object constancy. *Journal of Neuroscience, 35*, 12033–12046.

Tarhan, L. Y., Watson, C. E., & Buxbaum, L. J. (2015). Shared and distinct neuroanatomic regions critical for tool-related action production and recognition: Evidence from 131 left-hemisphere stroke patients. *Journal of Cognitive Neuroscience, 27*, 2491–2511.

Taylor, L. J., Evans, C., Greer, J., Senior, C., Coventry, K. R., & Ietswaart, M. (2017). Dissociation between semantic representations for motion and action verbs: Evidence from patients with left hemisphere lesions. *Frontiers in Human Neuroscience, 11*, Article 35.

Teneggi, C., Canzoneri, E., di Pellegrino, G., & Serino, A. (2013). Social modulation of peripersonal space boundaries. *Current Biology, 23*, 406–411.

Terrill, A. (2006). Body part terms in Lavukaleve, a Papuan language of the Solomon Islands. *Language Sciences, 28*, 304–322.

Tettamanti, M., Buccino, G., Saccuman, M. C., Gallese, V., Danna, M., Scifo, P., Fazio, F., Rizzolatti, G., Cappa, S. F., & Perani, D. (2005). Listening to action-related sentences activates fronto-parietal motor circuits. *Journal of Cognitive Neuroscience, 17*, 273–281.

Tettamanti, M., Manenti, R., Della Rosa, P. A., Falini, A., Perani, D., Cappa, S. F., & Moro, A. (2008). Negation in the brain: Modulating action representations. *NeuroImage, 43*, 358–367.

Thierry, G. (2016). Neurolinguistic relativity: How language flexes human perception and cognition. *Language Learning, 66*, 690–713.

Thierry, G., Athanasopoulos, P., Wiggett, A., Dering, B., & Kuipers, J. R. (2009). Unconscious effects of language-specific terminology on preattentive color perception. *Proceedings of the National Academy of Sciences, 106*, 4567–4570.

Tomasello, M. (1999). *The cultural origins of human cognition.* Cambridge, MA: Harvard University Press.

Tomasello, M. (2014). *A natural history of human thinking.* Cambridge, MA: Harvard University Press.

Tomasello, M., & Call, J. (1997). *Primate cognition.* New York: Oxford University Press.

Tomasello, R., Garagnani, M., Wennekers, T., & Pulvermüller, F. (2017). Brain connections of words, perceptions and actions: A neurobiological model of spatio-temporal semantic activation in the human cortex. *Neuropsychologia, 98*, 111–129.

Tomasino, B., & Rumiati, R. I. (2013). At the mercy of strategies: The role of motor representations in language understanding. *Frontiers in Psychology, 4*, 27.

Tononi, G. (2004). An information integration theory of consciousness. *BMC Neuroscience, 5*, 42.

Tononi, G. (2008). Consciousness and integrated information: A provisional manifesto. *The Biological Bulletin, 215*, 216–242.

Tononi, G. (2012a). Integrated information theory of consciousness: An updated account. *Archives Italiennes de Biologie, 150*, 290–326.

Tononi, G. (2012b). *Phi: A voyage from the brain to the soul.* New York: Pantheon.

Tononi, G., Boly, M., Massimini, M., & Koch, C. (2016). Integrated information theory: From consciousness to its physical substrate. *Nature Reviews Neuroscience, 17*, 450–461.

Tononi, G., & Edelman, G. M. (1998). Consciousness and complexity. *Science, 282*, 1846–1850.

Tononi, G., & Koch, C. (2015). Consciousness: Here, there, and everywhere? *Philosophical Transactions of the Royal Society B: Biological Sciences, 370*, 20140167.

Tranel, D., Damasio, H., Damasio, A. R., et al. (1997a). A neural basis for the retrieval of conceptual knowledge. *Neuropsychologia, 35*, 1319–1327.

Tranel, D., & Kemmerer, D. (2004). Neural correlates of locative prepositions. *Cognitive Neuropsychology, 21*, 719–49.

Tranel, D., Kemmerer, D., Adolphs, R., Damasio, H., & Damasio, A. (2003). Neural correlates of conceptual knowledge for actions. *Cognitive Neuropsychology, 20*, 409–432.

Tranel, D., Logan, C. G., Frank, R. J., & Damasio, A. R. (1997b). Explaining category-related effects in the retrieval of conceptual and lexical knowledge for concrete entities: Operationalization and analysis of factors. *Neuropsychologia, 35*, 1329–1339.

Tranel, D., Manzel, K., Asp, E., & Kemmerer, D. (2008). Naming static and dynamic actions: Neuropsychological evidence. *Journal of Physiology, Paris, 102*, 80–94.

Troche, J., Crutch, S., & Reilly, J. (2014). Clustering, hierarchical organization, and the topography of abstract and concrete nouns. *Frontiers in Psychology, 5*, Article 360.

Troche, J., Crutch, S., & Reilly, J. (2017). Defining a conceptual topography of word concreteness: Clustering properties of emotion, sensation, and magnitude among 750 English words. *Frontiers in Psychology, 8*, Article 1787.

Trumpp, N. M., Kliese, D., Hoenig, K., Haarmeier, T., & Kiefer, M. (2013). Losing the sound of concepts: Damage to auditory association cortex impairs the processing of sound-related concepts. *Cortex, 49*, 474–486.

Tsao, D. Y., Moeller, S., & Freiwald, W. A. (2008). Comparing face patch systems in macaques and humans. *Proceedings of the National Academy of Sciences, 105*, 19514–19519.

Turnbull, O. H., Beschin, N., & Della Salla, S. (1997). Agnosia for object orientation: Implications for theories of object recognition. *Neuropsychologia, 35*, 153–163.

Turnbull, O. H., & Laws, K. R. (2000). Loss of stored knowledge of object structure: Implications for "category-specific" deficits. *Cognitive Neuropsychology, 17*, 365–389.

Turnbull, O. H., Laws, K. R., & McCarthy, R. A. (2005). Object recognition without knowledge of object orientation. *Cortex, 31*, 387–395.

Turney, P. D., & Pantel, P. (2010). From frequency to meaning: Vector space models of semantics. *Journal of Artificial Intelligence Research, 37*, 141–188.

Tye, M. (1995). *Ten problems of consciousness*. Cambridge, MA: MIT Press.

Tye, M., & Wright, B. (2012). Is there a phenomenology of thought? In T. Bayne & M. Montague (eds.), *Cognitive phenomenology* (pp. 326–344). New York: Oxford University Press.

Tyler, A., & Evans, V. (2003). *The semantics of English prepositions: Spatial scenes, embodied meaning, and cognition*. Cambridge, UK: Cambridge University Press.

Tyler, A., & Jan, H. (2017). *Be going to* and *will*: Talking about the future using embodied experience. *Language and Cognition, 9*, 412–445.

Tyler, L. K., Chiu, S., Zhuang, J., Randall, B., Devereux, B. J., Wright, P., Clarke, A., & Taylor, K. I. (2013). Objects and categories: Feature statistics and object processing in the ventral stream. *Journal of Cognitive Neuroscience, 25*, 1723–1735.

Ulltan, R. (1978). Some general characteristics of interrogative systems. In J. Greenberg, *Universals of human language*, vol. IV (pp. 211–428). Stanford, CA: Stanford University Press.

Ungerleider, L. G., & Mishkin, M. (1982). Two cortical visual systems. In D. J. Ingle, M. A. Goodale, & R. J. W. Mansfield (eds.), *Analysis of visual behavior* (pp. 549–586). Cambridge, MA: MIT Press.

Urgesi, C., Candidi, M., & Avenanti, A. (2014). Neuroanatomical substrates of action perception and understanding: An anatomical likelihood estimation meta-analysis of lesion-symptom mapping studies in brain-injured patients. *Frontiers in Human Neuroscience, 8*, Article 344.

Valdés-Conroy, B., Román, F. J., Hinojosa, J. A., & Shorkey, S. P. (2012). So far so good: Emotion in the peripersonal/extrapersonal space. *PLoS ONE, 7*, e49162.

Valyear, K. F., Culham, J. C., Sharif, N., Westwood, D., & Goodale, M. A. (2006). A double dissociation between sensitivity of changes in object identity and object orientation in the ventral and dorsal streams: A human fMRI study. *Neuropsychologia, 44*, 218–228.

van Ackeren, M. J., Schneider, T. R., Müsch, K., & Rueschemeyer, S. A. (2014). Oscillatory neuronal activity reflects lexical-semantic feature integration within and across sensory modality in distributed cortical networks. *Journal of Cognitive Neuroscience, 34,* 14318–14323.

van Dam, W. O., & Desai, R. H. (2016). The semantics of syntax: The grounding of transitive and intransitive constructions. *Journal of Cognitive Neuroscience, 28,* 693–709.

van Dam, W. O., van Dijk, M., Bekkering, H., & Rueschemeyer, S. A. (2012). Flexibility in embodied lexical-semantic representations. *Human Brain Mapping, 33,* 2322–2333.

Vandenberghe, R., Price, C., Wise, R., Josephs, O., & Frackowiak, R. S. J. (1996). Functional anatomy of a common semantic system for words and pictures. *Nature, 383,* 254–256.

van den Heuvel, M. P., Kahn, R. S., Goni, J., & Sporns, O. (2012). High-cost, high-capacity backbone for global brain communication. *Proceedings of the National Academy of Sciences, 109,* 11372–11377.

van den Heuvel, M. P., & Sporns, O. (2011). Rich-club organization of the human connectome. *Journal of Neuroscience, 31,* 15775–15786.

Van der Auwera, J., & Malchukov, A. (2005). A semantic map for depictive adjectivals. In N. P. Himmelmann & E. Schulze-Berndt (eds.), *Secondary predication and adverbial modification: The typology of depictive constructions* (pp. 393–423). New York: Oxford University Press.

Van der Auwera, J., & Plungian, V. A. (1998). Modality's semantic map. *Linguistic Typology, 2,* 79–124.

van der Zee, E., & Slack, J. (eds.) (2003). *Representing direction in language and space.* New York: Oxford University Press.

van Elk, M., van Schie, H., & Bekkering, H. (2014). Action semantics: A unifying conceptual framework for the selective use of multimodal and modality-specific object knowledge. *Physics of Life Reviews, 11,* 220–250.

van Gaal, S., Naccache, L., Meuwese, J. D. I., van Loon, A. M., Leighton, A. H., Cohen, L., & Dehaene, S. (2014). Can the meaning of multiple words be integrated unconsciously? *Philosophical Transactions of the Royal Society B: Biological Sciences, 369,* 20130212.

van Gulick, R. (1994). Deficit studies and the function of phenomenal consciousness. In G. Graham & G. L. Stephens (eds.), *Philosophical Psychopathology* (pp. 25–49). Cambridge, MA: MIT Press.

Vannuscorps, G., Dricot, L., & Pillon, A. (2016). Persistent sparing of action conceptual processing in spite of increasing disorders of action production: A case against motor embodiment of action concepts. *Cognitive Neuropsychology, 33,* 191–219.

Van Overwalle, F., & Baetens, K. (2009). Understanding others' actions and goals by mirror and mentalizing systems: A meta-analysis. *NeuroImage, 48,* 564–584.

van Staden, M. (2006). The body and its parts in Tidore, a Papuan language of Eastern Indonesia. *Language Sciences, 28,* 323–343.

van Staden, M. (2007). "Please open the fish": Verbs of separation in Tidore, a Papuan language of Eastern Indonesia. *Cognitive Linguistics, 18,* 297–306.

Van Valin, R. D., Jr. (2005). *Exploring the syntax-semantics interface.* Cambridge, UK: Cambridge University Press.

Velazquez-Castillo, M. (1996). *The grammar of possession: Inalienability, incorporation, and possessor ascension in Guaraní.* Amsterdam: John Benjamins.

Viberg, Å. (2006). Towards a lexical profile of the Swedish verb lexicon. *Sprachtypologie und Universalienforschung, 59,* 103–129.

Vingerhoets, G. (2008). Knowing about tools: Neural correlates of tool familiarity and experience. *NeuroImage, 40,* 1380–1391.

Vinson, D. P., & Vigliocco, G. (2008). Semantic feature production norms for a large set of objects and events. *Behavior Research Methods, 40*, 183–190.

Visser, M., Embleton, K. V., Jefferies, E., Parker, G. J., & Lambon Ralph, M. A. (2010a). The inferior, anterior temporal lobes and semantic memory clarified: novel evidence from distortion-corrected fMRI. *Neuropsychologia, 48*, 1689–1696.

Visser, M., Jefferies, E., Embleton, K. V., Lambon Ralph, M. A. (2012). Both the middle temporal gyrus and the ventral anterior temporal area are crucial for multimodal semantic processing: Distortion-corrected fMRI evidence for a double gradient of information convergence in the temporal lobes. *Journal of Cognitive Neuroscience, 24*, 1766–1778.

Visser, M., Jefferies, E., & Lambon Ralph, M. A. (2010b). Semantic processing in the anterior temporal lobes: A meta-analysis of the functional neuroimaging literature. *Journal of Cognitive Neuroscience, 22*, 1083–1094.

Visser, M., Lambon Ralph, M. A. (2011). Differential contributions of bilateral ventral anterior temporal lobe and left anterior superior temporal gyrus to semantic processes. *Journal of Cognitive Neuroscience, 23*, 3121–3131.

Voeltz, F. K. E., & Kilian-Hatz, C. (eds.) (2001). *Ideophones*. Amsterdam: John Benjamins.

Von Der Heide, R. J., Skipper, L. M., & Olson, I. R. (2013). Anterior temporal face patches: A meta-analysis and empirical study. *Frontiers in Human Neuroscience, 7*, Article 17.

von Fintel, K., & Matthewson, L. (2008). Universals in semantics. *Linguistic Review, 25*, 139–201.

Wälchli, B. (2010). Similarity semantics and building probabilistic semantic maps from parallel texts. *Linguistic Disvovery, 8*. doi: 10.1349/PS1.1537–0852.A.366

Wallentin, M., Nielson, A. H., Vuust, P., Dohn, A., Roepstorff, A., & Lund, T. E. (2011). BOLD response to motion verbs in left posterior middle temporal gyrus during story comprehension. *Brain and Language, 119*, 221–225.

Wandell, B. A., Dumoulin, S. O., & Brewer, A. A. (2007). Visual field maps in human cortex. *Neuron, 56*, 366–383.

Watanabe, N., & Yamamoto, M. (2015). Neural mechanisms of social dominance. *Frontiers in Neuroscience, 9*, Article 154.

Watson, C. E., & Buxbaum, L. J. (2015). A distributed network critical for selecting among tool-directed actions. *Cortex, 65*, 65–82.

Watson, C. E., Cardillo, E. R., Ianni, G. R., & Chatterjee, A. (2013). Action concepts in the brain: An activation-likelihood estimation meta-analysis. *Journal of Cognitive Neuroscience, 25*, 1191–1205.

Watson, C. E., & Chatterjee, A. (2011). The functional neuroanatomy of actions. *Neurology, 76*, 1428–1434.

Waxman, S. R., & Gelman, S. A. (2009). Early word-learning entails reference, not merely associations. *Trends in Cognitive Sciences, 13*, 258–263.

Wegener, C. (2006). Savosavo body part terminology. *Language Sciences, 28*, 344–359.

Weinberger, E., & Paz, O. (1987). *19 ways of looking at Wang Wei: How a Chinese poem is translated*. New York: Moyer Bell.

Weiner, K. S., & Grill-Spector, K. (2013). Neural representations of faces and limbs neighbor in human high-level visual cortex: Evidence for a new organization principle. *Psychological Research, 77*, 74–97.

Weiner, K. S., & Zilles, K. (2016). The anatomical and functional specialization of the fusiform gyrus. *Neuropsychologia, 83*, 48–62.

Weisberg, J., Turennout, M., & Martin, A. (2007). A neural system for learning about object function. *Cerebral Cortex. 17*, 513–521.

Werner, S., & Noppeney, U. (2010). Distinct functional contributions of primary sensory and association areas to audiovisual integration in object categorization. *Journal of Neuroscience, 30*, 2662–2675.

Wernike, C. (1900). *Grundriss der Psychiatrie*. Leipzig: Verlag von Georg Thieme.

Westermann, D. (1930). *A study of the Ewe language*. London: Oxford University Press.

Whaley, L. J. (1997). *Introduction to typology: The unity and diversity of language*. London: Sage.

Wheatley, T., Milleville, S., & Martin, A. (2007). Understanding animate agents: Distinct roles for the "social network" and "mirror system." *Psychological Science, 18*, 469–474.

Wheatley, T., Weisberg, J., Beauchamp, M. S., & Martin, A. (2005). Automatic priming of semantically related words reduces activity in the fusiform gyrus. *Journal of Cognitive Neuroscience, 17*, 1871–1885.

Whelpton, M., Beck, þ. G., & Jordan, F. M. (2015). The semantics and morphology of household container names in Icelandic and Dutch. *Language Sciences, 49*, 67–81.

Whitehead, H., & Rendell, L. (2014). *The cultural lives of whales and dolphins*. Chicago: University of Chicago Press.

Whitney, C., Huber, W., Klann, J., Weis, S., Krach, S., & Kircher, T. (2009). Neural correlates of narrative shifts during auditory story comprehension. *NeuroImage, 47*, 360–366.

Whorf, B. L. (1956). *Language, thought, and reality: Selected writings*. Cambridge, MA: MIT Press.

Wicker, B., Keysers, C., Plailly, J., Poyet, J. P., Gallese, V., & Rizzolatti, G. (2003). Both of us disgusted in my insula: the common neural basis of seeing and feeling disgust. *Neuron, 40*, 655–664.

Wierzbicka, A. (1999). *Emotions across languages and cultures: Diversity and universals*. Cambridge, UK: Cambridge University Press.

Wierzbicka, A. (1996). *Semantic primes and universals*. New York: Oxford University Press.

Wierzbicka, A. (2007). Bodies and their parts: An NSM approach to semantic typology. *Language Sciences, 29*, 14–65.

Wierzbicka, A. (2014). *Imprisoned in English: The hazards of English as a default language*. New York: Oxford University Press.

Wiese, H., Kloth, N., Güllmar, D., Reichenbach, J. R., & Schweinberger, S. R. (2012). Perceiving age and gender in unfamiliar faces: An fMRI study on face categorization. *Brain and Cognition, 78*, 163–168.

Weissner, P. W. (2014). Embers of society: Firelight talk among the Ju/'hoansi Bushmen. *Proceedings of the National Academy of Sciences, 111*, 14027–14035.

Wilkins, D. P. (2006). Towards an Arrernte grammar of space. In S. C. Levinson & D. P. Wilkins (eds.), *Grammars of space: Explorations in cognitive diversity* (pp. 24–62). Cambridge, UK: Cambridge University Press.

Willems, R., Hagoort, P., & Casasanto, D. (2010a). Body-specific representations of action verbs: Neural evidence from right- and left-handers. *Psychological Science, 21*, 67–74.

Willems, R., Toni, I., Hagoort, P. & Casasanto, D. (2010b). Neural dissociations between action verb understanding and motor imagery. *Journal of Cognitive Neuroscience, 22*, 2387–2400.

Wilson, R. (2003). Intentionality and phenomenology. *Pacific Philosophical Quarterly, 84*, 413–431.

Wilson, S. (1999). *Coverbs and complex predicates in Wagiman*. Stanford: CSLI.

Winawer, J., Witthoft, N., Frank, M. C., Wu, L., Wade, A. R., & Boroditsky, L. (2007). Russian blues reveal effects of language on color discrimination. *Proceedings of the National Academy of Sciences, 104,* 7780–7785.

Witkowski, S. R., & Brown, C. H. (1985). Climate, clothing, and body-part nomenclature. *Ethnology, 24,* 197–214.

Wittenberg, E., Jackendoff, R., Kuperberg, G., Paczynski, M., Snedeker, J., & Wiese, H. (2014a). The processing and representation of light verb constructions. In A. Bachrach, I. Roy, & L. Stockall (eds.), *Structuring the argument: Multidisciplinary research on verb argument structure* (pp. 61–80). Amsterdam: John Benjamins.

Wittenberg, E., Paczynski, M., Wiese, H., Jackendoff, R., & Kuperberg, G. (2014b). The difference between "giving a rose" and "giving a kiss": Sustained neural activity to the light verb construction. *Journal of Memory and Language, 73,* 31–42.

Wittenberg, E., & Piñango, M. M. (2011). Processing light verb constructions. *The Mental Lexicon, 6,* 393–413.

Wolbers, T., Wiener, J. M., Mallot, H. A., & Büchel, C. (2007). Differential recruitment of the hippocampus, medial prefrontal cortex, and the human motion complex during path integration in humans. *Journal of Neuroscience, 27,* 9408–9416.

Wolff, P., & Holmes, K. (2011). Linguistic relativity. *WIREs Cognitive Science, 2,* 253–265.

Wolff, P., Jeon, G., Klettke, B., & Li, Y. (2010). Force creation and possible causers across languages. In B. Malt & P. Wolff (eds.), *Words and the mind: How words capture human experience* (pp. 93–110). Oxford: Oxford University Press.

Wong, C., & Gallate, J. (2012). The function of the anterior temporal lobe: A review of the empirical evidence. *Brain Research, 1449,* 94–116.

Woodruff-Smith, D. (2012). The phenomenology of consciously thinking. In T. Bayne & M. Montague (eds.), *Cognitive phenomenology* (pp. 345–372). New York: Oxford University Press.

Woollams, A. M., Cooper-Pye, E., Hodges, J. R., & Patterson, K. (2008). Anomia: A doubly typical signature of semantic dementia. *Neuropsychologia, 46,* 2503–2514.

Wright, P., Randall, B., Clarke, A., & Tyler, L. K. (2015). The perirhinal cortex and conceptual processing: Effects of feature-based statistics following damage to the anterior temporal lobes. *Neuropsychologia, 76,* 192–207.

Wu, D., Morganti, A., & Chatterjee, A. (2008). Neural substrates of processing path and manner information of a moving event. *Neuropsychologia, 46,* 704–713.

Wu, D., Waller, S., & Chatterjee, A. (2007). The functional neuroanatomy of thematic role and locative relational knowledge. *Journal of Cognitive Neuroscience, 19,* 1542–1555.

Wurm, M. F., Ariani, G., Greenlee, M. W., & Lingnau, A. (2016). Decoding concrete and abstract action representations during explicit and implicit conceptual processing. *Cerebral Cortex, 26,* 3390–3401.

Wurm, M. F., & Lingnau, A. (2015). Decoding actions at different levels of abstraction. *Journal of Neuroscience, 35,* 7727–7735.

Yamamoto, N., Philbeck, J. W., Woods, A. J., Gajewski, D. A., Arthur, J. C., Potolicchio, S. J., Levy, L., & Caputy, A. J. (2014). Medial temporal lobe roles in human path integration. *PLoS ONE, 9,* e96583.

Yang, Y., Dickey, M. W., Fiez, J., Murphy, B., Mitchell, T., Collinger, J., Tyler-Kabara, E., Boninger, M., & Wang, W. (2017). Sensorimotor experience and verb-category mapping in human sensory, motor and parietal neurons. *Cortex, 92,* 304–319.

Yee, E., Chrysikou, E. G., & Thompson-Schill, S. L. (2013). The cognitive neuroscience of semantic memory. In K. Ochsner & S. Kosslyn (eds.), *The Oxford handbook of cognitive neuroscience*. New York: Oxford University Press.

Yee, E., & Thompson-Schill, S. L. (2013). Putting concepts into context. *Psychonomic Bulletin & Review, 23,* 1015–1027.

Yi, H. A., Moore, P., & Grossman, M. (2007). Reversal of the concreteness effect for verbs in semantic dementia. *Neuropsychology, 21,* 9–19.

York, C., Olm, C., Boller, A., McCluskey, L., Elman, J., Seltzer, E., Chahine, L., Woo, J., Rascovsky, K., McMillan C., & Grossman, M. (2014). Action verb comprehension in amyotrophic lateral sclerosis and Parkinson's disease. *Journal of Neurology, 261,* 1073–1079.

Zacks, J. M., Braver, T. S., Sheridan, M. A., Donaldson, D. I., Snyder, A. Z., Ollinger, J. M., Buckner, R. L., & Raichle, M. E. (2001). Human brain activity time-locked to perceptual event boundaries. *Nature Neuroscience, 4,* 651–655.

Zacks, J. M., Speer, N. K., Swallow, K. M., & Maley, C. J. (2010). The brain's cutting-room floor: Segmentation of narrative cinema. *Frontiers in Human Neuroscience, 4,* Article 168.

Zadbood, A., Chen, J., Leong, Y. C., Norman, K. A., & Hasson, U. (2017). How we transmit memories to other brains: Constructing shared neural representations via communication. *Cerebral Cortex, 27,* 4988–5000.

Zeki, S. (2015). Area V5—A microcosm of the visual system. *Frontiers in Integrative Neuroscience, 9,* Article 21.

Zheng, C. C. (2017). *Priming in motion event description: An experimental study in English and Mandarin Chinese.* Ph.D. dissertation, Purdue University.

Zhou, X., Jiang, X., Ye, Z., Zhang, Y., Lou, K., & Zhan, W. (2010). Semantic integration processes at different levels of syntactic hierarchy during sentence comprehension: An ERP study. *Neuropsychologia, 48,* 1551–1562.

Zinszer, B. D., Anderson, A. J., Kang, O., Wheatley, T., & Raizada, R. D. S. (2016). Semantic structural alignment of neural representational spaces enables translation between English and Chinese words. *Journal of Cognitive Neuroscience, 28,* 1749–1759.

Zwaan, R. (2014). Embodiment and language comprehension: Reframing the discussion. *Trends in Cognitive Sciences, 18,* 229–234.

LANGUAGE INDEX

Tables and figures are indicated by *t* and *f* following the page number

AUTHOR INDEX

Tables and figures are indicated by *t* and *f* following the page number

SUBJECT INDEX

Tables and figures are indicated by *t* and *f* following the page number

actions. *See also* motion events
  concepts for, neurobiology, 128
  cortical activation patterns associated with,
    deficit-lesion relationships, 238
  images, conceptual processing of, cortical
    underpinning of, 131
  language-specific representation, and
    cognition, 228–29
  lexical partitioning of, studies of, 9
  linguistic representations, 221
  object-directed, brain areas linked to, 43–
    44, 148–49, 149*f*, 200
  research on
    in cognitive neuroscience, 115
    in semantic typology, 115
  sequences of generic verbs for, 7
  verbal and nonverbal tasks related to
    cortical underpinnings of, 238–40, 239*f*
    deficit-lesion relationships, 238
action verbs
  basic, cross-linguistic prevalence
    of, 138–39
  conceptual processing of, cortical
    underpinning of, 131–33
  cultural diversity and, 139
  idiosyncratic lexicalization (Dogon
    language), 146–47, 147*t*
  motor features of, 37–39, 48–49,
    134–38, 136*f*
    factors affecting, 48
    individual experience and, 50
    retrieval of, context and, 49–50
  specialized, cross-linguistic prevalence
    of, 138–39
  specifying detailed object distinctions, 259

actotopy, 135–38, 137*f*
adjective-based constructions, neural
  substrate of, 56–58
adjectives, inventories of, in various
  languages, 5–6, 5–6n1
Alzheimer's disease, picture-naming errors
  in, 44–45
ambiguity, resolution of, 34–36
American Sign Language, classifier
  constructions in, 113–14n9
amodal representations, 41–43n1
amygdala, and social status judgments, 97
amyotrophic lateral sclerosis (ALS), motor
  area damage in, 38*f*
Anglocentrism, 257
angular gyrus, 35*f*
  and categorical spatial relations,
    200–3, 201*f*
    deficit-lesion relationships, 205
  and conjunctions of lexical-semantic
    specifications, 43*f*, 43–44
  and cutting, breaking, and opening events,
    150–51, 152
  and event segmentation, 170–71
  and transmodal attributes, 44
  and verbal and nonverbal processing of
    actions, 238–40
animacy and related properties, 87–88, 93
  contextual cues for, cortical areas sensitive
    to, 74–75
  cortical topography of, 79
  four-way conceptual contrasts, 93–94
  linguistic versus biological, 93
  neurobiology, 94
  neurotopography of, 94–96